Shadows On The Track

Australia's Medical War In Papua 1942-1943: Kokoda – Milne Bay – The Beachhead Battles

Jan McLeod

16pt

Copyright Page from the Original Book

Copyright © Jan McLeod

First published 2019

Copyright remains the property of Jan McLeod and apart from any fair dealing for the purposes of private study, research, criticism or review, as permitted under the Copyright Act, no part may be reproduced by any process without written permission.

All inquiries should be made to the publishers.

Big Sky Publishing Pty Ltd
PO Box 303, Newport, NSW 2106, Australia
Phone: 1300 364 611
Fax: (61 2) 9918 2396
Email: info@bigskypublishing.com.au
Web: www.bigskypublishing.com.au

Cover design and typesetting: Think Productions
Proudly printed and bound in China by Asia Pacific Offset

A catalogue record for this book is available from the National Library of Australia

For Cataloguing-in-Publication entry see National Library of Australia.

Author: Jan McLeod

Title: Shadows On the Track, Australia's Medical War in Papua 1942–1943.
    Kokoda — Milne Bay — The Beachhead Battles

TABLE OF CONTENTS

ACKNOWLEDGEMENTS	iii
ABBREVIATIONS AND ACRONYMS	vi
A NOTE ON TERMINOLOGY	ix
INTRODUCTION: 'A HISTORY OF PROBLEMS'	xi
CHAPTER 1: FOUNDATIONS, EXPLORATIONS, ALTERCATIONS	1
CHAPTER 2: LEADERSHIP, MIDDLE EAST, LESSONS	38
CHAPTER 3: MEDICAL ARRANGEMENTS IN PAPUA	83
CHAPTER 4: THE PAPUAN CAMPAIGN BEGINS	108
CHAPTER 5: MEDICAL CARE DURING THE AUSTRALIAN WITHDRAWAL	150
CHAPTER 6: MILNE BAY	196
CHAPTER 7: GOODENOUGH ISLAND AND MILNE BAY	229
CHAPTER 8: MEDICAL CARE DURING THE AUSTRALIAN ADVANCE	260
CHAPTER 9: ONGOING CHALLENGES ON THE KOKODA TRACK	313
CHAPTER 10: SOPUTA	350
CHAPTER 11: THE BEACHHEAD BATTLES AND VICTORY	404
CHAPTER 12: YEAR'S END AT PORT MORESBY	447
CHAPTER 13: 'ONE WONDERS WHY ALL THIS STRIFE SHOULD BE'	474
APPENDIX 1: AIF AND AAMC FIELD AMBULANCE UNITS	489
APPENDIX 2: CMF/MILITIA	491
APPENDIX 3	492
APPENDIX 4: 2/6th FIELD AMBULANCE MDS MYOLA 2	496
APPENDIX 5: OVERVIEW OF MEDICAL UNITS AND FACILITIES IN PAPUAN CAMPAIGN 1942	499
ENDNOTES	506
BIBLIOGRAPHY	676

About the Author 702
Index 705

> 'What would I like done to me if I were severely wounded tonight?'
>
> Lieutenant Colonel Frederick Chenhall, Commanding Officer 2/6th Australian Field Ambulance

ARMY·HISTORY·UNIT

PROTECTING ARMY HERITAGE
PROMOTING ARMY HISTORY

This book is dedicated to my dad, Jack Kennedy, and written in memory of my great-uncles Bill and Nick Kennedy, who both served in the 2/4th Australian Field Ambulance, 7th Division, AIF (1940–1945)

ACKNOWLEDGEMENTS

My sincere thanks to all who helped me see this project through to publication. My PhD supervisor at the University of Newcastle, Associate Professor Wayne Reynolds, kept me on course during my studies. Wayne's carefully considered feedback, suggestions, belief and encouragement were invaluable. Thanks to my university colleagues and fellow PhD candidates for their continued support—especially my friend, Dr Ann Hardy. I am fortunate to have a great group of friends who I have known for decades, and who have never wavered in their belief and support. Thanks to you all for the chats, the coffees, the good laughs and the good times. Special thanks to Bill Sweeting and Lorie Thompson, who have sadly both passed away since I began this research. Bill and Lorie served with my great-uncles in the 2/4th Australian Field Ambulance, and generously shared their memories and experiences with me in letters and telephone conversations.

Staff at the Australian War Memorial and the National Archives were helpful and professional, making my research trips to Canberra and Melbourne extremely productive. Dr Andrew Richardson and Nick Anderson at the Australian Army History Unit were generous with their time and practical advice. I thank the editors of *Health and History*—the journal of the Australian and New Zealand Society of the History of Medicine—for publishing my article, 'The House That Jack Built: DGMS Rupert Downes and Australian Army Medical Preparations for World War II'. Some material from the article has been included in this book.

Thank you to Professor Peter Stanley and Dr Peter Hobbins who provided valuable suggestions and advice at various stages of the editing process. I also extend my heartfelt thanks to Professor Susan Magarey for her careful reading and feedback regarding Chapter Five. I am grateful to Denny Neave of Big Sky Publishing for believing in this book and seeing it through to publication. Working with editor, Cathy McCullagh, was an absolute delight. I sincerely thank Cathy for her keen eye, good humour, diligence and professionalism.

On a more personal level, I would like to thank my parents for a lifetime of love. Though they both unfortunately passed away before I was awarded my doctorate, Mum and Dad were always interested in my research and supportive of my studies. Learning about the wartime experiences of his two uncles, Bill and Nick, meant a lot to my father. My three McLeod men are fabulous, and I love them to bits. My sons, Andrew and Daniel, have always encouraged me in this project, while busily pursuing their own lives, loves, and university studies. Special thanks to Andrew for bringing his PhD qualifications and writing expertise to my raw manuscript. His finesse, constructive criticism and helpful suggestions, as well as his patience in wading through these thousands of words, have made all the difference. Finally, I thank my husband, Greg, who is my best friend. His unwavering love and encouragement in all things over the many years we have been together have made the tough times easier and the good times better.

ABBREVIATIONS AND ACRONYMS

AAMC	Australian Army Medical Corps
AANS	Australian Army Nursing Service
AASC	Australian Army Service Corps
ADGMS	Assistant Director General of Medical Services
ADMS	Assistant Director of Medical Services
ADS	Advanced Dressing Station
AGH	Australian General Hospital
AIF	Australian Imperial Force
AMD	Australian Medical Directorate
AMS	Army Medical Service
ANGAU	Australian New Guinea Administrative Unit
AN&MEF	Australian Naval and Military Expeditionary Force
ANZAC	Australian and New Zealand Army Corps
CCS	Casualty Clearing Station
CMF	Citizen Military Force (Militia)
CO	Commanding Officer
COSC	Combined Operational Service Command
DADGMS	Deputy Assistant Director General of Medical Services
DADH	Deputy Assistant Director Hygiene
DADMS	Deputy Assistant Director of Medical Services
DDGMS	Deputy Director General of Medical Services
DDMS	Deputy Director of Medical Services
DGMS	Director General of Medical Services

DMS	Director of Medical Services
Fd Amb	Field Ambulance
GOC	General Officer Commanding
HQ	Headquarters
HT	Hospital Transport
IGMS	Inspector General of Medical Services
LHQ	Land Headquarters
MAC	Motor Ambulance Convoy
MDS	Main Dressing Station
MO	Medical Officer
NCO	Non-commissioned officer
NGF	New Guinea Force
NSW	New South Wales
OC	Officer Commanding
OR	Other ranks
PIB	Papuan Infantry Battalion
PMO	Principal Medical Officer
PUO	Pyrexia (fever) of Unknown Origin
RAAF	Royal Australian Air Force
RAAMC	Royal Australian Army Medical Corps
RAN	Royal Australian Navy
RAP	Regimental Aid Post
RMO	Regimental Medical Officer
SAT	Sea Ambulance Transport
SB	Stretcher-bearer
SIW	Self-inflicted wound
SMO	Senior Medical Officer

SWPA	South West Pacific Area
US	United States of America
WE	War Establishment

A NOTE ON TERMINOLOGY

While the scope of this book reaches far beyond the Kokoda Track, there is a need to acknowledge the passionate and ongoing debate over whether the term 'Track' or 'Trail' should be used. Which is correct? The short answer is neither—and both. The longer answer recognises that both terms were used by those who encountered the route from Port Moresby to the village of Kokoda before, during, and after thousands of Australian and Japanese soldiers were confronted by its testing topography in 1942.

These included the hopeful sojourners making their way to the northern goldfields in the 1890s, the Australians surveying and mapping the pedestrian path from 1899, the European missionaries traversing the route to deliver Christianity to the local population, and the Papuans of the Armed Native Constabulary who delivered the mail once a government station was established at Kokoda in 1904. The settlers, scientists, plantation owners and company managers who came to Papua during the early twentieth century used both 'Track' and 'Trail' to describe the path, as did the wives, nurses, teachers, and female missionaries who accompanied them. The challenging route was also known to many 'lost and wandering white men' who simply stumbled on the path by accident.[1]

During World War II, Australian and American war correspondents unwittingly contributed to the terminology debate, as did the military engineers and surveyors from both countries who continued to survey and map the area long after the war had ended. Government reports, books, newspaper reports and accounts by Australian veterans of the Papuan campaign that refer to the route as 'Kokoda Road' further illustrate the difficulties associated with determining the 'correct' terminology.[2] Conspicuously absent from most discussions on the topic, however, are the voices of the Papuan peoples. The Motu people from the southern coastal region use the word 'Dala', which roughly translates as 'road', 'path', 'track', or 'way'.[3]

I have chosen to use the term 'Kokoda Track' primarily because this was the term used by my great-uncle throughout the diary that inspired this book.[4]

INTRODUCTION

'A HISTORY OF PROBLEMS'

The Papuan campaign of World War II is often commemorated as the battle that saved Australia. The soldiers who fought this campaign against the Japanese are popularly immortalised as the men who saved Australia. Few have paused to ask who saved the soldiers. More than 20,000 Australians served in Papua between July 1942 and January 1943, fighting the Japanese along the Kokoda Track, across the Owen Stanley Range, on the northern beachheads, and at Milne Bay on the eastern tip of the island. Responsibility for the medical care of thousands of front-line Australian soldiers fell to just a few under-strength and under-resourced field ambulance units. There was no real plan or provision made for the medical care of those initially sent over the Owen Stanley Range to confront the Japanese in July. By the time victory was declared, approximately 6000 Australian soldiers had been killed or wounded, and almost 30,000 had suffered from illness and disease.[1] These stark statistics lead to the inescapable conclusion that most of the Australian soldiers in Papua were cared for at some stage by medical personnel.

Papuan Infantry Battalion; 6th Aust. Independent Company

7th Aust. Division	30th Brigade	6th Aust. Division	32nd US Division	41st US Division
21st Brigade 2/14, 2/16, 2/27 Bns	53, 39, 49, 3 Bns	16th Brigade 2/1, 2/2, 2/3 Bns	126th Rgt 1, 2, 3 Bns	163rd Rgt 1, 2, 3 Bns
25th Brigade 2/31, 2/33, 2/25 Bns			127th Rgt 1, 2, 3 Bns	
18th Brigade 2/9, 2/10, 2/12 Bns			128th Rgt 1, 2, 3 Bns	

Allied ground forces in active contact with Japanese forces on Kokoda Track and at Beachhead.

Viewing the campaign through the lens of Australia's front-line medical units reveals a picture that is markedly different to popular representations which have been inclined to lionise the role of the indigenous Papuan carriers who made a vital contribution to the campaign waged in their country. However, the image of 'Fuzzy Wuzzy Angels' bearing wounded Australians to safety has become so ingrained in any representation of medical aspects of the Papuan campaign as to obscure a much more complex—at times inspiring, at times infuriating—reality. To this end, a more nuanced representation is possible by traversing a track less travelled—the track taken by Australian medical personnel. Examining the experiences of the Australian field ambulance units calls into question the mythology around the singularly evocative word that has come to represent the entire Papuan campaign—Kokoda.

Perhaps understandably, the mythology that inspired the words etched in stone at the Isurava memorial—'Courage Endurance Mateship Sacrifice'—has been founded on the experiences of the fighting soldiers. Those very words have become the cornerstone qualities on which the popular narrative is constructed.[2] A sense of inevitability about the hardships endured by the Australians lies at the heart of this account of events—whereby the ordeals they suffered are direct, inevitable, and unavoidable consequences of the harsh environment in which the campaign was fought.

This book challenges that narrative.

Japan's entry into World War II in December 1941 set in motion a cascade of events that brought home the consequences of Australia's long-standing ignorance and neglect of Papua. In February 1942, the recently elected Prime Minister, John Curtin, described the defeat of the Allied forces in Singapore as 'Australia's Dunkirk', telling the Australian people that, just as 'the fall of Dunkirk initiated the Battle for Britain, the fall of Singapore opens the Battle for Australia.'[3] The rapidity of the Japanese advance in the Pacific area pushed Australia and its defence forces to their limits, redefining this country's relationship with Britain, the United States (US) and Papua New Guinea.

Desperation and necessity pushed Australian defence policy closer to America to bring about a situation that proved mutually beneficial. Successive Japanese victories in the Pacific during 1942 challenged the Australian government, the defence forces and the general population to confront the nature and limitations of Australia's relationship with Britain, to question their Dominion status, and to cast off some of the more onerous obligations of empire. The initial military response to the Japanese threat was defensive and, indeed, 'the whole emphasis of the Australian war effort changed to the defence of the Australian mainland [as] appeals for strengthening the outer barrier gave place to anxiety for the security of the base.'[4] The Australian Army's medical response was certainly in line with a defensive strategy. Very little was done to quell fears of an invasion of mainland Australia, even after any real threat had passed.

The Australian government and its defence forces had long acknowledged the potential Japanese threat to their shores, yet had done little to address that threat. Rather, there had remained an unfathomable degree of faith in the ability of the British navy to protect Australian territory via the Singapore Strategy. This reliance on British naval supremacy was underpinned by a denial of the practicalities of such a strategy, and an unwavering belief that geographical barriers such as the formidable Owen Stanley Range and the dense jungles of Papua were enough to prevent any land-based assault on Australia from the north. Many knowledgeable, pragmatic and otherwise realistic men clung to the hope that outdated treaties, covenants and alliances would afford sufficient protection from Japanese aggression in the Pacific—even in a world whose political landscape had been irrevocably altered since 1914.[5]

Australia's geographical proximity to, and long-term relationship with Papua should have resulted in a more organised and effective military and medical response to the Japanese landings on its northern shore in July 1942. The soundness of the eventual decision to launch an offensive in Papua was questioned by some in the military at the time, and the wisdom of that decision remains arguable today[6] An unwillingness to sufficiently grasp and respond militarily and administratively to the Papua that existed beyond Port Moresby effectively neutralised any medical advantage over the Japanese that may have existed for the Australian soldiers fighting in Papua. The territory's proximity to Australia should have posed far less of a logistical challenge for the Australian Army Medical Corps (AAMC) than that presented by the distant Middle East. However, the fear of a Japanese invasion of Australia—whether real, imagined, or politically expedient—drove the decision to concentrate medical resources and facilities around capital cities on the Australian mainland. This served to divert attention away from the adequacy of medical facilities in the island territories to Australia's north.

Within the Australian Army there was a failure to reform outdated administrative structures in response to the changing military situation. The defence of the Australian mainland continued to take precedence over pre-emptive measures in the islands to the north, with the result that many responses—such as accurately mapping the islands—came too late to be of benefit. Similarly, the decision to nominate the under-strength and ill-prepared militia 39th Battalion as the unit which would initially take the fight to the Japanese in Papua proved costly. The correspondingly meagre medical response during the first months of fighting was proof of the failure to heed the carefully considered and documented medical lessons from the Middle East. Both the military and medical plans in Papua, such as they were, relied on a successful advance and a swift victory, with little thought given to the medical consequences should these fail to eventuate.

Along the Kokoda Track, a combination of factors that centred on supply, treatment and evacuation adversely affected the Australian field ambulance units (the 14th, 2/6th and 2/4th) during the first weeks of fighting, leaving them overwhelmed with casualties. Though the later Milne Bay campaign was comparatively brief in terms of fighting, the three medical units primarily responsible for maintaining the health of soldiers in this malarial morass (the 11th and 2/5th Australian Field Ambulance units, and the 110th Casualty Clearing Station) encountered similar challenges to those presented by the Kokoda Track and the northern coast of Papua. Ultimately, all medical units paid the price for the Army's serious underestimation of the enemy's ability, and for a failure to sufficiently recognise and address the unique medical challenges presented by the Papuan terrain.

Although geographically close to the Australian mainland, the medical units in Papua quickly found themselves effectively isolated. The difficulties they encountered there, however, did not occur in isolation. Adopting a comprehensive and longitudinal approach to the medical campaign in Papua allows consideration of the political machinations, military maladministration, changing priorities, ineffective leadership, poor planning, and logistical difficulties, as well as the nature of the campaign and the 'relentless nature' of the country itself. There is no doubt that such issues impacted to varying degrees on medical personnel and the soldiers entrusted to their care.

The Australian Army was responsible for the lives of thousands of soldiers, yet medical care was far from a priority at any stage of the campaign in Papua. Flaws in the higher planning and execution of the medical campaign reflected an ad hoc approach that was reliant on the ability of medical personnel on the ground to improvise and extemporise to save lives. Examining a range of sources relevant to the highest levels of government and the military provides a more traditional, empirical 'history from above' perspective, while critical analysis of less formal source material (unit diaries, service records, correspondence) can help to balance this view. Close reading of personal diaries and letters round out the history and add to an understanding of the medical campaign specifically, and the Papuan campaign more broadly.

The diaries of Gavin Long—talented journalist, teacher, historian, war correspondent, general editor of (and contributor to) the 22-volume official history series, *Australia in the War of 1939–1945*—unexpectedly provided the guiding principles for *Shadows on the Track*.[7] Long wrote of a conversation with two esteemed colleagues—the editor and official historian of the First World War, Charles Bean, and that conflict's official medical historian, Dr Arthur Butler—in Canberra on 17 November 1944. The meeting that Friday afternoon centred on how best to approach the writing of the medical history of World War II.

The three agreed that it was necessary to first note 'how things were at the beginning and then record the changes'[8] A succinct summary of the military campaigns was regarded as vital, though Butler raised the difficulty of applying this approach to the campaign in New Guinea before pointing out that 'the fundamental problem was to deal with the medical side'[9] The gentlemen agreed that the right balance could be found by including a concise treatment of the military aspects, before moving on to a more detailed account of the medical problems. There was also consensus that discussions of medical aspects needed to be kept crisp and to the point. Finally, it was agreed that the narrative should not 'deteriorate into a diary' of field ambulance movements.[10]

Before leaving to catch a cab to the aerodrome, Charles Bean clarified the approach that should be taken to writing the medical history of the war: 'People won't want to know the movements of fd ambs [field ambulances] ... You can stand that for part of one campaign but when it continues for several campaigns it is unreadable. A history of problems – that is the guts of it.'[11] Indeed, it is.

CHAPTER I

FOUNDATIONS, EXPLORATIONS, ALTERCATIONS

'Little By Little'

FOUNDATIONS

Australia's medical response to the military situation in Papua in 1942 encapsulated all that was admirable, and that which was less so, in the history of Australian military medicine. The first deployment of an Australian military medical unit was to the Sudan in 1885. An ambulance corps comprising of 34 men, five ambulance wagons and 26 horses accompanied approximately 700 volunteer soldiers as they sailed from Sydney, New South Wales (NSW), to the Red Sea port of Suakin in Sudan. Though the NSW contingent was under British command, this was the first time that military medical personnel from Australia served as a discrete unit in an overseas conflict[1] Although not a united and promulgated medical service until 1902, medical corps personnel were among the 15,000 volunteers from the six colonies—later, the Australian Commonwealth—who served in South Africa during the Second Boer War (1899–1902).[2]

As the twentieth century unfolded in war's long shadow, Australians remained British in heart, mind and spirit. It was inevitable that the country's military and military medical service would continue to reflect those strong links. Developments in the AAMC to this point had mirrored those of the nation.[3] Prior to Federation in 1901, the standards of military medical units varied across the country, with NSW far ahead of the other states in terms of numbers and training. This has been attributed to the determination of one man, William 'Mo' Williams for, as Jennifer Gurner observed in her account of the history of Australia's medical corps, 'while other states had the *opportunity* to develop as good a service, they didn't have Williams.'[4]

Montage of New South Wales Contingent to the Sudan campaign, 1885. Surgeon-Major W.D.C. Williams is third from left in the top row. The central portrait is Major General J.S. Richardson (AWM 100976).

Williams had served as staff surgeon to the NSW Artillery before volunteering as the Principal Medical Officer (PMO) for the contingent to the Sudan. This experience, coupled with further training in England, saw Williams promoted to the rank of major and appointed PMO for the Army in NSW on his return to Australia. An idea first mooted by Williams and the Commandant of the NSW Corps, Colonel John Richardson, for the formation of a NSW Ambulance Corps finally came to fruition in

1888.[5] The inaugural unit temporarily took the form of a medical staff corps, with one PMO, four surgeons and 63 other ranks. When Williams attained the rank of lieutenant colonel the following year, he stated that his objective was to produce a permanent departmental corps which 'not only should contain surgeons equal to any emergency, and men so thoroughly trained, that they would be able to act as Hospital orderlies, wagon drivers, or stretcher-bearers, but that they might be expert in tent pitching, in transport, dressing and feeding patients.'[6] A permanent 15-man medical staff corps was subsequently established.

Federation saw the imperative for legislative and administrative cohesiveness, with which to bind the disparate colonies, extended to the military and its medical services. To this end, the existing services in each state were reorganised into a single, unified corps. The various state Defence Acts were subsumed, with the result that control of state military forces eventually became the responsibility of the Commonwealth. Due largely to the commitment of Williams, NSW was comparatively well resourced and boasted a corps of 36 officers and 122 other ranks by 1901. By comparison, Western Australia had a total corps of just 20 men, while the South Australian Medical Staff Corps struggled along with 45 members and was 'in urgent need of modern equipment'.[7] The Commandant's Report of 1901 provided an overview of staff levels, training and equipment in each state force, including the medical corps. Until this time, there had been no provision for service corps in South Australia, Western Australia or Queensland.[8] Only the NSW military could boast an ordnance store depot—and no state had a military veterinary department, despite the crucial role that horses played in the Army. It was against such a background that the General Officer Commanding (GOC) Australian Military Forces, Major General Edward Hutton, undertook his 1902 nationwide assessment of military equipment and supplies, including that available to medical staff.[9] The AAMC was officially promulgated that same year.[10] This new organisation comprised the Permanent Army Medical Corps, Militia Army Medical Corps, Volunteer Army Medical Corps, Reserve of Officers, and the Army Nursing Service Reserve.[11]

In 1906, Britain united its bearer companies and field hospitals into a single unit which became known as the field ambulance, comprising 10 medical officers and 224 other ranks. These were subsequently divided into tent divisions (nursing and administration duties) and bearer divisions. There was also a Light Horse Field Ambulance which had four, rather than the usual six, stretcher-bearers. The field ambulances were each attached to a brigade and were organised into self-contained sections (A, B and C), each equipped to handle 50 cases. Australia followed Britain's lead, with this new field ambulance system forming the foundation for the front-line medical care of thousands of Australian soldiers who found themselves fighting in twentieth-century wars. In 1909 pharmaceutical officers were included in the Medical Corps Reserve and sanitary officers were eventually incorporated. The original 1902 establishments had made no provisions for these components, nor had they included dental or preventative medicine units.[12]

Refinements to the organisational and administrative framework of the AAMC were extensive and ongoing during the turbulent first decades of the twentieth century. Such changes reflected the maxim, first proposed by Williams in the 1880s and adopted by the newly promulgated AAMC in 1902: *Paulatim*—'little by little'. This aphorism suitably conveyed the incremental steps by which Australia finally achieved a united and permanent military medical corps.[13]

The field ambulance soon became the largest component of the AAMC. These units were responsible for the administration of medical care to all sick and wounded soldiers and were located as close to the fighting as possible. Mobility was the field ambulances' defining feature—they shadowed the soldiers, with the primary aim to return the sick or wounded to the fighting or, if this was not possible, to evacuate them via a series of medical installations. Each medical post was located progressively further away from the front line. The standard scheme of casualty evacuation meant that the wounded were initially attended to on the battlefield by fellow soldiers, with battalion medical officers (often assisted by field ambulance personnel) administering further rudimentary care at Regimental Aid Posts (RAP), which were located short distances from the fighting. The field ambulance units assumed responsibility for the provision of increasingly more comprehensive treatment via the Advanced Dressing Stations (ADS) and Main Dressing Stations (MDS). Casualties were evacuated from the MDS back to Casualty Clearing Stations (CCS) and on to Australian General Hospitals (AGH) in the base area, depending on their wounds and condition. The field ambulance units came under the command of the division in which they served, with each unit generally responsible for the casualties of a single brigade.[14]

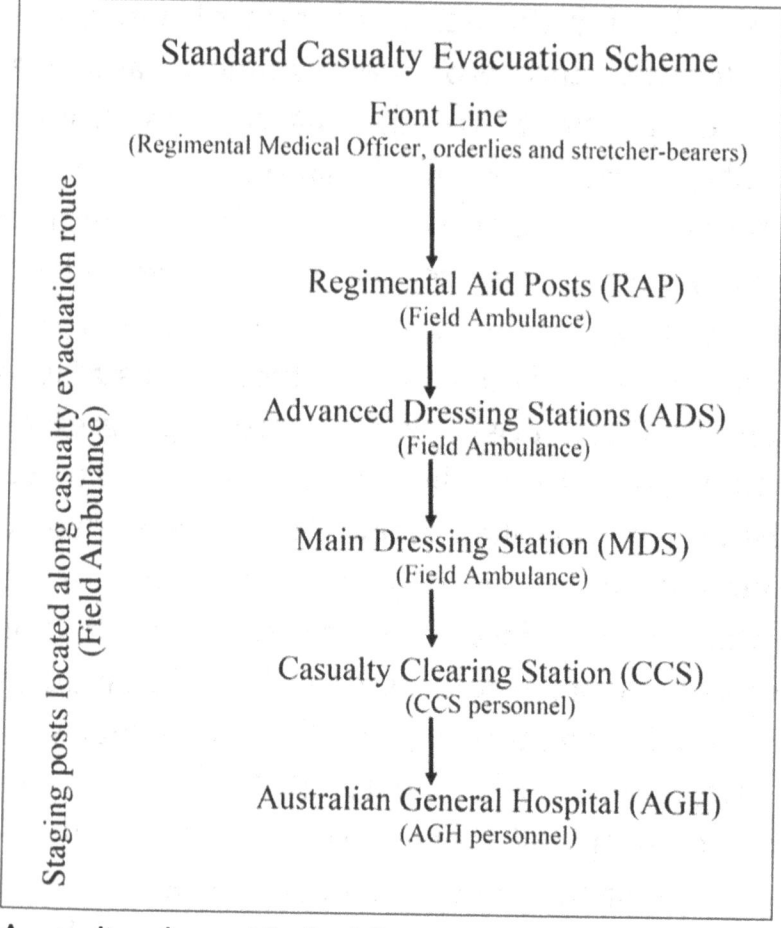

Australian Army Medical Service standard scheme of evacuation. Variations to the scheme were made over time and in response to the military situation.

The issue of funding proved to be a stumbling block to the evolution of a consistently well trained and well-resourced medical corps capable of supporting Australia's soldiers in time of war—and also providing medical care during peacetime. The introduction of universal military training in Australia in 1911 highlighted shortcomings in the medical services. At a time when more than 50,000 Australian males aged between 12 and 26 were training to fight for empire, king and country, no provision had been made for the acquisition of military medical stores. In addition, the medical supply and casualty evacuation systems both relied heavily on horse-drawn transport. Adding to the challenges was the issue of staffing: there were just four officers and 29 other ranks in the permanent AAMC, while the militia medical corps totalled 183 officers and 1649 other ranks.[15]

The fledging organisation was truly tested in World War I. On the eve of the conflict, the permanent medical services of the Australian Army had been in existence for a mere 23 years. The indefatigable Colonel 'Mo' Williams asked for, and was appointed to, the post of Director of Medical Services (DMS) and headed off to serve in his third war. He was 58 years old, overweight, not in the best of health, and with an outlook that was judged by some of his many detractors to be 'self-contained and restricted by his immersion in the past'.[16] The vast and bloody battlefields of Europe comprehensively tested DMS Williams, DGMS Major General Richard Fetherston and the AAMC as a whole. It was predictable, though not necessarily inevitable, that the effectiveness of twentieth-century battlefield medicine in places such as France and Turkey would be hampered by hauntingly familiar problems of resources, administration, logistics, command, communication, technology, transport, personalities and topography—factors which had so affected the administration of battlefield medicine in Europe, the Crimea, Africa and America throughout the preceding century, and which would arise in the Papuan campaign.

War inevitably brought change. Although this all-encompassing conflict produced carnage on an unimaginable scale, it also effected lasting scientific and technological developments—and heralded the emergence of medical men who were determined to fight for improvements to Australian military medicine. In the early years of the First World War the importance of rapid treatment was still not fully recognised as a crucial factor in the survival of wounded soldiers. However, by war's end it was this issue which drove key changes in military medical care as the importance of the swift collection, treatment and evacuation of patients was better understood. Another major advancement in medical care that evolved during these years was the development of specialty areas and specialist practitioners within the AAMC. This was largely the result of the medical profession worldwide finally taking a more scientific, less intuitive approach to medicine. Indeed, the official medical historian, A.G. Butler, contended that, by conferring the label of 'non-combatants' on the military medical service, the Geneva Convention of 1864 in effect stigmatised and isolated the military medical men of that time from civilian medical practitioners who were keenly embracing scientific developments.[17] Butler argued that the Great War not only redressed these issues but also came with the crest of a wave of technical 'scientific' activity unsurpassed, probably unequalled, in the history of man's cultural evolution ... [I]n the Great War medicine, almost alone among war's exploitations of peace, was able to 'save its soul alive' and, after some initial frustration, began to pick up the threads of peacetime scientific progress.[18]

War Establishment Personnel	Officers	Warrant Officers	Senior Sergeants	Sergeants	Other Ranks	Total
Current 3 Section	10	2	16	2	211	241
New 2 Section	8	3	4	6	190	211

Difference in personnel no.	-2	1	-12	4	-21	-30

Reorganisation of the Australian Field Ambulance from three sections to two sections December 1918.

The *raison d'être* for any military medical service in any war is to treat sick or wounded soldiers and return them to the front line as quickly as possible. However, the trinity of issues—supply, leadership and communication—which had vexed military medical men in earlier wars had once again stymied those charged with saving soldiers. During the turbulent years of World War I, millions of soldiers and civilians suffered death, disfigurement and disease on a scale hinted at, though barely imagined, by Henri Dunant and his contemporaries who founded the International Red Cross and drafted the first Geneva Convention.[19] This conflict that had pitted nineteenth-century men against twentieth-century machines impelled major technological advances, which paradoxically served both to destroy and save humanity.

EXPLORATIONS

From as early as the sixteenth century, a succession of Spanish, Portuguese, French and Dutch explorers sighted, charted and 'discovered' numerous South Pacific islands. Yet it was not until the 1840s that British naval officer Captain Owen Stanley surveyed the Great Barrier Reef, the waters of Torres Strait and the Arafura Sea, and the islands and coastline of south-eastern New Guinea.[20] Heeding the warnings of the British Admiralty to avoid the 'treacherous dispositions of [the] inhabitants', an ailing and trepidatious Stanley did not set foot on New Guinea itself.[21] Though reports on the area written by his contemporaries indicate that the Admiralty's warnings and Stanley's fears were not unfounded, a less anxious Captain John Moresby visited villages around the south-eastern part of the island in 1873. Moresby recorded his experiences, noting 'the kindness of the natives'.[22] Initial European efforts to establish permanent settlements in the western parts of New Guinea were short-lived, however, with most early attempts ending in suffering, sickness or death.[23]

The first permanent European resident of New Guinea was the English missionary William Lawes, who arrived with his family in Port Moresby (named by Captain John Moresby in honour of his father) in 1874. This decade heralded a period of exploration and exploitation that saw a seemingly disparate group of missionaries, adventurers, gold miners and government administrators wash ashore.[24] All were bound by the common desire to benefit—whether spiritually, scientifically or financially—from this untamed, untapped country and its people. Although Germany had played no role in its early exploration, the north-eastern area and surrounding islands of New Guinea comprised the first German protectorates claimed as part of that country's colonial expansion. In 1884, the north-eastern part of New Guinea was annexed by Germany, with the mainland area of Kaiser-Wilhelmsland and the islands to the east forming German New Guinea.[25] The south-eastern portion of the island of New Guinea became a British protectorate in the same year.[26] The area came under Australia's informal control in 1901, was named the Territory of Papua under the *Papua Act 1905*, and was formally placed under Australian administration in 1906, with Port Moresby as its capital.[27]

A series of tracks that criss-crossed Papua had long been used by the local population to travel from village to village, and between the interior and the coast. One such route, the 60-mile (approximately 96 kilometre) Kokoda Track, extended from some 25 miles north-east of Port Moresby in Central Province to Kokoda, in Northern Province. The village of Kokoda lies on a plateau to the north-east of the highest point of the Owen Stanley Range, Mount Victoria. From Kokoda, less-traversed sections of the track snake their way north to the coastal village of Soputa and the northern beaches.

Although predominately used by Papuans, a handful of nineteenth-century European settlers also walked the Kokoda Track. As the area north of the Owen Stanleys opened up to settlers, explorers and gold miners in the early years of the twentieth century, a government station was established at Kokoda and the track was improved to facilitate better communication between settlements. From 1904, a fortnightly mail delivery service was implemented along the Kokoda Track and in 1932 an airfield was constructed to the west of Kokoda village, with the aim of improving transportation for settlers.[28]

The arrival of the Europeans in Papua had implications for the island that went far beyond its physical landscape. An 1889 agreement between church representatives 'seeking only the best interests of the native population', determined their future 'spheres of influence' by effectively carving up the spiritual landscape of what was then British New Guinea. The Anglicans were allocated 'the whole of the north-east coast from Cape Ducie to the northern boundary', the

London Missionary Society and the Society of the Sacred Heart became responsible for the religious education of those on the south coast, while the souls of those in Milne Bay Province were assigned to the care of the Wesleyan missionaries.[29]

Map 1.1 Nova Guinea c.1600 (source: George Collingridge de Tourcey, The First Discovery of Australia and New Guinea: being the narrative of Portuguese and Spanish discoveries in the Australasian regions, between the years 1492-1606, with descriptions of their old charts, William Brooks, Sydney, 1906).

The peoples of the Milne Bay area encountered European explorers from as early as 1606, but it was not until the late 1800s that gold miners, pearl divers and missionaries settled there. This low, marshy coastal tract of land at the eastern tip of Papua is bordered by the mountains of the Owen Stanley and Stirling ranges. The deep body of water that forms Milne Bay itself is approximately 20 miles in length and 10 miles across. Nestled in the bifurcated tail of the island of New Guinea, the bay is spared the more turbulent moods of the Solomon and Coral seas. The wider Milne Bay District encompasses over 500 islands, including the D'Entrecasteaux group of Goodenough, Fergusson, Sanaroa, Dobu and Normanby islands.

The same series of legislative acts that opened much of Papua to European-owned plantations during the late nineteenth and early twentieth centuries saw the clearing of large areas of marshy land and jungle around the village of Gili Gili, towards the north-western shores of Milne Bay, to make way for coconut groves and copra factories. A 50foot jetty was later constructed to enable the loading and unloading of ships that anchored in the deep, protected waters of Milne Bay, while a narrow road that crossed the numerous and fast-flowing creeks of the area addressed some of the communication and transportation challenges.[30]

ALTERCATIONS

Britain's entry into a war with Germany in August 1914 stoked Australian suspicions of its near neighbours in the Pacific and heightened fear of the enemy in German New Guinea. Given that many Pacific Islands had long been 'carved up' and distributed geographically, politically and spiritually, the British now suggested that the Australian capture of German wireless stations and, eventually, their territorial possessions in the Pacific would constitute 'an important Imperial service'.[31] The Australian Naval and Military Expeditionary Force (AN&MEF) sailed for German New Guinea from Cockatoo Island, Sydney, on 19 August 1914 in response to the British suggestion.[32] This was to be the only time that Australia was entirely responsible for organising, supplying, mobilising and maintaining a military force overseas during the First World War.[33] The AN&MEF comprised approximately 1000 naval and army militia volunteers.

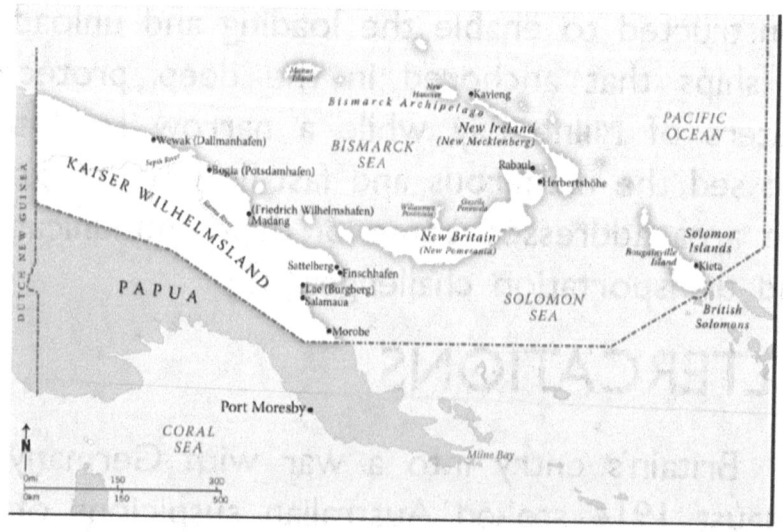

Map 1.2 German New Guinea

In many ways, the dire shortcomings of the medical component of the 1914 expedition represented a harbinger of the 1942 Papuan campaign. HMAS *Berrima*, which transported the force north to New Britain was unsuitable, having been hastily converted for the voyage just a week before embarkation. Because there had been no time to fit out *Kanowna*, a steamer originally intended to assist in transporting the troops, it was deemed too 'dirty and unsanitary' and was instead instructed to accompany the convoy—a decision that no doubt pleased the ship's company, who had not been told that the vessel was to be used for active service and so were 'not favourably disposed to the troops'.[34] The general ignorance among the men concerning hygiene and preventative health prompted instruction en route. Medical plans were virtually non-existent and the medical stores sent were 'defective ... indeed, the supply of drugs and dressings on board was ... nearly exhausted' before they reached their destination.[35]

This first joint operation undertaken by Australia's defence forces relied on 'undeveloped youths' who were physically unfit for service, ill-prepared and ill-equipped to fight a war in any theatre, let alone on a Pacific island.[36] The temperature at their destination of New Britain averaged c. to 90° Fahrenheit, with heavy rainfall all year round, oppressive humidity, dense jungles, steamy rainforests and rugged mountains. A medical detachment of just 40 men accompanied the AN&MEF. Among this group were two officers whose lives were to be woven into the tapestry of the Australian Army Medical Service.[37] Lieutenant Colonel Neville Howse VC was appointed PMO for the expedition, with Captain Frederick Maguire serving as second in command. Maguire would go on to write the official medical history of this expedition and the resultant Australian occupation of German New Guinea, while Howse was later appointed commander of the Australian and New Zealand Army Corps (ANZAC) medical services and its DMS.[38]

It was a portent of things to come that such little thought had been given to medical aspects of the hastily organised expedition or, indeed, to ongoing medical arrangements for the island's occupation thereafter. Howse was not consulted on the final medical arrangements and no naval medical personnel accompanied that service's 500 volunteers. With the expedition so poorly organised and medical aspects largely ignored, it had been left to Howse and Maguire to oversee the care of those sent north at the behest of Britain, and it was only the initiative shown by

Howse that equipped medical personnel with a few basic items suitable for the administration of medicine in tropical conditions. Voluntary organisations such as the Red Cross assisted his last-minute scramble for supplies of anti-malarial drugs such as quinine and other necessities, including microscopes and mosquito nets.

On 11 September 1914, the naval contingent landed near Herbertshöhe on the Gazelle Peninsula. The soldiers went ashore at Rabaul on the north-east tip of New Britain, kitted out in their heavy woollen uniforms. The advanced naval landing party consisted of 50 reservists and was supported by just one AAMC officer, Captain Brian Pockley. Leading Stoker William Kember, responsible for tending the furnace on the steamship, served as Pockley's medical orderly. Once ashore near Herbertshöhe and Kabakaul on New Britain, the men were charged with seizing the wireless station at Bita Paka, less than five miles inland. The fighting was over within 24 hours, with both sides sustaining casualties before the German Governor surrendered.[39] Captain Pockley was shot while attending the wounded and later died from his wounds, with Captain Maguire at his side. Pockley is widely acknowledged as the first Australian to die in World War I.[40]

The British government was so pleased with the operation at Bita Paka that it encouraged Australia to seize further German possessions in the Pacific, thereby enhancing its contribution to the 'great and urgent Imperial service'.[41] German New Guinea came under Australian military administration for the duration of the war, with Captain Maguire remaining there as PMO until February 1915. It was under Maguire's solid leadership that the small medical team, which had been 'extemporised for an expedition', faced the continuing challenges involved in dealing with the public health issues presented by Australia's occupation of German New Guinea.[42] His correspondence during the early months of 1915 indicated ongoing and serious medical supply problems. During January and February, for example, Maguire urgently requested a range of drugs as well as medical provisions such as castor oil, cough medicine, hydrochloric acid and methylated spirits. With a dearth of mosquito nets and quinine, and malaria becoming more prevalent among the men the longer they remained on the island, Australians began dying from the disease.[43] No nets had been sent with the most recently arrived soldiers and any thought that some use could be made of the nets sent earlier dissipated given that 'it was a week after the new troops arrived before the old troops could be sent away, and ... the nets in use by the old troops were so dilapidated and dirty that even if available they were quite useless.'[44]

Captain Brian Colden Antill Pockley, AAMC, AN&MEF, c.1914 (AWM H19316).

The dosage of quinine was increased in an effort to counter the heightened risk of malaria due to the lack of protective measures, thus further depleting already inadequate supplies. That many of the men were now taking 10 grains of quinine daily meant approximately one and a half pounds (more than half a kilogram) of the drug was required *per day* to treat 1300 troops. The medical supplies requested by Maguire had still not arrived six weeks later. This affected the local population as well as the soldiers, as there was no quinine with which to treat the many patients languishing in 'native' (non-military) hospitals.[45]

AN&MEF personnel queuing for their daily dose of quinine, August 1917 (AWM A02739).

Captain Raphael Cilento, an AAMC officer and one of the official medical historians of the First World War, observed that Australia's military occupation of German New Guinea in 1914 should serve to 'impress on all concerned the fact that, although Australia was close to tropical countries, and had, in fact, tropical dependencies, the training of medical staff for the responsibilities of tropical hygiene was still very deficient and ... the community could not risk being caught again in so serious a state of unpreparedness as at the outset of the War.'[46] Unfortunately these wise words went largely unheeded.

Australia was not alone in claiming, occupying and holding German possessions throughout the Pacific during and after World War I. Many countries not only capitalised on the opportunity to increase their presence and power in the area for the duration of the conflict, but sought to hold onto the islands long after hostilities had ceased. In accordance with Article 119 of the Versailles Treaty of 1919, the Council of the League of Nations dispersed all German overseas possessions among the Allied countries.[47] In the South Pacific, these included the Bismarck Archipelago, Western Samoa, Bougainville and Nauru as well as the Marshall, Caroline and

Mariana islands, which Japan formally took possession of in 1920.[48]

The pivotal role to be played by the 'novel and interesting little corner' of Papua, long obvious to Australia, was underscored by this changing world order. Prime Minister William (Billy) Hughes firmly believed that the key to Australia's security was to be found in that 'great rampart of islands which stretch around the north-east coast of Australia ...[as] those who hold [New Guinea] hold us.'[49] Hughes' determination to doggedly pursue his country's interests at Versailles finally handed control of German New Guinea to Australia. By May 1921, the eastern section of the island had become a League of Nations Mandated Territory under the administration of the Commonwealth Government of Australia.[50] Milne Bay, its districts and islands, represented the south-eastern extent of the Territory of Papua and so also came under Australian administration and protection. The western section of the island—Netherlands New Guinea—had been recognised as a Dutch possession by Britain and Germany since 1895 and remained under the administration of the Government of Netherlands East Indies.[51]

From the 1920s, successive Australian governments adopted a policy of colonial self-sufficiency regarding New Guinea. The minimal amount of expenditure intended for Australia's mandated territories was made clear in a 1921 budget speech by the Treasurer, Joseph Cook, who explained that 'After considerable pruning, the expenditure estimates have been reduced to a sum not exceeding estimated revenue. In accepting the mandate, Australia has entered upon additional responsibility, but no stone will be left unturned to prevent further financial burdens being entailed thereby.'[52] The financial ramifications of the budgetary 'pruning' were keenly felt, with one former district officer and goldfields warden pointing out that the cost of supplying medical services to the indigenous population was 'more than the head-tax collected [and] left no money for anything else'.[53]

The enthusiastic post-war carve-up of the South Seas had not only shattered German hegemony, but produced a 'political hodgepodge that ... by the early 1930s was hardly a satisfactory basis for a permanent status quo.'[54] Indeed, the post-war status quo continued to shift on already shaky foundations throughout the decade. The years that had passed since the signing of the peace treaty at Versailles in 1919 saw old enmities fester away in Europe just as new enemies emerged on the Pacific horizon, with the result that German aggression soon threatened world peace once again. The sovereignty of the mandated territories resulting from the Versailles Treaty was not clear—a fact that did nothing to allay fears in the Pacific over the growing power and influence of yet another threat to peace during the 1930s: Japan. That the Marianas, Palau, Caroline and Marshall islands became Japanese mandated territories in 1920 appeared to represent an ever-present threat to countries such as Australia—one which escalated in the years after Japan's withdrawal from the League of Nations in 1933. The Japanese decision to leave came in response to the League's adoption of the Lytton Report which recommended that Japanese troops be removed from Manchuria. The withdrawal by Japan was accompanied by statements which 'intimated quite plainly that she has no intention of handing back her mandate'.[55] Importantly, the League did not insist that Japan do so.

Although fortifications were prohibited in any of the territories covered by the League of Nations' mandates, Japan had built substantial naval bases on her Pacific islands during the interwar years.[56] Such action was construed by some as being in contravention of the mandate. However, there existed no clear delineation between the instigation of administrative processes and the building of civil constructions deemed necessary to promote development as well as free trade—but which might be also used in a military capacity if needed—and those processes and constructions which were established or developed *purely* for military purposes. Compulsory inspections of the Japanese mandates in the Pacific during the interwar years did not identify military fortifications. Regular reports delivered to the League of Nations also failed to highlight any violations. These facts have been drawn on to argue that Japan's actions during the interwar period did *not* constitute a clear breach of the somewhat ambiguous limitations imposed by the League of Nations' mandates.[57]

Given the uncertainty of the world's political and economic situation during the 1930s, a decision by Australia on the ongoing question of the relocation of Rabaul, the capital of its mandated Territory of New Guinea, was deferred.[58] The possible amalgamation of Papua with the Territory of New Guinea was instead prioritised by Australian politicians. There were various reasons the amalgamation question now reared its head. Proposals to amalgamate had previously been presented in an administrative context only, largely because full amalgamation of the territories was considered impracticable. Yet the issue had never been fully dismissed by the Australian government and was now deemed worthy of further investigation given the growing threat of conflict.[59] It was thought that amalgamation would strengthen this 'Australian outpost', with the Minister in Charge of Territories, Eric Harrison, arguing that 'the island of New Guinea, as represented by Papua and the territory of New Guinea, is vital to the life of Australia.'[60]

An associated issue came to the fore when Rabaul, located on the island of New Britain and approximately 35 miles off the coast of mainland Papua, was severely damaged by a volcanic eruption in May 1937. A visit to the area in 1938 by a group led by ex-Prime Minister, now Minister for External Trade, Billy Hughes, recommended Lae, on the Huon Gulf in north-east New Guinea, as the site for the new capital. Hughes' preference for Salamaua, approximately 20 miles south of Lae, was roundly criticised, with the location deemed 'extremely unhealthy'.[61] Some, such as the Administrator of the Mandated Territory of New Guinea, Sir Walter McNicoll, who were cognisant of the military value of locating the capital inland, favoured neither of these small coastal towns. The debate became academic when the growing threat of war interrupted any plans for relocation and turned the country's attention to other matters.[62]

An insight into the attitudes of Australian parliamentarians towards their northern neighbours in Papua can be gained by briefly considering discussions undertaken just prior to the 1938 visit to debate the location of the new capital. Much mirth had ensued in May that year when the wizened Hughes was asked by members of the Opposition to verify the accuracy of a statement contained in an earlier report by the Lieutenant Governor of Papua, Hubert Murray, which posited that 'men with tails roamed the interior of New Guinea'.[63] Hughes' United Australia Party colleagues rather unkindly noted his remarkable likeness to a sketch of the so-called 'monkey man' who they deemed to be 'Billy's living image'.[64] Ever the showman, Hughes played to the gallery and humoured the House by dutifully promising to look into the existence of the monkey men while in New Guinea. Although these discussions were conducted in a light-hearted fashion, they encapsulated Australian attitudes towards the peoples and history of the island of New Guinea and its component territories: Dutch New Guinea, the Australian Mandated Territory of New Guinea, and the Territory of Papua.

As diplomacy faltered and fractures deepened across Europe towards the end of the decade, the imperative for Australia to retain a mandate over New Guinea became more acute. It was thought that failure to adequately secure the area would 'place the adjoining territory of Papua in jeopardy [and] provide a jumping-off place which might prove a very serious menace to Australia itself.'[65] Australia's mandate in the Territory of New Guinea was bound by the same League of Nations' ruling that forbade Japan from building fortifications in her mandated territories. Indeed, the edict was the very reason that Australia 'had scrupulously avoided making defence preparations there until 1939, and there was great leeway to make up.'[66] A small military contingent left Australia to begin the construction of basic fortifications around Port Moresby in 1939, with the aim of implementing 'the [Australian] Government plan to make Papua the base for the defence of the whole territory'.[67]

In September 1939, Prime Minister Robert Menzies declared that Australia was at war with Germany. Two months later, the DGMS, Rupert Downes, attended a presentation by J.R. Halligan of the Prime Minister's Territories Branch regarding the overall situation in Papua and New Guinea.[68] Halligan was a respected authority on the country and had accompanied Hughes on his visit the previous year. According to Halligan, the two areas of primary importance to Australia in terms of administration and defence were the current capital of the Territory of New Guinea, Rabaul, on New Britain, and the southern settlement of Port Moresby, the capital of Papua.

Major General Rupert Downes, DGMS from 1934 to 1941 (AWM 043212).

Downes was familiar with the medical situation in Rabaul, having previously requested that the Acting Director of Public Health there undertake a survey of medical and hygiene conditions. That survey identified malaria, dysentery and dietary issues as the main health concerns. Downes, a diligent DGMS as well as an experienced and knowledgeable medical officer, was aware of similar health issues around Port Moresby and was keen to better understand the medical demands as well as learn more about the medical facilities already in place in Papua.[69] Halligan explained that there were two main 'native' hospitals located at Port Moresby and Samarai, which was the administrative capital of Milne Bay Province. Smaller medical facilities were located at various stations, missions and plantations. European medical personnel in Papua regularly attended patients at some of the facilities, assisted by local nurses. Common medical conditions treated included hookworm, venereal disease, ulcers and yaws.[70] This rudimentary health system was augmented by Papuans who trained for six months at the School of Public Health and Tropical Medicine in Sydney, before returning home to work as travelling medical assistants.[71]

Australia's medical unpreparedness for war had long concerned Downes, who served as the youngest lieutenant colonel (2nd Light Horse Field Ambulance) in the First World War, before his promotion to the position of Assistant Director of Medical Services (ADMS) for both the ANZAC Mounted Division and the Australian base in Egypt.[72] In 1936 he had organised a training exercise involving the Deputy Director of Medical Services (DDMS) and the Assistant Directors of the military districts then in existence: Queensland, NSW, Victoria, South Australia and Western Australia. The exercise was attended by 25 senior medical officers of the AAMC, the Deputy Director of the Australian Air Force medical service, as well as nonmedical members and staff. In what was the largest peacetime medical training exercise conducted in Australia to date, Downes presented the participants with a scenario predicated on a Japanese invasion of NSW, in which they were required to consider the military medical challenges of such an attack and propose the best methods for dealing with the casualties.[73]

In December 1939, DGMS Downes again travelled to Canberra to meet Halligan. This time the discussion centred on the logistics involved in expanding the medical facilities in Port Moresby. Downes was pleased with the outcome of the meeting, noting that 'Halligan considers our proposal for an adjoint ward quite reasonable [and] thinks there is room to build a good deal in hospital site.'[74] These discussions are notable for two key reasons: first, they indicate that there was some recognition of the imperative to improve medical care in Papua, and, second, they occurred two years before Japan's entry into the war.

There is a view that the Japanese threat to Australia and its territories 'had been foreseen and measures had been taken to establish some defence organisation, at Rabaul and Port Moresby in particular.'[75] Yet, it must be acknowledged that any such measures proved too little and far too late. The sluggishness of the implementation and the deficiencies associated with Army administration, the building of fortifications, and the provision of medical facilities suitable for a country at war, suggest a low level of strategic importance had been afforded the military medical services and the Territories of New Guinea and Papua, even at this relatively late stage.

CHAPTER 2

LEADERSHIP, MIDDLE EAST, LESSONS

'Our mutual feelings toward each other are quite unimportant'

LEADERSHIP

To better understand the medical situation that unfolded in Papua in 1942, it is important to appreciate the challenges facing the medical services on the eve of war, assess their response to the Middle East campaign of 1940–41, and consider the lessons learned—as well as those ignored. Medical lessons learned across Cyrenaica, Greece, Crete and Syria were not always heeded in the South West Pacific Area (SWPA) during 1942. In many ways, the Middle East campaign represented the nexus between the progression of the AAMC since its promulgation in 1902 and its regression in Papua 40 years later. The forefather of the military medical service in Australia, 'Mo' Williams, would have struggled to foresee both the highly mechanised war in which medical personnel found themselves embroiled in the first half of the twentieth century, and the primitive conditions later faced in Papua.[1]

By the time the country was again at war, the consequences of allowing the medical services to run down after 1918 and, indeed, actively pursuing their reduction, were clear. The harsh economic realities of the years following World War I, coupled with the peacetime somnolence that had been the hallmark of nations before and since meant that, rather than looking to the future, army medical departments worldwide remained mired in the past. Medical disasters such as the Gallipoli campaign left a bitter aftertaste for Australian medical officers who attributed such failings to a casual disregard for the importance of scientific research. Although wartime advances in science and technology progressed military medical practice to some extent, most Army medical units continued to be as outdated, under resourced, under-staffed and undervalued after 1918 as they had been throughout the long nineteenth century.[2]

Changes to the size and composition of the Australian Army had been effected over the decades, so that an Australian infantry division in World War II comprised 15,000 men—3000 fewer than in World War I. By contrast, the number of Australian Imperial Force (AIF) divisional support personnel had increased from

30,000 to more than 50,000 men.[3] In general, a division comprised three infantry brigades, two armoured brigades, artillery regiments and supporting arms and services. The organisation and size of the brigades changed during the interwar years and, by the 1940s, totalled between 2500 and 5000 soldiers. Although there had been major changes to the organisation and personnel numbers of the field ambulance units after World War I ended, it remained the case throughout World War II that three Australian field ambulance units were allocated per infantry division—with one unit assigned to provide medical care for each of the three infantry brigades and their attached troops.

By 1939, the war establishment of the Australian field ambulance units comprised 12 officers and 225 other ranks, including 56 Australian Army Service Corps (AASC) personnel. Ten of the officers were doctors, with two non-medical officers—one quartermaster captain and one officer—to command the AASC personnel. The other ranks included nursing orderlies, ward orderlies, quartermasters, carpenters, cooks—and later, motor ambulance and transport drivers. In accordance with the 1906 and 1929 Geneva Conventions, personnel were generally unarmed, permitted to carry only 'light individual weapons solely to defend their patients or themselves against acts of violence.'[4] Each of the three companies of the field ambulance unit included two medical officers with the rank of captain. In most battle situations, Headquarters Company was responsible for the MDS with the two bearer companies (A and B) manning the ADS. The field ambulance unit was commanded by an officer with the rank of lieutenant colonel, and each of the three companies was commanded by a major.[5]

Many of the medical officers who went on to play important roles in the Papuan campaign of 1942 had served in World War I, contributed to medical planning during the Army's lean interwar period, and played vital roles in the early years of World War II. Over time, the influences associated with rank, personality and patronage combined to determine the direction and effectiveness of the medical campaign in the Pacific. Manoeuvrings and machinations in 1940 irrevocably altered the leadership of the medical service at a time when Australian soldiers were fighting and dying in the Middle East. Sixteen months later the AAMC would face its greatest challenge in Papua.

The DGMS, Rupert Downes, was on a long tour of Army medical facilities in Britain, India, the Middle East and Canada in September 1939 when Prime Minister Robert Menzies declared that Australia was at war with Germany. Rising tensions in Europe coupled with the failure to prioritise the medical services during the interwar years should have made the benefits of undertaking such a trip as obvious to others as it had long been to Downes. This was not the case. Though Downes had sought permission many years earlier, a long delay in obtaining official approval ensued, with the result that 'the tour was begun too late for its full value to be attained.'[6] DGMS Downes did not return to Australia until October 1939, with his position as the most senior officer in the Australian Army Medical Service temporarily filled by Colonel William Johnston.

In anticipation of the range of medical issues that would confront the Army if again called to serve in an overseas theatre of war, two key bodies—the Central Medical Coordination Committee and the Medical Equipment Control Committee—had been established by Downes in 1938. Their aim was to ensure adequate supplies for overseas medical units as well as for the home front.[7] What Downes could not anticipate was the way in which myriad bureaucratic processes caused the wheels to turn ever so slowly. To take just one example, the cumbersome 10-stage process required to issue orders for medical equipment took a minimum of 22 days and a maximum of 60.[8]

As DGMS, it was Downes' responsibility to organise the mobilisation of the medical service. On his return to Australia in October, he quickly established the Army Medical Directorate as the body responsible for preparing the AAMC for mobilisation. The efficacy of the Directorate was soon tested when, in January 1940, the bulk of the 6th Division of the Second Australian Imperial Force (2nd AIF) sailed for the Middle East. Based at Victoria Barracks in Melbourne, the Medical Directorate initially consisted of just five members, including Downes' colleague and close friend, Colonel Samuel Burston. That their long-established friendship would come under considerable strain during these early years of war was not unrelated to Burston's developing professional and personal relationship with the GOC 2nd AIF and I Australian Corps, Thomas Blamey. Revered and reviled, Blamey was a complex and difficult character who strongly supported those he deemed worthy and callously cast aside those he did not. Importantly, in view of his friendship with Burston, he 'played favourites with some of his appointments ... and relegated able men ... and less able ones ... to the sidelines as much for personal as professional reasons.'[9]

While conscious of the importance of maintaining the traditional close relationship with British military command, the obligation to ensure the autonomy of the Australians as a distinct fighting force made Commander-in-Chief Blamey extremely determined to 'maintain the integrity of the AIF and his command over it.'[10] Although history has generally judged his efforts in this regard as successful, it nevertheless proved a difficult task for Blamey for reasons other than personality.[11] For instance, many of the problems later experienced by Australian military commanders in the Middle East were attributable to the 'fundamental flaw in Australian policy, namely that effective defence depended on a nation's ability to manufacture arms.'[12] The Australian Army had certainly been slow to adopt mechanisation and manufacturing policies during the 1930s and so continued to rely on its British counterpart for a great deal of support in the Middle East.[13]

Burston and Blamey arrived in Palestine together in June 1940. Downes had appointed Burston as DDMS for I Australian Corps—the most senior corps medical officer.[14] On reaching Jerusalem on 20 June, Burston and Blamey attended a cocktail party hosted by the commander of the 6th Division, Major General Iven Mackay, who introduced them to some of the British commanders. Burston was pleased with the Australian medical situation, stating that 'there has probably never been a force sent overseas from any country better equipped on the medical side.'[15] During his time in the Middle East, Blamey experienced various health issues and became increasingly dependent on Burston. In conjunction with his official position, which was 'always political', Burston willingly filled the unofficial role of Blamey's 'personal physician and counsellor wherever they served together ...[and] made it a habit to spend time with Blamey daily, often on the pretext of AAMC matters, to check on Blamey's physical condition and then give him medical and personal advice.'[16] Thus, the already strong bond between the two men was consolidated. This information is relevant to any discussion of AAMC leadership as, in time, that bond would prove crucial to Burston's controversial appointment to the coveted role of DGMS—a role proudly held by Downes since 1934 until it was wrenched from him in intriguing circumstances in 1941.

DGMS Major General Rupert Downes with senior medical staff, c. December 1940. Downes is seated in the middle of the front row (AWM 000485).

The outbreak of war in 1939 had highlighted the need for the rapid mobilisation of the three arms of the defence services. Yet the power vacuum that had been created by Downes' overseas tour meant that important issues such as the amalgamation of the medical services of the Army, Navy and Air Force, the coordination and distribution of medical supplies, and the training of medical personnel were either thrown into disarray or abandoned altogether.[17] Among the many considerations in planning the medical care of Australian soldiers fighting a distant war, two areas had demanded Downes' immediate attention: first, the AAMC had to be set up to function as a distinct entity and not merely serve as an extension to either the civilian medical service or the Army; second, it had to accommodate Australian, not British, circumstances and priorities.[18]

A report written by Downes in these early years of the war points to a medical service ground down by years of neglect—one that continued to rigidly adhere to outdated procedures, remained bound by severe financial limitations, and was too often hamstrung by the obstructionist behaviour of those in positions of military or political power. An insight into the composition of the medical service itself was provided by his observation that most of those who volunteered were older medical men—the corollary being that there was an absence of younger, fitter volunteers with medical training. There was certainly a marked difference in age between those volunteering in 1940 and those who had enlisted in the medical corps during World War I. Downes did not attribute this situation to a lack of suitably qualified personnel, but rather to a reticence to serve that he struggled to understand. In what seemed both a rebuke to the young doctors of the time and a surfacing of inter-state rivalry, Downes noted that, while only one of the registrars at

Melbourne Hospital had volunteered (and later withdrew, before subsequently re-enlisting), 'the holding back was particularly marked in Sydney from which all sorts of complaints on every subject connected with volunteering came.'[19]

The popular depiction of an altruistic group of young Australians eager to serve their country and rushing to enlist is somewhat dented by this description.[20] Given that he had strongly and consistently opposed the well-supported proposition of conscripting medical students and doctors, Downes must have been bitterly disappointed at this turn of events. His comments regarding the effectiveness of the committees which had been set up to oversee the organisation of medical services reflected this disappointment. While observing that the various committees were primarily engaged in directing the supply of medical equipment, he noted the ineffectiveness and confusion surrounding 'the control of medical practitioners owing to the lack of any executive power as regards calling up medical men [and] there was a good deal of misunderstanding and confusion with the State Committees. Some State Committees carried out their work to the limit, others did very little.'[21]

Relationships that were personally and professionally important to Downes changed dramatically during 1940. Despite the problems he encountered in dealing with military personnel and government departments, Downes enjoyed a good rapport with Prime Minister Menzies and the Minister for the Army, Brigadier Geoffrey Street, who recognised his expertise and often sought him out for advice on medical matters. A combination of respect and friendship saw Downes appear before the War Cabinet to discuss matters of varying importance, and he was often 'either sent for or was accorded interviews with the Prime Minister.'[22] Downes' bond with senior ministers was dealt a cruel blow when a Royal Australian Air Force (RAAF) Lockheed Hudson A16-97 crashed on its approach to Canberra Airport in August, killing six men on board—including Brigadier Street.[23] This 'shocking calamity' also claimed the life of the Chief of the General Staff, General Sir Cyril Brudenell Bingham White.[24]

The air crash had widespread and unanticipated ramifications for the nation, for Downes, and for the Army's medical service. In personal correspondence, Downes noted that Street had previously instructed him by telephone 'that nothing was to be allowed to hold up the provision of [medical] equipment and that it might be ordered whether the money was ready or not.'[25] Street had also issued this instruction to Downes on previous occasions.[26] For instance, the challenges of readying the medical services for war, the early battles to obtain access to sufficient medical resources, and Street's willingness to help smooth the way, were discussed by the two over dinner on 11 October 1939, not long after Downes had returned from overseas.[27] On 12 August 1940 (the day before the air crash), Downes asked Street to put his informal instruction 'to see him at once if blocked' in writing. That request was tragically 'thwarted in execution by his death'.[28]

The difficulties encountered by DGMS Downes in supplying the Australian medical units in the Middle East impacted on leadership issues that came to the fore towards the end of the year. In June 1940, 12 days after disembarking in Palestine, Blamey promoted Colonel Burston to the rank of brigadier—a promotion Burston foreshadowed as early as April:

> With regard to my position, I don't think there should be any difficulty at all as my appointment until the Corps concentrates will be D.D.M.S., A.I.F., and I will carry out the two jobs of D.M.S., A.I.F., and D.D.M.S., Corps. It is possible that I may be given the rank of Brigadier almost straightaway, as it is considered that with nine full Colonels under me there should be some upgrading in my rank.[29]

Brigadier Burston moved to the headquarters of I Australian Corps in Gaza, which remained his base until it was relocated to Alexandria in February 1941.[30] In Australia, Downes was struggling to supply equipment for the Middle East, as well as oversee the recruiting, equipping and training of the newly recruited medical men. These difficult tasks were made more so by reports of discontent among overseas personnel. Correspondence received by Downes from Burston and others was sometimes conspiratorial, ambiguous and confusing. Perhaps with one eye already focused on advancing his career prospects, Burston advocated a decreased reliance on Downes and the Melbourne Directorate over matters pertaining to the Middle East. In stark contrast to his initial impressions of a medical service that ranked among the best in the world in terms of equipment, Burston's private correspondence with other officers now included explicit or implicit complaints about the medical situation in the Middle East and Downes' culpability for problems encountered.[31]

Yet the impression Burston conveyed directly to Downes was quite different. He congratulated him on his organisational expertise regarding medical supplies, 'sincerely' expressed appreciation for everything Downes had done to 'make our part of the show a really first class one' and again opined that the Australians were probably the best equipped troops in the Middle East.[32] Critically analysed, the contradictory nature of Burston's correspondence suggests both disingenuousness and duplicity. This distancing of the relationship between senior medical personnel serving overseas and the medical hierarchy based in Australia was worryingly reminiscent of earlier attitudes in earlier conflicts.[33] Various interpretations of Burston's changing and divergent views on the medical situation in the Middle East are possible: it might be that there were (as Burston originally stated) sufficient medical supplies for the AAMC to satisfactorily treat Australian soldiers; it is possible that he was unaware of any supply problems until the Australians went into battle and the AAMC was called on to treat the wounded; or perhaps the issue of supply was used by Burston and others to undermine Downes' authority, with the aim of installing Burston as DGMS. Indeed, the explanation may well lie in a combination of these factors.

As forthcoming with criticism as Burston was in private, it seems he favoured a more circuitous route when it came to making his complaints official. Yet he could not have failed to foresee that his decision to take his grievances directly to General Blamey ensured that they would snake their way along the chain of command until ultimately reaching the ear of Adjutant-General Victor Stantke and Prime Minister Robert Menzies.[34] Further, 'Burston's serious complaints about the supply problem really only began in January 1941 ... previously, Burston's letters to Downes had given the impression that all was generally well.'[35] That Burston's complaints first emerged in the same month the Australians first saw action in Cyrenaica (Libya)—thereby exposing shortcomings in the medical services under the newly promoted DMS Burston's command—is surely no coincidence.

In the shadow of what some overseas personnel deemed a medical supply crisis primarily attributable to Downes, Blamey had appointed Burston to the position of DMS AIF in the Middle East in late November 1940. A leadership controversy quickly engulfed Downes when, at the behest of the new Minister for the Army (appointed after the air crash that killed Brigadier Street), Percy Spender, and the Adjutant-General, Victor Stantke, he temporarily relinquished the role of DGMS and was formally appointed DMS AIF in the Middle East—the same role that Blamey had just handed to Burston. It seems that both Spender and the Military Board that approved Downes' appointment were unaware that Blamey had already promoted

Burston to DMS. Equally oblivious to the situation, Downes set about making the necessary preparations to sail overseas to take up this new position.

Downes' correspondence on the matter provides some insight into the confusing and complex chain of command of the Army and its medical service. On 27 December 1940, he noted that the Military Board was not even aware that Blamey had the *power* to appoint the DMS, 'else they would hardly have appointed me'.[36] The lack of respect shown to Downes at this difficult time both surprised and disappointed him, with his DMS appointment 'not even cancelled officially or politely'.[37] When he asked the Chief of the General Staff, Vernon Sturdee, for some indication of when he would be leaving Australia to take up the position in the Middle East, Downes was 'casually' told 'oh, Blamey had appointed Burston already' with Sturdee informing him that he would not be heading overseas after all.[38]

Downes' letters regarding these events also make clear his unwillingness to take up the DMS appointment, the amount of pressure applied by Stantke, and the value Downes placed on maintaining his friendship with Burston. A letter written in March 1941 to another friend and colleague, Colonel William Johnston, who was in

Alexandria, explained that he 'did not ask for or desire the job of D.M.S., A.I.F., and definitely recommended that I should not be appointed.'[39] In one of the many letters to Burston that went unanswered, Downes attempted to explain the sequence of events to this man he still regarded as a dear friend. He explained that he had expressed concerns about taking up the position in no uncertain terms to Stantke, adding:

> to my thinking I was of more importance here, particularly from the point of view of supplying medical personnel and equipment, to say nothing of co-ordination. He thought the other way ... I wanted to tell you this so that you might not think I have been trying to rob you of your job.[40]

Burston was officially appointed to the position of DMS AIF in March 1941. Although his own appointment as DGMS should have continued until August 1943, Downes occupied this most senior role only until the time of Burston's promotion. As an interim measure, Spender appointed the former DDMS of the 2nd Military District (NSW), General Frederick Maguire, to Downes' DGMS position in mid-March and, notably, did not involve the Military Board in this decision. The role had been ably held and much valued by Downes since August 1934. Now, shattered and humiliated, he was effectively moved sideways to make room for Maguire, taking up the newly created position of Inspector General of Medical Services (IGMS).[41] The fact that Spender's appointment of Maguire occurred while Prime Minister Menzies was overseas, and was implemented without any consultation with the Military Board, highlights not only the strained relationships and tussles for power within and between the government and the Army, but also the political nature of the military appointments.[42]

Letters from Downes to Burston a few months after the turmoil say much about the man. On 2 March 1941, he wrote: 'Our mutual feelings toward each other are quite unimportant. All that matters is to do the best that lies in our power for the troops through the efficiency of the AAMC.'[43] Downes' removal from the most senior position in the AAMC represented both the climax of an intriguing narrative that had played out since the declaration of war, and the professional nadir for a man who had dedicated his life thus far to military medical service. A few weeks after returning to Australia, Burston was formally appointed to the coveted position of DGMS, taking over from Maguire on 1 April 1942 and remaining in the role until

1948. The nationally significant consequences of this leadership debacle were serious and long-ranging—not only for Burston and Downes, but also for the future of the medical service and the Australian soldiers entrusted to its care for the duration of the war.

Major General Samuel Burston (middle of front row) and officers of Headquarters 1 Australian Corps on troop transport ship HMT Orcades, returning from the Middle East to Australia in March 1942. Burston took over the role of DGMS from General Frederick Maguire on 1 April 1942 (AWM 011887).

THE AAMC IN THE MIDDLE EAST

An overview of the military situation lends context to the medical situation in the Middle East. The 6th Division, so named because five militia infantry divisions were already in existence, was the first Australian division to be raised and serve overseas in World War II.[44] Advance units arrived in the Middle East towards the end of 1939, with numbers bolstered throughout January and February 1940. A second convoy arrived in May and was followed by a third brigade in June. The Australians did not see action until the first Cyrenaican campaign in January 1941, by which time the 2nd AIF comprised four infantry divisions of three brigades, plus one armoured division. The 7th Division was raised on 28 February 1940 and arrived in the Middle East in November that year. The 8th Division was raised in May, the 9th in June, and the 1st Armoured Division was formed in January 1941. Independent companies as well as support and service units were also raised. The 6th, 7th and 9th divisions of the AIF served in the Middle East and the Pacific; two brigades of the 8th Division were captured in Malaya, while other members later surrendered to the Japanese on islands such as Ambon and Timor.[45]

A range of problems was in evidence even before the soldiers left Australian shores in 1940. To take one example, much of the equipment and weapons of the 2/1st Battalion was not only poorly labelled, but had been so hastily loaded and stored while the ship was berthed in Sydney that it was severely damaged once at sea. Adding to the men's misfortune, Red Cross Comfort Fund items, such as chocolates and cigarettes, were stolen while the ship was en route to Western Australia.[46] Health and discipline issues within the battalion also caused concern. Of the 1594 men on board, 14 were evacuated as medically unfit in Fremantle and one soldier was admitted to hospital. Twelve soldiers failed to report back to the ship and most of these were eventually deemed to be absent without leave and so were lost to the unit.[47]

The soldiers' health and discipline improved as the ship neared Ceylon, despite further pilfering of food stores that was not discovered until docking at Colombo. By the time the soldiers finally disembarked at El Kantara in Egypt, medical staff on board had treated a variety of ailments including sea sickness, influenza, venereal disease, rubella and pneumonia, as well as conditions requiring surgical intervention such as appendicitis, gastric ulcers and haemorrhoids.[48] The 2/2nd Battalion experienced similar dramas to those of the 2/1st. Prior to weighing anchor in Sydney, one of that battalion's soldiers on HMT *Otranto* was found 'with his wrists cut by [a] sharp instrument'.[49] Eight soldiers were reported absent without leave when the ship sailed from Fremantle for the Middle East via Ceylon. Adding to the medical challenges, an outbreak of gastro-enteritis that occurred after the men went on day leave in Colombo seriously affected many of the soldiers.[50]

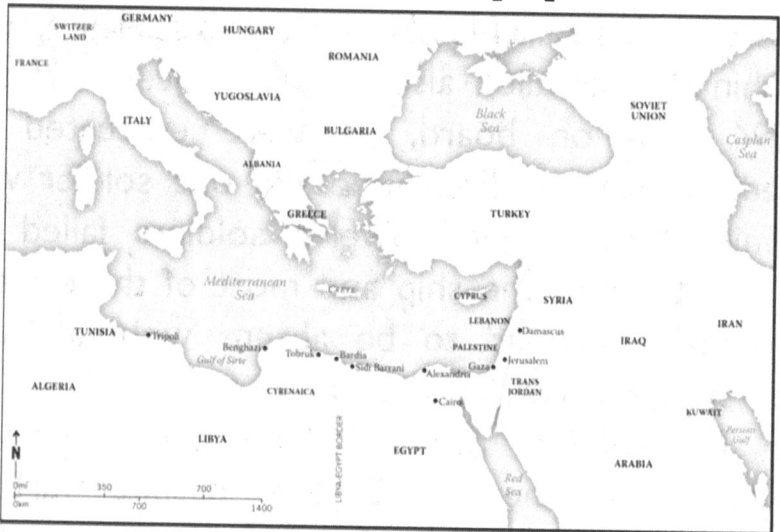

Map 2.1 The Mediterranean and Middle East theatre of war

DGMS Downes and General Blamey with staff nurses on board a ship, Melbourne, 5 May 1940 (AWM 001843).

It should have been no surprise that problems of supply emerged for the medical services in the Middle East. The immutable factors of geography and distance were always going to stretch supply lines to breaking point in this war, just as they had in the last. The resultant communication delays between the Middle East and Australia further slowed the already sluggish administrative processes. DGMS Downes was among senior medical personnel who foresaw that neglect and lack of preparedness during the interwar years would inevitably have dire consequences should the AAMC be called on to serve in another overseas conflict. And the root of many of the problems associated with the acquisition and control of medical supplies in this war extended as far back as World War I. The lack of appropriate measures to control the storage of obsolete medical equipment from that conflict and the failure to update the relevant processes for decades were undoubtedly contributory factors. Indeed, it seems extraordinary that it was not until the mid-1930s that the medical services finally wrested control of the medical supply system from the Army's Ordnance Department.[51]

While the consequences of such attitudes were manifold, there were other causes for the issues the medical service now faced. Not only were difficulties with medical supplies encountered long before the troops disembarked in Egypt, but the haste with which soldiers were recruited and despatched from Australia inevitably led to the emergence of physical health issues (including dental issues) once overseas. Similarly, it did not take long for administrative and communication problems to arise. Various incidences, such as the issuing of poor-quality medical equipment to AAMC personnel in the Middle East, exemplified key issues which would persist in Papua in 1942: a lack of detailed planning and a failure to prioritise the medical service when preparing to fight overseas. It is, however, important to reiterate that, unlike the medical situation that unfolded in Papua, Australian medical personnel in the Middle East could call on British support for administration, planning, treatment and supply.

The Australian soldiers in the Middle East were eventually supported by a complex network of AAMC units and medical establishments, including eight AGH, three CCS and nine field ambulance units.[52] Although each medical formation was headed by a series of officers, all were ultimately answerable to Burston. Even before his promotions, Burston's duties as DDMS were extensive. These encompassed the formulation of policy guidelines for the management of approximately 80 units of the Australian medical service overseas, the overseeing of medical supplies to ensure they were used economically, checking that hygiene measures were implemented and maintained, and overseeing disease control.[53] Samuel Burston was widely regarded as amiable and a good communicator. Playing to these strengths, he experienced few problems in establishing cooperation with either his British counterparts, or with the increasing number of senior Australian officers under his command. By contrast, Blamey's more forceful and forthright personality, coupled with the logistical challenges that immediately confronted him on arrival in the Middle East, sometimes gave rise to problems of communication.

Field Ambulances	2/1st, 2/2nd, 2/7th (6th Division)
	2/4th, 2/5th, 2/6th (7th Division)
	2/3rd, 2/8th, 2/11th (9th Division)
Casualty Clearing Stations	2/1st, 2/2nd, 2/3rd
General Hospitals	2/1st, 2/2nd, 2/3rd, 2/4th, 2/5th, 2/6th, 2/7th, 2/9th
Special Hospitals	8th
Convalescent Depot	2/1st

AAMC units under control of DMS Burston in the Middle East, December 1940.

Yet any perception that DGMS Downes and the Medical Directorate were sitting on their hands in Australia while battles raged and soldiers died in far-off places is inaccurate. Just as the hasty departure of the 6th Division provided a convenient explanation for shortages and problems in the recruitment, equipping and training of the fighting soldiers, so it was used by some to account for the difficulties experienced by the Australian medical units overseas. This may have represented an attempt to absolve the political and military hierarchy of any responsibility for the shortcomings. In truth, a range of issues—some inevitable, others avoidable—contributed to the medical situation in the Middle East during 1940.

As had been the case in earlier conflicts, the Australians retained a certain degree of autonomy, but were, nevertheless, heavily dependent on British leadership and organisation. This point is underscored by the experiences of Colonel Clive Disher, who was appointed by Downes as the ADMS for the AIF Overseas Base. On arriving in January 1940, Disher discussed the initial medical plans for the Australians with the DDMS for the British Army in Palestine, Colonel Large. The fact that Large had already prepared the medical appreciation and formulated the medical plan for the Australians prior to Disher's arrival demonstrates the unequal nature of the relationship. All that remained was for Large to submit these documents to Disher for his agreement, which he readily gave.[54]

The decision to send the 3rd Australian Special Hospital to England instead of its original destination in the Middle East 'pending opportunity for return to its correct destination', was another factor that compounded the difficulties faced by the medical units.[55] The flow-on effect of this loss of medical personnel as well as 'much wanted' medical equipment was felt by those already in the Middle East, who were now compelled to reorganise medical units and stores depots and reallocate staff accordingly. Ongoing shortages of personnel, equipment and building materials, as well as delays in the construction of facilities impacted on the medical plan to treat Australian soldiers in Australian hospitals. As a result, sick and wounded Australians often found themselves in British or New Zealand hospitals.[56] Further unexpected challenges that confronted the medical units in Palestine included damage to a long-awaited x-ray machine and the delayed construction of an operating theatre.

Seemingly minor issues had the potential for major consequences—for instance, there was a lack of flywire to screen the tents and decrease the spread of dysentery throughout hospital wards. The absence of Australian motor ambulances during the early weeks of the campaign only added to the continued reliance on the British, with their vehicles called on to transport Australian casualties.[57] At home, citizens worked with civilian organisations, such as the Red Cross, to find solutions to this lack of ambulance vehicles.[58] Newspapers reported in August 1940 that the Australian Red Cross was constructing 50 ambulances in Australia and in the Middle East, some of which were intended for the British Red Cross in Palestine.[59] A few months later, readers learned that public subscription to the Red Cross appeal had resulted in the handover of 15 field ambulances to General Blamey and Lord Somers, the British Red Cross Commissioner in the Middle East.[60]

The separate, though related, issue of the poor dental health of Australian soldiers saw the under-equipped dental units in the Middle East quickly overwhelmed with patients. The shortage of trained personnel, the high workload, and the supply difficulties were all eventualities that had been foreseen in 1939 when DGMS Downes protested the lowering of dental standards for AIF enlistment. Although the British now offered the Australians practical assistance in this area, their army also suffered—due largely to the 1938 abolition of the Dental Standard, under which British applicants with poor dental health had previously been excluded from enlistment.[61]

The medical issues in the Middle East were made known to those in authority by various means. ADMS Clive Disher had previously served with Burston as part of the medical service in France during World War I, and the two remained close friends.[62] Throughout 1940, Disher forwarded sections of his personal diary to Burston, describing the experiences of the medical units. Burston then passed these writings to his close friend and colleague, General Blamey, as well as to Downes back in Australia, thereby ensuring that the military and medical hierarchy both at home and abroad were well informed apropos the medical difficulties experienced during this period.[63] And while resolving the diverse range of medical issues was already a priority for some, this took on even greater urgency once the Australians engaged the Italians in Cyrenaica in January 1941.[64] Disher's front-line medical units encountered difficulties due to the lack of motor ambulances suitable for traversing the harsh desert terrain. The number of casualties sustained was relatively high and factors such as distance, geography and the speed of the advance affected the evacuation of sick and wounded. Nevertheless, after regular correspondence with Disher and a week-long visit to the medical units in Cyrenaica, Burston concluded that the medical arrangements had ultimately proven successful.

This was certainly not the case in Greece. Problems of supply, mobility and communication were encountered by those responsible for medical arrangements during the ill-advised campaign in Crete in May 1941.[65] Arrangements had initially been made for Australian, New Zealand and British units to provide medical support for the ANZAC force on the island. However, on 14 May the 'inexplicable' decision was made to withdraw most of the Australian medical units before the German offensive commenced.[66] This meant that the AAMC units that remained in Crete could play only a minor role. No details of what prompted this decision are provided in Walker's official medical history of the Crete campaign, and neither is there any mention of Burston's role. Explaining the 'subsidiary' part played by the Australian medical units in Crete, Walker wrote that it was only the 'Field Ambulances [which] were ever likely to play any significant part, and possibly not all of these.'[67] This account then sidestepped leadership issues by explaining that, 'in the further unfolding of this story only the experiences of these Australian medical units will be described.'[68]

The interim medical arrangements for the ANZAC force in Crete were made by the DDMS for I Australian Corps, Colonel William Johnston, in conjunction with Disher and the ADMS of the 2nd New Zealand Division, Colonel Kenrick. It seems that Burston 'had no direct involvement with Crete Force ... Crete was the one place where AAMC units had major commitments that he did not visit. He did, however, take a close personal interest in events there.'[69] It is difficult to accept that, in his capacity as the newly appointed DMS Middle East, Burston had no part to play in the key medical decision to withdraw the majority of the medical units, leaving those remaining in Crete hopelessly compromised in their ability to offer adequate care for the soldiers.[70] Regardless of whether more medical support could, or should, have been provided to the Australians in Crete, history has been kind to Burston who 'emerged from the debacles in Greece and Crete with his reputation intact.'[71]

LESSONS FROM THE MIDDLE EAST CAMPAIGN

Reports by officers such as the ADMS of the 6th Division, Colonel Clive Disher, the Commanding Officer (CO) of the 2/6th Australian Field Ambulance, Lieutenant Colonel George Maitland, and the ADMS of the 7th Division, AIF, Colonel Frank Kingsley Norris, summarised key aspects of the medical campaign in the Middle East.[72] Broadly speaking, Disher's observations highlighted organisational matters, Maitland examined aspects of field ambulance preparation, while Norris summarised the overall lessons learned from the campaign. The reports variously identified problems associated with mobility, mechanisation, transport, forward surgery, prompt evacuation, and reliable supply lines. While all reports contribute to any understanding of the medical campaign, that of Disher is representative of the level of consideration given by all three officers to the issues, the nature of the problems, and the recommended solutions. Consideration of his observations and recommendations is especially pertinent to the medical campaign in Papua.

Disher argued that substantial reorganisation of the field ambulance component of the medical service was necessary, concluding that 'the existing organisation ... is not entirely satisfactory for active Mobile Warfare however much it may be so for Static Warfare.'[73] His emphasis on the need for reorganisation, increased mobility and greater flexibility for these units preceded the official recommendations put forward by a committee convened in October 1941 by the British War Office, which had been tasked with considering the future role of the medical services in mechanised warfare. Its formation was prompted by the experiences of the British medical services in the Middle East, Greece and Crete, and the recognition that the traditional organisational structure of the field ambulance units was no longer suited to the mobile warfare they now confronted.[74] The committee's report supported the majority of changes already instigated by the units in the Middle East in response to the situation and stated that 'the object [of the modifications] has been to produce a flexible organization of mobile and elastic units capable of treating and evacuating casualties under any conditions.'[75]

Not content with the proven success of these modifications, Disher urged even more radical changes, centring on alterations to the war establishment for the field ambulance units. The challenge, as he saw it, was to introduce a system that relied on a headquarters company and three mobile sections without decreasing the number of personnel allocated to the unit or affecting the allocation of equipment and vehicles. He argued that such a system would achieve the goal of 'increased mobility, greater flexibility [and] preservation of the present number of personnel.'[76] Personnel issues were uppermost in Disher's thoughts, due to his observations that the traditional organisation of the field ambulance units (headquarters plus static A and B companies) was often unable to cope with sudden influxes of patients. Noting that the units were invariably under-strength, Disher highlighted factors that exacerbated the staffing problem, such as the wide dispersal of tents which necessitated a large number of stretcher-bearers to move casualties between facilities, and extra nursing personnel to care for patients across the various locations.[77]

Describing himself as a 'rebel' whose actions had sometimes been frowned on in peacetime exercises for his willingness to cut links in the casualty evacuation chain if needed, Disher fired off a series of questions regarding the AAMC's continued reliance on traditional structures and methods in the face of modern, mechanised warfare:

> Why should a man have to go through these channels when it would be quicker to go direct to a CCS? Is not our object to get the man back as quickly as possible to where he can get the best treatment, providing of course that the distance is not too great? ... There is no reason why a man could not go direct from an ADS to a Gen Hosp [General Hospital]. Why should Medical Units be opened up unnecessarily?[78]

Disher argued that medical challenges encountered during the campaigns in Cyrenaica and Crete proved what had long been acknowledged, but not acted on, prior to these campaigns—that the traditional CCS was largely stationary and virtually useless in mobile warfare.

Presaging the medical war in Papua, Disher reiterated that the MDS served as the focal point for the 'fan like evacuation areas in the front', and argued that the devastating effects of aerial attacks warranted the retention of a series of smaller medical posts throughout an area—rather than concentrating medical care in facilities that were less numerous, but larger, and therefore more susceptible to attack from the air.[79] Disher further explained that 'for the reason that I think C.C.Ss should not be too close to the front I am not in agreement ... that M.D.Ss should disappear.'[80] He argued that it was the MDS, rather than the CCS, which should be sited closer to the front line, reasoning that locating it in close proximity to the action saved lives by allowing the attachment of a surgical unit capable of performing emergency surgery. While noting that the tactical situation must be suitable for this to occur and that 'the use of surgical teams in forward areas opens considerable field for debate', Disher felt there could be no argument about their value, pointing out that their use in Libya and Tobruk had already proved their worth.[81] However, he again highlighted the importance of mobility and emphasised that any attached surgical units needed to be able to pack up quickly if required, lest they render the unit and its MDS immobile. Aware of the inherent dangers involved for medical teams stationed so close to the action, Disher believed that staffing such a unit required a special type of medical officer. He suggested that 'the team should be of young men prepared to improvise and adapt themselves to prevailing conditions. They should be self-contained as far as possible and must not expect to be spoon fed.'[82]

Finally, Disher suggested a change of name for the field ambulance units:

> Would not a change of name be wise to 'Casualty Clearing Stations' which they really are and so save the general confusion between M. Amb [Motor Ambulance] and Fd Amb [Field Ambulance]. A CCS might then well become a 'Mobile Field Hospital' which it is rather than a 'Casualty Clearing Station.'[83]

Considered superficially, this could be interpreted as little more than a brief discussion of semantics. But it was more than this. Disher's words underscored the flexibility required for the provision of medical care on the battlefield. They encapsulated the way in which developments in science, technology and medicine had affected the structure and function of medical units during these early years of the war, thereby irrevocably altering the roles of the various establishments of the Army's medical services.

A PERSONAL PERSPECTIVE

As important as reports by medical officers are, all too often it was the ordinary men on the ground who most keenly felt the effects of complex issues and decisions made by those in power. Though formal reports by senior medical men such as Disher, Maitland and Norris are invaluable in providing an overview of the medical aspects of war, they cannot offer an insight into the thoughts, feelings and personal experiences of the other ranks of the medical units. For an understanding of what life was like for these men, it is necessary to look elsewhere. Personal diaries add another dimension to front-line medical experiences.

Australian 2/4th Field Ambulance personnel, Palestine 1940. Back row (left to right): W. Clarke, G. Spence, W. (Bill) Kennedy, J. Tate, E. Lyndon, L. (Nick) Kennedy. Front row: W. Watt, Corporal Gribble, M. Lean (author image).

Private Lawrence Nicholis (Nick) Kennedy served as a nursing orderly in the Headquarters Company of the 2/4th Australian Field Ambulance, 7th Division, AIF, from the time of his enlistment in May 1940 until the unit's demobilisation in August 1945.[84] His older brother, William (Bill), served alongside him. The younger Kennedy kept a diary of his wartime experiences. Early entries evocatively convey the emotions of a 24-year-old man from Wyong in NSW taking in the sights, smells and sounds of places such as Damascus, Jerusalem, Bethlehem and Cairo. Kennedy wrote of olive groves, snow-covered hillsides and the Sea of Galilee. As a Catholic, Kennedy was awed by the holy cities of Bethlehem, Nazareth and Jerusalem, visiting sacred sites such as the Holy Mosque where the 'pillars consist of solid marble' and the Church of the Holy Sepulchre with its 'curtains draped with gold and silver'.

He recounted his visit to a Crusader castle in Tripoli and described wandering among the ruins of the Roman Temple of Baalbek, posing for photographs with mates atop the ancient stones. Kennedy thought that Beirut resembled 'a miniature cemetery' when viewed from the Lebanon Mountains, and contemplated the history held within the crumbling Roman walls of Damascus that encircled 'the outskirts of this old city ... a battlefield for many centuries past'.[85] Over time, the vivid descriptions of the beauty and history of his surroundings are juxtaposed with the reality and monotony of war. Kennedy wrote of marching 20 miles carrying a full pack and recounts passing 'several prison camps where there were some thousands of Italian prisoners of war'.[86] He lamented the mundane aspects of Army life: 'for four days we never changed [clothes] and the usual bully beef and dog biscuits served as our menu ... we took up our location in the desert. Dust storms every day. Sand and grit in everything. The desert sand proved a good bed on a couple of occasions.'[87]

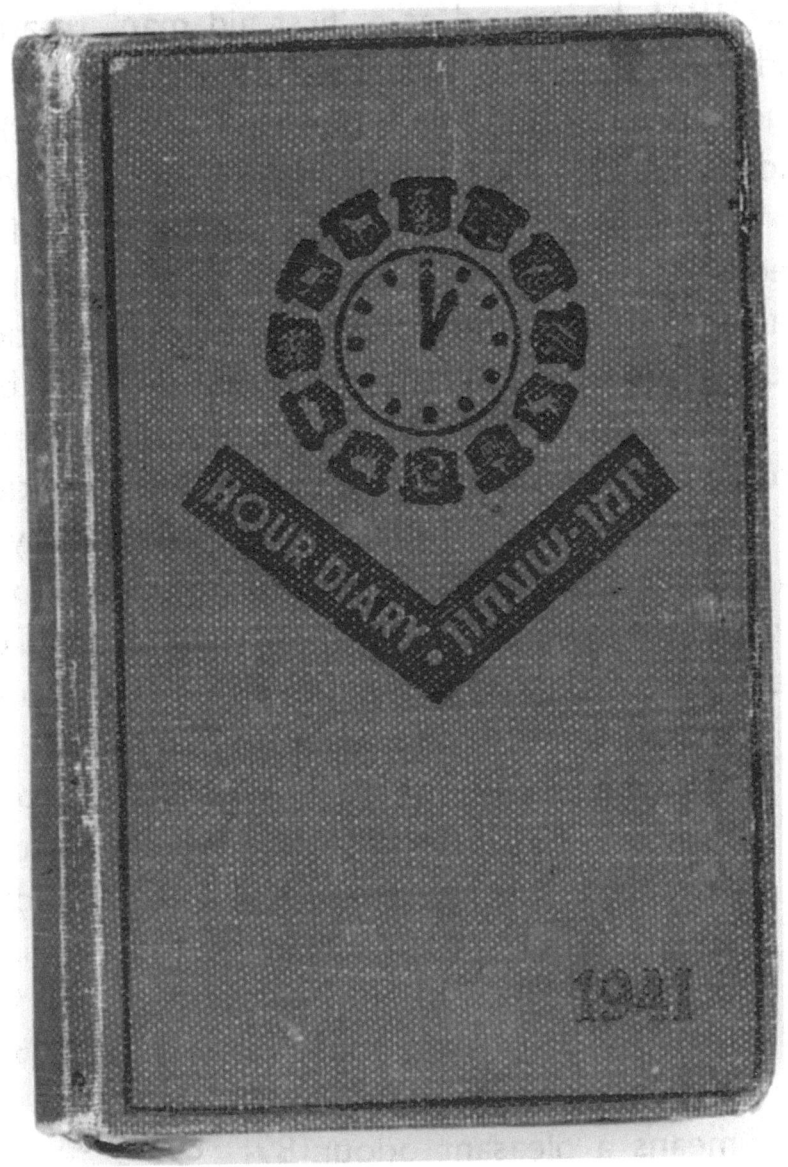

Diary of NX21854 Private L.N. Kennedy (author image).

Eight months after enlisting with his brother, Bill, at Moore Park in Sydney, Kennedy described his first experience administering medical aid to soldiers engaged in battle. Between January and

May 1941, he served as a 'first aid man', treating and evacuating wounded soldiers via convoys of trucks heading into and out of Egypt, Palestine and Syria. On finally rejoining his unit in Syria on 1 June and crossing the Syrian border a few weeks later, Kennedy noted that 'enemy aircraft machine gunned the road around our position causing casualties. Bombs were also dropped but no great damage was caused by these.'[88] Enemy aircraft again attacked close to the unit's position in the weeks before peace was declared in Syria on 15 July. Kennedy's vivid descriptions of the devastated towns his convoy passed through on the way to Tripoli allow the sights and smells of war to permeate the pages of his diary:

> [In] many of the towns we pass through, heavy fighting had taken place a few days before, leaving behind the scars and ruins of warfare. Many of the buildings of Damour, which had been under shell fire for days were in complete ruin ... the stench from the dead in places was by no means a pleasant odour.[89]

The 2/4th Field Ambulance in snow, Syria, December 1941 (author image).

It had not taken long for Kennedy's awe at the beauty of this ancient landscape to give way to more sombre descriptions of the 'scars and ruins' of war.

On an overcast day in early January 1942, Private Kennedy looked back on his experiences in the Middle East and mused on what the year ahead might hold:

> Xmas 1941 brings another Xmas abroad to us. Xmas day in Syria was a bleak cold day and New Year's day even colder still. 1942 looms in front of us. We look back on 1941 with its various happenings. No one would care to live it over again on this side of the world. We all feel confident that

1942 is going to be a more victorious year than the one past.[90]

Our knowledge of the brutality of the war in the Pacific and of what was waiting in Papua for Kennedy, his unarmed comrades, and the sick and wounded soldiers in their care, lends a poignant and bittersweet quality to these words.

Members of the 2/4th Field Ambulance at a café in Jerusalem c. December 1940 to January 1941. Private Nick Kennedy is third from the left (author image).

CHAPTER 3

MEDICAL ARRANGEMENTS IN PAPUA

'Situation and planning are satisfactory provided the attack is from the south'

WAR WITH JAPAN

The medical services of the Australian Army were rapidly overtaken by events once Japan entered the war in December 1941. The attack on Pearl Harbor and the advance of Japanese forces through the SWPA forced the Australian government and the military to confront centuries of ignorance and complacency concerning both Japan and Papua New Guinea. The military's forces were distributed far and wide, with three AIF divisions in the Middle East, two brigades from the 8th Division in Malaya, and one 8th Division brigade dispersed between Timor, Ambon and New Britain.[1] Japan's entry into the war provided further incentive, if any was needed, to learn the medical lessons from the desert campaigns and undertake training in tropical medicine.

The experiences of the AAMC in new theatres of operations were primarily shaped by those charged with formulating military strategy. Well before the Japanese attack on Pearl Harbor in 1941 and the fall of Singapore in February 1942, some military minds had recognised the possibility of an overland invasion of Papua. Most, however, failed to envisage such a thing. Events in Papua were further influenced when the Allies achieved their strategic objective in the Battle of the Coral Sea in May 1942 and attained a more decisive victory at Midway in June. The naval losses incurred by the Japanese during these encounters meant that the planned amphibious attack on Port Moresby would not eventuate in the near future.[2] Yet the Allies did relatively little in Papua in response to this crucial reprieve.

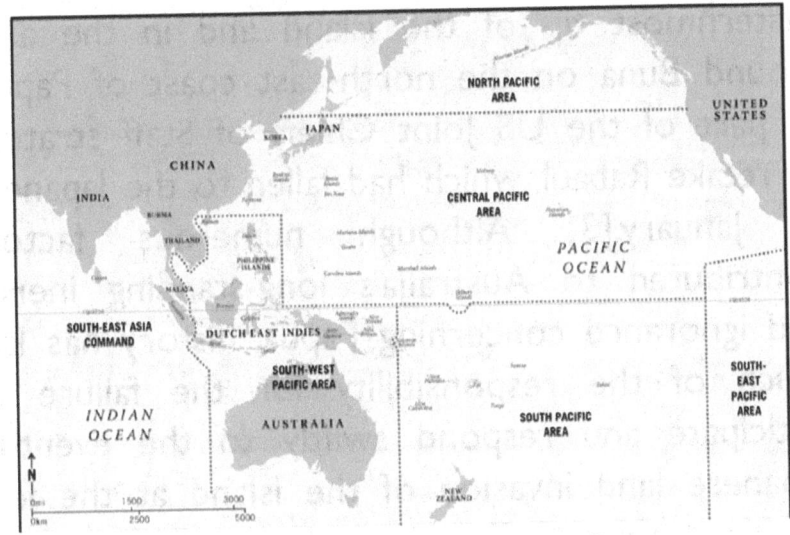

Map 3.1 The Pacific theatre of war

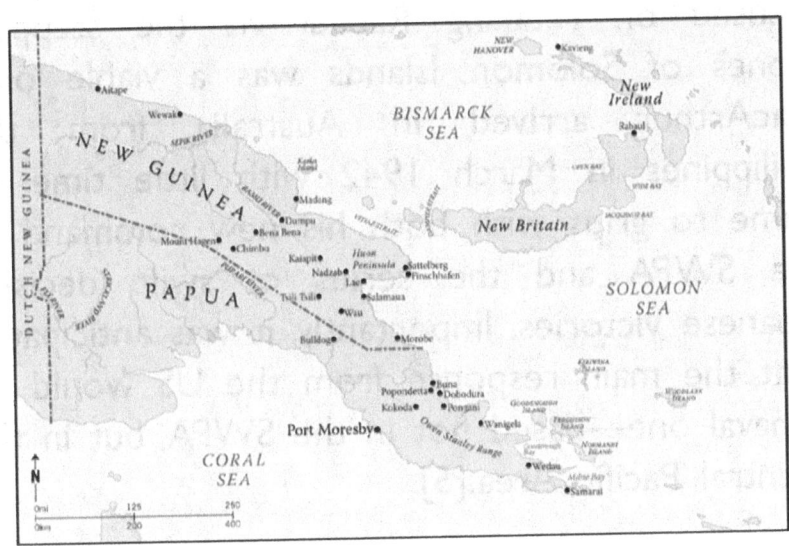

Map 3.2 Papua and New Guinea

In early July 1942, the Supreme Commander of Allied Forces in the SWPA, US General Douglas MacArthur, ordered the establishment and defence of airfields at Milne Bay on the easternmost tip of the island and in the area around Buna on the north-east coast of Papua, as part of the US Joint Chiefs of Staff strategy to retake Rabaul, which had fallen to the Japanese in January.[3] Although numerous factors contributed to Australia's long-standing inertia and ignorance concerning Papua, history has laid much of the responsibility for the failure to anticipate and respond swiftly to the eventual Japanese land invasion of the island at the feet of MacArthur.[4] This is understandable in one sense, though the initial US strategy which focused on retaking Rabaul via the stepping stones of Solomon Islands was a viable one. MacArthur arrived in Australia from the Philippines in March 1942 with little time to come to grips with both his new command of the SWPA and the series of swift, decisive Japanese victories. Importantly, it was anticipated that the main response from the US would be a naval one—based not in the SWPA, but in the Central Pacific Area.[5]

Australian service personnel and civilians being evacuated from New Britain, April 1942 (AWM 069397).

The land campaign that developed in the interior of Papua was instigated by the Japanese, whose leadership had long been aware of the need to establish and hold airbases in the South Pacific. Indeed, the action was regarded as key to strengthening their strategic position in the area. In July 1942, the Japanese Army Chief of Staff declared, '[w]e must hold the fronts in eastern New Guinea and Rabaul to the end. If they fall, not only will the Pacific Ocean be in peril, but it will allow the western advance of MacArthur's counter-attack through New Guinea and herald the fall of our dominion in the southern area.'[6] Not understanding that the Allied plan was to remain on the strategic defensive, the Japanese overestimated the resources available to MacArthur to mount the counter-attack they anticipated.

In terms of the preparedness of the Army medical services in Papua, progress on the expansion of hospital facilities in Port Moresby, as discussed by Downes and Halligan in 1939, had moved slowly despite the national awareness of the growing Japanese threat.[7] A report on the hospital situation in the north submitted by Downes to the weekly medical conference in September 1940 revealed that 'the Darwin position seems to have eased ... Moresby not yet settled.'[8] The medical facilities in Port Moresby were still 'not complete' by November that year.[9] A detailed account of facilities at the Darley and Seymour camps in Moresby suggested that this assessment was an understatement at best, with Seymour deemed to have 'many things totally wrong. Kitchens are completely closed in ...[the camp is] unfit to live in.'[10] Both camps were affected by the unhealthy combination of inadequate drainage and a non-existent sewerage system, which led to the fouling of the nearby river.

The poor conditions at the camps raised protests of a different kind from State Health Committee members when they learned that the estimated price to fix the sewerage problem was

£8000. The committee's consensus was that 'approval may not be given as cost is too high.'[11] The government did, however, approve expenditure to send an entomologist to assess the malarial risk around Port Moresby. The medical situation in Papua was not much improved by the following year, with a February 1941 summary of Port Moresby and Darwin stating that 'the hospital position in the North is definitely unsatisfactory. Battalion going up but there is nothing there. It is understood that tenders only are to be called next week ... it is said that the hospital will not be complete for at least 8 months ... I am pursuing the matter as it really is a serious thing.'[12]

By October, the War Cabinet 'encouraged' civilian women who were not engaged in essential work to gather their children and leave New Guinea and the surrounding islands. Yet official attitudes towards the looming Japanese threat had vacillated for months, with informal recommendations to evacuate the islands not fully enforced until the end of December 1941, by which time most of the Australian women and children were believed to have left.[13] This was not the case, however, and the exodus continued well into the following year, with almost 2000 women arriving in Australia from Papua and New Guinea between December 1941 and March 1942. In April, the newspapers announced that Mrs C.H. Lampo, who was 'bombed and machine-gunned by the Japanese but has escaped injury and wants to return to her home as soon as she can', was 'the last white woman out of Moresby'.[14]

Civilian and military administrations co-existed in Papua and New Guinea throughout 1941. Port Moresby was part of the 8th Military District, with medical care the responsibility of the medical units of the 9th Fortress Company and the 49th Battalion.[15] During March, reinforcements were sent to bolster the small Australian garrison at Rabaul in New Britain, where the senior civilian health officer in the Rabaul Civil Administration, Dr E. Brennan, oversaw the medical needs of the troops.[16] A detachment from the 2/10th Field Ambulance was among the reinforcements that trickled into Port Moresby during the year. There were also plans to send one much-needed pathologist trained in tropical medicine, once he had finished the relevant training course in Sydney. On 23 December 1941, the Australian Army Medical Service assumed responsibility for *all* medical care in the 8th Military District, with Brennan (now a lieutenant colonel) appointed ADMS for the area.[17] The civil administrations in Papua and New Guinea were amalgamated between February and April 1942 to form the

Australian New Guinea Administrative Unit (ANGAU). The Australian soldiers in both territories now became part of New Guinea Force (NGF).

Four officers from Lark Force of the Rabaul garrison, who were among service personnel and civilians evacuated from Rabaul, receive their tobacco issue on arriving in Port Moresby in April 1942. The ADMS, Lieutenant Colonel E. Brennan, is on the far left (AWM 069392).

There were unintended consequences of the increased military movements in Papua. Fears of malaria outbreaks across Australia escalated when it was revealed that the soldiers heading north had not been issued with mosquito nets.[18] These fears were heightened when the Japanese invasion of Java cut off access to the main source of the anti-malarial drug quinine. The possibility that tropical diseases would spread in Papua due to Australian soldiers mixing with the local population was recognised by authorities, though the initial solution to this problem was dangerously naïve. It was proposed that the garrisons being established in Port Moresby and Rabaul in early 1941 should be accompanied by a 'specially trained Sergeant [who] will try and keep men and natives as far apart as possible.'[19]

This response was consistent with the proceedings of a conference convened by Downes in his final week as DGMS before Major General Maguire replaced him. Documents hint at military and civilian medical organisations being reactive rather than proactive in the face of the rapidly changing circumstances. Ongoing problems for the Army's medical service included inadequate sterilisation processes for the 'catgut' used for sutures, a shortage of dental equipment in Northern Command that was attributed to administrative issues with requisition forms, the inconsistent quality of plaster of Paris used to treat fractures, doubts over the efficacy of a new 'cocktail' vaccine, shortages of medical equipment, and reserve medical stocks which had 'just disappeared'.[20] The potential for a catastrophe on the mainland as well as in the tropics was already obvious and undeniable. Finding and implementing the solutions to the cascade of concerns became the responsibility of others once Downes reluctantly stepped away from his role as DGMS in March 1941.

INSPECTIONS

On assuming the newly created position of IGMS, Downes discovered that his duties were not actually defined. Indeed, no official duty statement had been drawn up until the day that Downes commenced work as Inspector-General, and this document was brief, wide-ranging and lacking in detail.[21] He demonstrated his characteristic no-nonsense approach when explaining to a friend and fellow medical officer that, 'since no-one has had time to take an interest in making them [the duties] out – I have been doing so myself.'[22] The prosaic Downes set about compiling his own detailed job description over the following weeks.

It seems reasonable to conclude that Downes was supposed to simply while away his time in a role where very little was expected. This was not his way: despite the apparent indifference shown by others to his new appointment, IGMS Downes approached his new role with the same dedication, rigour and energy he had exhibited in all previous positions. As well as requiring him to inspect AAMC facilities around the world, this new appointment afforded Downes the opportunity to build on his knowledge of Papua and to more closely assess its medical preparedness for war. To this end, he briefly visited Port Moresby and Rabaul during April and May 1941, returning for more detailed inspections in February 1942. During 1941, IGMS Downes travelled throughout Australia, visited several Pacific islands, and flew as far afield as Africa, the Middle East and India.[23]

Downes' notes on inspections conducted during his initial visit to Papua included a three-page appreciation of the medical situation in Port Moresby.[24] He observed that more than 1000 troops were stationed there in May 1941, a number that included members of the Papuan Infantry Battalion (PIB). Papua's total population was estimated at 352,000, of whom 2000 were 'whites' spread throughout the territory. Accommodation to house the 49th Battalion at Murray Barracks in Port Moresby was not yet complete, fresh water was still being carted to the barracks as there was no pump system, there was insufficient fresh meat available and a worrying lack of fruit and vegetables for the soldiers. Despite this, the rate of sickness was relatively low, with few cases of malaria and no dysentery or diarrhoea. Members of the PIB who needed medical care were being treated separately in a section of an Army hut until a 'proper' hospital could be built for them.[25]

Because the military hospital in Port Moresby comprised just one hut measuring 42x16 1/2 feet (approximately 12x5 metres), the medical staff utilised either the civilian hospital or the RAAF hospital when necessary. The additional huts that had been discussed as far back as 1939 had been built, but were still not ready to accommodate patients at the time of Downes' inspection. There was just one motor ambulance available, no casualty rooms, and no convalescent facilities—though there was a proposal to build one over 20 miles (32 kilometres) away at Rouna.

While medical equipment was generally deemed to be adequate, requests for an anaesthetic machine and for the anti-malarial medications atebrin and plasmoquine were noted by Downes. Plans to construct a new hospital at nearby Simpson's Gap remained 'in abeyance because of high estimate of cost', with three alternatives proposed: a temporary hospital at Murray Camp, a permanent hospital at Murray Camp, or a permanent hospital at Murray Camp 'with provision for an M.D.S.[Main Dressing

Station] in the event of hostilities.'[26] The third option was chosen.

Later in 1941, IGMS Downes discussed his work thus far with the new Minister for the Army and Deputy Prime Minister, Francis (Frank) Forde.[27] As well as indicating the level of respect his opinions still garnered, Downes' notes of this meeting are of interest as much for what they do not say, as for what they do. He felt that the 'dissatisfaction in Darwin ... was largely psychological in that it was thought to be the custom to growl ... very depressing.'[28] He also offered his views on a wide range of medical matters in his typically forthright manner.[29] Issues canvassed included the maximum enlistment age of 40, which Downes believed was too old. The two men also discussed the role of the Red Cross and, interestingly, in line with a report on the medical situation in the Middle East that would subsequently be written by Colonel Disher, spoke of the need to consider the likelihood of aerial attacks when planning the dispersal and staffing of medical establishments. Downes also raised a long-standing bugbear regarding the lines of communication between himself, Minister Forde, and Adjutant-General Victor Stantke. He explained that it remained his intention to send his Inspector-General reports directly to Forde, despite the fact that the 'A-G had desired that they should be made to the Military Board.'[30] While their relationship had never been easy, there was added rancour between Downes and Adjutant-General Stantke in the wake of the leadership fiasco. His discussion with Forde about 'the circumstances of my appointment as temporarily I.G.M.S.' would have been interesting, to say the least.[31]

Although the pain caused by his demotion must still have been quite raw at this stage, Downes' magnanimity towards his friends and colleagues who had helped to bring about his demise as DGMS was evidenced in his meeting with Forde who 'asked my opinion on General Blamey's capabilities, which I answered enthusiastically on the approval side.'[32] Forde also sought Downes' opinion on other topics, with Downes candidly expressing his views on all manner of issues and emphasising the work that he had previously undertaken as DGMS:

> He [Forde] read me a letter from a Member of Parliament criticising medical arrangements in Southern Command ... I suggested to him that the writer did not know there was a war on, and it required special efforts and there had been a Committee in being, which was of my creation, for some years before the war dealing with this whole issue of medical

manpower, and that it was a large and active body at present.[33]

Downes' subsequent visit to Papua in early 1942 was at the behest of Forde. Throughout February, Japanese aircraft conducted raids over Port Moresby. The fall of Rabaul to the Japanese the previous month and reports regarding the inadequacy of medical facilities for the garrison stationed there prompted the Minister to ask Downes to investigate 'the adequacy of the arrangements made for the treatment of sick and wounded members of the Australian Forces who were scattered over the various areas in Northern Australian waters in the Pacific, and in the Far East.'[34] Aware that unforeseen difficulties had already affected, and would continue to affect, the efficacy of the AAMC, Forde expressed a desire that his request for information regarding the current medical arrangements should not be misconstrued as a criticism of the state of the medical service.

Forde emphasised the need for Downes to consult with all those in positions of responsibility, including the temporary DGMS, Maguire, before submitting an itinerary, time-frame and list of staff he would need in order to inspect medical facilities 'wherever Australian troops are located' within the Pacific and Malayan theatres of war.[35] This overly ambitious remit was presented at what was already a relatively late stage in terms of the war in the Pacific. It required Downes to submit reports on each medical station's location and situation, and to present detailed plans for the care, treatment and evacuation of sick and wounded soldiers. Included in Forde's request to Downes was a transcript from Mr M. Blackburn, who had written to inform the Minister of the 'hopelessness' of the situation in Rabaul. Blackburn told of the desperate situation and the sickness that constantly depleted the ranks of the one infantry battalion tasked with defending over 40 miles of coastline against the Japanese. He reported that 'our medical stores are falling quickly and the present small Field Ambulance detail is having more than it can handle with sickness and with the advent of bombing raids, casualties will not be in the race [to survive].'[36]

Downes diplomatically pointed out to the enthusiastic Minister that, at this stage, visits to places such as Rabaul, Ambon, Ocean Island and Malaya were ill-advised, impractical, and dangerous—if not impossible—due to the war's rapid progress.[37] Forde's stated aim was to ensure the adequacy of medical supplies, plans and facilities for all Australian troops overseas. He wanted to be certain that the medical service could 'meet any eventuality that may arise, and that where any defects occur, all possible action is taken to remedy them.'[38] The already dire situation in places such as Malaya and Rabaul, and the impending Japanese landings in New Guinea, meant that Forde's plan proved too little, too late. However, 10 days after receiving Forde's communiqué, Downes left on an inspection visit to Port Moresby. He and his staff officer, Lieutenant Colonel Galbraith, arrived on 20 February 1942 and spent their first night at the hospital at Murray Camp, 'sitting on [the] verandah dodging mosquitoes in the dark.'[39]

REPORTS AND CONCLUSIONS

Both Downes and Galbraith provided reports on their inspections which allow some insight into the state of the medical facilities in the Port Moresby area just months before the Papuan campaign began. The first section of Galbraith's report dealing with medical arrangements in terms of personnel, stores and equipment, is somewhat contradictory. He writes, for example, that the level of staffing in the medical facilities at Port Moresby was sufficient, before proceeding to highlight staffing problems. Other observations include the toll taken on medical officers living and working in this tropical environment. All were relatively advanced in age, and the harsh conditions affected their endurance, prompting the evacuation of some of these men. This seemed to vindicate the concerns that Downes had earlier expressed to Forde when he argued that the maximum enlistment age of 40 was far too old. That just two surgeons now remained at Murray Camp would seem to be at odds with any conclusion that staffing was adequate, with Galbraith himself concluding that 'a third [surgeon] is necessary, young and of cheerful disposition.'[40]

It is obvious from Galbraith's report that the Australian government's recent and sudden decision to evacuate all female nurses from Port Moresby had exacerbated hospital staffing problems. The Japanese aerial attacks on the north of Australia—which occurred just a few days prior to Downes' inspection of Port Moresby—killed and wounded members of the Australian Army Nursing Service (AANS) stationed there. This not only prompted the withdrawal of all nurses from Darwin, but the six nurses who were working at Murray Barracks in Port Moresby at the time were also instructed to return to Australia.[41] Galbraith observed that 'the withdrawal of members of the A.A.N.S., which has occurred in the last day or so necessarily lessens the standard of medical provision, both in the wards and operating theatre.'[42] This situation was to continue for most of the Papuan campaign, with no female nurses returning to Port Moresby until the end of October 1942.[43] By the time they did return, the Japanese had withdrawn to the northern coast of Papua and the threat to the Moresby area had long since passed.

Stores for the Army's medical units stationed in Port Moresby had, thus far, been supplemented by those of the civilian medical facilities. Though Galbraith wrote that these 'appeared to be satisfactory', he noted that Downes had left without conducting a full inspection to confirm that this was the case. His own report on the subject was frustratingly vague, with no figures given for the amount of quinine in stock, for instance, and only an estimate that 120 pounds of the drug would be required per month. Similarly, while noting that the full order of mosquito nets had not arrived, Galbraith did not state how many had been ordered or received. He observed that large supplies of both ether and adhesive plasters would be needed, but did not specify amounts. He did, however, discuss problems with the despatch of drugs, identifying labelling and packaging issues that would continue throughout the Papuan campaign, and proffering possible solutions: '[v]ouchers should show name of article and not just the number. Date and method of despatch should be intimated [and] dry ingredients rather than mixtures should be sent because of breakages.'[44] The locations of the various medical units widely dispersed around the Port Moresby area were listed before it was concluded that the medical organisation of the 8th Military District as a whole was extremely efficient.[45]

Noting that, in the past 'a few defects have been remedied as a result' of his inspections, IGMS Downes nonetheless opined that, in general, his reports were read by so few that they did little to improve the situation about which he was writing. Noting that the rapidly changing nature of the war had already rendered many of his earlier observations on the medical situation in Australia and the SWPA redundant, he ascribed the lack of weight afforded his words to a bureaucratic system which ensured that his reports 'are not read by one fixed man in the Secretary's Office before presentation to the Minister.'[46] This was regrettable, since his reports regarding medical posts in Port Moresby and surrounding areas at this time not only fleshed out the bones of Galbraith's report, but proved ominously prescient.

On his first day in Papua, Downes inspected the overcrowded dysentery hospital, which was due to be moved from its open site, and visited the mission from where the Australian nurses had 'suddenly' been evacuated the previous day. Downes also travelled to nearby headquarters buildings and inspected the Red Cross convalescent home as well as the convalescent depot, which was accessed via a 'new and very difficult road', before heading north-east to Koitaki. The trip inland to Koitaki highlighted the disparity between official military opinions regarding the possibility of a Japanese land attack from the north, and the views of those who had long been living and working in Papua.

The local population knew that an overland crossing of Papua from north to south was far from impossible. They knew, too, of the numerous rough roads and foot tracks, some of which led from Port Moresby in the south to villages as far north as Buna on the shores of the Solomon Sea. The large homestead at Koitaki Plantation, which harvested rubber and, later, coffee, had been built in the 1920s and comprised structures which Downes thought would prove useful as medical facilities. While pleased with the buildings themselves in terms of suitability, his initial reservations about locating a hospital at this site were not allayed on closer inspection. Downes observed that 'it was the furthest back station and so nearest to any approach by the Japs from the Salamaua side if this is practicable, which I was assured it was as there was an old road.'[47] With this in mind, and because a new camp hospital was already under construction closer to Port Moresby, an annex—rather than a complete hospital—was built at Koitaki a few months later. On his return from Koitaki, Downes inspected the new camp hospital site located on the Sogeri Road as well as stores depots near the Laloki River. The following day he headed south-east to Bootless Bay, approximately 12 miles south of Moresby, for an unexpectedly brief visit before returning to Townsville by aircraft.[48] He did not visit Milne Bay—a fact which may well have had repercussions in terms of the lack of medical facilities later allocated to the area.

Downes' summary of his 1942 visit to the medical facilities in and around Port Moresby indicated that staffing levels remained adequate, despite the evacuation of personnel, including one dental officer who was 'leaving at once with the jitters'.[49] Sickness rates were down after an earlier dysentery epidemic, and the overall statistics were generally quite good, considering seasonal influences. Downes identified the main areas of concern as the lack of trained nurses, communication breakdowns, low morale, the poor physical fitness of medical and military personnel, and ongoing problems with supply. He reported that the removal of the female nurses had 'caused alarm, leaves operating theatres without anyone with training. Bad delay in reply from A.H.Q.[Army Headquarters] to urgent telegrams asking for four to remain ... shortage of Quinine, 120lbs asked for and said to have been sent by air. Mosquito nets short.'[50] When commenting on the advanced ages of personnel and problems with the overall staffing situation, Downes was as forthright as ever: 'those 55 to 60 break up; no use sending them over 50. Many unfit on arrival, mostly from Queensland, some of whom were said not to have been examined ... thought morale of medical units poor. Spoke to Gunning re complaining attitude of his officers; he was one of the worst himself.'[51]

The ruins of the RAP at Murray Barracks following an air raid by Japanese bombers, March 1942 (AWM P03929.001).

History has shown that Downes and Galbraith were right to fear a Japanese approach from the north. When the Japanese Army came within a few miles of Koitaki in September 1942, patients were hurriedly evacuated and the hospital annex was moved south to Port Moresby.[52] A few months after the inspections, the battles of the Coral Sea and Midway damaged or destroyed many of the ships and aircraft the Japanese had intended to utilise in their amphibious assault on Port Moresby, thereby saving Papua from a seaborne attack from the south. That these encounters forced them to instead embark on an overland offensive towards Moresby from the north coast of Papua saw Downes' fear and Galbraith's worst-case medical scenario realised:

> Situations and planning are satisfactory provided the attack is from the south. An attack from the north will mean rapid revision of plans. Transport of casualties from certain areas ... offers great difficulties. There is urgent need for pushing on with road making in these areas. Arrangements for evacuation to mainland fortuitous and depending on maintenance of freedom of sea and air.[53]

CHAPTER 4

THE PAPUAN CAMPAIGN BEGINS

'Accidental Wounds'

THE MILITARY AND MEDICAL SITUATION TO JULY 1942

The possibility of a land invasion from the north had been flagged by a handful of senior Australian officers in the months before the Japanese landed in Papua. In February 1942, DGMS Downes had identified the very real possibility of a Japanese land attack from the northern coastal village of Salamaua in the Territory of New Guinea.[1] That same month, the Deputy Chief of the General Staff, Major General Sydney Rowell, wrote to the commander of the Australian forces in Papua, Major General Basil Morris, observing that 'You will probably have already considered possibility of [Japanese] landing [on the] New Guinea mainland and advance across mountains but think it advisable to warn you of this enemy course.'[2] In mid-June, General MacArthur drew General Blamey's attention to the 'increasing evidence of Japanese interest in developing a route from Buna through Kokoda to Port Moresby'.[3] On Blamey's orders, Major General Morris sent Australian militia troops from the 39th Battalion and members of the PIB to Kokoda on 23 June with the aim of 'preventing' any Japanese movement towards Port Moresby.

On 21 July, an advance party of the Japanese Army's *South Seas Force* and a company of the *Sasebo Special Naval Landing Party* landed unopposed near Basabua, close to the village of Gona on the north coast of Papua.[4] The force, under the command of Major General Horii Tomitarō, was instructed to 'promptly land near Buna, quickly advance along the Kokoda Road, and attack the airfields in the Port Moresby area.'[5] Two days later, Major General Morris ordered Lieutenant Colonel William Owen to make his way to Kokoda, take command of Maroubra Force and block the Japanese advance towards Port Moresby:

> at the same time (so deep rooted was the belief in the effectiveness of the mountains as a barrier against invasion) he was told that an attempt to move overland against Port Moresby was not likely and that the Japanese intentions were primarily to

establish an advanced air base in the Buna-Gona area.[6]

The Japanese had prior knowledge of the rugged topography and the precarious nature of existing tracks due to intelligence gathered over decades—including detailed information on Australian defences in Port Moresby and maps of the area to its north.[7] On landing, the Japanese troops immediately began the overland journey of approximately 100 miles south (around 160 kilometres) towards Port Moresby via the Owen Stanley Range and the Kokoda Track, preparing roads and supply lines as they went. One week after the initial landing, an additional 3000 Japanese troops came ashore.[8] The enemy force in Papua eventually comprised the *South Seas Force*—three infantry battalions attached to the *17th Army*, the *35th Infantry Brigade, Ryuto Unit, 1st Landing Group*, direct Army units, Army reserve units, and the *Aoba Detachment*.[9] Like the Australians who would soon confront them, these men were destined to suffer mightily as their medical units struggled to treat illnesses and wounds in profoundly difficult circumstances.

The goal of the Japanese offensive operations in the Pacific, which began with the attack on the American fleet at Pearl Harbor in December 1941, was to secure for their expanding empire the resources of the Netherlands East Indies.

Coordination and cooperation between their naval and infantry forces saw the Japanese swiftly occupy a series of northern Pacific islands, including Luzon in the Philippines as well as Guam, Truk, Saipan, and Palau in the Marianas. By mid-1942, Japanese forces had overrun Allied forces in Malaya, Singapore and Borneo, seized Ambon in the Moluccas Islands and Java in the Dutch East Indies, secured both Dutch (West) and Portuguese (East) Timor, invaded Bougainville and Guadalcanal in Solomon Islands, and occupied Rabaul, Lae and Salamaua in New Guinea.[10]

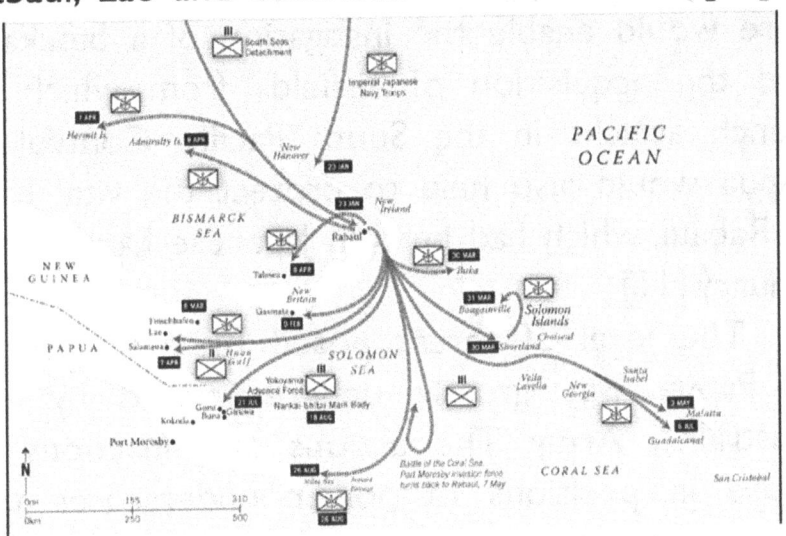

Map 4.1 Japanese invasions in SWPA between January and August 1942

To hold these conquests, secure further territories, establish new bases in the area, and avoid an Allied counter-attack, the Japanese Imperial Headquarters sought the isolation of mainland Australia from its US ally. This could be achieved via a Japanese advance towards the South Pacific islands of Fiji, Samoa and New Caledonia. It was anticipated that the newly formed *17th Army* and the *8th Fleet* of the Imperial Japanese Navy would drive this offensive. Changing circumstances compounded by heavy losses incurred in the battles of the Coral Sea and Midway contributed to a change in plans. Imperial Headquarters instead issued orders for the land-based invasion of Papua and the capture of Port Moresby. It was anticipated that success here would enable the instigation of a blockade and the acquisition of airfields from which to launch attacks in the South Pacific. Control of Papua would also help to protect the vital base at Rabaul, which had been in Japanese hands since January.[11]

The level of threat posed by the Japanese in Papua was grossly underestimated by the Australian Army. The actions and inactions of those in positions of power underscores this point. Hostile terrain and a lack of suitable vehicles meant that the area around the Kokoda plateau remained largely unknown to all but the local Papuans and the plantation owners who lived and worked in the harsh environment to the north of the Owen Stanley Range.[12] While the development of airfields in Papua meant that aircraft increasingly provided a means of travel for civilians, the Australian military did not readily embrace the technology. It remained the case that, while 'the Territories of Papua and New Guinea had produced, before the war, a remarkably air-minded class of white inhabitants ... military transport in the island was not so advanced. The importance of Kokoda [and its airstrip] in the coming land struggle for Moresby was obvious.'[13] On 9 June 1942 an order to secure the still unprotected Kokoda airfield gave some indication that its strategic importance had been recognised—albeit belatedly.

In response to concerns over the security of the area, Major General Morris 'implied that the defence of Kokoda was sufficient'.[14] He reassured the Commander of the Australian Military Forces, General Thomas Blamey, and others at SWPA Headquarters that all was under control. Morris explained that 'native' patrols were present in the villages and small parties of PIB personnel were also patrolling the area. In addition, he pointed out that ANGAU officers were equipped with radios and were 'in the region [while] an infantry company stationed in Port Moresby [was] preparing for immediate deployment to Kokoda'.[15] The reality was that, in these crucial weeks before thousands of

Japanese troops landed in the north, the Australian soldiers remained in the south.

Kokoda village and airfield, 14 July 1942 (AWM 128400).

The size of the Port Moresby garrison had been bolstered in May with the arrival of the partially trained militia 14th Brigade. More than 1000 AIF soldiers, over 12,000 Citizen Military Force (CMF)—militia—personnel and 2208 American troops were now stationed in the Port Moresby area.[16] Maroubra Force was raised by Morris in early July in response to Blamey's urgent instructions the previous month to immediately take 'adequate measures ... to prevent Japanese offensive landings north of Buna ... prevent Japanese use of the grass airstrip at Kokoda, and ... secure the pass at Kokoda.' Morris formed Maroubra Force from the incomplete 39th Battalion of the CMF 30th Brigade and approximately 300 members of the PIB, with attached units in support.[17]

Personnel from an Australian infantry brigade dressed as 'chorus girls'. The soldiers were performing in a show presented by the Port Moresby Concert Party to entertain Australian and American troops, July 1942 (AWM 026040).

The 30th Brigade comprised the 39th, 49th and 53rd battalions and the 13th Field Regiment, and had been in Port Moresby since January 1942. In April, Brigadier Selwyn Porter assumed command of the brigade from Brigadier Neville Hatton.[18] The 39th Battalion was under-trained and significantly under-strength; at just 32 officers and 923 men, it fell far short of the authorised battalion strength of 1500. The battalion's B

Company was stationed at Kokoda, C Company remained at the base area in Port Moresby, and the rest of the battalion was dispersed across the general Moresby area.[19] Just 20 Australian officers and 280 members of the PIB were based on the northern side of the Owen Stanley Range, at Awala.[20] When Kokoda and its vital airfield fell to Japanese forces on 29 July, it seemed to many that the Australian Army's '"penny packeting" with bits and pieces against a fanatical enemy, highly trained in jungle warfare, was doomed to fail.'[21]

NO FRONT-LINE MEDICAL UNITS

Australia's military preparations had been shaped by the increasing likelihood of fighting the Japanese in defensive manoeuvres on mainland Australia—not in an offensive campaign in the islands to the north.[22] Medical preparations for soldiers in both Australia and Papua mirrored this approach. As DGMS, Major General Rupert Downes planned, oversaw and drove the upgrade and expansion of the military hospital system from 1939 until his removal from the position of DGMS in early 1941. Japan's entry into the war in December that year gave added impetus to the modernisation of existing military and repatriation hospitals, and the construction of new facilities across Australia. To this end, expenditure and resources were funnelled to the more densely populated centres, such as Sydney and Melbourne, at the expense of the far-flung towns and territories.[23]

The need to now prepare for the possibility of a war fought in tropical environs was obvious. The allocation of medical personnel for the thousands of soldiers in Papua had been a low priority, leaving those who were already in the Port Moresby area severely overstretched.[24] In the days immediately prior to the Japanese landing, Australian medical support for the 15,000 Allied troops in Papua centred on the 3rd Field Ambulance and a base hospital, which later evolved into the 46th Camp Hospital. Personnel had been stationed at the base hospital since December 1941, with the 3rd Field Ambulance arriving in January 1942 in support of the 30th Battalion. Further build-up of medical personnel was slow; despite the obvious implications for Australia's defence once Singapore fell in February, the 3rd CCS did not sail for Papua until May and the 14th Field Ambulance did not arrive in Port Moresby until June.[25]

In the same week that Japanese forces landed in Papua, illness forced the return to Australia of the ADMS NGF, Lieutenant Colonel Brennan, who was temporarily replaced in Port Moresby by Lieutenant Colonel Gunning.[26] Gunning's transition to the role was not made any easier by indications that medical aspects of the military campaign were not uppermost in the minds of the hierarchy—even at this late stage. As Australia's military preparations ramped up in early 1942, requirements for completed materiel destined for the fighting forces in the SWPA were prioritised according to an alpha-numerical system. Goods with an A1 listing were most important, those with an A2 rating slightly less so, with the priority decreasing through categories such as B1, B2, and so on. For example, an A1 classification was allocated for 'airplanes' and 'airplane parts' by the Supreme Commander, General MacArthur, while medicine and medical supplies were prioritised as B8. At a ranking of B15, materials for the construction, repair and maintenance of military hospitals sat two levels below that of railroad transportation facilities—and two places above shipbuilding.[27]

Revised military and medical strategies for Papua needed to acknowledge that the enemy would now be engaged on land, that the battles would be fought in extreme terrain, far from the relative security of Port Moresby, and that medical care and casualty evacuation must rely on a combination of ground-based front-line medical units and aerial support. Indeed, aerial supply and evacuation did play a pivotal role in the original medical plans for soldiers fighting the Japanese on the northern side of the Owen Stanley Range. Such plans, which were predicated on the expected scenario of a swift and decisive Allied victory against an inferior enemy, required the establishment of medical staging posts located successively back from the northern coast and towards the Kokoda airstrip. It was envisaged that the sick and wounded Australian soldiers would then be transferred by air to further medical care at Port Moresby.[28] In theory, this medical plan hinged on a successful Australian advance in conjunction with ready access to airstrips and suitable aircraft. Little thought was given to an alternative scenario. In reality, once Kokoda was occupied by the Japanese, the Australians lost control of the village, the airstrip and any reliable means of aerial supply, troop reinforcement and casualty evacuation.

Though many Australian and American medical units would go on to serve in various capacities, strengths and locations over the course of the six-month campaign in Papua, front-line medical support for Australian soldiers was primarily and most consistently provided by just three under-strength and under-equipped Australian field ambulance units. The militia 14th

Field Ambulance, and the AIF 2/6th and 2/4th field ambulances tended the sick, treated the wounded and buried the dead. They cared for the soldiers around Port Moresby and shadowed the troops along the entirety of the Kokoda Track, providing medical support across the Owen Stanleys and beyond to the northern coastline.

The 14th Australian Field Ambulance was an inexperienced and ill-equipped militia unit under the command of Lieutenant Colonel Malcolm Earlam. The unit disembarked at Port Moresby on 3 June 1942 with reinforcements, but with no vehicles or attached AASC personnel such as drivers or cooks.[29] As none of the unit's medical officers was experienced in either the diagnosis or treatment of tropical diseases, two were immediately detached to the camp hospital in Port Moresby for instruction in this field. It was thought advisable to encourage more medical officers to undergo such training, however, due to the shortage of personnel none could be spared.

Factors that contributed to the staffing shortfall included the detachment of one officer to the Infectious Diseases Hospital and recent changes to the composition of the field ambulance establishments that meant one medical officer in each forward company was replaced by a bearer officer, thereby making it 'impracticable to detach more'.[30] As DGMS Downes and his staff officer, Galbraith, had observed on their visit to Port Moresby in February 1942, the withdrawal of female nurses contributed to the critical shortage of medical personnel available to provide daily care for patients. The decision to call on field ambulance personnel to fill the gaps left by the nurses' departure meant that a further six orderlies from the 14th Field Ambulance were detached to the hospital. The long delay in the return of the nurses to Port Moresby was a contributory factor in the ongoing and severe staffing shortages that affected all medical facilities, and which persisted for the duration of the Papuan campaign.[31]

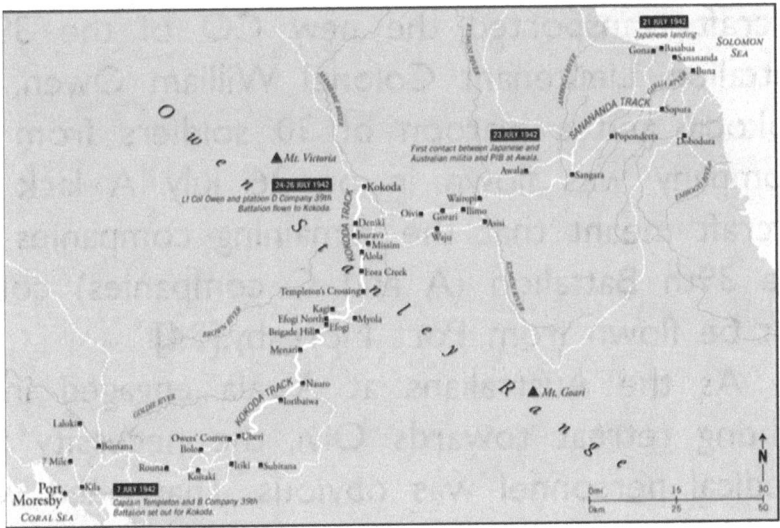

Map 4.2 The Kokoda Track (from Port Moresby to Kokoda) and the Kokoda–Sanananda Track (from Kokoda to Sanananda) showing key events July 1942.

On 7 July, 129 soldiers from B Company of the 39th Battalion, under Captain Sam Templeton, were ordered to walk from Port Moresby to Kokoda to secure the village and its airstrip.[32] That they were ordered to do so without either a dedicated medical officer or a field ambulance unit suggests supreme confidence, complete ignorance, or extreme neglect. The Regimental Medical Officer (RMO) attached to the 39th Battalion, Sergeant J.D. Wilkinson, later joined the soldiers as they made their way on foot over the Owen Stanley Range.[33] On 23 July, this small band of militia men and 38 PIB members encountered the advancing Japanese troops at Awala in what was to be the first engagement of the Papuan campaign. The next day, an Allied aircraft transported the new CO of the 39th Battalion, Lieutenant Colonel William Owen, to Kokoda, and a platoon of 30 soldiers from D Company was flown in on 26 July. A lack of aircraft meant that the remaining companies of the 39th Battalion (A and C companies) could not be flown from Port Moresby.[34]

As the Australians at Awala engaged in a fighting retreat towards Oivi, the necessity for medical personnel was obvious. That need was met from an unexpected source. Captain Geoffrey 'Doc' Vernon was a 59-year-old civilian, World War I veteran, and current medical officer with

ANGAU. Charged with the care of the Papuan carriers, this resilient and resourceful doctor travelled—on foot and on his own initiative—from the medical base and hospital he had established at Ilolo to Deniki, to offer his services to the 39th Battalion. It is important to reiterate that Vernon's presence was not due to any formal arrangement instigated by the Australian Army. Arriving on 27 July, he reported to Owen, the battalion CO, and immediately began administering much-needed medical care to the Australians, using only the small amount of basic equipment he could carry.[35]

After retreating as far back as Deniki, Owen and 140 of his men returned to Kokoda in an unsuccessful attempt to receive aerial supplies and reinforcements. On 28 July, the Japanese forces attacked the Australians. Owen was shot above the eye during the fighting. He was taken, with the other battle casualties, to the small aid post set up by Vernon near the village. Vernon cleaned his patient's wounds, moistened his lips, and observed that Owen was 'dying as comfortably as possible' as the soldiers withdrew from Kokoda, leaving their CO behind.[36] The 'inevitable' Australian retreat that saw Kokoda 'left in its misty silence' meant that 'most of the medical equipment except the instruments had perforce to be left behind' also.[37] Variously reported as 'mortally wounded and captured at Kokoda' and 'mortally wounded in action prior to being captured', Owen's death was later recorded as 'killed in action'.[38] He was one of many to suffer from the failure to prioritise medical support for Australia's front-line soldiers in Papua.

THE FIELD AMBULANCE UNITS AND THE FIGHTING

On 23 July 1942, C Company of the 39th Battalion (considered by the CO of the 30th Brigade, Porter, 'to be the best of his bad battalions') was ordered to make its way to Kokoda, accompanied by one RMO, Captain Shera.[39] A detachment of the 14th Field Ambulance comprising one medical officer, Captain William McLaren, and five other ranks was sent to Kagi, south of Templeton's Crossing, to set up a medical dressing station. Each man set off with 47 pounds (21 kilograms) of equipment, 17 pounds (seven kilograms) of which was transported by each of the 20 Papuan carriers who accompanied the group. The local carriers also transported medical and ordnance stores.[40] Shera, Wilkinson and 'Doc' Vernon, who joined B Company as its RMO, along with the small 14th Field Ambulance detachment, provided all medical support for the frontline soldiers until they were temporarily relieved by the AIF 2/6th Field Ambulance on 8 September.

McLaren's detachment reached C Company at Nauro towards the end of July. Making their way further north along the Kokoda Track, the men established a medical post at Eora Creek to treat the first battle casualties as the soldiers withdrew south.[41] A military withdrawal was not part of the original medical plan, which had aimed to move patients *forward* for evacuation by air from the Kokoda strip. At Eora Creek, Vernon, who had remained in support of Owen's men as they retreated from Kokoda, argued that the medical post was badly sited on the side of a hill and was too far from the medical post at Kagi for the Papuan carriers to travel. Despite the difficulties, patients were treated for exposure, their wounds were dressed and prophylactic sulphanilamide (an antibacterial agent) was administered orally. The last members of the exhausted 39th Battalion had made their way back to Eora Creek from the Kokoda area by the end of the month. Because much of the battalion's equipment was left behind during the frantic fighting withdrawal from Kokoda and Deniki, there was now a severe shortage of blankets, clothing and food. To relieve the pressure on the rations that remained, any sick or wounded soldier thought capable of the journey was sent on foot towards Port Moresby.[42]

The 14th Field Ambulance detachment advanced as far north as Isurava, where it established a medical post to treat the battle casualties, the sick, and the exhausted. At 4500 feet above sea level, Isurava was extremely cold and torrential rain regularly fell throughout the night. The small medical group pressed on ever closer to the advancing Japanese soldiers and arrived at Deniki by 8 August, before coming under mortar fire and attack from a Japanese patrol. Along with a few members of the 39th Battalion and PIB on patrol in the area, the detachment was forced to withdraw. The men carried their medical equipment as well as casualties—including three patients on stretchers—back towards Isurava as Allied aircraft bombed and strafed the Japanese forces.[43]

It was not until the middle of August that the 14th Field Ambulance detachment at Isurava was bolstered to 16 personnel with the arrival of Captain Wallman and other ranks from the unit's main body at Ilolo. Wallman's arrival was particularly welcome as he brought a much-needed and 'more complete kit of surgical instruments than taken [forward] originally.'[44] Because there were no medical personnel on the ground between the forward field ambulance detachment at Isurava and the hospital back at Port Moresby, nursing orderlies and three drivers from the 14th Field Ambulance had earlier been sent to Ilolo to fill the geographical gap in medical care by establishing a staging post there.[45]

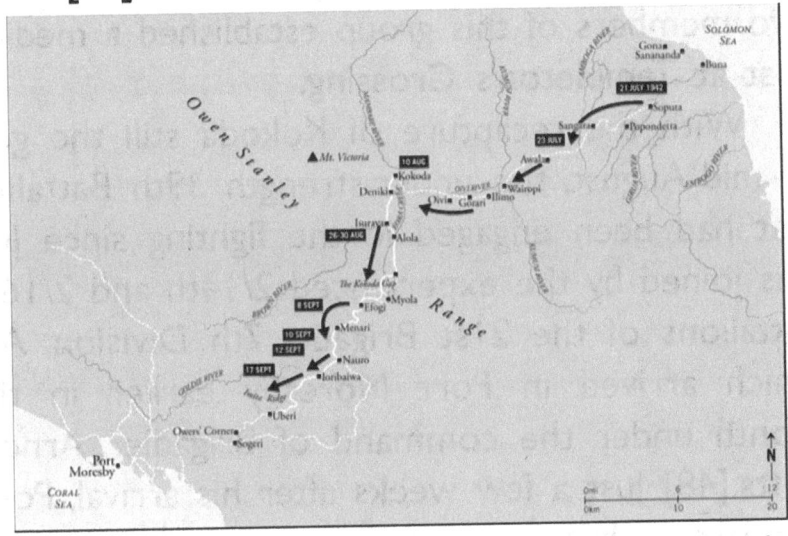

Map 4.3 The Japanese advance along the Kokoda Track 21 July–17 September 1942

Meanwhile, the casualties, 'both walking and stretcher, continued to arrive in fairly large numbers' at Isurava.[46] Adding to the challenges was a diarrhoea outbreak, which necessitated a reconnaissance of Alola village, 40 minutes to the south, to assess the feasibility of establishing a specialised diarrhoea hospital there.[47] The original detachment of the 14th Field Ambulance subsequently withdrew to Alola on 13 August.

The militia 53rd Battalion, on its way north to relieve the 39th, had arrived at this village a few days earlier. Wallman's second detachment of 14th Field Ambulance personnel finally made its way to Alola on 16 August and moved on to Isurava to set up a forward medical post 20 minutes from the constantly shifting front line. Two members of this group established a medical post at Templeton's Crossing.

With the recapture of Kokoda still the goal by mid-August, the under-strength 39th Battalion that had been engaged in the fighting since July was joined by the experienced 2/14th and 2/16th battalions of the 21st Brigade, 7th Division, AIF, which arrived in Port Moresby earlier in the month under the command of Brigadier Arnold Potts.[48] Just a few weeks after his arrival, Potts increased hygiene measures and improved discipline among the soldiers. Regular doses of salt tablets and ascorbic acid were deemed necessary and any 'deficiencies of medical equipment were listed with the object of obtaining these from Moresby.'[49] Potts' plan to recapture Kokoda was thwarted by the alarming dearth of suitable aeroplanes with which to transport supplies to forward troops—the only two aircraft available had returned to Australia on 5 August. Requests from Morris, the CO of Maroubra Force, for aircraft to be permanently based at Port Moresby had grown increasingly urgent: 'personnel cannot be fully maintained by native carriers ... [p]rocedure for obtaining transport planes outlined is too slow and has already cost us Kokoda.'[50] Yet the overall medical plan continued to hinge on the success of the military strategy to recapture Kokoda, because this would allow the aerial evacuation of casualties. Continued confidence in the Army's ability to achieve this aim prompted the plan for the 'unusual' forward movement of casualties, in the hope that they could soon be transported from Kokoda to Port Moresby by air.[51]

On 11 August, Lieutenant General Sydney Rowell—who had warned Morris months earlier of the likelihood of an overland attack by the Japanese—arrived in Papua with Headquarters Company, I Australian Corps, and assumed command of NGF from Morris the following day. On 24 August, Potts ceased suppressive quinine treatment among troops in and around Port Moresby, with a view to conserving supplies of the drug.[52] While ultimate responsibility for this controversial decision became increasingly difficult to determine as the malaria situation worsened during August, the evidence points to the man who had now assumed the role of DGMS, Samuel Burston, making the final decision to cease quinine treatment. The route to this decision was complex. The original advice that up to 1500 newly arrived troops in and around Port Moresby (NGF and 7th Division Headquarters) should cease taking suppressive doses of the drug was given by Colonel Neil Fairley, Director of Medicine at Land Headquarters, and supported by the Deputy Assistant Director of Hygiene, Major McDonnell. For administrative and disciplinary reasons—as well as the fear that 'his number of effectives' would be diminished—this advice was 'strongly' rejected by Rowell, who was 'emphatic' in opposing any cessation of treatment for troops who had been stationed in Port Moresby for months. Despite such objections, it was 'considered by DGMS that Suppressive Quinine should be discontinued [given] the comparatively small numbers of men concerned [and] it is requested that a direction be issued to that effect.' The devastating health repercussions of this action became obvious and the decision was reversed. On 3 September the DDMS, William Johnston, reported that 'all troops in NG Force are now on Suppressive Quinine.'[53]

The plan to quickly recapture the village of Kokoda from the Japanese was unsuccessful and the Australians were again forced to fall back along the track. A modicum of relief was afforded the exhausted and overstretched 14th Field Ambulance detachment still caring for the casualties at Eora Creek with the arrival of Major Rupert Magarey and three members of his 2/6th Field Ambulance, AIF, who had only recently landed in Papua to support Potts' 7th Division troops. When the forward medical post at Isurava came under mortar fire on 25 August, personnel from the 14th Field Ambulance were forced to evacuate equipment and casualties, including 22 stretcher cases, back to Eora Creek. Wallman established a surgical unit to treat the many casualties from the fighting, with over 160 arriving in a single day.[54] The field ambulance detachment withdrew further back along the track four days later, taking with it medical equipment, 43 stretcher cases and numerous walking wounded. This beleaguered and bedraggled group eventually made its way to Templeton's Crossing, where casualties were fed and their wounds tended before being sent on to Myola.

The flat, dry lake beds of Myola had served as a dropping area for supplies until Japanese air raids on Seven Mile Drome near Port Moresby destroyed the Allied transport aircraft. The continuing failure to recapture the Kokoda airstrip meant that the latest extemporised medical plan now centred on the evacuation of casualties by air from Myola. The sorry procession slowly making its way to Myola was supported by medical personnel, with one nursing orderly assigned to every three stretcher cases. The journey took between 12 and 24 hours, with the move completed by 31 August. A lack of Papuan carriers that had persisted since the beginning of the month added to the difficulties and meant that 'stretcher cases could not be evacuated behind [the] medical post, ... until 29 August, none were so evacuated.'[55]

There was to be no relief in September as the exhausted, ill and wounded Australians continued their fighting withdrawal from the advancing Japanese. When the promised aerial evacuation of casualties at Myola failed to eventuate, the 14th Field Ambulance assumed sole responsibility for their survival. Accordingly, a detachment of unit personnel plus three medical officers (Wallman, Oldham and McLaren) walked south to Menari to establish a medical post.[56] Sixty stretcher cases and over 200 walking sick and wounded were received at the medical post at Menari on the first day. Two days later, 14th Field Ambulance personnel from the detachment, along with 24 members of Magarey's recently arrived 2/6th Field Ambulance, moved the medical post and its patients further back to Nauro, where all necessary surgery was undertaken by the unit's medical officers.[57]

The relentless Japanese push south forced the Australians to continue their withdrawal along the track. The AIF 2/14th and 2/16th infantry battalions were pulling back from Myola, the 39th Battalion was fighting in the Kagi area, and the 2/27th Battalion was in position around Efogi. An outbreak of dysentery among the troops placed even greater pressure on the overstretched medical posts, where up to eight new cases were arriving daily. Adding to the burden was the ongoing lack of medication with which to treat the condition since 'no supplies of sulphaguanidine were available, despite repeated appeals over the preceding weeks, and only very small supplies (1/2 lb lots) of Mag Sulph [Magnesium Sulphate].'[58] The 14th Field Ambulance withdrew from Nauro to Uberi then back to Ilolo on 7 September, before finally reaching the relative safety of Port Moresby. Captain Wallman, however, remained on the track and continued to perform surgery at Uberi for a further 10 days before returning. By this time the exhausted 14th Field Ambulance had been relieved and all established medical posts along the track were taken over by the 2/6th Field Ambulance.

PROBLEMS AND DIFFICULTIES

The CO of the 14th Field Ambulance, Lieutenant Colonel Malcolm Earlam, summarised the 'problems and difficulties' encountered by this militia medical unit during the first weeks of the Papuan campaign. That many of the issues identified at this early stage were never adequately addressed throughout the six-month campaign in Papua undoubtedly hampered and compromised the health of the Australian soldiers. As well as engaging in a wide-ranging discussion of medical issues, Earlam identified seven key areas of concern: the collection and evacuation of the wounded; the conduct of 'waifs and strays'; the incidence of accidental wounds; supply problems; the composition of medical detachments; the rate of sickness among the soldiers, and the protection of the non-combatant medical units.[59]

The issue of protection of the front-line field ambulance units and their patients would become ever more relevant as the Papuan campaign continued. The Geneva Convention of 1929 stipulated that the Red Cross flag (a red cross on a white background) should be displayed by medical establishments to indicate their non-combatant status and protect them from enemy attack. Fighting units or any establishments *not* associated with medical care were denied use of the flag. Medical personnel were also required to carry proof of identity and wear a Red Cross brassard (armband) when undertaking medical duties.[60] Earlam's 14th Australian Field Ambulance detachments made the decision not to fly the Red Cross flag at their various medical posts during this stage of the campaign, primarily because of their proximity to the fighting soldiers and to supply dumps containing ammunition.[61] This principled decision effectively meant that they had forsaken any claim to protection. A less altruistic reading is possible when one considers that displaying the Red Cross symbol in any guise was often regarded as akin to providing a bullseye for the enemy to target.[62]

In terms of the level of personal protection that medical personnel might expect in war, the relevant articles of the Geneva Convention, although seemingly straightforward, were open to some interpretation on the battlefield. Under Rule 25, for example, the medical men were permitted to carry 'light individual weapons solely to defend their patients or themselves against acts of violence.'[63] The units in Papua, such as the 14th Field Ambulance, were affected by a lack of weaponry in ways other than the obvious, with Earlam's report identifying a situation that effectively placed his unit in a metaphorical no man's land. The five pistols issued to the unit's medical officers prior to embarkation 'were of old pattern and all efforts to obtain ammunition to fit them were unavailing. They were therefore returned ... Efforts to draw pistols from NGF and 7 Aust Div [the 7th Australian Division] were unsuccessful.'[64] This might well have been for the best, given that none of the officers had received any firearms training.[65] Whatever comfort the unarmed officers may have taken from knowing that, under the Convention, the unit could request armed guards to be posted on the perimeter of its medical posts, surely dissipated on learning that no soldiers could be spared for this duty in Papua. In what seemed a rather unsatisfactory compromise, the unmarked medical establishments of the 14th Field Ambulance instead occasionally relied on unarmed picquets (a small group of soldiers placed in a forward location or on the perimeter), who were accompanied by local Papuans supplied by ANGAU.[66]

Problems with personnel numbers, as well as supplies of medical and general stores that impacted on the unit were identified in Earlam's report. The ongoing shortage of personnel affected the allocation and execution of specific duties essential to patient wellbeing and the unit's smooth running, such as feeding and bathing patients, and changing their wound dressings. The need for forward dumps of reserve medical supplies supervised by an officer who was experienced in handling medical stores was noted. The implementation of such an arrangement would mean that medical personnel need only carry minimal equipment as they made their way to the front.[67] Much of the medical equipment Earlam received in Papua was unsuitable, poorly packed or 'damaged by water and rough handling, in particular by dropping from planes into swamps.'[68] Both the Thomas arm splint (a ring at one end, two shafts down either side and a cross-piece for the application of traction) and the standard Army stretcher, for example, proved cumbersome and were judged to be useless in the jungle. Vital medical supplies including plaster of Paris, strapping, morphine, quinine and sulphaguanidine 'were always inadequate, possibly because of losses in dropping, and requisitions going astray.'[69]

Ordnance stores and food rations were deficient, lacking in both quantity and quality. There was no reserve of blankets or clothing, and what was available proved woefully inadequate to meet the needs of the soldiers, who were constantly soaked to the skin by driving rain and exposed to bitterly cold nights. The innovation and extemporisation that proved vital in negotiating the daily challenges presented in Papua led field ambulance personnel to fashion cooking utensils, water containers and bed-pans from a wide range of objects, such as bully beef tins and helmets. Earlam explained that sterilisers and cases for carrying medical stores were fashioned from the metal linings of ammunition cases.[70]

Earlam discussed the importance of a good cook to medical posts and the qualities he should possess. Military medical personnel recognised the strong links between diet and disease, and the serious repercussions of neglecting this aspect for a fighting force: 'a cook is essential, and can make or mar the post ... and should preferably be made responsible for the drawing of rations.'[71] This link between nutrition and disease was noted by respected authorities, including the Deputy Assistant Director of Hygiene and Pathology in New Guinea, Edward Ford, who acknowledged the direct correlation between poor diet and an increased incidence of malaria.[72] The effect of poor nutrition on the efficacy of a fighting force and its medical units soon became obvious in Papua. Food rations were so short during these early months that, at one stage, the 14th Field Ambulance was solely reliant on procuring vegetables from the villagers. When Army rations *were* available they were monotonous—bully beef, biscuits, and wheatmeal. There was a scarcity of sugar and salt, with the occasional inclusion of rice regarded as a highlight. Sick soldiers received equally scant consideration as that afforded the fighting troops, with those suffering diarrhoea or dysentery given only black tea and biscuits.[73] It is likely that, without the aid of the Red Cross—whose delivery of 30 bundles of stores during this period alleviated many diet-related problems—the sick, the wounded, and the fighting soldiers would all have remained under-fed, and under-nourished.[74]

When reflecting on the effects of malnutrition during the campaign, the official medical historian, Walker, recorded that members of the 2/27th Battalion, who were cut off near Nauro after encountering the Japanese at Kokoda, suffered 'famine oedema'—a condition which took approximately six weeks to subside.[75] These soldiers also experienced a type of diarrhoea that did not respond to traditional treatment, as well as atrophic tongues and symptoms of pellagra (Niacin deficiency). Similarly, the exaggerated or non-existent reflexes in the legs and the burning pain in their feet suffered by soldiers of the 39th Battalion were indicative of the Vitamin B deficiency 'found to be a feature of the unhappy experiences of the 8th Division in captivity.'[76]

In other words, many soldiers in Papua suffered from the same poor nutrition and diet-related illnesses as prisoners of war—and were still expected to fight.

Walker drew attention to another factor that affected the nutrition of the soldiers in Papua, noting in typically eloquent style that 'an intrinsic weakness in the distribution of rations was that the innate selfishness of man intrudes: the temptation to abstract the more popular and varied items and to pass the remainder to those beyond was not always resisted, despite the greater needs of the forward troops.'[77] Simply and less eloquently put, rations that were intended for soldiers who were fighting, suffering and dying in Papua were being pilfered by their fellow Australians before reaching them. While the rugged terrain and environment undoubtedly affected supply, this revelation shows that other, more nefarious factors were sometimes at play.

Earlam's report also considered the conditions under which the Papuan carriers were expected to work. In June 1942, General Morris had introduced a regulation conscripting the local male population for employment with ANGAU during the war in Papua. The Employment of Natives Order stipulated that these men, employed for up to three years, could not 'desert ...[be] absent ... without leave, [or] refuse or neglect to perform work which it is his duty to perform.'[78] The conditions were arduous at best. Though many Australians, such as 'Doc' Vernon, showed empathy and concern for their welfare, the Papuan carriers were often treated harshly, underfed, overworked and subjected to coercion, bullying or cruel punishments while in the service of ANGAU.[79] Australian war correspondents in Papua observed that 'the majority did their work only because the white men in command bullied them into doing it. Few if any were serving voluntarily and most would have deserted if possible.'[80]

Indeed, Earlam recognised that war did not always bring out the best in men. Two aspects of his report regarding the Papuan carriers are of particular interest, given the mythology that later grew around this group. Earlam indicated that they did not provide a regular and reliable method of transporting Australian casualties during the early weeks of the campaign and neither did they act as a panacea in the care of the sick and wounded soldiers. The lack of Papuan men available to carry stretcher cases, and the effect of this shortage on casualties and medical personnel, are detailed in Earlam's chronology of events:

It is difficult to get them to RAP's [Regimental Aid Posts] under fire ... great difficulty was also encountered in getting natives at the right time ... another factor in delaying evacuation was the fact that native carriers would not travel at night ... all available carriers were required to carry supplies [forward] so that if patients were awaiting evacuation at the time of arrival of supplies they were taken back, while any arriving after this necessarily waited until the arrival of the next supply train ... owing to shortage of carriers, as mentioned above, no stretcher patients were evacuated behind Euro [Eora] Creek until 29 Aug 42, when the general withdrawal commenced ... there were approx. 45 patients at Euro Creek who were still stretcher cases.[81]

Logistical problems arose even when carriers were available to transport casualties, with many unforeseen issues requiring extemporised solutions. It was difficult, for example, to know if, and when, the last of the stretcher cases had arrived at a new medical position. The varying pace at which the different groups of carriers made their way along the track was a key factor—some teams would overtake others who had set out earlier, thereby affecting both treatment and administrative processes at medical posts located further down the track. This situation was not helped by many carriers 'sitting down to rest as they felt [d]isposed.'[82]

Uncertainty regarding the time and distance between medical posts added to concerns over the health and nutrition of casualties who were often forced to endure long periods on the track, sometimes spending as much as 'four successive nights in the rain'.[83] The Australian medical personnel attempted to address the adverse consequences of the situation by posting an orderly to the rear of the column of casualties and positioning orderlies within the column so they could administer medical care, including injections of morphine, en route.[84] It was clear that the extreme conditions, difficult carries, and long intervals between care had not been adequately anticipated in the medical planning for Papua. The nutrition of the patient during transportation had similarly been afforded little consideration. In keeping with the underlying principle of war medicine that relied on science 'interwoven with all the extemporisations that ingenuity could compass', field ambulance personnel found that the routine inclusion of a tin of bully beef and a packet of biscuits on each stretcher went some way to alleviating nutrition problems.[85]

Not all problems were so easily resolved, however, with some transportation challenges requiring harsh solutions. Many casualties who walked into medical posts unassisted were unable to walk out a few days later, once sickness and exhaustion took their inevitable toll. Because the uncertain supply of Papuan carriers made it extremely difficult to arrange transportation for urgent stretcher cases at short notice, it was imperative that all walking casualties remained upright and ambulant for as long as possible. However, well-intended 'interference' by soldiers sometimes hindered the evacuation of urgent cases. Empathetic to the suffering of their comrades, the Australians would order a team of Papuan carriers to construct a stretcher on which to transport casualties who, though undoubtedly in pain, were capable of walking.[86]

Papuan carriers moving supplies on the Kokoda Track, August 1942. Almost 5000 Papuans were conscripted by ANGAU during this month. The average load carried by each man was approximately 50 pounds (22 kilograms) (AWM 013004).

Just as Earlam's frank discussions regarding the Papuan carriers influences subsequent portrayals of their role in the campaign, so other incidents mentioned in his report call into question the popular image of the quintessential Australian soldier. The lack of Australian Army Provost Corps personnel (military police) contributed to ill-discipline on the track, which manifested in various ways. Soldiers sometimes arrived at medical posts with no authority to do so and, while some were genuinely in need of medical care, others simply 'walked out of the front line and bi-passed [sic] their RAP and other medical posts in an attempt to get themselves evacuated.'[87] Similarly, while the majority of soldiers headed towards the front line and the advancing Japanese, some disinclined 'stragglers' dropped out of lines at the ADS in an attempt to avoid the fighting. In the absence of Provost personnel to police such matters, it fell to the medical units to resolve this difficult issue. The soldiers knew that the medical officers had no means or authority to enforce any order to return to their infantry units, and so these reluctant soldiers 'spent much of their time in this part of the campaign wandering up and down the line between staging posts ... the situation was not rectified during the withdrawal.'[88]

Problems associated with ill-discipline occasionally presented as self-inflicted wounds. Earlam reported that such wounds, traditionally categorised as 'accidental wounds', were 'very prevalent during the whole period of advance and withdrawal.'[89] He observed that self-inflicted wounds shared certain characteristics, with most involving injury to either the left big toe or the left hand and were more prevalent during periods of heavy fighting. The presence of soldiers with self-inflicted wounds contributed to congestion at medical posts at times of highest demand, placed unnecessary strain on medical personnel, and hindered their ability to treat battle casualties. Self-inflicted wounds to lower limbs were more prevalent in the opening weeks of the campaign. Injuries to upper limbs became more common once the soldiers learned that those with lower limb injuries which had been classified as self-inflicted wounds or accidental would no longer be evacuated as stretcher cases.[90] During the relatively brief period when those who had sustained wounds categorised as self-inflicted were returned to their unit rather than being evacuated, the number of wounds subsequently categorised as 'accidental' fell dramatically—to nil.[91]

While self-inflicted wounds posed a concern for the military in broader terms of policy and public perceptions, the added strain that such wounds presented was felt most acutely by the already overstretched medical personnel. When news of the soldiers' growing discontent concerning the treatment of 'accidental wounds' reached the ears of the military and medical hierarchy, the field ambulance units in Papua were issued with new instructions stating that *all* such casualties must be evacuated.[92] ADMS Norris stymied further discussion on the question of classification of self-inflicted wounds by ordering that 'a wound was not to be labelled as self-inflicted unless the medical officer had actually seen the shot fired.'[93] Earlam did not record whether incidences of 'accidental' wounds subsequently increased in response to Norris' order.

The experiences of the 14th Field Ambulance in these early months indicate that factors other than the commonly accepted challenges of climate and terrain impacted on their work in Papua—the effects of which could have been mitigated, if not avoided. The cumulative effect of the lack of priority afforded the medical units, the acute shortage of suitably trained personnel, inadequate planning, insufficient medical equipment, and discipline problems among the soldiers, exacted an unnecessarily heavy toll on this unit. Many problems were exacerbated by seemingly separate yet related issues, such as the recalling of all female nurses from Port Moresby or the failure to train medical officers in tropical diseases before sending them to Papua.

The initial medical situation in Papua did not bode well for unit personnel or their patients in the months to come. Medical planning at even the most basic level—the logistics of transporting medical equipment across the mountains and the provision of adequate nutrition for patients—was overlooked right up until the moment when it could be ignored no longer. One result of such failures was that medical officers on the ground were increasingly forced to rely on improvised solutions and make decisions in a reactive, rather than proactive, fashion. Earlam's report allows some insight into how a small band of medical personnel was left to cope with illness and wounds, and deal with issues of logistics and discipline along the Kokoda Track. Through his words, the enormity of the difficulties encountered by the Australian field ambulance units and the soldiers in their care in Papua during these early weeks is more fully understood.

CHAPTER 5

MEDICAL CARE DURING THE AUSTRALIAN WITHDRAWAL

'It seems inevitable that this should occur in this type of warfare'

THE PORT MORESBY MEDICAL SITUATION

The 21st Brigade (comprising the 2/27th, 2/16th and 2/14th battalions), 7th Division, AIF, was badly depleted when it set out for Kokoda from Port Moresby in mid-August 1942. The ADMS 7th Division, Colonel Frank Kingsley Norris, who had arrived in Papua with Potts, the AIF soldiers and the 2/6th Australian Field Ambulance, observed that 'all units were under strength and my one field ambulance lamentably so.'[1] Indeed, the 2/6th Field Ambulance was 20% under-strength when it sailed from

Australia—down three officers and 40 other ranks. This AIF field ambulance had received no reinforcements for seven months. Unit personnel had totalled nine officers and 174 other ranks on returning to Australia from the Middle East in March 1942. The fact that 'certain personnel had been retained on the mainland' contributed to staffing difficulties in Papua—even the newly appointed CO, Lieutenant Colonel Frederick Chenhall, was yet to return to Australia from the Middle East.[2] This lack of personnel had repercussions all along the Kokoda Track, delaying relief at the rear and increasing the strain on forward medical units—a situation that persisted throughout the campaign.[3]

In highlighting the cumulative effects of under-staffing, Norris made the point that, while personnel of other units in the rear of the action, such as AASC and Ordnance, could simply walk away and leave behind the stores and dumps for which they were responsible, this was not the case for the medical personnel, who were responsible for the lives of Australian soldiers. ADMS Norris' efforts to formulate a medical plan in Papua were severely hampered by this lack of manpower: 'I was allotted only two medical officers and thirty-two other medical ranks, but was denied hygiene duty personnel. In the battle area there was still a detachment of a militia field ambulance [the 14th], two medical officers and thirteen other ranks in support of militia troops in contact with the enemy.'[4] The rest of the 14th Field Ambulance had returned from the Kokoda Track to the area around Port Moresby by mid-August. Along with the other base area medical units (3rd Field Ambulance, 46th Camp Hospital, 113th Convalescent Depot), the staff of the 14th Field Ambulance cared for newly arrived troops as well as those who returned sick or wounded from the fighting.

Seasoned by the Middle East campaign, the 2/6th Field Ambulance was well acquainted with challenges of the unexpected kind. Shortly after disembarking in South Australia in March, the men learnt that 23 vehicles and some of their personal belongings, which had been sent ahead from Palestine to Woodside Camp (east of Adelaide) 'for safe keeping', had been damaged, vandalised or stolen on the voyage home:

> Headlights have been wrenched off, tools are gone, stretchers broken, radiators, tail-lights broken, bumper bars torn off, canopies [of ambulance vehicles] broken, bolts stolen. Officers' baggage had been 'ratted' locks were wrenched off and the contents of the cases stolen ... all were complete and new when we left Palestine.

One shudders to think at the catastrophe that must have eventuated if we had been disembarked in Far East to fight[5]

This incident not only affected morale, but also delayed the unit's training exercises in Australia—some of which were later deemed to have been of dubious value.[6]

On disembarking at Port Moresby on 14 August, 2/6th Field Ambulance personnel were transported to Koitaki—without the knowledge of the medical officers, who remained on the ship overnight. When the officers came ashore the next day, they could find no senior medical staff and no-one in Divisional Headquarters knew of their whereabouts. Fortunately, both ADMS Norris and the DDMS, Johnston, were eventually located near Koitaki and Itiki. Lieutenant Colonel Chenhall arrived in Port Moresby a week later and took command of the 2/6th Australian Field Ambulance. Not all members of the unit immediately set off on the Kokoda Track, however, with vital work undertaken at Itiki, Koitaki and Ilolo by those who remained in the area between Port Moresby and Owers' Corner.[7] Essentially, the lack of personnel meant that field ambulance units in Papua 'developed into holding units and thus had to forego any real attempts at field training ... they were in effect stationary Hospitals without the proper equipment or personnel for such.'[8] Members of the 2/6th Field Ambulance were also tasked with transporting the sick and wounded on the final stage of their arduous journey back to Moresby, caring for them once they reached the camp hospital and surrounding medical facilities.[9]

The 2/9th AGH located at 17-Mile (so named because of its distance from Port Moresby). The hospital did not arrive in Papua until 23 August—one month after the first Australian engagements with the Japanese. The operating theatre did not open until November 1942 (AWM 026603).

The 2/9th AGH, under the command of Colonel A.H. Green, did not arrive in Port Moresby until 23 August—one month after members of the PIB and elements of the 39th Battalion had first engaged the Japanese at Awala.

The hospital did not prove to be the panacea it promised. It did not begin functioning until almost a fortnight later, and its limitations were soon obvious—no nurses, poor location, poor water supply, poor hygiene measures, and no functioning operating theatre. The most pressing restriction, however, was its size.[10] Eighty-one of the 120 hospital beds were occupied by the end of the first day of admissions on 5 September and, although the AGH had expanded to 605 equipped beds by 25 September, it could still barely cater for the 560 patients requiring treatment at that time.[11]

Green's later requests to increase bed numbers to 1200 and establish another 600-bed hospital were initially refused, despite his unambiguous statement that 'a 600-bed hospital can continue to function normally only if the average daily admissions were 30'.[12] The average daily admission rate during September was 43. By way of compromise, the hospital was enlarged to 800 beds, but continued to lack tents, fly-proofing materials and a fully functioning operating theatre. Because the operating theatre did not open until November only minor surgery could be performed throughout September and October.[13] Overcrowding was made worse by the fact that few of the 1200 casualties admitted between 5 September and 2 October 1942 were discharged. The average hospital stay was 20 days, with sick and wounded soldiers placed on stretchers on the floor beneath occupied beds in a less than ideal means of coping with the congestion.[14]

DATE	EQUIPPED BEDS	OCCUPIED BEDS not including stretchers)
5 September	120	81
25 September	605	560
6 October	800	732
5 November	884	829
25 November	1081	1010
30 November	1374	1347
2 December	1610	1431
4 December	1664	1566
13 December	1853	1606
19 December	2054	1707
23 December	2172	1803
25 December	2261	1901

The 2/9th AGH bed state September–December 1942.

THE 2/6th AUSTRALIAN FIELD AMBULANCE

ADMS Norris considered Major James Rupert Magarey to be the 'ideal medical officer' and chose him to act as ADMS of Maroubra Force in Papua as well as the Senior Medical Officer (SMO) of the forces in the forward area.[15] True to the form he had shown in the Middle East, Magarey adroitly took command of medical matters along the Kokoda Track.[16] Unforeseen challenges presented themselves from the start. While unloading and repacking stores in preparation for the arduous trek over the Owen Stanleys, Magarey realised that the non-arrival of supply trucks meant that much of the required medical equipment was missing.[17] It was an ill-equipped Magarey and 33 members of the 2/6th Field Ambulance who set out on 19 and 20 August to assist—and eventually relieve—the beleaguered 14th Field Ambulance. A further detachment comprising 12 other ranks from the 2/6th Field Ambulance supervised Papuan bearers as they evacuated patients from Isurava and Eora Creek.

Magarey made his way towards Templeton's Crossing, setting up a staging post and organising the establishment of additional medical stations at strategic points along the track. He assigned two or three medical personnel to each post and allocated a medical officer wherever he thought his services might best be utilised. The man himself was 'here, there and everywhere' on the track as he sought to do all he could to improve the medical care available to the front-line soldiers.[18] By the end of August, a medical plan that took into account the military plan for the 'capture of KAKODA [sic] and the severance of enemy communication between KAKODA and OIVI' was formulated and submitted to Brigade Headquarters for approval.[19] It is important to emphasise that, a month after the Japanese landing and rapid advance past Kokoda, the Australian medical plan continued to be predicated on a successful Australian advance—despite the reality of troops withdrawing back down the track from Kokoda since July.

The medical plan, though approved, was still being finalised as late as 28 August. The delay was perhaps due to the unusual decision to advocate for the forward evacuation of casualties. Magarey informed the RMOs of the 2/14th and 2/16th battalions, 7th Division, of the new scheme. He explained that shortages of supplies and carriers meant the evacuation of any patients forward of the RAP would be undertaken by Australian regimental stretcher-bearers, rather than the Papuan carriers. Anticipating problems with the scheme due to the fluidity of the military situation, Magarey nevertheless surmised that 'at this stage the whole plan was made for an [advance] and it was felt that if an RAP had to move [forward] and leave its lying cases behind, they could subsequently be picked up without difficulty.'[20] In other words, any wounded soldiers left behind as the Australian advance pushed the Japanese north would be treated by field ambulance personnel who were also advancing, with casualties, towards Kokoda.

The routing of the Australians by the Japanese during a series of engagements at Isurava between 26 and 29 August compelled Brigadier Potts to order the full withdrawal of Maroubra Force to Eora Creek on 30 August.[21] It was this development that rendered the plan for the forward evacuation of casualties completely unworkable. Magarey and the few medical personnel available were forced to adopt—and adapt—the traditional rearward system of patient evacuation through the series of small medical posts established along the track. By utilising posts at Alola, Eora Creek, Templeton's Crossing, Myola, Efogi, Menari and so on, the casualties were to be effectively 'leapfrogged' all the way back to the hospital at Port Moresby. Although the military's failure to advance meant that the forward medical evacuation scheme did not come into operation in its entirety, the consequences of the plan were far from negligible. The decision to push all medical posts forward and 'hold all patients as far forward as possible' with no assurance of a successful Australian advance or reliable supply lines was always an inherently risky plan—one which placed the sick, the wounded, and medical personnel quite literally in the firing line.[22] In addition, the number of hours and the amount of manpower that had been spent on devising this ambitious—though short-lived—scheme, had taken precious time and focus away from the planning and implementation of a more workable, more orthodox, evacuation and treatment plan.

The final days of August were tough days indeed as medical personnel were forced to treat battle casualties under the most difficult of circumstances during the fighting withdrawal. The obvious priority was to move patients away from the encroaching front line and back to relative safety as quickly as possible. On 30 August, personnel began the task of evacuating casualties from Eora Creek. The precarious military situation called for this to occur as rapidly as possible, and meant that only life-saving surgery could be performed. The objective was to move patients to Templeton's Crossing and then further back along the track to Myola, from where the military and medical hierarchy remained inexplicably confident that the aerial evacuation of casualties was still possible.

The success of a hurriedly devised five-stage evacuation plan hinged on Papuan carriers coming forward with supplies before being back-loaded with stretcher patients for the return trip. Three hundred of the carriers were to be 'lightly loaded' and staged along the track between Myola and Eora Creek to clear the more recent battle casualties. The Papuan carriers from Templeton's Crossing to Eora Creek were to carry stretcher cases as part of the final evacuations, while the battalions would be responsible for the evacuation of their own casualties to Eora Creek via the returning supply lines. This plan required Captain William McLaren of the 14th Field Ambulance to remain at Eora Creek with minimal personnel and equipment, while Captain Douglas Wallman and the rest of the medical personnel were instructed to carry their own equipment and make their way to Templeton's Crossing.[23] Magarey was initially accompanied by 140 Papuan carriers as he left Eora Creek that morning, but within hours that number had dwindled to 60. It says something about the onerous nature of the work, that many of the Papuans chose to accompany the militia 53rd Battalion towards the Japanese enemy at Eora Creek, rather than assist medical staff with the evacuation of casualties away from the area. Their reasons are perhaps more easily understood through Magarey's succinct observation that 'it is much easier to carry a pack than a stretcher'.[24]

Australian soldiers and local Papuans at Eora Creek, 28 August 1942 (AWM 013250).

LIFE AND DEATH DECISIONS AT EORA CREEK

It was during this frantic time that Magarey and his fellow medical officers faced an unenviable medical, ethical, and moral dilemma, when brutally confronted at Eora Creek by the many and varied ways in which war can kill a man. The situation in which they found themselves had echoes of Vernon's grim decision to leave the wounded Lieutenant Colonel Owen to die in the 'misty silence' of Kokoda.[25] On the afternoon of 30 August, Magarey was informed that the AIF 2/14th and 2/16th infantry battalions would be falling back to take up defensive positions around Eora Creek. The geography here was extremely challenging with 'slopes so steep and undercut that you had to be careful at night that you did not slide down into the water ...[it was] a dreary, windswept, sunless perch with great mountain walls towering on each side.'[26] It became necessary to quickly move the 30 stretcher patients who remained at Eora Creek back and away from what would soon become a dangerously exposed location.

This was a heavy task undertaken with great difficulty. Those few casualties who could walk at least a few steps did so with encouragement and assistance, while others were carried by PIB members or Papuan carriers. The move to the rudimentary medical staging post, which had been established in a safer location on a nearby hill, was initially deemed a success. On closer inspection, however, it was discovered that several stretcher cases had been abandoned by the carriers a few hundred yards up the hill and were now lying helpless, vulnerable and out of reach of medical attention. These patients were retrieved from their dangerously exposed position by members of the PIB who, under the cover of darkness, headed back down the hillside equipped only with a single torch.[27]

Not all casualties were evacuated from the medical post at Eora Creek. Three gravely wounded Australian soldiers—one with a 'sucking' chest wound and two with severe abdominal injuries—remained there. They were left behind by neither accident nor oversight, but because initial examinations led the medical officers to conclude that all three men were 'extremely unlikely to live'.[28] Further examination determined that two of the men were 'in very poor condition', while one of the soldiers with abdominal wounds was reportedly in a 'fair' condition.[29] The order to administer intravenous morphine to all three soldiers was given, though the records do not make clear on whose authorisation that instruction was issued. Magarey's later report on the incident stated that a severe shortage of labour was the reason for the order. In other words, had it even been possible to operate on the soldiers, there was neither the medical personnel to care for them nor the carriers to stretcher them to the medical staging post now located atop the nearby hill.

At Eora Creek, Captain McLaren administered five grains (approximately 300mg) of morphia intravenously to two of the patients, and eight grains (approximately 500mg) subcutaneously to the third patient.[30] The morphine was originally in tablet form, but had been made up into a solution. The standard injection of morphine for pain relief was half a grain (30mg).[31] The traditional system of measurement, long used in Britain for pharmaceutical items was the Apothecaries' Weight. This system was based on the grain as a unit of weight, where one grain was equivalent to 0.06 grams (60mg).[32] The high dosages, in conjunction with Magarey's observation that 'after half an hour none of these men were dead', leave little doubt that the intended outcome for these patients was not pain relief, but a painless death.[33]

Death did not come quickly.

McLaren and his men were instructed to leave the medical post at Eora Creek with utmost haste and take with them any remaining medical equipment. A decision was needed as to what should be done with the three wounded soldiers who despite—not because of—medical intervention, continued their fight to live. A further dose of morphine was considered, presumably to hasten their demise. That this action was rejected was primarily due to supply problems, which continued to impact on the unfolding tragedy in the cruellest of ways—Magarey explained that 'as all of them appeared moribund and [as] supplies of morphia were getting low this was decided against.'[34]

Further examinations led to the consensus that all three soldiers would be dead within half an hour. The medical officers then made their way to the safety of the new post as night fell, leaving the three dying men to their fate. The following morning, Magarey returned to check on his patients. His report on the aftermath of the macabre situation is included here with its original punctuation:

> ...three patients left for dead in Eora Creek were examined. Two were dead, but the lower abdominal wound (who had morphia gr V intravenously) asked whether he was to be left behind!!! Arrangements

were made ... to get him out, which was done. This man lived for several days; but died before reaching the road head.[35]

An account of the incident by ANGAU officer Major Tom Grahamslaw provides another perspective on the men's final hours:

> I spoke to Captain McLaren, who was evacuating patients from the hospital [at Eora Creek] ... He also told me that there were two mortally wounded soldiers in the hospital whose end was near. I still recall the eerie feeling which overcame me as I entered the hut in the gathering dusk. The lantern was almost empty and its fitful light made little impression. Shortly afterwards one of the men died. I'd heard of the death rattle but this was the first time I heard a sound resembling it. The other lad died a few minutes later.[36]

It is not possible to know with certainty the degree of suffering endured by the soldiers throughout that long night, nor the amount of time it took for two of them to die. It is also difficult to know whether the surviving soldier, who continued to cling to life for days after, might well have lived if appropriately treated in those first crucial hours after being wounded.

The events at Eora Creek shed light on how lesser known factors affected military medical care in Papua. Broader issues such as the harshness of the terrain, the rapidly advancing enemy, the long distances from the front line to Port Moresby, and the lack of surgical facilities, undoubtedly contributed to the deaths of these soldiers. Ultimately, though, it was specific shortcomings in the medical planning—the lack of personnel and carriers, the dwindling supplies of morphine—that dramatically limited Magarey's options, influenced his decisions, and sealed the soldiers' fate.

Magarey's reflections on the treatment of abdominal wounds during the Papuan campaign are crucial to any understanding of the challenges of fighting a medical campaign in such a place. Given the circumstances leading up to the soldiers' deaths, Magarey's words remain significant—not only for what they do say, but for what they do not:

> Abdominal wounds were invariably fatal. Only three were encountered in rear of RAPs and these all died. With one other death from a sucking chest wound – inflicted during the withdrawal from Alola and unsutured for some hours – these were the only deaths which occurred after the wounded had passed through the RAP. No major abdominal or thoracic surgery was possible at any time.[37]

Major Magarey's colleague, Captain McLaren, reached a more succinct though similarly bleak conclusion regarding the fate of soldiers who suffered abdominal wounds in Papua at this time: 'Few reached medical aid. All were of more than 12 hours duration, and all died.'[38]

SCRAMBLING BACK TO SAFETY

Dawn on 31 August saw the 40 stretcher cases who had been hastily transported to the hillside staging post carried back down the hill by Papuan bearers and on to the next stage of treatment at Templeton's Crossing. Here they were fed, cared for and rested ahead of a further 10-hour journey back to Myola, from where aerial evacuation was still anticipated. The casualties were accompanied on the long trek by small teams of field ambulance personnel who moved among the patients and tended them along the way. Papuan carriers were also called on to evacuate casualties directly from the fighting to Myola. That evening, amid this pitiable scene of suffering, news was received that the crucial and much-awaited aerial evacuation of casualties from Myola, which had formed the basis of the medical plan, was now 'impossible'.[39] This was a devastating blow for the patients, carriers and medical personnel who were all laboriously making their way towards safety.

The original rationale for choosing Myola was that, if an area was considered suitable for forward supply—and if the means of supply (Douglas aeroplanes, known as 'Biscuit Bombers') could also be used for evacuation, 'the casualty problem can be solved'.[40] That not even the first part of this statement was applicable to Myola did not seem to faze the military hierarchy. The area known as Myola I was reconnoitred by long-time resident, plantation owner and ANGAU officer, Herbert Kienzle, in early August and identified by him as a suitable dropping ground for supplies. Initial wastage from the subsequent airdrops was high and remained so throughout the month. In response to this problem, Kienzle explored the area around the second dry lake bed, referred to as Myola 2, and reported that 'reconnaissance of area east of Myola found suitable for possible landing ground ... approach 295 degrees first 700 yards soft but could be improved with steel matting ... Foxmoth [sic] Junker or Ford with wide tyres can land with safety.'[41]

The type, size, and availability of aircraft identified by Kienzle as being capable of landing at Myola should have indicated that this was not a suitable place from which to effect the large-scale evacuation of casualties. The A41 DH 83 Fox Moth was a five-passenger light transport aircraft. Four such aircraft were used as air ambulance and communication aircraft by the RAAF between 1941 and 1943. The A44 Junkers G31 and W44, which carried up to six passengers, were used as transport utility aircraft. Three Junkers were in service during February and March 1942, but by November that year all had been either written off or scrapped. The A45 Ford Trimotor could carry up to 14 passengers and Guinea Airways operated two of these aircraft. They were pressed into service by the RAAF to be used as air ambulances and for patient evacuation from February 1942. However one was destroyed in a Japanese strafing attack in March, while the other later crashed at Myola, injuring the civilian pilot.[42]

Despite these obvious limitations, all plans for evacuation and supply were centred on Myola and the Australian command remained hopeful that they could hold the area against the Japanese advance. That hope dissipated by the end of August when patients and medical staff awaiting evacuation from Myola were ordered to leave on foot. Casualty evacuation assumed even greater urgency once Brigadier Potts was advised that Myola could not be held against the advancing enemy and he would have to pull his troops back towards Efogi. Potts' plan was to adopt defensive positions approximately two hours north of Efogi, from where it was still hoped he could hold back the Japanese troops 'for some time'.[43] Medical personnel were ordered to destroy any stores that could not be taken with them on the next stage of the withdrawal to Menari, to prevent them falling into enemy hands.

Two crashed aircraft at Myola 2 airstrip in October 1942. The aircraft in the foreground (right) is a Stinson Reliant which crashed on landing. The upturned aircraft in the background (left) is a Ford Trimotor which crashed on the same day, injuring the pilot. Both pilots were experimenting to see whether it was possible to evacuate patients from the 2/6th Field Ambulance MDS at Myola (AWM P02423.014).

A key consideration in the decision to abandon Myola was the large number of casualties and the shortage of Papuan carriers. The use of the 'Fuzzy Wuzzy Angels' to evacuate Australian casualties was a secondary consideration born of necessity—one that stretched the carrier system to breaking point and contributed to the decision to abandon this site on which so much hope had been pinned. Casualty numbers had increased after the battle for Isurava (26–31 August) and saw the already over-extended chain of Papuan carriers stretched beyond its limits 'when they were further called on to carry back the wounded'.[44] Adding to the pressure was the increasing rate of desertion among the Papuan carriers, which placed an extra burden on those who remained and pushed them beyond the point of exhaustion. The labour-intensive nature of the work can be better understood by considering that the transportation of each stretcher case required eight bearers. Therefore, the evacuation of 42 stretcher cases—a feat which was undertaken as a single exercise during this period—necessitated the availability of 336 Papuan carriers. Events at Myola underscored the reality that the primary role of the Papuan carriers was to function as a human supply train. Estimations of the numbers required and their recruitment were determined solely on this basis.

The situation that unfolded throughout August makes it clear that the difficulties experienced by the forward field ambulance units at this stage did not relate purely to supply and demand issues. Any oversimplification that attributes the problems which beset the campaign thus far to poor timing and difficult terrain risks distorting the realities of the medical situation.[45] For example, medical personnel kept supply requests to a minimum, yet urgent requisitions for medicines were only partially filled—for reasons that were never explained. Medical equipment was regularly damaged and rendered useless, simply because it had been poorly packed before being dropped from a great height from aircraft that could not land.[46]

On 1 September, Major Magarey and his colleagues at Myola began evacuating most of their equipment as well as all patients and personnel who had arrived from the Templeton's Crossing and Eora Creek area. All were to make their way back towards the ADS at Efogi. Despite the added urgency resulting from the military decision to abandon Myola in the face of the advancing Japanese troops, much care was taken to ensure that all patients—including 40 stretcher cases—remained overnight once they had arrived at Efogi. Here they were sheltered, fed and had their wounds tended before setting out on the arduous next stage of the withdrawal. Stretchers were renewed and each patient received four new blankets, a groundsheet and a water bottle.

It was from this point in the campaign that the nature of the casualty evacuation problem changed, as patients and supplies were now transported in the same direction. Prior to this, supplies were taken towards the front line, unloaded, and the unburdened carriers were then 'back-loaded' with stretcher cases to be taken down the track on the return trip. An unforeseen consequence of the fighting withdrawal and the resultant casualties was that the 'natives carrying stretchers were written off by the [supply] people.'[47] In the ensuing chaos, Magarey was again forced to formulate a medical plan while literally on the run. The aim of the plan was to ensure that casualties and medical personnel remained at some distance from the pursuing enemy.

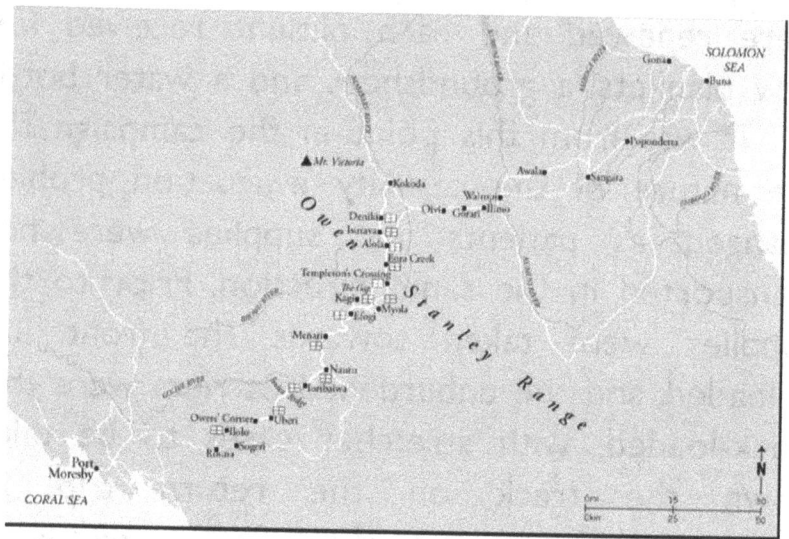

Map 5.1 Location of medical units in the area around Myola, August–September 1942

After consultation with supply personnel, it was decided that the ADS at Efogi would function as a staging post and not hold any patients. An MDS was to be established at Menari under Captains Wallman and McLaren. Captain Oldham was to accompany patients to Menari and take over command on arrival. In addition, a holding post would be established at Nauro to accommodate patients considered fit to return to their unit within 10 days. ADMS Norris was asked to supply additional medical officers and orderlies at Nauro to assist with implementing the plan.[48]

This latest improvised scheme was put into effect at dawn on 2 September and, to avoid confusion, a guide was stationed at the junction of the track to direct newly arriving casualties away from Myola and towards Efogi. A cookhouse was set up between the two locations to feed exhausted personnel, carriers and casualties. By 7.00am the next morning, all patients held overnight at Efogi had been evacuated back towards Menari, though arrangements were yet to be made for the evacuation of stretcher cases beyond this point. Magarey was instructed to remain at Efogi to receive any arriving casualties and so did not accompany the others to Menari. He was then asked to go forward again to Myola to attend to the few patients who had arrived there despite the newly formulated plans and to arrange for their immediate evacuation.

All battle casualties continued to be evacuated from the front-line area by Papuan bearers, under the supervision of Warrant Officer Robert Preece of ANGAU.[49] Magarey returned to Efogi from Myola on 4 September after organising the distribution of food, tea and cigarettes for the many casualties and carriers still traversing the Kokoda Track.[50] His assessment of the advancing soldiers who were resting overnight at Efogi noted good morale among the men, despite their generally poor physical condition, the high rate of diarrhoea, and the prevalence of foot problems. He emphasised to the soldiers the importance of undertaking preventative measures along the track, including the burying of excreta. On arriving back at Brigade Headquarters on 5 September, Magarey discussed the troops' health and the latest medical plans with Potts, organised the building of shelters to act as staging posts on the way to Menari, and implemented a hygiene plan for the headquarters. He noted that an earlier requisition for foot powder, methylated spirits, new socks and boots had been received and implemented by Norris, but because these were air-dropped at Menari after the soldiers were cut off from Brigade Headquarters by the advancing Japanese 'very little of them reached the [troops]'.[51]

The rapidly changing military situation along the Kokoda Track continued to influence medical planning into September. It became necessary, for example, to evacuate most casualties from Menari back to Nauro within days of their arrival. Only minimal medical personnel and equipment, as well as those soldiers well enough to return to their units within 24 hours, were left at Menari. The fluidity of the military situation also affected the location, number and composition of additional medical staff required. In a move that reflected the dire situation, a request for extra field ambulance personnel to be sent to

Nauro was cancelled. As the Japanese relentlessly pursued the Australians south, it was suggested that one medical officer and four orderlies should instead make their way to locations progressively closer to Port Moresby, at Ioribaiwa, Salvo Dump and Uberi. Holding three medical teams at Menari would allow the rest and rotation of staff, enabling them to deal more effectively with the large number of sick and wounded soldiers arriving there. A rare quiet day allowed Magarey to 'adjust minor matters such as failure of men to return to their units when discharged by medical services, and men being discharged too soon at Nauro'. He also oversaw the evacuation of Captain McLaren, who had fallen victim to malaria.[52]

Earlier reference has been made to the fact that Brigadier Potts ceased the administration of suppressive quinine to soldiers in the Port Moresby area on 24 August. The decision exposed the men to the continuing malaria epidemic in the base area, detected as early as March 1942, when the monthly rate of hospital admissions for malaria increased from seven per 1000 to 36 per 1000.[53] As the AIF 7th Division's 25th and 16th brigades advanced along the Kokoda Track during August and September, ADMS Norris decided that 'suppressive Quinine was unnecessary' for these forward troops. The reasons given for his 'strong representations' on the issue included that distribution of the drug was 'extremely difficult if not impracticable', that rough handling and wet conditions in the mountains caused the tablets to disintegrate, and that 'under the geographical and climatic conditions ... being encountered, anophelines [malaria transmitting mosquito of genus Anopheles] and malaria were non-existent.'[54]

By the middle of August, the malaria situation around Port Moresby was coming under some control, due to 'the taking of 5 grains of quinine in the relatively safe areas and 10 grains in those more heavily infected [however] the medical appreciation of the situation prophesised heavy casualties from malaria when action took place at Milne Bay and in the Buna area on the north coast.'[55] Yet suppressive quinine was not recommenced for the front-line soldiers until mid-November. Between 9 November and the end of the month, over 696,000 quinine tablets were sent by air to Ward's Drome near Port Moresby for distribution at Kokoda, Wairopi and Popondetta.[56] However, malaria had already severely affected the front-line soldiers by this time. DDMS Johnston later accepted 'full responsibility' for the decision to cease suppressive treatment in the forward area, believing at the time that it was the best answer to 'the quinine question'. This decision had not been Johnston's alone—before suppressive quinine was ceased, Johnston had sought and obtained from senior medical and military officers their 'concurrence ... in this action and subsequent confirmation by DGMS [Burston].'[57]

The medical situation became increasingly desperate once the three AIF infantry battalions were cut off from Brigade Headquarters due to outflanking manoeuvres by the Japanese. The battalions' isolation meant that the field ambulance could not reach the casualties. It was hoped that Warrant Officer Preece and his Papuan carriers, who remained with the battalions 'might be able to bring them out, but this was doubted.'[58] The direct impact of military decisions on the medical units was again highlighted when it was suggested that the formation of a 'fortress area' at Efogi Ridge might become necessary to defend against the advancing enemy troops. Major Brummitt, who was holding casualties at the 2/6th Field Ambulance's post at Menari, was instructed to have all patients fed and to be ready to evacuate men and equipment either forward to the area around Efogi or back to Nauro, with the direction of the evacuation entirely dependent on operational decisions regarding Efogi Ridge. With consideration given to their proximity to the Japanese, as well as the lack of soldiers who could be spared for such duties, a few armed medical personnel stood guard over the patients held at Menari overnight.

Walking wounded from the 39th Infantry Battalion on a six-day trek back to medical care in the base area around Port Moresby, August 1942. All sustained gunshot wounds in the fighting against the Japanese around Kokoda (AWM 026319).

The area around Efogi was abandoned by the Australians on 8 September. When the decision was made to evacuate casualties to Nauro, Captains Oldham and Wallman—already at Nauro—were instructed to fall back to Ioribaiwa.[59] The next day, all remaining patients and personnel were evacuated from Menari and more than 100 patients were fed, dressed and had their wounds tended at the Nauro staging post. Brigade Headquarters re-established communication with two of the three infantry battalions and were incorrectly informed that neither the 2/16th nor 2/14th had sustained casualties.[60] It was at this stage that ADMS Norris, accompanied by Major Ronald Humphery, arrived at Nauro having walked from Port Moresby.[61] All patients and most of the medical personnel were evacuated to Ioribaiwa by the following morning, and Major Humphery relieved Major Magarey as SMO of the unit.

MEDICAL OFFICERS' REPORTS AND RECOMMENDATIONS

Major Magarey wrote his report of the experiences of the 2/6th Australian Field Ambulance during the August withdrawal largely from memory, having destroyed his original diary when forced to evacuate from Alola, north of

Eora Creek. His considered comments, in conjunction with reports by other medical officers who were on the track during the Australian withdrawal, allow a comprehensive assessment of the medical situation.

Magarey observed that the medical posts during these early months of the Papuan campaign did not fit accurately any training picture. Each MO [medical officer] as he arrived in the area brought with him a certain number of personnel and a certain amount of eqpt [equipment]. This was regarded as one 'medical team' ... as a rule medical posts were regarded as being staffed by one or more 'medical teams'. This system was found more satisfactory than trying to work in terms of Lt Secs [Light Sections], ADS etc. The personnel of the 'teams' had to be prepared [to], and did, turn their hands to anything, from building huts to cooking, from nursing duties to guard mounting.[62]

It was clear that, for the medical units to function effectively in Papua, adaptation and team work were required. Such cooperation extended beyond the medical personnel, with ANGAU staff supervising the construction of huts to serve as medical posts at various locations on the track and stretcher-bearers from the field ambulance working as cooks, occasionally assisted by 'co-opted' locals. Indeed, the traditional role of

Australian stretcher-bearers came under scrutiny during this period, with Magarey concluding they were of little use in jungle warfare and recommending they be trained as nursing orderlies, so that they could supplement the severe shortage of trained personnel within the standard field ambulance unit.[63]

The role of the indigenous carriers was also considered and suggestions made for improvements. To alleviate the severe shortage of carriers needed to assist in the evacuation of patients it was suggested that some be placed under the control of ANGAU staff for the *sole* use of the medical services.[64] Magarey's admiration for the resilience, innovation, care and compassion shown by these 'native' stretcher-bearers and the ANGAU officers who supervised them was obvious. He was less enthusiastic, however, about the quality of the actual stretchers they were bearing, declaring them to be of little use due to design flaws, rotting canvas, and handles that were too short. A separate report written by Staff Sergeant Alan Bentley which included comprehensive lists of medical and general equipment, supplementary stores and 'native loads' (that is, supplies to be transported by the Papuan carriers) used during the campaign was endorsed by Magarey and incorporated into his own report, as was a long list of additional equipment which should have been taken by field ambulance personnel.

Whereas Earlam, as CO of the 14th Field Ambulance, reported a prevalence of self-inflicted wounds 'during the whole period of advance and withdrawal', Magarey did not believe this to be the case.[65] However, unlike Earlam, he had not been present during the initial weeks of the campaign and so could not dismiss such claims outright. It was possibly due to inclination rather than necessity that soldiers classified as suffering from self-inflicted wounds were, according to Magarey, given 'scant sympathy and treatment' by medical personnel.[66] While conceding that there were instances where the location of the wound pointed to the conclusion that it was self-inflicted, Magarey noted that because few such wounds were examined for gunpowder burns it was unreasonable to assume that the wound was self-inflicted. Indeed, he expressed anger that many soldiers he knew to have been wounded in battle were categorised, stigmatised and treated as suffering from self-inflicted wounds by those charged with their care.[67]

EVACUATED ON STRETCHER	34
WALKING WOUNDED	32
GUN SHOT WOUNDS/SHRAPNEL	34
MALARIA/QUERIED MALARIA	7

OTHER (diarrhoea, dysentery, scrub typhus, infection, skin complaints)	25
TOTAL CASUALTIES EVACUATED	66

Summary of casualties evacuated from Kokoda area by No. 2 Light Section, 14th Field Ambulance, 9 September 1942 (see Appendix 3 for further details).

The issue of 'malingering' was similarly dealt with by Magarey. He acnowledged that such behaviour did occur and that it usually took the form of inventing or exaggerating the effects of diarrhoea. Nevertheless, he felt much the same way about this topic as he did about self-inflicted wounds, stating that it was 'difficult and often impossible to prove one way or the other.'[68] The challenges involved in proving a charge of malingering were also noted by Captain McLaren—though he was of the view that the difficulties were based less on medical or forensic reasons and more on the practicalities of war, where 'under the existing conditions, especially during a withdrawal, many [suspected malingerers] escaped past medical posts.'[69]

There was no denying that problems were encountered in persuading fit personnel to return to their fighting unit, with Magarey echoing Earlam's views on the burden of responsibility placed on field ambulance personnel to control the matter during the initial stages of the campaign. He recommended the allocation of 'some form of policing ... to control waifs and strays.'[70] McLaren also saw the need for increased policing in this regard and lamented the lack of appropriate authorities to control these men he unapologetically labelled 'deserters'.[71]

McLaren also identified the collection and evacuation of casualties as the main medical challenge in Papua. Like Magarey, he concluded that such an environment not only demanded an increase in the number of trained medical and nursing personnel, but rendered Australian stretcher-bearers 'useless'. He considered that the bearers would be better utilised in the supervision of stretcher convoys or the administering of first aid. Members of the PIB received high praise, primarily for their work in retrieving the wounded from the battlefield and taking them 'to an area where the ordinary native carriers could take over'.[72] McLaren praised the carriers for their pride in their work and the measures taken to care for the wounded Australians. His report also included numerous suggestions regarding medical supplies: that all supplies for forward areas should be packed in small boxes for ease of carrying; that larger quantities of supplies such as plaster of Paris should be made available, and that the main medical supply dump should be located safely away from the action.[73]

While conditions and geography played a major part in the difficulties experienced by the Australians in obtaining adequate stores and equipment at this stage of the campaign, the human element cannot be overlooked. It was noted that priority for medical supplies was usually obtained without too many problems and that some stores were dropped relatively soon after requesting; however, there were instances where the lack of planning and common sense simply beggared belief. A high percentage of loss was attributed to easily rectifiable issues, for example, 'a 10000 tin of Quinine tabs was dropped, unwrapped and not sealed with solder, and only 200 recovered.'[74] Glass bottles with no protective packaging were dropped in sacks from aircraft. Entire requisitions were sometimes lost due to a failure to advise those on the ground of the planned time and location of the drop. Medical stores were regularly dropped long after sites had been abandoned, with 'no natives left to recover it from scrub':[75]

> Practically at no time was there an adequacy of stores, mainly due to the nature of the action, misunderstanding as to the of requisition ... stores lost in scrub and swamp, and breakages due to dropping. Requisitions from the front were for quantities urgently required. The practice of

the Base medical stores of 'chopping down', which happened on practically every occasion, made [forward] supply very difficult. On re-ordering, the balance of original requisition was [forwarded], showing no acute shortage at Base. It was found necessary quite frequently, to break into [Battalion] reserve RAP Stores to enable us to carry on.[76]

A focus on the difficulties associated with supply and evacuation, and issues around the treatment and transportation of stretcher cases was understandable. Yet Magarey felt that attention should also be given to the plight of the walking wounded and sick, who made up the greater percentage of casualties. He acknowledged that the tactical situation made it impossible to adequately treat these patients, noting that it was often necessary to be ruthless in moving them on from medical posts while simultaneously praising them for their 'fortitude and cheerfulness ... and [the] feats of endurance performed by some of the wounded.'[77] There was general agreement among the medical officers that the foremost causes of sickness and ill-health were an inadequate diet, the harsh living conditions, and poor hygiene facilities. These issues were blamed for the prevalence of bowel disorders such as dysentery and diarrhoea.[78] Seemingly minor health issues easily became major concerns in an environment where the days were wet, nights were cold and rainy, the atmosphere was constantly damp, clothes did not dry, and fires either could not be lit due to the weather, or were forbidden due to the proximity of the enemy.

There was a lack of warm blankets and waterproof clothing, with the single groundsheet issued to each soldier offering scant protection from the weather. While the prevalence of foot problems was attributed to the individual failure of the soldiers to regularly remove their boots and change socks, the systemic failure to regularly resupply troops with foot powder, new boots and socks undoubtedly contributed to the problem. It was difficult enough to survive, let alone fight in Papua and 'the condition of fighting was such that often, even when things were apparently quiet, the men dare not take their boots off in case they were caught with them off.'[79] The paucity of exchange dumps from which forward units could acquire replacement items such as blankets added to health problems. Some medical officers argued that this could be addressed by maintaining an adequate supply of these items at all medical posts and sending them forward with carriers to replace those which accompanied the casualties. The main hindrance to a more effective medical supply system was identified as an unnecessarily complex requisitioning process and a lack of bulk stores situated close to the front line.[80]

Malaria undoubtedly contributed to the number of sick casualties incurred between July and September 1942. Magarey explained that anti-malarial precautions 'were considered unnecessary' by some and were not put in place because there were practically no anopheles mosquitoes in the Owen Stanleys.[81] While it is true that there were relatively few new malaria cases among the soldiers in the forward area, there were certainly relapses. The 14th Field Ambulance, for example, encountered recurrent malaria among the soldiers who had been as far north as Kokoda and Oivi.[82] Many of the militia troops who had been stationed in the Port Moresby area for months prior to the advance along the Kokoda Track had already been exposed to the disease and again succumbed once they found themselves cold, wet, under-nourished, exhausted, in the mountains, and without quinine. Because the fresh 7th Division soldiers had spent little time in Port Moresby before advancing over the track, their exposure to malaria was significantly less than their militia comrades.

Though conditions for the walking wounded and the sick were grim, the situation for the more seriously wounded was dire. Until the withdrawal from Alola, the field ambulance units were permitted to undertake all surgery the medical officers thought was possible. After the withdrawal, the only surgery possible 'for some days ... was the arrest of haemorrhage and similar measures for the immediate saving of life.'[83] Any operations performed during this phase were necessarily minimal, and undertaken in accordance with the prevailing military situation and anticipated need for further withdrawals. Despite these challenges, most of the wounded received basic first aid and adequate wound care, as well as anti-tetanus serum and morphine as required.

For prosaic reasons, including the outflanking and infiltration tactics of the Japanese, the need for rapid withdrawal, and the potential danger to unarmed medical personnel, Magarey recommended that no major surgery should be attempted closer than two days' travelling distance from the forward soldiers. That this decision guaranteed the death of all those suffering massive injuries was regarded as a price that must be paid: 'This means the loss of all abdominal wounds, but it seems inevitable that this should occur in this type of warfare. If these wounds are to be saved a surgeon would usually need to be placed with, or in front of, the RAP.'[84] The fact that many casualties arrived at the road head in relatively good condition seemed to surprise even Major Magarey. With more first-hand knowledge of the situation than most, he noted that while some soldiers with chest wounds did recover, 'there is no doubt that the majority did not reach medical aid.'[85] Certainly the incident at Eora Creek demonstrated that survival was not an option for the seriously wounded during these desperate days. The fact that no major surgery was undertaken sealed their fate.

Some 45 years after the harrowing events at Eora Creek, Rupert Magarey ruminated on the nature of suffering and death in war. Agreeing with the proposition that penetrating stomach and chest wounds equated to a death penalty in a place like Papua, because of the difficulty in getting the patient to an operating theatre, Magarey explained:

> If you got an abdominal wound on the Kokoda Trail, you might as well have given up. You never told the troops that, but you knew bloody well that that was what would happen ... so you gave them a shot of morphine...[86]

[original punctuation]

Simply put, deliberate inaction or deliberate intervention by medical personnel sometimes ended the life of a soldier. The general nature of Magarey's comments in combination with the use of ellipses in the quotation, work to soften the overall impact of the statement and leave the reader to ponder the silence and spaces between his words.

CHAPTER 6

MILNE BAY

'One of the most malarious places in the world'

THE MILITARY SITUATION

While the Papuan campaign has become synonymous with the Kokoda Track, the fight for Papua also erupted as a series of land battles in the east of the country, around Milne Bay and Goodenough Island. In a sequence of engagements in late August and early September, Australian forces encountered strong and determined opposition from the Japanese. In many ways, this theatre proved a microcosm of the larger campaign, yet also presented the Australian medical units with a number of unique situations and challenges.

The Battle of Milne Bay was not a single, decisive land battle. The series of land and air engagements began with the unchallenged amphibious landings of approximately 2000 troops from the Japanese *Special Naval Landing Force* on 25 August and formally ended with the amphibious evacuation of thousands of surviving

Japanese troops on 7 September 1942. The relatively small size of the initial landing party reflected the need for the Japanese High Command to divert troops to Guadalcanal in Solomon Islands, with the aim of countering the US landings there. Further, the Japanese underestimated the size of the Allied presence in Milne Bay Province, which totalled over 9000 men.[1] The recently reinforced and renamed Milne Force, under GOC Major General Cyril Clowes, comprised approximately 4500 seasoned AIF soldiers, 3000 'unblooded militia', 600 RAAF personnel, and 1350 US troops.[2] Despite the numerical superiority of the Allies, the Japanese landings on the shores of Milne Bay initially went unchallenged. As the troops advanced towards the airstrips they came under sustained aerial attack, before clashing with the Australian militia soldiers who were charged with defending these valuable assets.[3]

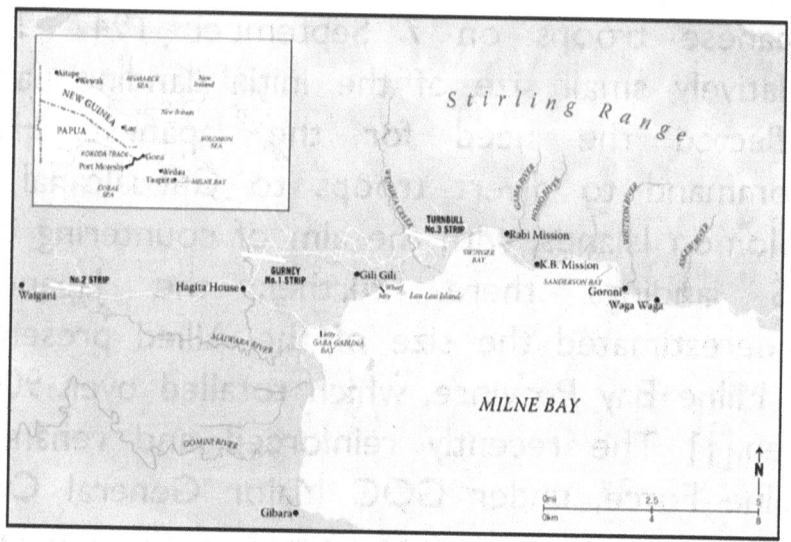

Map 6.1 Milne Bay

AIF AND MILITIA	RAAF	US FORCES
7th Infantry Brigade	No. 32 Squadron	709th US Airborne Anti-aircraft Battery
9th Battalion		
25th Battalion		
61st Battalion		
18th Brigade	No. 75 Squadron	101st US Coast Artillery Battalion
2/9th Battalion		
2/10th Battalion		
2/12th Battalion		
2/5th Field Regiment	No. 76 Squadron	43rd US Engineer Regiment (2nd Battalion)
101st Anti-tank Regiment 4th Battery		46th US Engineer Regiment (E Company)

6th Heavy Anti-aircraft Battery	US MEDICAL Station Hospital
9th Light Anti-aircraft Battery	
24th Field Company	
AAMC UNITS	
11th Field Ambulance	
2/5th Field Ambulance	
110th Casualty Clearing Station	
2/1st Casualty Clearing Station	

Units at Milne Bay, August–September 1942.

Control of the Milne Bay area on the eastern tip of Papua was considered vital to the war in the South Pacific. The strategic advantages of its location and geography were summarised by the CO of the 110th CCS, Lieutenant Colonel Frederick Wall:

> [Its] geographic situation renders it of high significance as an Air Base. It is a 300 miles due-north flight to Gasmata in New Britain, an easy range for medium bombers, but just too far for land-based pursuit planes ... it is 635 miles to Townsville and almost the same distance to Tulagi in the Solomons, but only 430 miles separate Milne

Bay from Buin in the Solomons ...[it] is well protected from attack by sea.

Nature, too, makes impossible any overland invasion across the mountain ranges ... successful air attack is difficult ... on the other hand, this well-protected spot is an ideal sally port for our reconnaissance, pursuit and bomber planes ... Australia owes a great debt of gratitude to the man whose brain first envisaged the strategical possibility of this area, as it must seem the Allies occupied the place just in time.[4]

Lieutenant Colonel Frederick Wall, CO of the 110th CCS at Milne Bay (AWM P00440.003).

Identifying Milne Bay's significance early in 1942, General MacArthur decided to establish an advanced base from which to patrol Bootless

Inlet and Port Moresby, the waters of Goodenough Bay, the China Strait, and the Solomon Sea. MacArthur knew that airbases here would help to protect Port Moresby against naval attack from the east and enable ground troops to make their way towards the area around Buna and Gona by sea, rather than cross the formidable Owen Stanley Range.[5] Known initially as the Fall River Force, three Australian battalions of the 7th Brigade (the 9th, 25th and 61st) joined elements of the 55th Battalion, US anti-aircraft batteries, and a company of American engineers tasked with establishing roads, wharves and airstrips to facilitate the defence of the area. The build-up of personnel, aircraft and materiel began in June 1942, followed by advance parties of the 7th Brigade under the command of Brigadier Field in early July. The first of three airstrips was completed by 21 July and the first three Kittyhawk aeroplanes landed on 24 July.[6]

After coming ashore near Buna and advancing south towards Kokoda in July, the Japanese aim was to prevent the Allies developing an airbase at Milne Bay, so as to open up the possibility of launching a second land-based offensive on Port Moresby from the area. Weeks before landing on the northern shores of Milne Bay, the Japanese attacked from the air, following their initial attack on 4 August with a series of aerial engagements against pilots from Nos 76 and 75 squadrons, RAAF, throughout the month.[7] On the morning of the Milne Bay landings, seven Japanese barges were observed approaching the coast of Goodenough Island, which was part of the wider Milne Bay Province. The Japanese vessels were destroyed by RAAF aircraft, but not before they had landed an estimated 350 marines on Goodenough. A US Army Air Force aircraft sighted a convoy of Japanese ships consisting of three cruisers, two transports, two minesweepers and two tankers, 'or vessels resembling tankers', sailing towards Milne Bay.[8] Once the sightings were confirmed, aerial attacks by Kittyhawks and a Hudson bomber commenced, but these failed to prevent the Japanese fleet approaching Milne Bay.[9]

Dogged by communication and transportation problems, and lacking intelligence on the true strength of the recently landed enemy force, Major General Clowes held the experienced AIF 18th Brigade in reserve—a decision later heavily criticised by MacArthur and the Commander-in-Chief of the Allied Land Forces in the SWPA, General Thomas Blamey. Clowes' decision saw the task of defending the Milne Bay area fall primarily to the 'relatively inexperienced militiamen of the 61st and 25th Battalions [who bore] the brunt of the early fighting.'[10] Attacks on No.3 Airstrip by the reinforced Japanese soldiers between 28 and 30 August met strong resistance, with a heavy casualty toll prompting their fighting withdrawal. From this point on, Allied tactics centred on clearing the enemy from the area around the northern shore of the bay. These efforts continued until 6 August with the RAAF playing a key role in the victory.[11] This aerial support was vital as there was no naval base at Milne Bay from which to direct a defence from the sea. Indeed, the 'practically nonexistent' naval presence effectively ruled out any maritime engagement of the enemy's ships.[12]

MACARTHUR'S 'VICTORY'

The broader historiography has depicted the Battle of Milne Bay as a landmark and decisive victory over the Japanese. This has its roots in the words of the British commander of Allied Forces in India and Burma, Field Marshal Sir William Slim, who declared that the Australians at Milne Bay were the first to break 'the spell of invincibility of the Japanese Army'.[13] Although it was an important strategic victory that boosted morale, the military operations at Milne Bay had far less impact than those of the Kokoda Track or the Papuan beachheads in terms of scale, duration and casualties. The standing that was subsequently afforded the fighting at Milne Bay rests with its continued representation as 'the first defeat of the invincible Japanese in the Pacific ... the turning point [whereby] the seemingly unstoppable Japanese had been stopped.' This is despite acknowledgements that 'no large forces were engaged ... and that it never reached the stature of a major battle.'[14]

The Australian victory at Milne Bay hinged on an unprecedented level of cooperation between the Army and the RAAF and was not as concise, clear-cut or absolute as generally portrayed. In fact, thousands of Japanese marines survived the fighting and withdrew to a series of amphibious landing points on the shores of Milne Bay from where they were successfully evacuated by sea. This meant that the troops could be redeployed in other battles. The pockets of determined Japanese troops who remained behind after most of their comrades had sailed away ensured that sporadic fighting continued well beyond the Battle of Milne Bay's accepted end date of 7 September 1942. And though there were relatively few Australian battle casualties, thousands later fell victim to illness and disease.

None of these details stopped the mercurial MacArthur from claiming a decisive victory at Milne Bay less than a week after the Japanese landing, and before the fighting had concluded.

On 31 August, he issued war correspondents with a special statement entitled 'Chopping Japs to Pieces', which was reproduced in newspapers across Australia.[15] Yet the ignominiously labelled 'mopping-up operations' over the following weeks saw further Australians killed and wounded well after MacArthur's victory statement. Indeed, the attack on Japanese machine-gun posts at Goroni which saw the posthumous awarding of a Victoria Cross to Corporal John French of the 2/9th Infantry Battalion took place four days *after* MacArthur claimed victory at Milne Bay.[16] Intermittent fighting continued across the area as the thousands of Japanese survivors withdrew towards the shores in preparation for evacuation. It was not until the nights of 6 and 7 September that their successful evacuation by sea brought an end to the organised land engagements at Milne Bay. At this stage, Australian casualties totalled 377, with 167 soldiers killed in action.[17] Fourteen Americans and an estimated 700 Japanese also died in the fighting.[18]

The wreck of the supply ship MV Anshun lying on her side in Milne Bay after coming under attack from Japanese ships on the night of 6 September 1942 (AWM 026666).

But the suffering was not over yet. In October 1942 Australian soldiers were tasked with eliminating the Japanese troops still languishing on Goodenough Island. This three-day engagement, codenamed Operation Drake, caused further Australian casualties and again saw hundreds of Japanese evacuated by sea before the island was secured by the Allies. Arguably, it was the Battle of Goodenough Island that more accurately represented the end of the organised fighting in Milne Bay Province. The Milne Bay area continued to function as an Allied base and staging zone for the duration of the war, with

Australian and American service personnel stationed there until 1945.

THE MEDICAL SITUATION

The relatively small scale nature of the Milne Bay campaign provides an opportunity to assess the medical strengths and weaknesses of the broader medical campaign in Papua. As was the case on the Kokoda Track, the ability of the soldiers at Milne Bay to fight, survive their wounds and illness, and return to the front line was contingent on the efforts of the medical men. Maintaining a healthy fighting force in this malarial morass, with its 'black and tenacious' soil, ankle-deep mud, and average annual rainfall of 108 inches (2743mm) represented a mighty medical challenge.[19] The trinity of issues that plagued medical units elsewhere in Papua—communication, supply and evacuation—also hampered medical care at Milne Bay. Again, in a scenario similar to that which unfolded on the Kokoda Track, three key medical units were primarily responsible for the Australians at Milne Bay. Occasionally reinforced and eventually relieved, the 11th and 2/5th field ambulances and the 110th CCS ensured the survival of thousands of soldiers stationed there between mid-1942 and early 1943.

Like those who sailed into Port Moresby, the Australian soldiers disembarking at Milne Bay did so with inadequate training, preparation and intelligence. In his understated manner, Clowes noted, for example, that 'the absence of any suitable map of the theatre of operations proved a considerable handicap' and all requests for aerial photos with which to produce such maps locally remained outstanding for weeks.[20] It was estimated that 10 to 20% of the troops had trained for between six and nine months while, unbelievably, the rest 'had received training for not more than 1 month to 6 weeks'.[21] In some cases, that training did not include even basic elements, such as use of small arms (musketry). Some of the soldiers who were sent to the front line to face the Japanese were mere 'lads', less than 19 years old.[22]

Australian soldiers and truck bogged in mud at Milne Bay, October 1942 (AWM 026682).

These shortcomings in training and preparation saw young men with little or no weapons experience sent forward into the swamps and jungles of Milne Bay to fight a seasoned enemy who showed 'initiative, imagination and originality both in regard to their tactics and their equipment which one feels has been lacking in the past in our own approach to this type of warfare.'[23] Despite such challenges, many of these 'unblooded' soldiers performed extremely well in battle, with Clowes commenting 'most favourably [on] the meritorious nature of the services performed by certain units of the A.M.F. in their baptism of fire.'[24] However, the soldiers' lack of maturity, knowledge and skill inevitably affected the medical units as well as their battalions. The Minister for the Army, Frank Forde, declared that the lack of training was 'nothing short of a calamity' that rendered such men 'a menace to themselves [and] a menace to the men with whom they are serving.'[25]

Before the Papuan campaign began in July 1942, the DDMS, Brigadier William Johnston, knew that inadequate facilities and the severe shortage of beds would necessarily compromise medical care, make it extremely difficult to maintain the strength of NGF as a whole, and prevent those requiring treatment being retained on the island.[26] A malariologist's report at this time similarly identified the need for 'at least twice the number of hospital beds usually provided in training areas in the north of Australia, for good laboratory facilities, reserve supplies of all kinds, an active malarial control unit, and provision of protection for troops.'[27] None of these measures was in place at Milne Bay.

These facts render the order, logically attributed to General Blamey in his capacity as Commander-in-Chief of the Allied Land Forces in the SWPA, that 'no man would be evacuated from the [Milne Bay] area for malarial infection except for serious medical reasons', unworkable, unsustainable and destined to stretch all medical facilities to breaking point.[28] The long-standing awareness of the malarial risk posed by Milne Bay juxtaposed with the acknowledged inadequacy of medical facilities there makes it very difficult to defend such an order from a medical standpoint. These factors also lend perspective to Major General Clowes' instruction that contracting malaria at Milne Bay was to be regarded as a self-inflicted wound.[29]

MALARIA

The view that the soldiers themselves were to blame for the high rate of malaria in Milne Force was one perpetuated by the military and medical hierarchy—despite overwhelming evidence to the contrary. The soldiers' medical preparedness to fight in an environment such as at Milne Bay was certainly poor. Hygiene standards were low, the men wore shorts and rolled-up shirtsleeves and 'with the exception of a few individuals ... the force at Milne Bay was not malaria-conscious at any time during the first few months.'[30] It must be remembered, however, that the first soldiers arrived with no mosquito nets, no effective repellents, and no Director of Hygiene.[31]

The devastating effects of malaria in much earlier wars, coupled with more recent advice from doctors, malariologists, entomologists and pathologists, ensured that the military and medical hierarchy not only understood how the disease was transmitted, but were aware of its continued and insidious presence in Milne Bay. Surveys from as early as the 1930s, and as recently as 1942, clearly showed that the malignant tertian strain of malaria was endemic.[32] In August, the Assistant Director General of Medical Services (ADGMS), Land Headquarters, Brigadier Alec Dawkins, read a report on the range of diseases prevalent in New Guinea. That report (attributed by Dawkins to AAMC Director of Entomology, Major Ian Mackerras) observed that leprosy, sandfly fever, hookworm and venereal disease were present in all villages in Milne Bay Province. Mackerras also noted that the malignant tertian strain of malaria was 'found in this area in abundance'.[33] Indeed, it was because the malarial hazard was 'known to be great' that soldiers were instructed to start taking quinine tablets within a week of arriving at Milne Bay.[34]

The risk of contracting the disease was deemed so high because 'Milne Bay had a dire reputation, subsequently borne out to the full, as one of the most malarious places in the world.'[35] The province was certainly regarded by 'old timers' as 'one of the worst malarial areas' in the Eastern Division of Papua. Mackerras knew that it would be almost impossible to control the numbers of mosquito vectors (transmitters) of malaria at Milne Bay, given the lack of means, men and materiel with which to do so.[36] He therefore warned that 'the greatest possible care in every detail of personal preventive measures must be exercised, or heavy losses are certain.'[37] He was soon proved right. Almost 6000 patients were admitted and treated for the disease at Milne Bay in the six months from July to December 1942.[38] Around 25% of Milne Force was admitted to the field ambulance units and CCS suffering from malaria between September and November, with an average recovery time of 17 days. Confirming the accuracy of the malariologist's concerns expressed months before, it was obvious that there would soon be no beds for the sick. In November, the 'daily admissions exceeded discharges by forty-three, with 1151 of 1252 beds occupied.'[39] Various means were suggested to overcome the crippling shortage of beds. These included increasing the rate of evacuation by sea or air to Australia, establishing an additional hospital to cope with demand, and expanding the existing medical facilities.

The fact that medical personnel themselves were not immune to malaria only added to the problems faced by those who remained at Milne Bay long after the fighting ended. The CO of the 11th Field Ambulance, Lieutenant Colonel John Crakanthorp, reported that most who worked the night-duty shift fell victim to the disease, and staffing levels across all units were affected by various illnesses. In the week ending 21 November, for example, 28 members of his field ambulance were on sick parade, five were unfit for duty, and a further five were evacuated to the MDS. This represented an improvement compared to the first week of November, when 48 of the unit's personnel reported for sick parade.[40] A survey of medical personnel of the 2/5th Field Ambulance, whose average daily strength was just 108—less than half the war establishment—revealed that, between September 1942 and February 1943, 100 personnel were struck down by malaria. Some 55% of these men experienced more than one attack, with 60% of cases occurring in December and January.[41]

Superficially, these figures seem to contradict the statement by Crakanthorp that 'the strictest anti-malaria precautions have been maintained throughout the unit's stay of approx. 7 months in New Guinea.'[42] However, another interpretation is possible: that the malaria situation by this stage was so bad and the risk of exposure so high, that it was virtually impossible for medical staff *not* to fall victim to the disease—even when taking all possible precautionary measures. Yet, when impressing on infantry brigades that 'the measures adopted by troops in general have fallen far short of what is possible', Lieutenant Colonel Esmond (Bill) Keogh cited the extremely low rate of 'only 3 cases' of malaria among medical personnel of the 110th CCS as 'evidence' of best practice.[43]

Conversely, the ADMS Milne Force, Colonel George Maitland, stated that a more 'realistic picture' of the malaria situation at Milne Bay could be gained by considering the *high* incidence of the disease in medical units. As well as noting the 'unhappy story of failure to supply malaria control stores and medical stores', Maitland pointed out that holding patients in the CCS and MDS quickly brought the facilities to saturation point, overstretched staffing levels that were far below war establishment numbers, and necessitated evacuations to Australia 'at the rate of 2 Battalions per month'.[44]

Despite increased casualty evacuations by sea towards the end of the year, almost 1700 beds in the medical facilities at Milne Bay remained occupied in December, with daily admissions over discharges averaging 64 patients and increasing rapidly. The overall admission rate stood at an alarming 1914 patients per month.[45] The CO of the 110th CCS, Lieutenant Colonel Frederick Wall, later stated that malaria was the cause of 67% of all medical admissions during the nine-month period to May 1943, observing that 'whatever feverish illness a man suffered, he usually produced a positive blood film for Malaria.'[46] Maitland succinctly summarised the issue thus: 'the major problem in Milne Bay was not the collection and care of battle casualties, but the conservation of the force against the ravages of malaria.'[47]

In Australia, DGMS Burston was kept informed on the malaria situation across NGF. While yet to visit the area, he was aware of the medical issues at Milne Bay. Burston expressed frustration with 'the very grave lack of any proper implementing by combatant officers of Anti-Malarial measures ...[and] no supervision of the distribution and taking of quinine.'[48] He also questioned whether there was 'any subversive activity connected with the widespread propaganda concerning quinine and impotence?'[49] Although seemingly ready to blame the officers and soldiers for the situation, detailed reports had already made it clear to Burston that the causes of the high incidence of malaria at Milne Bay were many and varied.

This awareness is obvious from Burston's correspondence. In December 1942, he discussed with his recently appointed DDMS, Brigadier Clive Disher, the Army's failure to deliver anti-malarial equipment 'due to faulty handling by Movement Control and Docks Operating Units ... A great deal of it has got to Moresby instead of Milne Bay'—over 200 miles away.[50] Burston opined that the only way to overcome the malaria problem at Milne Bay was to send thousands of men to 'clean the place up and get it drained as far as possible', before adding a qualification that lent a fatalistic edge: 'Even then of course, it isn't going to make a very vast difference as from all reports that area would take a year or two to make it anything like safe to live in.'[51] Yet thousands of soldiers *had* been living, training, and fighting at Milne Bay for months. Remarkably, just three deaths at Milne Bay were definitively attributed to malaria. Such a low mortality rate was ascribed by some to changes to the suppressive quinine regime, while others credited the high standard of care provided by the medical personnel.[52]

The most severe form of the disease, cerebral malaria, caused the death of a patient in the 11th Field Ambulance MDS on 7 December 1942.[53] Another soldier who had been admitted for typhus died two days later—ironically, not from the disease itself, but from the 'toxic effect of Plasmoquine', with which he had been treated.[54] This drug was routinely given at a rate of 0.01 grains three times a day for five days to all patients diagnosed with malaria, with atebrin and quinine also administered. A report on plasmoquine toxicity found that, in the six weeks to 9 December, 80% of patients showed slight symptoms of poisoning, noting this was not confined to slightly built men—in other words, the cause was not simply attributable to dosage miscalculation and resultant overdose. Symptoms included abdominal pain, anorexia, headache, dizziness and weakness as well as 'considerable cyanosis'.[55] Further investigations led to the conclusion that 'so called plasmoquine poisoning is due to insufficient interval between the administration of Atebrin and plasmoquine', with treatment adjusted accordingly.[56]

The majority of casualties evacuated from Milne Bay during the final three months of 1942 were suffering from malaria in its various stages and forms (malignant tertian, benign tertian, cerebral). Illnesses also associated with the disease, including anaemia, affected the soldiers' energy levels and, therefore, their ability to march and to fight.[57] While other diseases such as dengue fever, scrub typhus and dysentery affected the soldiers at Milne Bay, malaria was by far the predominant disease and its ubiquity presented the major challenge to the medical units there. Overall, more than 8000 soldiers suffering from battle wounds and illnesses *other* than malaria, such as dengue fever, scrub typhus and dysentery, were admitted to medical facilities between July and December 1942, with a total of 14,189 casualties treated by medical units during this time.[58]

THE FORDE REPORT

The Minister for the Army, Frank Forde, visited Milne Bay in the first week of October 1942 as part of his remit to evaluate the situation in Papua and report back to Prime Minister Curtin. Referring to all Australian units across Papua, Forde observed that, 'practically every fighting unit was at least 25% below establishment and an urgent need exists for reinforcements from Australia. The number required at the time of my visit being 6,000 personnel, but this being added to every day by further casualties particularly from malaria and dysentery.'[59] This was certainly borne out by the Milne Bay statistics. Of almost 12,000 Allied troops stationed there at the end of September, 8350 were AIF and CMF (militia) personnel. The number of combatants was approximately 300 below the Australian Army war establishment strength of 6986, with non-combatants numbering 1666 (558 fewer than the war establishment).[60] More than 600 RAAF servicemen were also based at Milne Bay. There were 2445 US troops, with an additional 442 in transit.[61]

While acknowledging that the true numbers were higher than those available to him at the time of writing, Forde listed Australian casualty statistics to October as 353, with 161 killed or missing, and 192 wounded.[62] Challenges that hampered the gathering of accurate statistics included communication problems and the harsh realities of jungle fighting. These factors made it especially difficult to categorise any soldiers classified as missing, with Forde noting that 'it is one of the most tragic and pathetic features of jungle warfare that, in many instances, where the member's life is taken, it is not possible in this type of fighting to discover the body or trace his whereabouts.'[63]

Minister for the Army, Frank Forde (far left), with General Douglas MacArthur and General Thomas Blamey on their arrival in Papua, October 1942 (AWM 013427).

Confirming what medical personnel already knew, Forde reported that most of the sick soldiers at Milne Bay were suffering from 'malarial and other tropical diseases ... there was an influx of 50 new malarial cases daily and ... the average treatment period extended over three weeks, with an average number in hospital suffering from malarial and other tropical diseases in the vicinity of 850 patients.'[64] Such high numbers at this time were worrying because the hospital transport ship, *Manunda*, had already evacuated hundreds of the more seriously sick and wounded to Australia. It was clear that admissions due to illnesses, such as dysentery and malaria, remained high—and that there were insufficient personnel to care for them.[65]

As was the case at Port Moresby, the withdrawal of AANS personnel in February was still being felt in Milne Bay as late as October. While accepting the reasons for their withdrawal and agreeing that women should not be sent to areas where Japanese troops were present, Forde argued that their role in staffing the static medical facilities, where field ambulance personnel had now been called on to fill the void, far outweighed other considerations. He considered that 'little, if any, risk is involved' at this stage of the Papuan campaign, adding that, 'while I would not recommend that nurses should be permitted to go into any area in which the Japanese were likely to penetrate, I consider that nurses should be available in all the theatres in which it is possible readily to evacuate them should enemy penetration of the area in which they are located become a possibility.'[66] The nurses themselves were very keen to return and, arguably, no theatre of war met Forde's criteria better than Milne Bay, where large-scale land battles had ceased since September and there remained 'few, if any, Japanese troops in the area'.[67] The Allies were also gaining air superiority and hundreds of casualties continued to be evacuated by sea without coming under enemy attack. The nurses did slowly return to Milne Bay and Port Moresby in the latter part of 1942—the end of October and start of November respectively—and maintained a welcome presence in Papua for the duration of the war.

Even allowing for the obvious challenges involved in maintaining a fighting force in a place such as this, failures of the systems that underpinned the supply of medical equipment demanded Forde's attention. Despite the inevitable difficulties presented by 'relentless nature' that brought the wind, rain, mud, mosquitoes and malaria to Milne Bay, most of the problems encountered in this area were exacerbated by human factors—poor planning, communication, supply—leading to the conclusion that much suffering could have been avoided. This uncomfortable truth was recognised by Forde, who identified numerous weak links in the chain of supply that could have been strengthened with relatively little effort. To end the problem of inappropriately packaged supplies being dumped in unsuitable locations on a regular basis, for instance, a need for more (and better trained) labourers, dock workers and transport personnel was identified. Forde found it distressing to see huge dumps of Army supplies exposed to the tropical weather conditions, in the majority of cases without any cover and, in other cases, without adequate protection ... supplies of flour exposed in dumps to the weather was rapidly deteriorating, causing a wasted effort of shipping, unloading and transport facilities, culminating in a waste of essential supplies.[68]

He added that much-needed hospital equipment was left 'lying out in the open where it had been dumped at the side of the roadway, evidently awaiting the provision of accommodation before it could be utilised.'[69]

Unloading supply ships at Milne Bay, September 1942 (AWM 026697).

In calling for a review of 'our whole set-up', the Minister was primarily motivated by the incongruity of financing a large number of expensive projects in Australia, which focused on housing personnel, supplies, munitions and equipment in 'relatively elaborate structures', while the money, supplies and buildings in operational areas such as Milne Bay remained either non-existent or 'elementary'.[70] His palpable anger regarding these issues prompted him to not only call for a new appreciation of the situation, but to urge the Australian government to make a policy decision as to 'whether projects now based on probable invasion of Australia (other than those with a defensive tactical or operational objective) should receive priority over pressing requirements in the New Guinea Area.'[71]

Forde was similarly forthright in linking the high number of malaria casualties to the scarcity of quinine available. Further, he unambiguously connected the deaths of soldiers to a lack of the anti-malarial medication, while also highlighting its importance as a suppressive agent:

> Two deaths from malaria had occurred in the Milne Bay Hospital because the members concerned had run out of supplies of quinine tablets through being in an isolated post. In consequence, malaria

attacked them with much greater severity and resulted in their deaths, clearly demonstrating the value of quinine and the necessity of ensuring its continued supply to troops operating in the tropics.[72]

A seemingly unrelated supply issue that was nonetheless identified by Forde as contributing to the high rate of illness at Milne Bay was the lack of tents. This shortage exposed the soldiers to the harshness of the weather and forced them to sleep on the ground or on piles of leaf mould, further weakening their compromised immune systems and making them more susceptible to diseases such as dysentery. The exasperated Minister recounted how he had already given approval for the urgent manufacture in Australia of two-man tents and mosquito nets 'some time ago', stressing that 'their non-supply to date requires explanation'.[73] The Australians would later turn to the Americans in the hope of securing a supply of this basic equipment.

Further inspections of the Army's supply situation encompassed the methods used by stores depots in Australia, the level of cooperation with other service arms at Milne Bay, and the transportation, storage and collection of goods. One inquiry found that, of 234 cases of stores despatched from Australia on 5 August, only 171 could be traced as having ever arrived at Milne Bay.[74] However, a later investigation checked and cross-checked inventories and associated paperwork to conclude that 'of the 1500 (approx.) cases sent forward, less than seventy are missing.'[75] Key factors such as the duplication of consignment numbers, the mixing of medical stores with ordnance goods during transportation, incorrect storage, and the use of unsuitable containers, specifically and directly affected medical supplies. In one incident, Hydrogen Perchloride (an acid used in medicines which, if inhaled can lead to breathing problems, collapse and death) was sent in paper bags with the name of the drug and the word 'poison' handwritten, smudged, and barely legible. Highly volatile and flammable Ether, which was used as an anaesthetic, was packed in five-pound (two kilogram) lots and put into tins that were unsuitable for air dropping.[76]

Forde's summary of what was required to improve the overall medical situation at Milne Bay highlighted the need to pay greater attention to precautionary hygiene measures, deliver more four-wheel drive vehicles and ambulances, establish convalescent depots, send more anti-malarial drugs and equipment, and implement major changes to the overall supply system. While not shrinking from the many criticisms he had made throughout the report, Forde was nevertheless keen to distinguish between those issues relating directly to shortcomings in Army administration on the mainland and the continued efforts of personnel in Papua. In what was perhaps an attempt to placate the military and political hierarchy, Forde expressed a 'quiet confidence' in a successful outcome, stating that the fighting forces in Papua were 'ably maintained and efficiently administered'.[77] Forde's report was sent to Prime Minister Curtin who noted his recommendations.[78] Meanwhile, those at Milne Bay continued to deal with the medical situation as best they could.

CHAPTER 7

GOODENOUGH ISLAND AND MILNE BAY

'Keep your chin up, things ain't really too bad'

GOODENOUGH ISLAND

Goodenough Island, 20 miles long and 15 miles wide, lies just off the north-east coast of Papua. Part of Milne Bay Province, this strategically important island on the sea route to New Britain and the Trobriand Islands is the northernmost land mass in the D'Entrecasteaux group of Goodenough, Fergusson, Normanby, Dobu and Sanaroa. The climate and geography of Goodenough Island is as spectacularly unforgiving as that found across mainland Papua. Typically receiving an annual rainfall of between 60 and 100 inches (1524–2540mm), the centre of the island is dominated by Mount Vineuo, which rises to over 8000 feet, while its shores are skirted by a coastal belt measuring six miles at the widest point. Health surveys conducted by Australian researchers across the D'Entrecasteaux group in the 1930s painted a picture as challenging as the geography. The indigenous population, estimated at less than 25,000, suffered from a range of tropical diseases, with 'malaria hyperendemic. High spleen rates [an indication of malaria] even in villages on the mountain slopes – habitation ceases at about 2000ft.... Hookworm is 100% in many localities examined ... lesions due to yaws and filaria common ... scattered cases of leprosy on Normanby and Dobu.'[1]

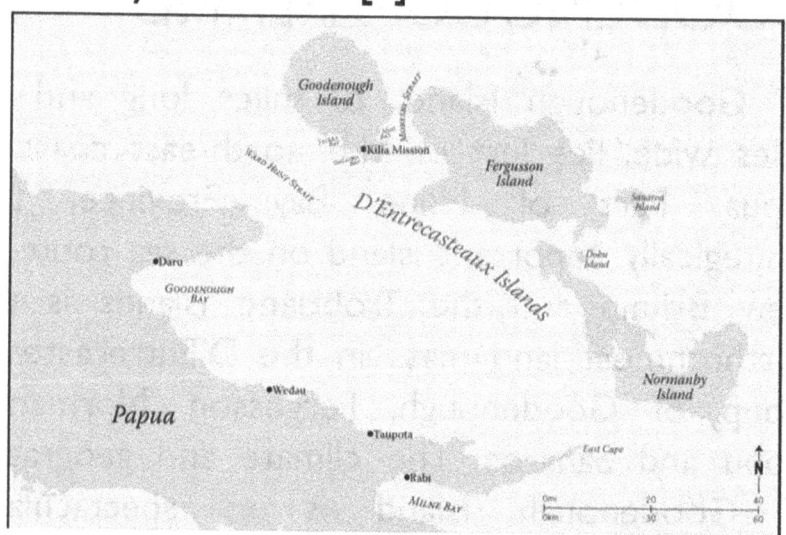

Map 7.1 The D'Entrecasteaux Islands

Recognising the vital role that Goodenough Island could play in providing advance warnings of approaching enemy ships and aircraft, and the monitoring of the Ward Hunt Strait separating the island from mainland Papua, an American fighter control squadron detachment was stationed there in early August 1942. The Japanese were eager to gain control of Goodenough as part of their quest to control the entire island of New Guinea. On 25 August, the day before the Japanese amphibious landing at Milne Bay, a small detachment of the *5th Sasebo Special Naval Landing Party* went ashore on Goodenough Island intending to sail by barge to Taupota, on the north coast of Milne Bay Province, proceed overland to Milne Bay, and launch an attack on the Australians from the rear. However, the Japanese soon found themselves stranded on Goodenough Island when the RAAF's No.75 Squadron destroyed their landing craft shortly after coming ashore. Though unsuccessful in terms of the larger goal, the Japanese landing on Goodenough Island prompted the Americans to destroy their own equipment on the island and withdraw, abandoning the island to the enemy.[2] In September, seaborne attempts by the Japanese to rescue those stranded on Goodenough saw their destroyer, *Yayoi*, sunk by Allied aircraft. The survivors from *Yayoi* made their way on rafts to Normanby Island—the most southerly of the D'Entrecasteaux Islands. These men languished on Normanby until the Japanese destroyers *Isokaze* and *Mochizuki* sailed from Rabaul and rescued some 83 of them on 25 September.[3]

Although neither those who remained stranded on Normanby nor those on Goodenough Island posed any discernible military threat, there were concerns among the Australians over their ability to be reinforced and to undermine Australian authority in the islands by winning the hearts and minds of the local population. Accordingly, a company from the 2/10th Battalion, AIF, was ordered to 'eliminate' the Japanese from Normanby Island. No Australian casualties resulted from this action, and some of the captured Japanese troops were taken to Milne Bay for interrogation.[4] However the determined Japanese command did not abandon those who remained on Goodenough Island, using aircraft, submarines and landing craft to deliver food, ammunition and medical supplies to the starving men. In a remarkable example of compassion that challenges popular representations of a ruthless enemy who abandoned their sick and weak, more than 70 Japanese casualties and the bodies of 13 men who had died during their time on Goodenough Island were taken back to Rabaul by submarine in October 1942.[5] A further attempt in the middle of the month to rescue the 285 sick and starving men who remained was anticipated and thwarted by Allied aircraft.[6] After two months on the island, the fate of the Japanese survivors would now be determined by the Australians.

The shoreline of Goodenough Island with the schooner Maclaren King in the background. In 1942, the Australian government requisitioned Maclaren King from the Anglican missionaries who had used it as a ferry between the islands (AWM 150997).

OPERATION DRAKE

In late October, the 2/12th Infantry Battalion, 18th Brigade, AIF (Drake Force), stationed at Milne Bay under the command of Lieutenant Colonel Arthur Arnold, was tasked with the mission 'to eliminate the Japanese force of approx. 300 and deny Goodenough Island to the enemy'.[7] This mission, codenamed 'Operation Drake', hinged on simultaneous attacks from two directions by two forces. Mud Bay Force comprised 520 soldiers (one battalion less one company), while the 120 soldiers in Taleba Bay Force represented one company plus detachments. The names of the forces reflected the locations on Goodenough Island from which the attacks would be launched.[8] Arnold provided a succinct overview of Drake Force's subsequent engagement with the Japanese:[9]

> The Task Force from Milne Bay that landed on the south tip of Goodenough Island on the night 22/23 Oct was divided into two forces. The larger force attacked from Mud Bay towards Kilia Mission and made two unsuccessful attacks. During the morning of the third day, these troops again attacked the enemy position to find that the enemy had escaped during the night. A smaller force attacked from Taleba Bay on the morning of 23 Oct, but failed to gain their objective and as a result of Japanese pressure returned to Mud Bay early the next day, 24 Oct.[10]

Mud Bay Force then discovered that the remaining Japanese defenders had been evacuated by sea from Goodenough Island, undetected by the Australians.

History records that Operation Drake was successful in its mission to 'eliminate' the Japanese from Goodenough Island. Arnold's men reportedly counted the bodies of 32 dead Japanese marines who were in good physical condition, well clothed and well equipped. However, no accurate assessment could be made as to the total number killed because the Japanese had 'apparently been successful in removing most of their dead'—action that surely indicated the 'orderly and unhurried' nature of the evacuation.[11] The organised nature of both the Japanese defensive action and their evacuation was commented on by the official army historian, Dudley McCarthy, who noted that the defenders were well aware of the Australian landings on Goodenough 'from the time they began' and that 'all of the survivors were taken in two barges to Fergusson Island soon after they broke off the engagement. A cruiser picked them up there and took them to Rabaul.'[12] McCarthy recorded 20 killed and 15 wounded Japanese marines, which is substantially fewer than Arnold reported.[13]

MEDICAL CARE ON GOODENOUGH ISLAND

Consideration of the medical situation on Goodenough Island humanises the experiences of Arnold's men in a way that military accounts alone cannot.[14] The insidious effects of tropical diseases were again underscored as soldiers, who had long since completed the full course of malaria treatment and returned to their unit, were so severely weakened by the disease that they were unable to cope with the demands of marching and fighting in the jungles of Goodenough Island. Similarly, one soldier who had completed a long recuperation at Milne Bay after being struck down with typhus remained so exhausted while on Goodenough Island that he was unable to reach even halfway to the forward area before being forced to return to the rear. Throughout the operation, the number of soldiers available for front-line fighting was affected by the 'large proportion of men who were kept in the rear party and who showed intermittent pyrexia [fever] of 100 ... or 99.' Although these sick and weakened men were undergoing suppressive malaria treatment, their high temperatures suggested that they were, in fact, already suffering from the early stages of the disease.[15]

Illness was not the only problem confronting the soldiers and medical personnel on Goodenough Island. The inevitable battle casualties that resulted from fighting in such an environment presented their own set of problems for the field ambulance detachments. Captain John Scott, the medical officer from A Company, 2/5th Field Ambulance, who was sent in support of Mud Bay Force, reported that five soldiers wounded on the first day could not be evacuated back to the ADS due to the military situation and a lack of personnel. Those responsible for staffing the ADS were unable to obtain details of any further casualties sustained in the forward area because of 'scant and difficult' communications.[16] There were challenges too for those who were treating casualties awaiting evacuation in tents set up on the sand. Captain Roland Holmes, the medical officer from B Company with Taleba Force, explained that on 23 October 'a message was sent for the ketch in Taleba Bay to come round with reserve ammunition and evacuate wounded. When a dingy had rowed ashore the Japs opened fire with heavy machine gun and the ketch was forced to retire with several holes in her.'[17]

A brief consideration of this incident in terms of the Geneva Convention lends perspective to events. Most of the vessels used to evacuate casualties from Goodenough Island had long served in various capacities, sailing between Australia and the island of New Guinea since the start of the Pacific War. Whether the reserve ammunition requested by Holmes was on board the ketch is unknown. It is also unclear whether the vessel that was fired on by the Japanese displayed the official Red Cross markings, or met other conditions of the relevant articles that would entitle it to protection from enemy attack under the Geneva Convention.[18] It is known, however, that the Australian Army requisitioned the two-masted schooner *Maclaren King* from Anglican missionaries in Papua early in 1942 and armed it with a .50 calibre machine-gun and 20-millimetre cannon.[19] Photographs of the schooner off Goodenough Island in August and November 1942 show Papuan crew and Australian anti-aircraft gunners posing with 'the 50-calibre water-cooled Browning anti-aircraft gun with which Australian Army gunners shot down a Japanese attacking aircraft.'[20] A further unknown factor is whether the weapons were removed during the intervening months between when these photographs were taken—that is, the period when the schooner was used to ferry casualties from Goodenough Island.

The evacuation of casualties from Goodenough Island continued nevertheless. At 7.00am on 24 October, 10 wounded and three sick soldiers were transferred from the ADS at Mud Bay to *Maclaren King*, which 'did not stop' on its voyage back to Milne Bay, despite being strafed by machine-gun fire from three enemy aircraft. When a further 11 casualties unexpectedly arrived on the sands of Goodenough at 10.00pm that night they, along with one nursing orderly and three sick patients, were transferred on board two ships (*Minerva* and *Tieryo*) and sailed for Gili Gili at midnight.[21]

It was not just this final link in the evacuation chain that proved challenging. Transportation of casualties on Goodenough island was extremely difficult, primarily due to having 'more stretcher cases than stretchers', insufficient men to carry them, and little time to improvise.[22] The nursing orderlies treated their patients in conditions described by Holmes as 'bad ... continually under machine gun fire in a not very well protected spot.'[23] The stretcher-bearers worked under constant fire from machine-guns and mortars. Such actions culminated in the deaths of two stretcher-bearers and the wounding of two others as they retrieved wounded soldiers from the forward area. Captain Holmes reported that 'Blackburn and Miles going forward to bring back wounded, received a burst from an enemy mortar. Miles was killed instantly and Blackburn died a few minutes after being brought back to the RAP.'[24] Another stretcher-bearer, Private Marriott, received two gunshot wounds to the back, and a soldier from the 2/12th Battalion, Sergeant

Hughes—who was also acting as a stretcher-bearer—sustained shrapnel wounds to his arms and back.[25]

Australian anti-aircraft crew and .50 calibre machine-gun on board Maclaren King, August 1942. Goodenough Island is in the background (AWM 013500/05).

These attacks by the Japanese troops on Australian personnel engaged in the collection of the wounded cannot unequivocally be regarded as breaches of the Geneva Convention. The reason lies in a statement by Captain Scott, the medical officer with Mud Bay Force, who explained that 'most of the Field Ambulance personnel were armed at this stage for self-protection'.[26] The Convention of 1929 permitted the possession of a 'light individual weapon' to protect medical personnel and the casualties in their care.[27] However, Scott acknowledged that this type of 'commando' raid by the Australians, undertaken in a jungle environment requiring a narrow perimeter defence against counter-attack, made it extremely difficult for the enemy to discriminate between the fighting soldiers and the medical establishments, even 'if he wishes to do so'.[28] Further, Scott recommended that all medical personnel in these situations carry weapons, specifically pistols or light sub-machine guns, for their own protection and that of their patients, and to 'boost morale'.[29]

Despite the killing and wounding of their mates, the five remaining stretcher-bearers from the 2/5th Field Ambulance company continued evacuating casualties. Eleven wounded men were literally carried along three miles of sandy beach with the help of infantry soldiers '[Corporal] Hewett showed great stamina by carrying a very big man on his back over the ¾ mile to our perimeter and later a considerable part of the further distance back to the ketch, at times under fire.'[30] The determined efforts of these stretcher-bearers had a positive effect on the fighting soldiers, who were understandably heartened to witness the wounded being taken from the front as quickly as possible. The wounded stretcher-bearer, Private Marriott, was to garner further recognition for his actions as part of Operation Drake when *McLaren King* was fired on by enemy aircraft as it left Mud Bay on 24 October. Marriott was on board as both a patient and a medical orderly. When many of the casualties who were lying on the deck were wounded afresh in the Japanese attack, Marriott became solely responsible for tending to them. He was later awarded the Distinguished Conduct Medal, with the recommendation stating in part:

> Pte Marriott was the only AAMC man aboard ... during the strafing Pte Marriott showed great fortitude by attending to those freshly wounded while under fire. In spite of his wounds, which seriously hampered his movements, and exhaustion due to haemorrhage, Pte Marriott improvised splints and splinted the engineer's fractured leg. He continued to attend all wounded until the ship arrived at Gili Gili wharf several hours later.[31]

On disembarking at Gili Gili, Private Marriott further impressed officers, soldiers and his field ambulance comrades by insisting that all other casualties be attended to before his wounds were treated.

On 30 October, the bulk of the field ambulance personnel on Goodenough Island and a further 14 casualties sailed from Mud Bay to

Gili Gili on *Tieryo* and HMAS *Warrego*. Two nursing orderlies stayed behind on Goodenough in support of the soldiers who remained.[32] In summarising the experience of the medical detachments during Operation Drake, both COs (Scott and Holmes) felt that the equipment available to them was generally adequate, though the stretchers were found to be 'unsuitable for transport over rough jungle tracks'.[33] Special praise was given to the Papuan carriers who accompanied the soldiers for their stamina, improvisation and ability to 'carry large weights for long distances', all of which were crucial to the efficiency of the operation.[34] The excellent discipline, high morale and determined efforts of all field ambulance personnel were noted, with the prompt retrieval of the wounded by the stretcher-bearers especially commendable. The work of the nursing orderlies in caring for the casualties in the ADS while under fire was prosaically summarised as 'less spectacular [though] very good'.[35]

When tallying up the casualties among the 280 Japanese marines who defended Goodenough Island in October 1942, Colonel Arnold recorded 'Enemy: Killed 39. Wounded unknown.'[36] Drake Force had suffered 27 casualties from the 640 Australians sent to reclaim Goodenough—12 dead (10 killed in action, two wounded in action later dying of their wounds) and 15 wounded (one officer and 14 soldiers, including one battalion stretcher-bearer). Of the 24 members of the 2/5th Field Ambulance who served on Goodenough, one stretcher-bearer was wounded and two were killed, bringing the overall Australian casualties to 30—14 dead and 16 wounded.[37]

Poor weather, difficult terrain, and a determined enemy had all affected Operation Drake. Inadequate preparation, an absence of suitable weapons and equipment, a lack of reconnaissance and unreliable lines of communication complicated what was a supposedly straightforward mission. Quite apart from the intrinsic perils of battle, the deployment of so many sick soldiers who, even before the battles began, lacked the 'physical toughness ... stamina and endurance' required to fight a commando-style jungle war, made casualties inevitable.[38] A hastily composed medical plan that failed to consider the obvious challenges of casualty evacuation from Goodenough Island undoubtedly contributed to the shambolic way in which Operation Drake unfolded.

The medical work on Goodenough Island continued after Operation Drake concluded. On 6 November, Captain Holmes and six members of the 2/5th Field Ambulance were sent to vaccinate the Drake Force detachment that had been ordered to remain on the island as part of General MacArthur's planned 'Pygmy' movement. This operation would see a force of between 6000 and 7000 troops construct, maintain and defend an airfield on Goodenough. The AAMC hierarchy felt that the 200-bed hospital suggested by General Headquarters would not be sufficient for 'Pygmy' and hoped to eventually send enough personnel and equipment to allow the bed capacity to expand to 600. DGMS Burston was sure that 'a 10% holding capacity will be necessary as the sick rate will be high and ... evacuation will be difficult.'[39]

The deferral of Pygmy in December was due largely to General Blamey's request for MacArthur to reconsider the merits of the operation in light of the ongoing fighting around Buna, the availability of sufficient garrison troops, 'the continued shrinkage in the combat numbers of the Australian Military Forces ...[and the] inability ... to have the 9th Division returned from the Middle East and to obtain reinforcements from the United States.'[40] A complex deception scheme, known as Operation Hackney, was instead implemented on Goodenough Island to convince the Japanese of the ongoing presence of a large Allied force and so deter further enemy attacks.[41]

Towards the end of November, the Drake Force personnel on Goodenough Island were assessed by Captain Holmes as being in relatively good health, despite virtually all (including Holmes himself) having a history of malaria. The usual issues had, nevertheless, followed the medical detachment to Goodenough: an RAP tent that was not waterproof, irregular supplies, and shortages of basic items such as iodine and bandages, despite repeated requisitions. Holmes' initially positive assessment of the health of the Drake Force detachment was short-lived. Between 30 November and 5 December 1942, 76 cases of malaria were admitted for treatment, rising to 97 from a total of 143 casualties just a few days later. Of the malaria cases, almost 70% had experienced at least one previous attack, with some suffering three bouts since their time with Drake Force in October. The decision to alter the treatment regime from quinine only, to the inclusion of atebrin and plasmoquine, was a response to the inadequacy of the regime used to date.[42] Despite this change, the average daily sick rate on Goodenough rose from 20 cases in mid-November to 52 by mid-December, with the majority attributed to recurrences of malaria.[43] Hopes that aerial casualty evacuations would ease some of the burden were dashed when the aircraft allocated to the task was finally sighted:

'We have just seen the plane – a Moth – which will be somewhat uncomfortable for the patient. Would it be possible to have larger planes for stretcher cases?'[44] As had occurred during Operation Drake, hundreds of casualties were eventually evacuated from Goodenough Island back to Milne Bay by a small flotilla of vessels.

Imitation tank made from hessian stretched over wooden frames, used as part of the Operation Hackney deception scheme on Goodenough Island (late 1942 to mid-1943) (AWM 090203).

YEAR'S END AT MILNE BAY

Australian truck and bulldozer bogged in mud near Gili Gili, October 1942 (AWM 026680).

While the medical services on Goodenough Island continued to respond to their unique situation, fellow medical personnel back on the Papuan mainland at Milne Bay were similarly strained as troop numbers increased throughout September and October, despite the lack of an enemy presence on the ground. The number of casualties rose in line with the arrival of these fresh troops. The 2/1st CCS that had only recently been established at Gili Gili was soon caring for more than 500 sick patients, while a much-needed Convalescent Depot opened at

Waigani to ease the load.[45] By 12 October, the 70 patients remaining in the poorly located 110th CCS had been transferred to the 2/1st CCS, enabling Lieutenant Colonel Wall's unit to move to a more suitable site 'of which we all entirely approved ... situated three miles further inland and 700 yards off the main road it consisted of an elbow-shaped elevated portion of plantation ... [and] 15 to 20 feet above the level of the surrounding groves and jungle.'[46] This too was quickly overwhelmed—so much so that the 'rate of expansion was embarrassing', with 350 patients admitted within 10 days of the establishment of the CCS at the new location.

The unit was further overstretched when it transferred 12 nursing orderlies to the 2/1st CCS for a six-week period to replace personnel from that unit who had already been struck down with malaria.[47] The latest order that *any* casualty requiring hospital treatment must now be returned to Australia relieved some pressure. A daily scheme to collect patients for evacuation from the various facilities scattered across the Milne Bay area was implemented to ensure the order was followed. An additional field ambulance unit (the 2/2nd) arrived on 27 October in support of the advanced group of the 17th Brigade, 6th Division, AIF, which in turn had been sent to relieve the 18th Brigade.[48] Lieutenant

Colonel Crakanthorp's 2/5th Field Ambulance was kept busy caring for new admissions as well as preparing a steady stream of patients for evacuation.

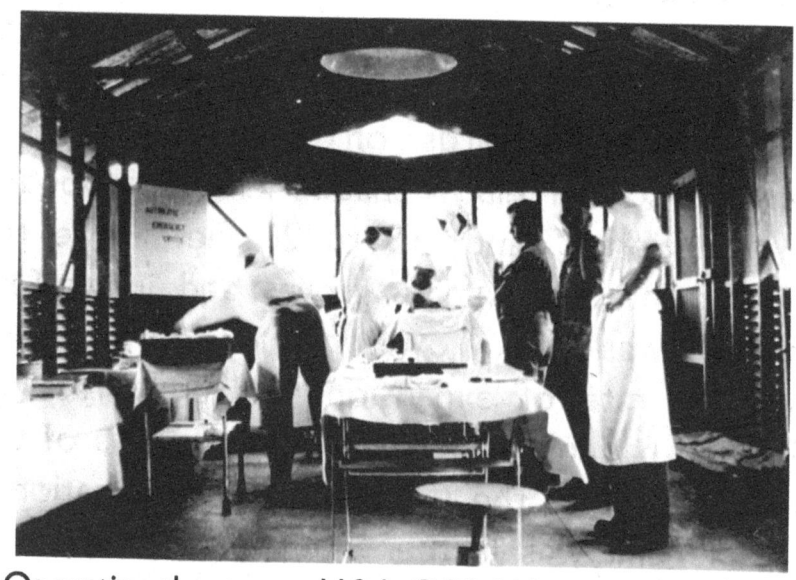

Operating theatre at 110th CCS, Milne Bay, December 1942 (AWM P00440.005).

Although some duties across the Milne Bay area understandably changed in accordance with the fluctuating military situation, the core task of the medical units remained focused on the care of casualties admitted to their fixed establishments—the MDS and CCS. However, this aspect of their work came under considerable stress during the final months of 1942 when light sections were formed from small medical detachments and sent to support troops stationed in villages on the north coast of Milne

Bay Province and beyond. Personnel shortages added to the pressure once these sections were regularly despatched to care for soldiers stationed at isolated locations where the work undertaken included casualty care, as well as inoculations and blood typing to minimise potential problems if men later needed a blood transfusion.[49]

The overstretched 2/5th Field Ambulance was particularly affected, with Captain Scott leading a detachment in support of Hanson Force, and Captain Howard Edelman plus two orderlies establishing an ADS at Wedau-Taupota on the north coast of Milne Bay in support of a 2/9th Battalion detachment.[50] Living conditions in these far-flung places were rudimentary at best, with basic medical equipment for the soldiers at Wedau, for example, sourced from the Mission hospital. When a group of medical personnel set out to walk the 30 miles between the hut that was serving as a medical post at Taupota and the larger eight-bed hut at Wedau, the heat, lack of wind, and difficult terrain exhausted the men, forced them to stop frequently and limited their progress to approximately two miles per hour.[51] Evacuation of casualties from such locations was extremely difficult: the Mission's whaleboat proved an 'unsatisfactory arrangement' for urgent cases, while the rugged coastal and inland tracks made stretcher-bearing 'almost impossible'.[52]

Captain Edelman soon discovered that he was responsible for caring for 'half the Force [plus] 30 in Hospital and 35 in [Convalescent] Depot'.[53] Edelman's account of his experiences makes interesting reading. Outlining his dual roles as medical officer to the unit and the commander of the light section of the field ambulance, he explained that the increasing 'sick wastage' among the soldiers in the Wedau area coupled with the dire situation 'further up'—presumably, the unfolding action around Buna and Gona—prompted his decision to delay the vaccination of the troops.[54] Edelman based his decision on the likelihood that the vaccinated soldiers would suffer temporary disabilities due to side-effects, resulting in a loss of manpower at the front line. He was not only keen to avoid this scenario, but also 'any unusually strong complaint from the "G" [General Staff] side' that might follow.[55] Another important consideration was casualty evacuation arrangements, which Edelman described as practically nil. The whole situation is deplorable. Air evacuation to Moresby is haphazard, and this route is used for US personnel. Sea evacuation is more so-there seems to be a certain amount of one-way traffic going on, and I am encumbered with 5 very sick patients which should not be kept here any longer.'[56]

The lack of arrangements for evacuation also plagued Captain Scott and Hanson Force, with instructions regarding casualty evacuation specifically—and future medical arrangements more generally—less than encouraging: 'If you require Air Evacuation, signal ADMS [repeated] to us, and we will do our best. For really urgent air evacuation, try liasing [sic] direct with Wanigela and/or Poingani, signalling us results. Keep up the chin, we will get you back when possible.'[57]

Captain Verco, the CO of B Company that Edelman was initially sent to assist, had been ordered elsewhere by the time Edelman arrived, leaving him to care for soldiers suffering from complaints ranging from malaria to tinea, boils and ulcers—all in a 'hospital' with no lights. The fact that so many soldiers who were already on a course of anti-malarial treatment succumbed to the disease within weeks of its completion was 'maddening' to Edelman, who predicted that 'it will only need another month or two to turn the majority into physical wrecks.'[58] Further adding to the misery, there were no thermometers in the surgical haversack and the primus stove—as well as the medical comforts—had been 'stolen by the miserable thieving unloading party'.[59] The problem of theft was not confined to these more isolated areas, with the 'pilfering of comforts' that had occurred for months at Gili Gili depriving soldiers of cigarettes, tobacco and writing materials.[60] An exasperated Edelman concluded that, to work as a medical officer in such a place, 'all you need is the ambition of a slug, the mentality of a paranoiac, the skin of an armadillo, and complete paralysis of both olfactory nerves.'[61] The less than sympathetic reply to Edelman's 'gigantic moan' from the acting CO of his unit, Macintosh, ended with the facile advice to 'keep your chin up, things ain't really too bad.'[62] It could be argued, however, that 'things' were really not all that good for any of the detachments sent to the far reaches of Milne Bay Province.

A pattern of reinforcements, reassignments and evacuations continued across all medical units, some of which had been at Milne Bay since July. At the start of December, news was received of the impending arrival of the 2/3rd Convalescent Depot and AAMC reinforcements, totalling 10 officers and 185 other ranks. With relief in sight, some of the sick medical men who had struggled on for months at Milne Bay were finally evacuated to Australia for treatment of malaria and other illnesses. Unfortunately, this loss of personnel only added to the workload of those who remained. The fighting escalated on the northern beaches of Papua in the final months of 1942, around Buna, Gona and Sanananda, and drew in medical personnel from Milne Bay where, though the risk of death or wounding from enemy attack had long since passed, the risk of disease remained ever present. Indeed, the work had barely eased for those tasked with maintaining the soldiers' health in the MDS and CCS facilities around Waigani, and their units were further taxed as light sections were continually sent elsewhere in support of Drake, Hat and Hanson forces.

On 12 December, a light section initially comprising one officer (Major Lavarack) and 11 members of A Company, 2/5th Field Ambulance, set out from Waigani to provide medical support for Hammer Force as it prepared to attack the Japanese near Buna.[63] The difficult journey included a full day of sailing in waters regularly patrolled by enemy ships, on a voyage described as 'one of the world's most treacherous, with uncharted reefs and shifting sandbars dotting the coastline.'[64] This experience was followed by a 'dreadful trek' along the malarial northern coast of Papua until the men finally arrived at Hariko, two miles south of Buna Mission, on the night of 15 December—just hours before the Battle of Buna-Gona was scheduled to commence.[65]

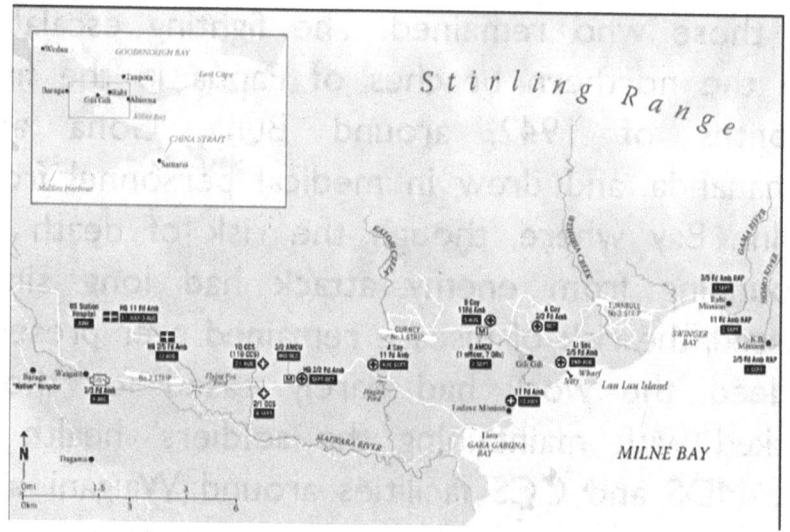

Map 7.2 Location of medical units at Milne Bay

The pressures on the medical facilities at Milne Bay continued to mount. It was clear to all that here, as at Port Moresby, 'mass evacuation to the [Australian] mainland was the only solution [to] the problem.' The rate of casualty evacuation did gain momentum as Christmas approached. Pleased that the tide was finally turning in this regard, the CO of the 110th CCS, Colonel Wall, was nevertheless dismayed that many of those who returned to Australia were subsequently struck down with malaria. Wall wrote that 100% of casualties evacuated to Australia developed malaria after reaching the hospitals there—suggesting, perhaps, that these were undiagnosed cases or recurrences of the disease. He mentioned—though did not elaborate on the point—that the way the evacuation process was executed was 'a wrong procedure, and was rather demoralising, as well as depleting the area.'[66] Flagging spirits were lifted somewhat when the festive season brought a performance by the visiting New Guinea Concert Party, and all medical units enjoyed an impressive Christmas dinner of roast meat and vegetables, followed by plum pudding topped with brandy sauce—sans brandy.

These medical men had undoubtedly earned the luxury of good food and 'excellent entertainment'.[67] Almost 2000 beds remained occupied across all medical units. The daily bed occupation rate for the 110th CCS during December was 438, and the daily patient average for the 11th Field Ambulance was recorded as 279. The ratio of sick to battle casualties was striking: 58 battle casualties and 1400 sick had been admitted to the 2/5th Field Ambulance MDS between 28 August and 31 December 1942. This number did not include those 'passing through' or those who received treatment from the unit's light sections, ADS, or while at sea.[68] Of the 1400 suffering from illness, 912 or 65% were diagnosed with malaria.[69] Lieutenant Colonel Wall was undoubtedly expressing the views of many when he looked out across the shores of Milne Bay on Christmas Eve 1942:

Perhaps the finest sight of all was the Hospital Ship "Manunda" riding at anchor in the Bay, her snow-white frame contrasting finely with the deep blue hills beyond. Perhaps, too, our minds were influenced by satisfaction that she would bear away some of our medical responsibilities.[70]

As 1942 ended, both the Australian Army and the Australian government were forced to weigh up the medical, military and financial costs of keeping so many sick soldiers in Port Moresby and Milne Bay, against the advantages of bringing them home for treatment, recuperation and, eventually, a return to the front line. Consideration was also undoubtedly given to the societal and public relations benefits associated with returning loved ones to their families at Christmas, and before January heralded yet another grim year of war—and a Federal election eight months later.

Milne Force was redesignated the 11th Division in December and sent to Port Moresby in January 1943, having been relieved of duty at Milne Bay by the 5th Division under Major General Edward Milford. The arrival of the new year also prompted recommendations for the relief of some of the medical units that continued to languish at Milne Bay. Plans for the 2/1st and 110th CCS to support First Army in Queensland were dependent on when the 2/11th AGH and 106th CCS could be sent to Milne Bay. There was to be no immediate relief in sight for the exhausted 2/5th Field Ambulance, however, with the unit remaining at Milne Bay until March 1943.[71]

CHAPTER 8

MEDICAL CARE DURING THE AUSTRALIAN ADVANCE

'After three years of war, it would seem reasonable to expect a higher standard'

THE 2/4th FIELD AMBULANCE PREPARES

By September 1942, the depleted 14th and 2/6th Field Ambulance units were struggling to cope with the casualties incurred during the Australian fighting withdrawal along the Kokoda Track. It was clear that additional medical units were needed urgently and some relief materialised in the form of the experienced 2/4th Australian Field Ambulance, 7th Division, AIF, on 17 September. Lieutenant Colonel Arthur Hobson had assumed command of this unit six months earlier from Colonel Stanley Lovell, the unit's

CO in the Middle East.[1] Lovell's final report in March 1942 indicated satisfaction with his unit's progress since returning to Australia, noting the men's initiative and problem-solving skills.[2]

The new CO, Hobson, was well respected by the men. At 35, he was the oldest officer in the unit. Nicknamed 'Silent Sam', Hobson was 'a man of few words, but whenever the need arose they were well chosen'.[3] A week before the unit sailed for Port Moresby, Hobson met with Colonel Alec Dawkins, ADMS for Advanced Land Headquarters, in Brisbane. Hobson was slightly taken aback when Dawkins offered him 'no further medical instructions' regarding the unit's work in Papua.[4] It was not clear to Hobson whether the lack of instructions indicated that Dawkins was satisfied with the unit's level of fitness and training, or whether there was simply nothing more he could say that might adequately prepare them for what lay ahead. These men had trained for months in Australia, were physically fit, and were experienced in administering medical treatment in the deserts and towns of the Middle East. Nevertheless, they were ill-prepared to fight a medical war in a place such as Papua.

To illustrate this point, there is value in briefly describing the men and their training—both of which were typical of other

Australian medical units. The personnel of the 2/4th Field Ambulance were certainly an eclectic group. They were drawn from a wide range of social circumstances, educational backgrounds and civilian occupations—tram conductors, railway officers, wharf labourers, clerks, shopkeepers and psychiatric nurses. Once recruited to the 2/4th, however, this seemingly disparate group was bound together by its core function of providing medical care for the fighting soldiers:

> the medical heart of the unit ... was centred round a group of male nurses, ... gentle and kind men who had devoted their lives in peace to the care of the sick and mentally ill. In the main the transition from peace to war came easily to them ... they included Wally Johns, George Spence, the Kennedy brothers, Nick and Bill, Ken Short, Jack Tate as well as others ... their equal in the nursing world would have been hard to find.[5]

The men were often given nicknames based on their personalities and idiosyncrasies, such as Mumbling Minnie, Sweet Pea, Charlie the Crane, The Orangutan, and Tiny Flowers—an ironic description for 'a six-foot tall bullocky, who preferred bare feet to boots, and on long route marches invariably swung his No.13s over his shoulder.'[6] The Regimental Sergeant Major, Kim

Williams, had served in the Coastal Defence Artillery. A big man, Williams possessed 'a voice like a foghorn when raised in anger ... [and] a heart not merely of gold, but as soft as table margarine.' In 1940, Lovell had given him the job of 'making a military unit out of some unlikely looking material'.[7]

The B Company cook, 'Doover' Brown, was a heavyweight wrestling champion for the Permanent Military Forces prior to the war and continued wrestling during his time in the Middle East in 1941. Indeed, Doover enjoyed a fight in and out of the ring. His trainer was Private 'Squeaky Joe' Walker, who 'knew more about training greyhounds and horses than men' and struggled to 'keep Doover (and himself) off the grog'.[8] Described as 'a lean and handsome Scot' who women found 'irresistible', Lance Corporal Arthur Mowbray Moodie was a well-educated accountant fluent in Hindustani and French, who wrote loving letters from the Middle East to his long-time girlfriend in Australia, 'Tuppence'. The medical officers of the unit were civilian doctors with private practices in various towns and cities. Among them were Major Hew McDonald from Victoria and Major Ian Firth Vickery of Sydney—both 'handsome young men, whose appearance was matched only by their devotion and skill.'[9] Moodie, McDonald and Vickery were among those later killed in a Japanese aerial attack at Soputa in Papua.[10]

The 2/4th and 2/6th field ambulances were both experienced AIF units that served in the Middle East between 1940 and 1942, and both units accompanied the soldiers of their AIF brigades (21st and 25th) to Woodside Camp on their return to Australia. Here, they attended lectures on topics ranging from morale to chemical warfare. The focus for all troops, however, was on physical conditioning and optimum fitness—including regular two-day route marches with full packs across 55 miles of rugged terrain. Despite the hard training and discipline, many found enough energy to wreak havoc while on leave in Adelaide. Routine Orders of 16 March commented on the generally poor behaviour of soldiers on leave, noting that some were drunk, accosted women, or were found sleeping in gardens and streets. In response, an order was issued that liquor was not to be carried away from Adelaide hotels.[11]

The tough training schedule continued into June, when the 2/4th Field Ambulance was sent to Caboolture in Queensland. The curriculum was broadened to incorporate lectures on the diagnosis of malaria and dysentery using blood films, giving some indication to the men—who remained ignorant of their ultimate destination—that the unit was heading north. The changing nature of training activities and the increased intensity of exercises undertaken by the 2/4th during August suggested that the rugged terrain in which the unit would soon find itself was known to those in command. Regular route marches now incorporated night exercises and river crossings, with the men carrying stretchers over hills and heavily timbered ground, and taking volunteer stretcher 'patients' across rivers using flotation devices made from drums, saplings and tarpaulins.[12] Lieutenant Colonel Hobson was especially pleased with the physical fitness of his A and B companies by this stage, observing that 'the intensive training of all combatant troops is making them unbelievably fit and tough.'[13]

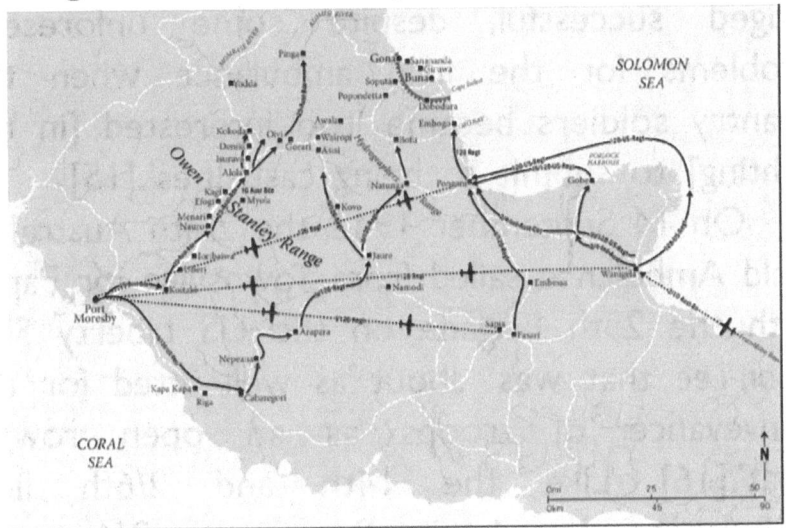

Members of the 2/4th Field Ambulance at Ingleburn Military Camp, NSW, 1940. Private L.N. (Nick) Kennedy is second from the left in the back row (author image).

The need for a training regime designed to combat Japanese fighting methods was obvious. The theatre of war had changed from distant dry deserts to the nearby islands of the South Pacific as Australia faced an unfamiliar enemy—one that employed tactics and weapons with which the Army was relatively unacquainted. Yet it was not until 27 August that the medical officers of the 2/4th Field Ambulance—who had been in Australia since March—attended a lecture entitled 'Jap methods and how to combat them'.[14] Simulated battles conducted a few days later exposed the unit to the fighting methods of the Japanese forces, as they were currently understood. The simulated battle exercise was judged successful, despite some unforeseen problems for the field ambulance when the infantry soldiers became 'too interested [in the fighting] to submit to being casualties'.[15]

On 14 September 1942, the 2/4th Australian Field Ambulance sailed from Townsville for Papua with the 25th Brigade on the US Liberty Ship *Jason-Lee* that was 'about as well fitted for the conveyance of troops as an open rowing boat'.[16] Like the 14th and 2/6th field ambulances already in Papua, the 2/4th was under-strength on its arrival in Port Moresby Harbour three days later. The unit's strength of five officers and 153 other ranks was 18 fewer than had sailed to Australia from the Middle East in March.[17] Their arrival in Port Moresby was long anticipated by ADMS Frank Norris who, on learning of their voyage, critically and unflinchingly reviewed the medical situation in Papua:

> 25 Aust Inf Bde arrived in this area 9 Sep 42 – after two days march they engaged the enemy and the brigade has continued in action since then.[Information] is just to hand that 2/4 Aust Fd Amb in support of this brigade is two days out on the high seas. If all goes well this Fd Amb will be in position to support 25 Aust Inf Bde ten days after the brigade has been in action. Could steps please be taken to ensure in future an improvement in such tactical movement? After three years of war, it would seem reasonable to expect a higher standard.[18]

It was indeed reasonable to expect not only that the Australian soldiers would go into battle supported by a medical unit, but that this unit was well trained, well equipped and at full strength. Yet B Company of the 39th Battalion had been sent over the Owen Stanley Range in July with no field ambulance unit in support. The 14th and 2/6th Field Ambulance detachments that were subsequently sent to support the militia and AIF soldiers on the Kokoda Track were under-strength and under-resourced.

As mentioned, a full-strength Australian field ambulance unit comprised 12 medical officers and 225 other ranks. Yet they rarely operated at full strength at any time during World War II, and there was never a time when they did so in Papua. That the 2/4th Field Ambulance was 79 men under-strength before its Papuan campaign even began underscores the military priorities of the Australian Army and the ongoing failure to fully grasp the medical situation in Papua, despite almost two months of fighting there. What is also indicated by the failure to swiftly deploy a complete field ambulance is the level of miscommunication between the medical men who were on the Kokoda Track and experiencing the difficulties first hand, the senior officers who remained in and around Port Moresby, and the military medical hierarchy ensconced almost 2000 miles away in Melbourne.

On disembarking at Port Moresby, the 2/4th Field Ambulance personnel were greeted by air raid sirens when 'hostile aircraft passed over but no damage [was] done'.[19] They were loaded into trucks and driven to nearby Murray Barracks where they 'slept under the stars that night'.[20] The unit's transport company and the numerous vehicles that had taken up precious space on the ship were left behind at Port Moresby as the men made their way to the road head marking the start of the Kokoda Track. The decision to move forward without the transport personnel seemed reasonable given that there were no vehicles for the men to operate beyond Owers' Corner. However, their absence 'left the Field Ambulance weak in numbers for the kind of routine tasks with which they were to be confronted in the mountains.'[21] That the number and type of vehicles and men needed in Papua was not anticipated at this stage of the campaign is difficult to comprehend.

'Some of the boys having a dip', Papua 1942. Identified members of the 2/4th Australian Field Ambulance: NX20515 James McAlpin, NX50787 Norman Lemcke, NX17630 William Greaves, NX57666 Ronald Allen, NX54298 Edward Latta, Roley Watkins (author image).

THE MILITARY SITUATION

The 2/4th Field Ambulance arrived in Port Moresby in the same week that the Japanese advance was finally halted by the Japanese High Command.[22] The Japanese decision to cancel their land offensive in Papua was made on 14 September, with the *South Seas Force* ordered to 'leave a minimum force at the front line and despatch all remaining troops to the rear to carry provisions'—the aim to reassemble on the northern side of the Owen Stanley Range.[23] The Japanese soldiers, who had been doggedly fighting their way south and away from their base around the Buna area in the north, now experienced the same logistical issues that confronted the Australians who had earlier fought their way north from the Port Moresby area. Overstretched supply and communication lines, difficulties in administering medical care and evacuating casualties, physical exhaustion, tropical diseases, sickness and hunger, all took their toll on the Japanese troops. Such blows to morale were compounded by their defeat and withdrawal from Milne Bay, in conjunction with a series of costly battles against the Americans at Guadalcanal during August and September. However, the extent of the Japanese supply crisis in Papua was not immediately obvious to the

Australians. ADMS Norris later reflected on the situation around Ioribaiwa and Imita Ridge at this time, noting that 'the pressure was increased [on the Japanese] until one morning our patrols found the Japanese defences abandoned. Shelled, mortared and shot at, starved and sick, they had reached beyond their limit.'[24]

The fighting had come perilously close to Port Moresby, when the desperate situation saw Maroubra Force engage in a fighting withdrawal as far south as Ioribaiwa—just 25 miles away.[25] Brigadier Ken Eather and the 25th Brigade, 7th Division, AIF, had been ordered to halt the Japanese advance by engaging in offensive action as far forward as possible. The aim was to regain control of the route to Kokoda before going on to recapture the village itself. The battle around Ioribaiwa raged for three days and nights until the evening of 16 September when it was successfully occupied by the Japanese. Meanwhile, the 2/4th Field Ambulance, which should have been in support of the 25th Brigade, still had not arrived in Papua.

Brigadier Eather explained in a telephone conversation to the commander of the 7th Division, General Arthur 'Tubby' Allen, that he was unable to estimate the number of casualties suffered thus far by either the Australians or the Japanese.[26] However, some idea of the number of Australian casualties sustained at Ioribaiwa is possible by considering that Eather sent 180 carriers to evacuate the stretcher cases the previous night. Given that eight carriers were generally allocated to each stretcher patient, this would indicate approximately 22 casualties. The Japanese *144th Infantry Regiment* lost 36 men and suffered 106 battle casualties.[27] Japanese reports claimed that 'the Australians had abandoned approximately one hundred and twenty bodies'.[28]

When Eather asked Allen for permission to withdraw further back along the track to Imita Ridge, the General reiterated the importance of holding Ioribaiwa—but left the final decision on whether to withdraw to Eather. A resolute General Rowell, Commander NGF, was less than impressed with this advice, surmising that the Japanese troops would be at least as exhausted as the Australians. He told Allen that 'however many troops the enemy has they must all have walked from Buna. We are now so far back that any further withdrawal is out of the question and Eather must fight it out at all costs.'[29] Eather nevertheless reasoned that a withdrawal would allow him to regain the initiative and strengthen his defensive position, and so began to withdraw to Imita Ridge on 16 September. The subsequent 'marked lack of activity on the behalf of the Japanese encouraged Eather to begin a cautious advance on 22 September', however, the Australian advance did not fully commence until 27 September, when the 25th Brigade, AIF (joined later by the 16th Brigade), pursued the withdrawing Japanese troops.[30]

THE MEDICAL SITUATION IN THE BASE AREA

As noted by ADMS Norris, the 2/6th Field Ambulance was 'grossly understrength' when it left Australia in late August. Compounding this problem was the lack of skilled reinforcements and time to train those who did join the unit. This, in turn, affected the unit's overall efficiency as well as the ability of its medical nucleus to maintain its previous high standard.[31] The 2/6th provided medical care for the Australian soldiers as they withdrew back along the track as far south as Itiki and Ilolo in September. With the majority of the unit back in the base area, their CO, Lieutenant Colonel Frederick Chenhall, now focused on stabilising the medical situation there and readying the unit to provide support during the forthcoming Australian advance back over the Kokoda Track. When the unit later moved forward to Uberi in early October, the Ilolo post was taken over by the fresh 2/4th Field

Ambulance. The now rested 14th Field Ambulance subsequently took over at Ilolo when the 2/4th and 2/6th were sent forward in October.[32]

The field ambulance units around Port Moresby were further stretched by the need to treat and evacuate casualties sustained during the initial Australian withdrawal, while also planning the provision of medical care during the forthcoming advance. That the 2/6th Field Ambulance was still attempting to function with minimal personnel inevitably meant 'any casualties would cause chaos'.[33] This unit was responsible for implementing the proposed medical evacuation plan for the Uberi and Ilolo sections, which centred on the movement of casualties back to the base area around Port Moresby. Chenhall was also asked by Norris to investigate the current evacuation system in this area and recommend changes to the processes if necessary. Chenhall accordingly classified cases into medical and non-medical categories, meaning severe medical cases in need of urgent evacuation were to be sent to King's Hollow Hospital (21 miles from Port Moresby), while mild cases would proceed to the 2/9th AGH located at 17-Mile.

The lack of properly constructed roads and a scarcity of reliable vehicles by which evacuations could be undertaken meant that, regardless of their medical classification, 'all cases [were] to proceed to Owens [sic] Corner by their own efforts except stretcher cases which will be carried.'[34] A melange of motor vehicles transported the casualties from Owers' Corner back to the base area, via a series of medical relay posts. Although this improvised approach to medical care was judged successful overall, transport issues impacted on its effectiveness. Bad weather meant that jeeps, trucks and ambulance vehicles—with or without tyre chains—all became bogged in the muddy quagmires around Koitaki and Ilolo. Heavy rain worsened the condition of the track and delayed both the evacuation of casualties to the base area and medical preparations for the advance.

The DDMS NGF, Brigadier Johnston, responded to urgent requests for additional transport vehicles by arranging for two trucks and extra motor ambulances equipped with chains to assist in the evacuation of the wounded. Although all were cleared from Ilolo by 8 September, persistent rain continued to hamper the evacuation process, leaving 13 stretcher cases, 27 walking wounded and seven sick patients at Uberi and four stretcher cases plus 41 walking wounded still at Ioribaiwa. The incessant rain forced road closures and isolated these medical posts, leaving them with insufficient medical supplies until a break in the weather a few days later finally allowed supplies in and patients out.[35]

Casualties from as far north as Nauro eventually made their way back to Ilolo. Accompanying the sick and wounded soldiers were ADMS Norris and Major Magarey of the 2/6th Field Ambulance Norris reported that all wounded except one had been evacuated successfully.[36] Chenhall noted that Magarey 'had done a fine piece of work acting as ADMS Maroubra Force, since its inception. It was a particularly fine effort of Norris to have gone forward so far over such a difficult track – beyond Owers' Corner it was another world.'[37]

The sorry procession of casualties slowly wending its way down the track towards Port Moresby during September soon overwhelmed the small hospital at Koitaki. The bed state at the 2/9th AGH at 17-Mile was 'precarious', with the hospital still not fully functioning due to a lack of water.[38] In an attempt to address the overcrowding problem, DDMS Johnston requested that the field ambulance units hold the 'light sick' and refrain from sending further casualties to Koitaki. The effect of this was to simply shift the problem back along the chain of evacuation, resulting in a bottleneck at the medical posts further up the track. When evacuation procedures were modified later in the campaign, the availability of beds in the base area again became an issue. Casualties taken by motor ambulance to the overcrowded base hospital at King's Hollow were 'in the habit of being asked to go from medical centre to medical centre until beds could be found. A truly terrible state of affairs.'[39] Another 'terrible state of affairs' was the 'continued pilfering' of Red Cross comforts on the wharf at Port Moresby, which meant these could not be supplied to the sick and wounded soldiers.[40]

The inability of the medical facilities in the base area to cope with the influx of casualties was the subject of correspondence between DGMS Burston in Melbourne and DDMS Johnston in Port Moresby. On 3 September Burston asked about the hospital situation and mentioned that six prefabricated huts had recently been sent from Australia for use by the 2/9th AGH. These huts were intended to function as operating theatres and so relieve the pressure to evacuate casualties to Australia for surgery. Burston concluded that 'if the Manunda [hospital ship] called regularly you could probably do with what you have for the present.'[41] Burston encouraged Johnston to supply a thorough appraisal of the medical situation when time allowed.

A week later, Johnston replied that, because the 2/9th AGH had arrived in Papua earlier than expected, the reconnaissance to determine a suitable site for its construction was necessarily rushed. Consequently, the hospital was located in an area which was not 'an altogether happy one' despite the 5th CCS and an American hospital already functioning nearby.[42] It also emerged that the hospital was in very close proximity to an area that had been earmarked for a reserve NGF. The hospital was then forced to relocate to a site that was even less suitable, with its 'various hillocks and bumps and valleys'.[43] The task of ensuring an adequate water supply was made more difficult by a shortage of pipes and the same scarcity of labour that had dogged the hospital's establishment.

Existing problems were further exacerbated when some of the men involved in getting the hospital facilities up and running at 17-Mile were called on to replace exhausted comrades who had been 'overworked for months' in other units. This lack of a reliable labour force affected both the construction and the functioning of the hospital, with the CO of the AGH, Colonel Arthur Green, reporting that the scarcity of men meant tents could not be erected, latrines could not be dug, and hospital staff 'have had to take in and nurse patients whilst erecting their hospital'.[44] Johnston also explained that the decision to send the personnel and equipment of the 2/1st CCS to Milne Bay instead of Port Moresby as originally intended had serious ramifications for the base area medical facilities, which had been holding out and holding on for the relief its arrival would bring.[45]

On the same day that the Australian advance commenced (27 September), the 2/9th AGH expanded from 600 to 800 beds. Within 10 days, 732 of these were occupied and by mid-October plans were in place to reorganise the facility to accommodate 1200 patients. This was just as well since NGF had increased in size with the arrival of the 16th Brigade, 6th Division, AIF, on 21 September.[46] Australian Army Field Service Regulations stated that hospital accommodation should be supplied for 10% of the total force. It was later determined that 'the total number of beds equipped was only 5% of the forces'.[47] This total included all field ambulance beds in Papua.

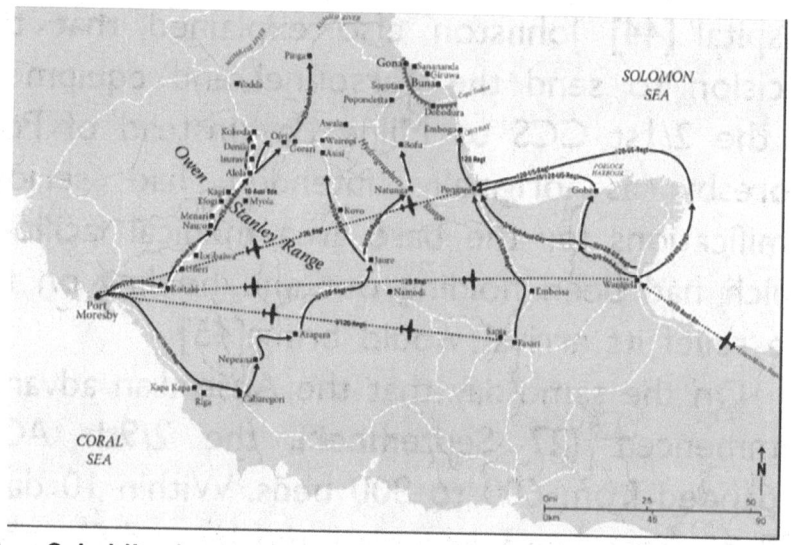

'Map 8.1 Allied advance towards the northern beachheads of Papua, 26 September–15 November 1942 (source: McCarthy, Australia in the War of 1939-1945, Series 1, Army, vol. V, South-West Pacific Area – First Year Kokoda to Wau, p.353).

THE FIELD AMBULANCE UNITS ADVANCE

In late September, the 2/4th and 2/6th Field Ambulance units began the first stage of their long journey north in support of the soldiers of the 25th and 16th brigades. Personnel of the 2/4th had spent the previous weeks reconnoitring the area around the foothills of the Owen Stanley Range. As well as familiarising themselves with the country, the officers liaised with other medical staff to discuss the most recent plans.

The unit then moved forward to relieve the detachments of the 2/6th Field Ambulance at various staging posts and MDS, often 'leapfrogging' them or 'budding off' men from their own unit to provide fresh medical staff and establish extra medical posts as needed.[48] By the end of the month, the 2/4th Field Ambulance had assumed responsibility for the evacuation of casualties from Jawerere back to the base area. The unit then left the relative safety of the area between Port Moresby and Owers' Corner to embark on the Kokoda Track proper:[49]

> We found the first stage to be fairly easy, but even so, burdened as we were with essential stores and our own personal gear, and soft from a sea voyage and a few days at Ilolo, it was not long before a condition aptly described as 'laughing knees' developed. This was a violent trembling of the legs, for which the only cure was rest ... we cut ourselves stout walking sticks from the bush ... they helped us negotiate slippery slopes, and they were a kind of a jack to help drag us to our feet after we had slipped and fallen, or tiredness had forced us to the ground.[50]

As the 2/4th Field Ambulance began the advance, the men encountered the challenges of the Papuan terrain already faced by their comrades in the 14th and 2/6th Field Ambulance units—the 'dense jungle, its silence, rent by eerie sounds ... the narrow tortuous tracks, the knee-deep mud with its vice-like grip.'[51] They too confronted the bloody aftermath of battle. In his diary, Private Kennedy described the brutal juxtaposition of nature and man as the first vistas of this new and very different theatre of war opened up before him:

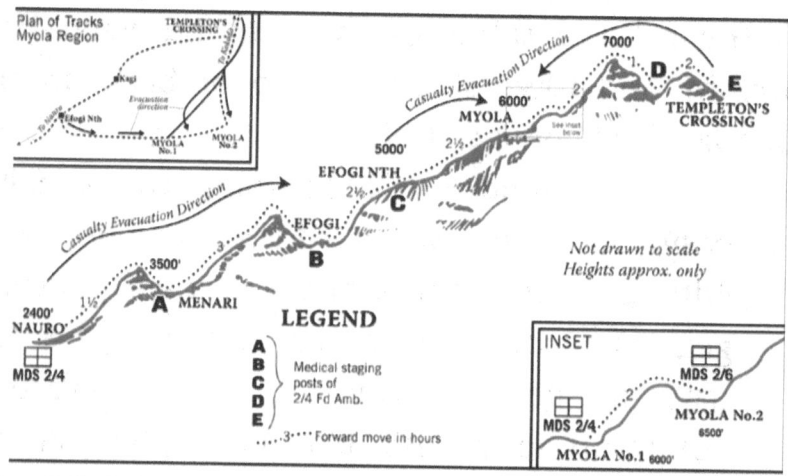

Map 8.2 Advance of the 2/4th Australian Field Ambulance from Nauro to Templeton's Crossing, September–October 1942

We set out for Ioribaiwa Ridge. The track winded [sic] in and out of gorges ... steps had been cut by the natives and engineers to make it possible to climb these steep mountainsides. In many places thousands of these steps had to be climbed to reach the top, and then there was ridge after ridge to travel over. Everyone carried their big pack, water bottle, picks, shovels, and other material that would be needed later.

That evening we reached Ioribaiwa Ridge where some fierce fighting had taken place previously. Abandoned Japanese equipment was to be seen in many places, particles of blood stained clothing, hand grenades, ammunition, tin hats, rifles ... on the side of the track were many Jap graves and the graves of our AIF that fell during the attack on this ridge ... we would have been happy that night to have kept on marching, but the night was as black as ink and to attempt to cross some of these ranges in a black out may prove fatal.[52]

Seventy-five men from the 2/4th Field Ambulance spent a long, uncomfortable and wet night among the dead of Ioribaiwa before setting out across the Maguli Range, where 'young though we were, our hearts pounded and we panted for breath'.[53] On finally arriving at Nauro, the men—now covered in mud and exhausted beyond measure—lay down on their groundsheets and slept. Morning revealed the tents that formed the medical post in a jungle clearing near the track and some field ambulance personnel set about building bunks from blankets stretched between poles so that the casualties did not have to lie on the ground. Small detachments, led by Majors Vickery and McDonald, were sent ahead to medical posts such as Menari, Efogi and Myola. Airdrops of supplies brought boxes containing equipment, bully beef, biscuits and boots. The sight of the goods falling from the bellies of Hudson transport aircraft reminded Private Kennedy of the song, 'Pennies from Heaven'. The hazardous nature of the airdrops had already caused deaths and injuries on the ground, so men took care to watch from a safe distance as 'tins and boxes ... would bounce like an Indian rubber ball, fragments of boxes and tins of bully beef would be seen flying in all directions ... and the contents would be like someone had broken them up into particles with a sledge hammer.'[54] The likelihood of the much-needed but poorly packaged medical supplies sustaining damage from this mode of delivery was obvious.

The type of casualty and the nature of the medical response altered in line with the changing military situation. Most of the sick soldiers who passed through the Nauro MDS were suffering from malaria. Battle casualties were relatively light because the soldiers had not yet encountered Japanese opposition—this would occur when they reached the Templeton's Crossing and Eora

Creek area a week later. Those who were badly wounded were kept overnight so that their dressings could be changed before they were transported towards Port Moresby by Papuan carriers the next day.

While no surgery had been undertaken in the forward areas thus far, a perceptive recommendation that a surgeon be sent to Uberi as part of the advance had been proposed at a meeting between Lieutenant Colonel Chenhall and ADMS Norris on 21 September.[55] Similar discussions regarding the feasibility of assigning a surgical team to accompany the advance took place between Chenhall and Colonel Ross, the officer commanding the surgical division of the 2/9th AGH. When Major Vickery of the 2/4th Field Ambulance added his voice to the push for a surgeon to be sent to the forward area, the initial medical plans for the advance were thrown into disarray and a decision on the matter from DDMS Johnston was not immediately forthcoming. Chenhall did not mince his words in his support of Vickery and his request:

> This officer is undoubtedly first class and only adherence to staff corps interests has prevented his promotion. His appreciation of the situation cannot be waived aside as of no consequence. To anyone who has been [forward] only our

Crimean mentality, so persistent throughout this war to date would allow a doubt to exist of the necessity of a surgeon with good judgment to be present at least as far as Uberi...

Since Sep 5 one feels a great deal has been done and organised but no one with a surgical conscience could feel happy or jubilant at the end result so far achieved. If anyone should doubt this statement let him ask himself the question 'what would I like done to me if I were severely wounded tonight.' The fact that very few severely wounded cases have been seen at Ilolo only beggars the argument. This is a difficult situation in a difficult terrain but it is thought that much more can and should be done.[56]

Vickery and Chenhall got their way and Captain Douglas Leslie was detached from the 2/9th AGH to act as surgeon in the forward areas. There are discrepancies in accounts concerning Leslie's remit. Some maintain that he was given scant medical equipment and instructed by ADMS Norris to assist in the early management of casualties, but *not* to operate.[57] DDMS Johnston, however, noted that several medical orderlies as well as full surgical equipment were made available to Leslie.[58]

Lieutenant Colonel Chenhall later reported that 'Leslie, Surgeon from 2/9 AGH, with Watson as anaesthetist, Stanleigh-Clarke and McBean as theatre orderlies, had come through with Major McDonald, from Uberi, and were functioning as a surgical team at Nauro.'[59] Whatever the real situation regarding the allocation of equipment, personnel and duties, there is no doubt that the provision of a forward surgical team would prove crucial to survival rates at places such as Myola where casualties were accumulating at a rapid rate.

The continuing shortage of medical personnel coupled with the nature of the terrain meant that the systems of 'budding off' and 'leapfrogging' that had been employed during the withdrawal were again used as the field ambulance units advanced along the track. Personnel from the 14th Field Ambulance staffed the Uberi post.[60] A severe shortage of Papuan carriers meant that attached Australian service personnel carried medical stores and rations via a series of relay posts. After three days at Nauro, the order came for the main body of the 2/4th Field Ambulance to move forward to Myola, leaving behind a detachment of a medical officer and 12 men to care for the remaining patients at the pared-back post of 50 beds. As the main body of the 2/4th Field Ambulance under Hobson, and 31 men of the 2/6th Field Ambulance under Chenhall, slowly made their way north through the villages of Menari and Efogi they stumbled over slippery slopes, sheer precipices, and narrow tracks with 'black evil smelling mud halfway up our legs'.[61] A meeting between Hobson, Norris, Vickery, and the commander of the 7th Division, General Allen, at Menari led to the decision to send Captain Leslie and his surgical team ahead to Myola.[62]

The journey to Myola via the medical post at Efogi North was not an easy one, as the track climbed ever higher into the mountains, the rain fell constantly, and the air grew colder. As the main body advanced, the discovery of Japanese dead lying close to the river near South Efogi led to fears that the water could be contaminated, prompting the medical officers to abandon the idea of spending the night there. The exhausted men were instead forced to continue across greasy ground in driving rain, scaling 'ridge after ridge [where] sun never penetrates and the track zig zags up the steep slopes' until arriving at North Efogi.[63] Here they were welcomed and given tea and jungle porridge (made from Army biscuits and powdered milk) by the small detachment of the 2/6th Field Ambulance caring for 30 casualties at the aid post there. They all spent a cold and wet night huddled under half-blankets before heading to Myola the next morning. As the men emerged from the mountains, they looked down on Myola and began 'hurrying towards it as though it was the promised land ... seeing in stark contrast to the past days the 2/4th MDS, with its white tents, set on a sward of green kunai grass, glistening in the sunshine.'[64]

MAROONED AT MYOLA

The earlier failure to wrest Kokoda from the advancing Japanese in August stymied the planned forward movement of Australian casualties for aerial evacuation from the Kokoda airstrip. In the face of the rapid Japanese advance, the Australians withdrew further south down the track towards Myola, where the promised aerial evacuation of casualties did not eventuate. The continuing southward advance of the Japanese during September had caused the Australians to abandon Myola, throwing supply and casualty evacuation plans into chaos. As a result, a pathetic procession of sick and wounded men was forced to make its way from Myola back towards Port Moresby on foot. These events make it difficult to comprehend the decision to again focus on Myola as the hub around which the latest medical plan revolved.

By October, the Australians were advancing north in pursuit of the withdrawing Japanese troops, while the RAAF and US Air Force effectively dominated the skies over most of the track. Once the route to the dry lake beds of Myola had been cleared of the enemy, the 25th Brigade established a supply depot approximately a mile and a half from the 2/4th Field Ambulance MDS. Ignoring the lessons of the recent past, the area once again became 'the goal for settled medical work on the range until Kokoda was taken'.[65] It was decided that casualties would no longer be sent to Efogi to be evacuated on foot, but would instead be held at Myola, where the surgical team under Captain Leslie was to be made available. It was hoped that casualties for whom evacuation was deemed urgent could be flown from Myola directly to Port Moresby. It was thought that, once Kokoda was back in Allied hands, the remaining casualties would make their own way *forward* to the Kokoda airstrip, from where they would be evacuated by aircraft. When a series of engagements against the Japanese at Templeton's Crossing and Eora Creek in mid-October produced the inevitable battle casualties, these latest medical arrangements were tested and found wanting.

The intrinsic value of Myola to the medical plan lay solely in the belief that it was a suitable site for a landing strip and a suitable dropping ground for supplies. However, this had been disproved in August, when the high rate of supply wastage around Myola 1 forced a reconnaissance of Myola 2 to assess its potential as a site. The second location was considered suitable only as a 'possible landing ground' for aircraft such as the Fox Moth Junker.[66] Although ordnance and some medical supplies were successfully dropped by low-flying Douglas transports and Hudson bombers at Myola, many missed the dropping ground and were scattered through surrounding jungle—never to be recovered. As had occurred throughout August, requisitioned items often failed to arrive and acute shortages of ordnance supplies, such as tents and eating utensils, persisted. In addition, much of the equipment that was recovered from the airdrops was damaged beyond use.[67]

A US Army Air Force aircraft drops supplies to the 2/4th and 2/6th Australian Field Ambulance units at Myola, October 1942 (AWM P02424.071).

On arriving at Myola 1, field ambulance personnel erected tent flies in preparation for the battle casualties they knew were being held at the 2/33rd Battalion RAP overnight. By 5.00pm the next day, the MDS held 75 patients, including 34 battle casualties. The need to undertake an urgent arm amputation at Efogi North delayed the arrival of Captain Leslie and his surgical team until midday on 16 October, but once at Myola he got straight to work, operating that same afternoon. By 6.00pm the MDS held 130 patients, including 41 battle casualties. Within three days, there were 200 patients in the MDS that was 'short of men, short of medical supplies, cooking utensils and even rations. We fed in relays, lying patients first, then walkers, then personnel. There was no evacuation route. Patients were coming forward ... from Efogi North, or direct from the front.'[68]

The 2/4th MDS was staffed by approximately 60 personnel—five officers, 49 other ranks plus Captain Leslie's surgical team and a dental officer, Captain Alan Watson, who worked as the anaesthetist.[69] Leslie was described as 'a small unassuming man' who often worked for 18 hours straight at Myola, undertaking complicated operations such as head surgery, amputations and abdominal surgery in the 'primitive' theatre built from a tent fly with blankets at either end and a 'couple of bush tables' where the operations were performed.[70] There was an acute shortage of items crucial to an operating theatre such as torches, lamps, drugs and dressings. Much of the equipment that was available was rudimentary at best—'a primus [portable kerosene-fuelled stove] of Syrian origin ... assorted tins for sterilization'.[71] Private Kennedy's writings provide some insight into how caring for seriously ill patients at Myola affected the nursing orderlies:

> We are more than busy attending to our wounded here – fourteen, sometimes eighteen hours without a break ... some of these wounds are terrific. One wonders at

times how the human body can live being mutilated like some of these poor fellows. But one cannot express his feelings towards them. We have got to try and keep them cheerful, but this is a hard job under these conditions.[72]

The 2/4th Australian Field Ambulance MDS at Myola, October 1942. The men to the right of the photograph appear to be drying clothing on the tent fly. Note that the MDS is situated in the open (AWM P02424.080).

Lieutenant Colonel Chenhall and 30 members of his 2/6th Field Ambulance arrived at Myola on the evening of 16 October. The following morning they walked approximately two hours to Myola 2 and established an MDS there.[73] Word reached the field ambulances that day that the 25th Brigade was now advancing after successfully breaking through the Japanese defences near Templeton's Crossing. The veracity of this claim was tested when the CO of the 2/4th Field Ambulance, Hobson, travelled to within 400 yards (365 metres) of the front line to report to Brigadier Eather on 20 October. Hobson noted that the Japanese 'still held Templeton's Crossing and their mountain gun kept personnel ... close to the ground.'[74] Despite the obvious dangers to unarmed medical personnel, Hobson returned to his unit at Myola and sent Kennedy and his mate, Corporal Walter Lovett, to the No.1 AASC dump near Templeton's Crossing, with a view to establishing a forward medical post. An uncertain, yet surprisingly optimistic Kennedy described what unfolded:

> On the 20th Oct I leave Myola, accompanied by Wally Lovett, to go to Templeton's Crossing to a forward post. A few shells from the Japs' mountain gun have landed here this evening before we get there, but they say they have been routed out of the position where the mountain gun was and should be fairly safe now for a medical post. We hope so anyhow.[75]

In anticipation of further battle casualties from the fighting at Templeton's Crossing and Eora Creek, Hobson sent for more personnel to assist him in dealing with the wounded at

Myola 1, where the MDS was holding more than 40 battle casualties. Medical personnel continued to search the skies for the promised aircraft that would transport the sick and wounded from Myola strip to the safety of Port Moresby. By 20 October the battle casualties had been prepared for evacuation by air. Of the 40 casualties, 17 were 'seriously ill' and several others were classified as 'dangerously ill'. The situation at Myola became increasingly desperate the next day, when fewer than 50 medical staff struggled to care for 184 casualties.[76]

It was now that the major weakness in the Myola medical plan became apparent. While this flat, marshy place—situated at 6000 feet above sea level and ringed by mountains—had once again been considered suitable for aerial supply, it remained as patently unsuitable and unsafe for the aerial evacuation of casualties as it had been months before. Even if it had been possible to safely and regularly land an aircraft on the Myola airstrip, there were not enough aircraft that could function as air ambulances—nor enough suitably trained pilots to fly them. Many of those responsible for military and medical planning long knew this to be the case. Lieutenant Colonel Chenhall described the moment when the tragic consequences of this fundamental flaw became obvious to the medical men at Myola:[77]

A request had been made and refused for an attempted plane landing at a dry lake about a mile from Myolo [sic]. Had the request been granted and successful a very rapid means of evacuation would have been afforded, whereas now B. Cs [battle casualties] will be held until Kokoda falls. This means a three to four day carry at least, and there is still doubt whether native SBs [stretcher-bearers] will be available. Hence the request for further personnel.[78]

Yet another flaw in the medical plan had revealed itself. The failure of aerial evacuation caused a backlog of patients and meant that the overcrowded MDS and its overworked 'little medical community marooned at Myola' was now in dire need of extra personnel and medical supplies.[79] The shortage of trained medical personnel was exacerbated by the lack of a guaranteed supply of Papuan carriers, meaning that additional AASC personnel were required to assist with stretcher-bearing and general duties for the field ambulance units. When the request for all fit personnel in the rear details to be sent forward was met with the response that none were available, weary 14th Field Ambulance personnel from various medical staging posts on the track were rounded up and used to plug the gaps at Myola. The ensuing scramble for men also meant that medical posts—such as the Uberi MDS—were directly affected. There were insufficient personnel to staff this post and the lack of carriers affected supply lines.[80] The 'extremely small number of patients held' at posts such as Uberi meant that these issues did not have a major impact in terms of the level of care. On 28 October, for example, there was one admission, five evacuations, and a total of 19 patients in the Uberi MDS.[81]

Small medical posts were rendered virtually redundant during this period—first, because medical care was now concentrated at Myola, and second, because the anticipated resistance from the retreating Japanese had not occurred until the Australians were in the area around Templeton's Crossing. The excess of unused equipment coupled with a shortage of personnel at Uberi would make any future move forward impossible. To avoid the 'embarrassment' of not being able to comply with orders when this time inevitably came, arrangements were put in place to send excess medical equipment *back* to the base area, prior to the post being ordered to move forward.[82] The result was a cruelly bizarre situation in which redundant equipment from the orderly room at Uberi was taken back down the track to Ilolo on 30 October, while medical staff in the forward MDS at Myola scrounged for the supplies, personnel and facilities needed to treat an ever-increasing tide of sick and wounded.[83]

NX57856 Norman Smith and NX46566 Fred 'Tiny' Flower of the 2/4th Australian Field Ambulance at Myola, October 1942 (author image).

The final days of October saw 200 casualties evacuated from Myola 1. These men were not being flown back to Port Moresby, however, but evacuated by foot on the two-hour journey to the 2/6th Field Ambulance MDS at Myola 2. Lieutenant Colonel Hobson and his 2/4th Field Ambulance were ordered to close Myola 1 MDS and move forward to Alola, north of Eora Creek. It was left to Chenhall and his 2/6th Field Ambulance to care for the casualties at Myola 2. Chenhall's unit was now effectively removed from future operations. The task of providing medical care for the 16th and 25th brigades, as well as any reinforcements fell solely to the under-strength 2/4th Field Ambulance.

A single-engine Stinson aircraft used to evacuate casualties from Kokoda and Myola. The aircraft could evacuate just two patients per trip (AWM 107135).

The first aerial casualty evacuation from Myola 2 on 27 October was a cause for celebration—even though just one patient with an eye injury was flown out and over 100 patients remained. By 1 November, the MDS was holding 450 patients and the unit was 'obliged to remain at Myola 2 until the last of its patients had either recovered or died.'[84] Because there was 'still no word' regarding aerial evacuation, ADMS Norris informed Chenhall that some of the casualties from Myola 2 would have to make their own way on foot to Port Moresby—a distance of almost 50 miles (80 kilometres) across the Owen Stanley Range.[85] Fifty patients duly shuffled their way towards the promise of hospital care over the next few days. Eventually, more of the 212 battle casualties and 226 sick soldiers 'literally took up their beds and walked, walked back to Moresby with arms in plaster and legs in bandages – an odd procession.'[86] During November, some of the more serious cases who still languished at Myola were stretchered forward to Kokoda in the hope of being flown out.

They would not be evacuated from Kokoda until late December.

'THIS CRIMEAN MENTALITY'

On 2 November, a platoon of the 2/31st Battalion, 25th Brigade, entered Kokoda unopposed and Brigade Headquarters was established in the village. The next day, Major General George Vasey—who had relieved General Allen as commander of the 7th Division—raised the Australian flag at Kokoda. Back at Myola, a frustrated Lieutenant Colonel Chenhall sent a desperate telegram to Land Headquarters and repeated it to ADMS Norris and DDMS Johnston. Chenhall's communiqués which were 'not couched in terms as temperate as they might have been', presented a grim picture of the situation at Myola 2:[87]

> Admissions have ceased. Still holding 428 patients 197 surgical. No further primary operations necessary. Drugs, Dressing ... still very necessary. Holding no, repeat, no Vaseline, Pop soluvac, N Saline, Saline Soluvac, G Saline, Catgut, Cotton Wool, Iodine etc. All medical supplies very short in spite of repeated indents [official requisitions] nightly since Oct 21. All substitutes nearly finished. Lighting still 4 Hurricane, one torch. Is air evacuation impossible? Portable x-ray and plaster shears will be required. Secondary operations will

become necessary. When will this Crimean mentality be replaced? This effort impossible 1842—a disgrace 1942.[88]

This was very much at odds with the picture painted by DDMS Johnston, who had been keeping DGMS Burston informed of the medical situation in Papua, via both official and personal correspondence. On 30 October, a few days before Chenhall's communiqué, Johnston had presented a far less dramatic—and far less accurate—account of the casualty situation. In a handwritten addendum to a personal letter, Johnston wrote that the 'proportion of sick to BC [battle casualties] is comparatively low—this gives a fair indication that casualties are not so bad.'[89] In language that was worryingly vague and inaccurate for the Deputy Director of Medical Services, Johnston wrote that there were 'something like 200 patients' in the care of surgical teams at Myola whose work was 'reasonably good, though of course rough'.[90] In fact, there were more than double this number of casualties at Myola, with Captain Leslie saving many lives by undertaking highly complex and delicate procedures—'many a soldier owed life and limbs to the miracles he performed there.'[91]

Johnston's comments on the aerial evacuation issue succinctly encapsulated all that was wrong with the medical plan that relied so heavily on its success—that is, it had long been known that the airstrip, the location, the conditions and the aircraft were unsuitable:

> Air evacuation has been a great bone of contention. The truth is that the comparatively short runway at Myola and the altitude (6500 feet) makes taking off a hazardous procedure for all but the one plane we have available – a single engine Stinson Dragon Fly. This can only take out 2 sitting patients at a time. General Herring [and] Whitehead are doing their best to get suitable planes.[92]

It seems Johnston had been aware of the mounting discontent among field ambulance personnel. Keen to ward off any criticism, he downplayed the seriousness of the dire situation at Myola and assured Burston that all was under control:

> Don't be misled by colourful or critical descriptions. The casualties are not lying on beds of roses but Norris, Chenhill [sic], Vickery, Hobson etc are looking after them well.[93]

Chenhall's November telegram succeeded in ensuring the transportation of long-awaited supplies (and DDMS Johnston himself) to Myola, though not without generating a flurry of heated correspondence. Some senior medical officers acknowledged the desperate circumstances which had led to such an impassioned request for assistance. Others denied the existence of supply problems at Myola and questioned both Chenhall's state of mind and his suitability for command. Once this noxious seed was planted, it quickly germinated and spread as others sought to distance themselves from this latest medical disaster in Papua.

A Stinson aircraft evacuates one sitting and one lying patient from Kokoda airstrip (AWM 107154).

'A LOST LEGION'

On the same day that Land Headquarters received Lieutenant Colonel Chenhall's telegram, Johnston wrote again to Burston to provide a more detailed account of the situation at Myola—one which unintentionally contextualised and justified Chenhall's rage. Johnston clarified his earlier figures by citing those originally compiled by Chenhall. These showed that the 2/6th Field Ambulance MDS at Myola held 426 patients and almost 200 of these cases required surgery. The juxtaposition of the total patient numbers against those needing surgery presented a far more striking picture than Johnston's earlier vague reference to 'something like 200 patients' in the care of the surgical team. With just one aircraft capable of even attempting medical evacuation (and only able to carry two patients at a time), Johnston now canvassed the varying opinions regarding the aerial situation before explaining that General Ennis Whitehead, the Commander of the US Air Force in Papua, had refused requests from Generals Vasey and Blamey to attempt evacuation with the few aircraft available.[94] It was only at this late stage that Johnston asked DGMS Burston to intervene directly by contacting the RAAF Director of Medical Services, Victor Hurley, to see what could be done to evacuate the casualties.[95]

Johnston incorporated an incongruous and implausible sentence into this important piece of correspondence to Burston, explaining he 'had meant to write the above to you and post last night, but was unable to do so.'[96] He expressed amazement at the content and tone of Chenhall's telegram before reiterating three points: all indents for supplies at Myola had been filled—either by aerial dropping or by landing via a small plane, recovery of supplies had recently been 100%, and there was no dire shortage of equipment. Johnston signed off by adding his voice to those now lining up to cast doubt on Chenhall's state of mind, adding that both he and Vasey felt Chenhall's outburst 'indicated a want of balance to say the least of it'.[97]

The Quartermaster General NGF and Deputy Adjutant-General, Brigadier John Broadbent, was most keen to absolve himself and his section from any blame concerning supply problems at Myola. Broadbent wrote that 'in view [of] our fulfilments of medical indents [and] also strenuous attempts [at] air evacuation cannot understand reason for attitude. Suggest under strain. Do you consider replacement ambulance [commander] necessary?'[98] Broadbent was not alone in questioning Chenhall's suitability to command his field ambulance, though Johnston was not keen to relieve Chenhall of command and so did not act immediately.

Over the next few weeks, he sought opinions and noted the difficulties presented by the 'abnormal conditions' at Myola. Among the advice received was that from Lieutenant Colonel William Tredinnick of the Australian Army Legal

Corps, who recommended Chenhall be replaced because of his 'wrong action' and because ADMS Norris had judged him to have 'a peculiar temperament better suited to a hospital appointment than forward command.'[99] Johnston eventually concurred, stating that Chenhall's message had raised 'grave doubts regarding his judgements during a period of stress [and] it would seem desirable that at a convenient opportunity, Lt Col Chenhall be allotted duties ... where his professional attainments could be suitable exercised.'[100]

It was left to Adjutant-General Victor Stantke, a man who had been a thorn in the side of two previous Director Generals (Maguire and Downes), to bring about the beginning of the end of Chenhall's career as CO of the 2/6th Field Ambulance. Writing from Allied Land Forces Headquarters at Victoria Barracks in Melbourne, Stantke sent Headquarters NGF an extract from personal letters that Chenhall in Papua had written to his brother in Bellevue Hill, NSW. The correspondence explained the conditions at Myola. Lieutenant Colonel Chenhall described the facilities, wrote that patient numbers had reached a peak of 458 and included 200 surgical cases, and explained that 'Air Force would not play' regarding aerial evacuations.[101] His most passionate words were reserved for the casualties, and his strongest criticisms for those in charge:

> These men have done and given their best for the nation and I can assure you it has been a glorious best. They are your only trained soldiers. Are you going to let them die or become cripples by not making any organised effort to get them out? Because that is what it means ... we can do little ... we have practically nothing with which to treat them. God forgive the blind stupid people who are responsible for such a state of affairs existing. Div [7th Division has moved on and we are left a lost legion.[102]

Stantke made clear his views regarding this personal and private correspondence between the two brothers, both of whom were doctors.

Arguing that the tone of the letter did not inspire confidence 'in the relations between Army and the public or the morale of the latter', he referred the matter to NGF for further enquiry and recommendations 'as to action you may consider desirable'.[103] The contrast between Chenhall's powerful writings from Myola and the reactions of Johnston, Broadbent, Stantke and other senior officers exemplifies the chasm between those directly responsible for the soldiers' lives on the Kokoda Track and those ultimately responsible in Port Moresby, Brisbane and Melbourne.

Lieutenant Colonel Frederick Chenhall (photograph taken in Damascus, October 1941) (author image).

Undeterred by the acrimony, Chenhall continued to discharge his medical duties at Myola until all remaining patients had been evacuated. He finally returned to Port Moresby in December 1942—by aircraft.[104] On 11 January 1943, Lieutenant Colonel Frederick

Chenhall disembarked in Cairns. He relinquished command of the 2/6th Field Ambulance five days later and was appointed to command of the 114th Convalescent Depot in Australia.

CHAPTER 9

ONGOING CHALLENGES ON THE KOKODA TRACK

'Knowledge was not translated into action'

LEADERSHIP

The defeat of the Japanese at Milne Bay in September and their withdrawal along the Kokoda Track throughout October foreshadowed an improved military situation as the Australians pursued the enemy north in the final months of 1942. Yet September and October proved tumultuous months for military leadership with Brigadier Potts, Lieutenant General Rowell and Major General Allen all dismissed in quick succession and General Blamey taking command of NGF. Brigadier Arnold Potts was recalled to Port Moresby in September and replaced as commander of the 21st Brigade in October primarily because he 'had the misfortune to command a retreat in the early stages of the Pacific War.'[1] As commander of 1 Australian

Corps, it was Lieutenant General Sydney Rowell who had relieved Potts of his command. Rowell was, in turn, relieved of his command by General Blamey in controversial circumstances that are examined in this chapter. On 29 October, Blamey relieved Major General Arthur Allen of his position as commander of the 7th Division 'for alleged lack of progress against the Japanese'.[2]

The leadership of the medical services was intertwined with key aspects of the military command in Papua in ways that were not immediately obvious or expected. After a series of meetings with the various bodies concerned with the conduct of the war—War Cabinet, Advisory War Council, Chiefs of Staff, the Supreme Commander of the SWPA, General MacArthur, and Prime Minister Curtin—in mid-September, Blamey returned to his office at Victoria Barracks in Melbourne and told DGMS Burston of his instructions to fly to Papua and take over command of NGF from Rowell. Reports of the conversation between Blamey and Burston indicated that, although Blamey continued to have confidence in Rowell's abilities, he felt pressured into action. In the end, Blamey's concerns for his career trumped his faith in Rowell: 'Canberra's lost it! ... I remember what happened to the Auk [British Field Marshal Claude Auchinleck] in the desert, and I'm off ...

I'm satisfied he [Rowell] has the situation under control, but I feel I must go.'[3]

Blamey was right to be concerned, given that MacArthur had told Curtin that General Blamey should proceed to New Guinea and take personal command, not only to energise the situation but to save himself, because, in the event of the situation in New Guinea becoming really serious, it would be difficult for General Blamey to meet his responsibility to the Australian public.[4]

Correspondence advising Rowell of Blamey's impending arrival indicated that he had not initially planned to take Burston with him to Port Moresby. Blamey focused on reassuring Rowell of the relatively innocuous nature of the visit, explaining that he had no intention of establishing a full headquarters there: 'At present I propose to bring with me only my P.A., [personal assistant] Major Carlyon, two extra cipher officers, and Lieut. Keith Lawson.'[5] When General Blamey flew from Brisbane on 23 September he was accompanied by this small group—as well as Brigadier Ronald Hopkins and DGMS Samuel Burston.[6]

Whether Burston invited himself to Port Moresby, or whether Blamey asked Burston to accompany him, is not clear. It is also unclear whether Blamey had planned to directly involve his close friend and confidante in this most important military episode. Nevertheless, DGMS Burston had placed himself at the centre of the tumult that was the Rowell affair. It is reasonable to question his decision to accompany Blamey to Papua when he had no official role to play in the dismissal of Rowell. Some questioning of Burston's priorities is also valid—the trip was instigated and organised for Blamey to deal with Rowell, and not for Burston to inspect and evaluate the medical services in Papua. Given the nature of their close relationship, as well as the long-standing professional and personal differences between Blamey and Rowell, it is not unreasonable to argue that Blamey recognised Burston's potential as a mediator in what promised to be a difficult situation—especially if consideration is given to the fact that Burston was a fellow South Australian, friend and colleague of Rowell.[7] It is also possible that the motivation for Burston's involvement was far less calculated and it was simply an opportunity for the DGMS to inspect the medical units in Papua for the first time.[8]

Whatever the rationale, General Blamey met with Rowell on arriving in Port Moresby on 23 September and, as he later explained in correspondence to Canberra, these discussions did not go well. It was now that DGMS Burston became a central player in the unfolding drama.

Blamey explained that 'on the second evening I asked General Burston, as an old friend of Rowell to endeavour to induce a proper frame of mind, but Burston met with no success.'[9] What constituted 'a proper frame of mind' and how Burston was meant to 'induce' such a state in Rowell is not known. Evidence suggests, however, that Burston simply served as Blamey's spokesperson in this first meeting, repeating sections of a conversation that had taken place between Burston and Blamey on their way to Moresby.

During this earlier conversation while en route to Papua, Blamey had reportedly confided to Burston: 'You know, I feel Rowell might think I've gone up to steal his thunder just as he's getting everything under control. But one thing is certain. If he plays, he won't lose by it.'[10] While various interpretations of these comments are possible, accounts of the meeting that followed indicate that Burston paraphrased Blamey and advised Rowell 'the only thing for you to do is play, and play as if it was the one thing you were looking for.'[11] This has since been construed as a cryptic comment intended to convince Rowell that his cooperation would result in reinforcements and supplies being sent to Papua.[12] Yet when considered in conjunction with the reported earlier conversation between

Burston and Blamey, it would seem that the crux of the statement is crystallised—if Rowell agrees to 'play' by going quietly, his career would not suffer. The next day, an increasingly frustrated Blamey asked Burston to intervene again. When Burston agreed to meet with Rowell a second time he 'found that Rowell's attitude had not mellowed since their earlier meeting.'[13] An angry Blamey then removed Rowell as commander of NGF and later reported to Curtin and MacArthur that he was 'difficult ... recalcitrant [and] of a temperament that harbours imaginary grievances.'[14]

The significance of DGMS Burston's visit to Port Moresby in late September 1942 lies in the fact that his close relationship with General Blamey directly affected matters of military leadership during the Australian advance and the later beachhead battles. Any direct impact of Burston's visit on the medical situation in Papua is more difficult to discern—he was there for five days and did not venture beyond Port Moresby.[15]

Left to right: Lieutenant Colonel F. Berryman; Colonel S. Rowell; Colonel S. Burston; Lieutenant General T. Blamey and Lieutenant General J. Lavarack at the embarkation of the second convoy of AIF troops in April 1940 (AWM 001389/28). At the time of this photograph, Major General Rupert Downes was the DGMS. Burston was appointed DDMS on 18 April 1940.

RESPONSES TO THE MALARIA SITUATION

Given the improving military situation in Papua during October, it is concerning that the same issues which had so dogged the Australian medical services across the Owen Stanleys continued to impact on the efficacy of the field ambulance units as they moved into the northern beachhead areas of Soputa, Popondetta, Gona, Buna and Sanananda. It was here, during the final months of 1942 that the continuing lack of priority afforded the medical services by military leaders keen to achieve absolute victory in Papua had its greatest impact, as thousands of soldiers were drawn into the malarial morass of the northern coastline.

Malaria and other illnesses felled thousands during the beachhead battles between November 1942 and January 1943, with the disease poised to devastate the already weakened force. Men whose resistance was already low due to exhaustion, illness and poor nutrition were sent into battle in piteous condition. One of the few positives about the fighting in the Owen Stanley Range had been that the incidence of new malaria cases was low because the main vector, the Anopheles mosquito, did not inhabit the mountainous regions. Surveys of mosquito populations undertaken by the Australians did not find Anopheles in the mountains north of Uberi. However, it was known that malaria was hyper-endemic in the northern coastal region of Papua and it was here that abundant breeding grounds inevitably led to increased numbers of mosquitoes, increased rates of infection, as well as 'the creation of a reservoir of parasites in the blood of the troops, and finally an epidemic.'[16]

To briefly recap the malaria situation during the first half of 1942: the high incidence of the disease in members of NGF had been the subject of an investigation in June by the Army Director of Medicine, Colonel Neil Hamilton Fairley, and senior Medical Entomologist (later Director of Entomological Services), Major Ian Mackerras. Their research revealed that little had been done during the previous 12 months to address the issue. They observed a fatalistic attitude among the Australian soldiers, who were 'not malaria minded', and noted that 'many mosquito nets are unserviceable, and many of the later types supplied are quite useless ... some are without nets altogether ... Certain troops do not possess appropriate protective clothing.'[17] Although the force of approximately 6000 men was taking suppressive quinine treatment for malaria, more than 1000 cases had already been treated during these first six months.

There was little atebrin and no plasmoquine available.[18] The lack of these newer, synthetic anti-malaria drugs in conjunction with the dearth of hospital facilities adversely affected the quality and uniformity of treatment. Since these two factors meant that the course of medication was often incomplete, many of those discharged from makeshift camp hospitals and CCS remained infected and 'still harboured detectable gametocytes in their blood', which allowed the disease to spread once the men were on the Kokoda Track.[19] The suffering was not confined to the fighting troops—of 90 field ambulance personnel examined by Mackerras and Fairley, 28 presented with enlarged spleens (a symptom of the disease), while pathology testing proved positive for malaria in 31 of these men. Further, examinations of the indigenous population across various locations confirmed suspicions that 'the areas likely to be occupied by troops were hyperendemic'.[20]

The report later submitted to DGMS Burston contained an unambiguous warning that 'to take liberties with the mosquito vector in New Guinea is to guarantee malaria.'[21] To underscore this point and consolidate the conclusions of numerous earlier reports, it was noted that at least 50% of the troops who had been in Port Moresby for six months or more had already contracted malaria and so represented an ominously dangerous reservoir of the disease within the soldiers themselves. This seemed to contradict the accepted view that Port Moresby and surrounds were only *mildly* malarious compared to the rest of the 'hyperendemic' island. The final paragraph of the report warned that:

The malaria position of our forces in the S.W. Pacific is serious ... troops are being sent to highly malarious areas without adequate anti-malarial instruction or training. Malaria is capable of decimating the force, and deciding the issue of the campaign in the S.W. Pacific. Action to make good our deficiencies calls for the highest possible priority.[22]

That early predictions by Fairley and Mackerras regarding the devastating effects of malaria in Papua were borne out again and again is obvious; that those in charge subsequently gave the 'highest possible priority' to the prevention and treatment of the diseases as recommended is less apparent. DGMS Burston had established the Anti-Malaria Advisory Committee in August 1942 and delegated management of the committee to his Deputy Director, Colonel McCallum, with the respected Doctor Fairley serving as one of five members. Burston did not attend these monthly meetings.[23] The first meeting noted that the Army had stocks of approximately eight million quinine tablets, excluding those already sent to New Guinea. Less reassuring was the fact that a consignment of three million tablets of atebrin and plasmoquine shipped to Australia from America was 'lost in transit'.[24] The minutes of the committee's second meeting noted that, despite the worsening malaria situation in Papua, mosquito netting ordered from America continued to receive a very low ranking in terms of supply prioritisation.[25] It was also at this time the committee recommended that suppressive doses of quinine be doubled for those soldiers stationed at Milne Bay, that all troops on active duty in the 'jungles' be given two tablets per day, and that those stationed at Port Moresby continue to receive one tablet daily.[26]

On Burston's advice, General Blamey sent a delegation to America and Britain in September to convey the urgency of the malaria situation in the Pacific, to secure supplies of synthetic anti-malarial drugs, and to ensure continued access to preventative measures such as netting.[27] This mission did raise awareness of the situation among Australia's allies and prompted important discussions on the future supply of anti-malarial measures. Burston believed that various factors contributed to the high incidence of malaria among Australian soldiers in Papua: a lack of discipline among the troops; lack of compliance by officers; the fear of impotence as a side-effect of the medication, and the deliberate avoidance of the daily malaria medication in the belief that contracting the disease was 'a much easier and safer method of ensuring evacuation than a SIW [self-inflicted wound].'[28] By the end of the year, Burston 'argued to Blamey that LHQ [Land Headquarters] should be giving primacy to malaria policy in order to "keep an efficient striking force in the field" in the SWPA.'[29]

Colonel E. (Bill) Keogh, Director of Pathology (AWM 126249). This photograph was taken in March 1946 and shows Keogh in his role as Assistant Director General of Medical Services.

The primacy case presented to Blamey was underpinned by the work of others, notably Lieutenant Colonel Esmond Keogh, Director of

Pathology.[30] Keogh's earlier forthright report to Burston recounted how, in just a few short months, malaria had 'reduced a first rate combatant force to an ineffective fraction of its original strength.'[31] He apportioned blame for this troop wastage to the failure of both military and medical hierarchy to heed the lessons of history and to act on professional advice, arguing that it was known that Malaria is hyperendemic in the Combatant areas. It was known that failure to appreciate the importance of Malaria as a strategical factor in previous wars had led to military disaster. **Knowledge** was not translated into *action* [original emphasis].[32]

These unambiguous statements were omitted from Burston's correspondence to Blamey and his report did not acknowledge receipt of Keogh's frank assessment of the malaria situation—in fact, it made no reference to Keogh. The recommendations regarding future training, protective clothing, enforcement of anti-malarial measures, the appointment of Fairley to General Headquarters, and Lieutenant Colonel Edward Ford (Assistant Director of Pathology NGF) to Australian Operational Headquarters were prefaced in Burston's report as being essential 'in my opinion'.[33] The similarity between the two documents leaves little doubt that the key suggestions for tackling the malaria problem in the Pacific stemmed from Keogh's original report—by the time Keogh's impassioned words roused Burston and Blamey to action, Australian soldiers had been fighting the tenacious Japanese troops, the malarial mosquitoes and the harsh Papuan environment for five months.

Keogh underscored the already dire consequences of the continued failure to act on numerous reports, advice and recommendations from those best qualified in the field. He also expressed the view that the decision by ADMS 7th Division (Norris) and others to cease administering suppressive doses of quinine to soldiers in the northern areas of Papua resulted in 'practically 100% of the wounded reaching Port Moresby from the Buna – Gona area [suffering from] malaria'.[34] Keogh further argued that it was not the need to conserve supplies of the drug that caused the cessation of suppressive quinine treatment, but rather it was a 'deliberate decision of responsible administrative medical officers'.[35] Keogh's claims that the quinine supply was adequate were supported by others. In December 1942, Adjutant-General Stantke dismissed allegations of shortages of anti-malaria drugs for the Army and the civilian population in Australia, stating that his department had consistently secured adequate supplies as well as stock in reserve. Stantke explained that 'any serious shortages would have been promptly brought to notice on the lines of the action recently taken ... to secure Quinine from N.E.I.[Netherlands East Indies] ...[and] when action in this was abortive to procure its synthetic substitute from America.'[36]

ADMS Norris proffered a very different explanation for perceived quinine shortages in Papua, explaining that 'a quantity of Quinine had been forwarded to Brisbane but with the limited space available those responsible for loading supplies to New Guinea had considered this of low priority and there it remained for months.'[37] Similarly, it was anticipated that anti-malaria drugs and prophylactics, such as creams and nets, could (and would) be airdropped at Kokoda for the soldiers advancing towards the coast. These supplies never reached the men. Norris explained decades later that he had 'signalled earlier for prophylactic facilities to be landed at Kokoda but unfortunately these supplies were dropped by an inexperienced pilot some miles away in the jungle, and no suppressant drugs, no repellents, no nets were available as we advanced into this danger.'[38]

In December 1942, Burston admitted that there had been 'a certain amount of wrong thinking, even in the Medical Service' in relation to the cessation of suppressive quinine treatment in Papua. He maintained that he had only just been made aware of a conference held 'some little time ago' between Johnston, Norris and the Deputy Assistant Director of Hygiene, McDonnell, in which the decision had been made to stop suppressive treatment in certain areas.[39] This differs markedly from DDMS Johnston's account (discussed in Chapter Five) that confirmation was received from DGMS Burston before the suppressive quinine was ceased.[40] An examination of the minutes of the Daily Staff Conference at Advanced Land Headquarters in Brisbane reveals yet another explanation for the perceived shortage of quinine. In early November 1942, Lieutenant Colonel Ross declared that the amount of quinine currently in transit but 'not yet located' was more than that held in the Army stores in Melbourne, and that the loss of medical stores between Melbourne and Port Moresby was becoming serious.[41]

Whatever the reasons, the reality was that field ambulance personnel in Papua, whose physical state was just as poor as that of the fighting men, were faced with the prospect of caring for an increasing number of casualties. By November 1942, the situation necessitated the establishment of a series of smaller medical posts specifically for the treatment of malaria sufferers. ADMS Norris explained that the already overstretched 2/4th Field Ambulance was now strained beyond breaking point:

> None of my Field Ambulances had arrived in New Guinea complete in establishment and a number of officers and other ranks were still marooned at Myola II out of the picture with their hundreds of casualties. This peeling off of medical personnel from those units already under strength for malarial posts severely taxed our meagre medical resources.[42]

The ramifications of crucial decisions manifested themselves across the Buna and Gona areas in December, with DDMS Johnston telling Burston:

> I think the troops should have been supplied with suppressive Quinine for the past week or so. But for a period of a week or so after leaving Kokoda there would appear to have been none issued ... it is possible that had suppressive Quinine been available all that time there would not have been so much appearing all at one time as at present.[43]

MYOLA

On 3 November Johnston sent a message to DGMS Burston informing him that there were more than 900 casualties in the MDS at Myola. The DGMS replied less than a week later explaining that General Blamey had postponed Burston's planned inspection of medical facilities in Papua for at least 10 days. He went on to explain that while 'we have done everything possible' to organise aerial evacuation from Myola, the lack of suitable aircraft meant that a solution remained doubtful. Various combinations of pilots and aircraft had attempted to deliver supplies and evacuate patients with limited success, and it was now felt that the only possible solution was to transport enough equipment to establish a CCS there 'until some means can be found of getting them out'.[44]

Johnston went to Myola to see the medical situation first-hand on 9 November. He made the journey as a passenger in a single-engine Stinson, which was being used as an ambulance aircraft. His stated reason for not visiting earlier was that he did not wish to take up space that might otherwise be used for transporting supplies and patients. Indeed it was the passionate and persistent urging by Colonel Chenhall—the CO of the 2/6th Field Ambulance, whose strongly worded telegram had caused such uproar and who had been at Myola with his 'lost legion' since early October—that persuaded Johnston to make the trip.[45]

Johnston's subsequent report to Burston noted that the Myola MDS held 349 patients, almost half of whom were battle casualties. There were 125 surgical and 185 medical in the MDS, and a further 16 medical patients awaiting aerial evacuation. It was thought that all remaining patients 'should eventually be able to walk back along the track. If native bearers were available (of which there is some slight hope), a number of those for air evacuation might be disposed of in this way.'[46] The DDMS calculated that, based on four patients being evacuated by aircraft per day, all air evacuation cases could be out of Myola within seven weeks. Yet in seemingly contradictory sentences, Johnston concluded that conditions were 'quite reasonably good, rough, of course, but compatible with recovery by all except those of the very worst class of case ... certainly the patients, except those who are very sick, look well and show a healthy glow.'[47] The regular aerial evacuations anticipated by Johnston never eventuated. Hundreds of patients and medical men were instead forced to walk across the Owen Stanleys—either back to the overcrowded 2/9th AGH at Port Moresby or forward to rejoin their depleted units in the front line.[48]

Despite the hardships they endured, those walking back to Port Moresby were considered better off than the patients left behind at Myola because, 'as heart-rending as it was, the situation of those who could not be moved at all was more so.'[49] Jim Bell was a soldier in the AIF reinforcements of the 3rd Battalion who first saw action at Ioribaiwa. He was wounded in the arm during fighting at Templeton's Crossing, when a bullet severed most of the nerves from his wrist to his elbow. He was operated on at Myola 1 and remained at Myola 2 for approximately six weeks. Jim and his mate, Sid, who been wounded in the hand, were part of a sorry group of seven soldiers who set out on the week-long walk from Myola to Port Moresby in November 1942.[50] The medical assistance available to these groups as they made their way back along the track was meagre at best. Jim and Sid's difficult situation was made worse when the fellow casualty assigned to help them on their journey 'cracked up' (presumably suffered a mental breakdown) soon after their departure and returned to Myola, leaving the two men to continue unassisted.[51] Warrant Officer Lorie Thompson of the 2/4th Field Ambulance described the helplessness felt by those posted along the Kokoda Track, charged with caring for the men from Myola:

> Men badly wounded and grievously ill made this torturous journey every day for weeks, going from stage to stage hobbling

painfully and arriving at the posts drenched and exhausted. All we could do was to ensure that pairs of our picked men were at posts along the track to receive the patients when they arrived at night, attend to urgent dressings, bed them down and spell [rest] over a day or so those who were too exhausted to go on in the morning. I shall never be able to forget the agony of those mornings when we despatched these chaps on the cruel ordeal of such a trip.[52]

The 2/4th Australian Field Ambulance MDS at Myola 1, October 1942. When the 2/4th moved north to Alola at the end of the month, all patients were evacuated from the Myola 1 MDS to the 2/6th Australian Field Ambulance MDS at Myola 2—a two-hour journey undertaken on foot (AWM P02424.103).

There were many times when Jim and Sid felt they could not go on—falling face down in the mud 'absolutely buggered' and unable to take another step. Somehow, they found the strength to continue. As Bell explained: 'I'd help Sid up, he'd help me up, and we'd go on.'[53] On arrival at the comfort stations set up along the track the two mates received a cup of tea and little else. When Bell asked for something to ease the shocking pain in his shattered and fly-blown arm, someone threw disinfectant on his wounds 'to keep the flies off a bit'.[54] Arriving at the 2/9th AGH seven days later, Bell was told that medical staff would not treat him immediately because of his generally poor condition and the filthy state of his wound. He was reprimanded for the amount of mud that covered his legs and feet—an unavoidable consequence of walking barefoot on the Kokoda Track for a week. Seemingly unfazed by the lack of empathy for what he had endured, Jim simply replied that 'it was hard to do [my] boots up with one hand.'[55]

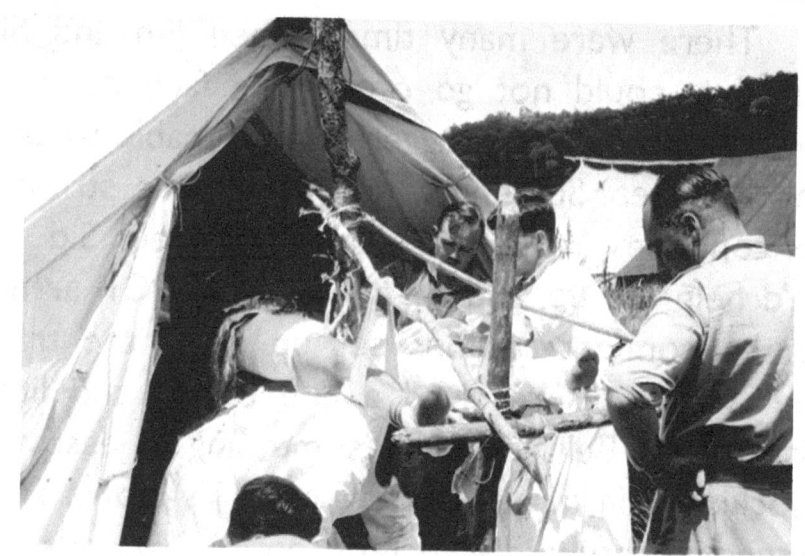

Applying plaster to a soldier's broken leg at Myola 1 MDS in October 1942. Lieutenant Colonel Chenhall, CO of the 2/6th Australian Field Ambulance, is on the far right, with his back to photographer. Captain Douglas Leslie, in the white coat, is applying the plaster, with Captain Peter Greenwell observing—both officers are from the 2/4th Australian Field Ambulance (AWM P02424.058).

Though thousands of sick and wounded soldiers still languished in Papua when Jim Bell returned to Australia at the end of November, the ship taking him home (HMAS *Katoomba*) was almost empty, with just 20 casualties on board. Bell remained in hospital until February 1943.

KOKODA

In early November 1942, the recently appointed commander of the 7th Division, Major General George Vasey (replacing Allen) and the brigades now under his command finally emerged from the treacherous track that had taken them over the Owen Stanley Range. The two brigades then separated, with Eather's 25th Brigade headed for Kokoda, while the 16th Brigade—originally a 6th Division brigade 'lent' to the 7th Division—under Brigadier Lloyd bypassed Kokoda and made its way towards Oivi. The 25th Brigade encountered no Japanese resistance when entering Kokoda village on 2 November 1942. Unlike Myola, the promised aerial evacuations of casualties from Kokoda did eventuate, though less regularly than anticipated. Changing military circumstances meant that it was now possible for seriously ill and wounded casualties to reach Port Moresby by air in less than 40 minutes, rather than a journey of six days or more along the track. This literally meant the difference between life and death.

The 2/4th Field Ambulance MDS at Kokoda, November 1942 (author image).

Private Kennedy was among 55 medical personnel of the 2/4th Field Ambulance who set out from Myola for Kokoda on 3 November, leaving Lieutenant Colonel Chenhall and his 2/6th Field Ambulance to care for the hundreds of casualties.[56] Hopes of an improved survival rate and reduced suffering as a result of the aerial evacuations from Kokoda so lifted Kennedy's spirits that the continuous torrential rain could not dampen them. He could even find beauty in the jungle as the sun shining brightly on the wet foliage made 'the leaves dazzle like diamonds'. Kennedy described the sight of Kokoda village as it finally came into view:

> At noon we reach Deniki, a native village on the crest of a steep ridge. We

have a spell here and boil the billy. From here we look down on Kokoda. It is a great sight to see this flat country with its rubber plantations spread out like a green carpet. They say it is only three hours and we are at the bottom of the ridge – the last of the Owen Stanley Range has been accomplished ... the going is quite flat now and we hike along the track winding in and out of the rubber trees. It seems as good as walking through Centennial Park in Sydney after the mountain passes. We reach Kokoda at 3.30pm.[57]

On arrival at Kokoda, the Deputy Assistant Director of Medical Services (DADMS) Munro Alexander directed the CO of the 2/4th Field Ambulance, Lieutenant Colonel Hobson, to the site already chosen for the unit's MDS. An MDS consisting of six tent flies was soon established. Recently landed medical equipment and items such as blankets and tents meant that the medical personnel could get straight to work tending the patients. The unit's new surgeon, Captain Gatenby (previously of the 2/2nd CCS), performed complex operations at Kokoda, including amputations, in conditions similar to those experienced by Chenhall and his men at Myola. The main difference was that the patient could now be airlifted to hospital care at Port Moresby within days of an operation. The prompt administration of blood transfusions helped to keep the patient out of immediate danger while waiting for evacuation.

Walking Wounded at Kokoda, November 1942 (author image).

The journey from the MDS to the Kokoda airstrip to await evacuation required casualties to be carried across a river before proceeding for at least a quarter of a mile. Patients and attending medical personnel then waited in the open or under scarce (and scant) shelter until supplies were unloaded and the empty aircraft could be backfilled with the human cargo. The dental officer of the 2/4th Field Ambulance, Captain Alan Watson, was responsible for ensuring that the greatest number of casualties possible was evacuated by air. He explained that 'when U.S. transport planes were off loaded, some pilots would take patients back to Port Moresby ... their loads varied – some taking two and others, eighteen patients. In all, approximately three hundred and fifty patients were evacuated by this method from Kokoda.'[58]

When the soldiers of the 7th Division had re-entered Kokoda, it was anticipated that the availability of the established airstrip would mean regular casualty evacuations and an improved medical situation overall. It was not long, however, before the medical hierarchy acknowledged that casualty evacuation arrangements at Kokoda were 'rather disturbed'.[59] Aerial evacuations did commence on 5 November 'with a flourish' and the aircraft transported 16 casualties. However, the MDS still held almost 100 patients at dusk that same day.[60] It was possible to evacuate over 100 casualties in a day when the weather was fine, but frequent heavy rain and poor visibility meant that the Douglas transport aircraft were often unable to land.[61] Other factors—the condition of the runway, irregular and unpredictable landings and take-offs, limited space on the aeroplanes to accommodate stretchers, and increasing casualties from the fighting taking place north of Kokoda—meant that the MDS was soon overcrowded and under-resourced.

The uncertainty regarding regular aerial evacuation directly affected those casualties transported to the Kokoda airstrip in anticipation of a flight. They remained there, sick and in pain, for extended periods when the aircraft failed to materialise. On 7 November, a number of seriously wounded soldiers were admitted to the MDS with wounds to the head, chest and limbs sustained after encountering Japanese troops around Oivi-Gorari, yet no evacuations took place and no medical stores were landed. By the end of the day, the MDS held over 52 battle casualties and more than 200 sick.[62] This number soon rose to well over 300, with far fewer patients evacuated than held at the Kokoda MDS. The constant influx of soldiers suffering from diarrhoea, dysentery, scrub typhus and malaria only added to the strain.[63] ADMS Norris requested that DDMS Johnston send another surgeon and a detachment of 14th Field Ambulance personnel to Kokoda.[64] Despite the obvious and stated need for extra staff to assist the 2/4th Field Ambulance, by 13 November their number had, in fact, decreased because it had again become necessary to 'bud off' smaller groups from this unit to staff the medical posts along the Ilima Track that led from Kokoda to Oivi.

Australian soldiers watch the raising of the Australian flag at Kokoda in November 1942. The Japanese abandoned Kokoda prior to the arrival of a patrol from the 2/31st Battalion, 25th Brigade, 7th Division, AIF, on 2 November (AWM 013572).

The situation at Kokoda improved during the second half of November, with increased aerial evacuations and the delivery of numerous boxes of Red Cross comforts and medical stores, including quinine tablets. Medical personnel numbers were increased by the arrival of the detachment of the 14th Field Ambulance requested by Hobson. These men had been waiting for days at Ward's Drome to be flown to Kokoda to relieve the exhausted members of the 2/4th, and their arrival had been a long time in the planning.[65] On 27 October, Johnston had requested that a light section of the 14th Field Ambulance be readied for flights to Kokoda in anticipation of battle casualties expected from the fighting north of the village. On 15 November, after a series of delays due to weather conditions and 'alterations in priority', four officers and 34 other ranks from this unit arrived at Kokoda, where the 2/4th Field Ambulance was holding 184 patients at the MDS.[66] The 14th Field Ambulance took over the running of the MDS the next day, allowing the 2/4th to join the Advanced Headquarters of the 7th Division, AIF, further north at Wairopi. Personnel from the 14th Field Ambulance were variously moved forward to Wairopi, back to Port Moresby, or forward to Popondetta—either by aircraft or on foot—to treat the casualties now scattered along the various jungle tracks.

General MacArthur's final push for victory at all costs on the northern beachheads of Papua was gaining momentum during November and 'Kokoda became a back-water when the campaign moved forward.'[67] Many of the patients in the MDS were too sick to return to their units in the front line, despite undergoing treatment. These men were transferred to the nearby transit camp, which had been transformed into a convalescent camp. Though the number of convalescing patients varied, at times this site held 100 men. Life for those left behind at Kokoda was tough, with the CO of the 14th Field Ambulance, Lieutenant Colonel Earlam, reporting that, at one stage, no rations or mail arrived at Kokoda for a period of 10 days and there were '300 whites and 1,300 natives [carriers], all hungry'.[68] Hundreds of Papuans from the surrounding villages had also gathered at Kokoda in the hope of being fed. Urgent requests for assistance went unanswered by both NGF and 7th Division Headquarters.

Like the Australians at Myola, the forgotten men of Kokoda were effectively marooned and left to fend for themselves. They received no news of the Papuan campaign or the wider conflict, except that which could be gleaned from listening to the news broadcasts from London on a 'wireless set belonging to ANGAU'.[69] The 14th Field Ambulance improvised to overcome issues such as poor hygiene brought about by 'mud, lack of sunshine, [the] lethargy of troops, and foul ground left by the Japanese.'[70] The availability of water was an issue because, although clean water was plentiful, it was not easily accessed due to the location of the MDS high on the Kokoda plateau and some distance from the source. The unit's cooks constructed a 'flying fox' to overcome this problem.[71]

On 28 November, the 14th Field Ambulance finally welcomed an aircraft at Kokoda. Unfortunately, the pilot was oblivious to their dire circumstances and carried no supplies. He had flown into Kokoda on his return journey from Popondetta to pick up a fellow pilot who had walked there from Myola. On learning of the medical situation, he agreed to take nine patients with him to Port Moresby.[72] Australian pilots did their best to drop supplies such as bread and cigarettes drawn from their own messes rather than from official stores. The situation slowly improved with organised ration drops as well as fresh fruit and vegetables brought into the village by local Papuans. More aircraft landed as the weather improved, allowing more patients to be evacuated.[73]

Almost 400 casualties were treated at the 14th Field Ambulance MDS at Kokoda and a further 800 soldiers received medical treatment in the line (that is, while serving with their unit in the forward area). Most suffered badly from the effects of the malaria that further debilitated these already weakened men. In a comment that contrasted sharply with the earlier arguments used to justify the cessation of suppressive quinine for the troops advancing on the Kokoda

Track, Earlam noted that 'the impression was given to 14 Aust Fd Amb on arrival in Kokoda that it was not a particularly malarious area. However, primary malaria developed in an extremely high proportion of personnel who remained in the area for 3 or 4 weeks.'[74] The consequences of the inadequate response to malaria and other illnesses is evidenced by Earlam's analysis of patients treated by his unit at the Kokoda MDS during this period. The statistics also illustrate the suffering that resulted from the inadequate medical evacuation policy. Approximately 80% of battle casualties (44 of 51) treated were later evacuated to Port Moresby. Of 332 sick, 52 were evacuated. The majority of the remaining 280 patients at Kokoda were transferred to the nearby convalescent camp, 12 soldiers returned to their units, and one died.[75]

At Myola, the supply of rations was 'parlous again' in December, though medical supplies were now adequate to treat the decreased number of casualties.[76] Since setting up the MDS in early October, the 2/6th Field Ambulance had treated thousands of soldiers and still held 58 sick and more than 30 battle casualties. Papuan carriers had recently evacuated 26 patients forward to the Kokoda MDS, while hundreds of sick and wounded soldiers were making their own way back to Port Moresby. On his last day in Papua

(15 December), DDMS Johnston telephoned Lieutenant Colonel Chenhall at the Myola MDS.[77] Interestingly, in light of the response elicited from Chenhall's October telegram, Johnston thanked him for his help and cooperation throughout the campaign so far, before advising that 150 pounds (68 kilograms) of Red Cross stores were on their way to Myola. Chenhall explained that the supplies were now of no use because the MDS was in the process of closing and most of the patients and personnel had been evacuated. He asked that the Red Cross packages be sent forward to his medical colleagues struggling on at Kokoda. The Myola MDS, set up on the promise of aerial supply and evacuation almost four months earlier, was finally closed on 19 December. The last patient from Myola arrived in Port Moresby just after Christmas 1942.[78]

Like the ongoing challenge of malaria, difficulties associated with supply and evacuation had plagued the field ambulance units at both Myola and Kokoda for months. Lieutenant Colonel Keogh's judgement that 'knowledge was not translated into action' in relation to malaria was certainly applicable to the conduct of the broader medical campaign in Papua.[79] Control of the airstrip at Kokoda, coupled with a more favourable military position in early November, had filled medical men such as Private Kennedy with optimism. Yet problems of supply, treatment, evacuation and leadership continued to impact on the efficacy of the field ambulance units at the Kokoda MDS until, like Myola, it finally closed in the days before Christmas. Unlike Myola, the aerial evacuation of casualties from Kokoda to medical facilities at Port Moresby reduced suffering and saved lives. However, the infrequency and unreliability of these flights did adversely affect supplies and communication—men went hungry, and were also starved of news of the Papuan campaign and the outside world. Medical personnel and their patients spent long hours beside the runway at Kokoda, searching the skies for aircraft that never came.

CHAPTER 10

SOPUTA

'Dead, mangled bodies, blood, guts and mud'

MILITARY SITUATION

The beachhead battles of Gona, Buna and Sanananda were fought in an extremely hostile environment—even for a country not lacking in harsh terrain. Approaches to both Gona and Sanananda were punctuated by swamps, mangroves, and the wide and winding Girua River—one of many bodies of water which fed into the creeks and lagoons before disgorging into the Solomon Sea. The area around Sanananda was the site of the main Japanese hospital and their military headquarters. The villages fanned out from the central hub of Soputa: Gona to the north-west, Sanananda in the centre, Buna and Cape Endaiadere to the north-east. Soputa lay approximately seven miles inland on the banks of the Girua River. The patchwork of foetid swamps and muddy quagmires between Soputa and the coast was interspersed with scintillas of land cloaked in jungle, sago palms and dense coconut plantations, and peppered with razor-sharp kunai grass harbouring mites that carried scrub typhus.[1] Thousands of men endured debilitating illness on these coastal battlefields as the scourge of malaria and other tropical diseases emerged from the marshlands and stagnant swamps to once again devastate the woefully unprepared forces. Geographically speaking, this truly was 'about as vile a country as any that exists'.[2]

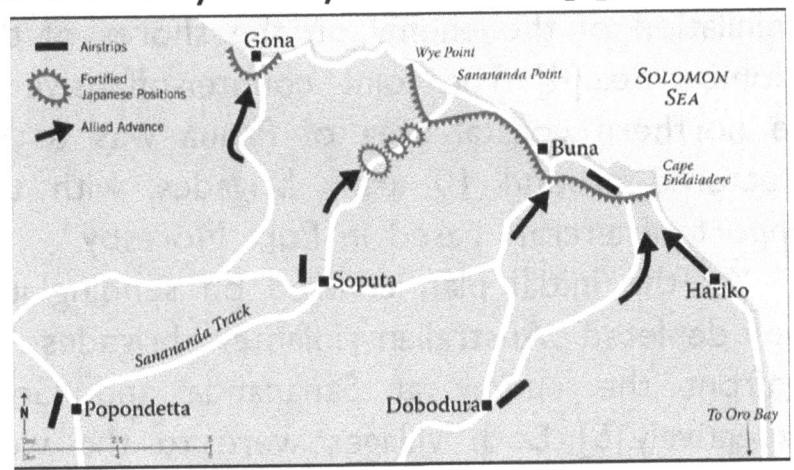

Map 10.1 The beachhead battles—Gona, Buna and Sanananda—were fought between November 1942 and January 1943. These battles marked the final phase of the Papuan campaign.

The Japanese had been withdrawing towards the northern coast since late September, pursued by the Australians. By mid-November 1942, the Kokoda airstrip was in Allied hands and the Australian flag flew over the village once again. US intelligence estimated that fewer than 4000

Japanese troops remained in the northern areas, 'believing them to be tattered survivors of Milne Bay and the Kokoda Track.'[3] It was against this backdrop that Major General George Vasey decided to take the advantage presented to him by the open environs around Oivi-Gorari, the next village on from Kokoda. The ensuing success here encouraged MacArthur and Blamey in their decision to push on towards a complete annihilation of the enemy on the shores of the Solomon Sea.[4] The joint counter-offensive in the northern coastal area of Papua was to be structured around 10 army brigades, with the support of aircraft based in Port Moresby.

Yet the initial plan centred on sending just two depleted Australian infantry brigades to confront the enemy at Sanananda and Gona respectively.[5] Both villages were to the west of Buna and Cape Endaiadere, where inexperienced troops from the US 32nd Division were tasked with engaging the enemy. Access to Buna was from the Solomon Sea or via a 'corduroy' (log) road, which snaked through swamps towards the Government Station and Buna Mission.[6] Approaches to Cape Endaiadere, situated to the east of Buna, passed through the low-lying Duropa coconut plantation, which was thickly planted with trees and criss-crossed with drains. The areas around Gona, Buna and

Sanananda were defended by determined Japanese soldiers, entrenched in well-concealed bunkers.

After crossing the Kumusi River in November the soldiers of the 16th and 25th brigades, 7th Division, AIF—who had been fighting along the Kokoda Track since September—made their way north towards the beachheads. The two infantry brigades were functioning at just one-third of their normal strength. The 7th Division Advance Headquarters and a detachment of the 2/4th Field Ambulance followed the men across the river a few days later. Soldiers from the 2/5th Field Regiment, AIF, at Milne Bay made slow progress along the north coast towards Buna by land and sea, bringing much-needed weapons.[7] The Australian forces were to link up with the Americans, some of whom had walked across the Owen Stanleys via the gruelling Kapa Kapa Track (to the south-east of, and roughly parallel to the Kokoda Track), and others who were airlifted from Port Moresby to the Wanigela airstrip.[8] With a plan in place and the Australian ground forces bolstered by the Americans, the military leadership anticipated a quick and relatively easy triumph over a weakened enemy.

They were wrong.

The belief that the battles would be over quickly had influenced the decision not to airlift the rested 21st AIF Brigade from Kokoda to the front line.[9] The idea that the victory would be relatively easy prompted the despatch of the inexperienced and under-trained US 32nd Division, rather than the better trained 41st Division still in camp in Australia. This decision also favoured practicality over preparedness—the 32nd was due to move to another training camp within Australia and it was thought that it might as well be put to good use while training, so the men were sent to Papua instead. Lieutenant General Eichelberger later conceded that the wrong division had been sent.[10] It was not long before MacArthur and Blamey were forced to confront the reality that their much-anticipated swift and decisive victory on the Papuan beaches against a depleted group of 'tattered survivors' would not materialise.[11] In reality, the condition of the Allied forces being sent into battle was not much better than that of the Japanese.

The role of the Allied air forces was ramped up in order to wrest control of the skies over land and sea and enable regular resupply of the forward troops during this period of intense action.[12] However, the overall success of the bombing missions was tempered by incidents of 'friendly fire' that wounded or killed Allied soldiers.[13] The Allied air forces were strengthened somewhat with the arrival of additional aircraft in the lead-up to the beachhead battles. Importantly too, Japanese aerial superiority over Solomon Islands and New Guinea had been diminished.

While there had been a weakening of the Japanese position on land and in the air, the Allies remained particularly vulnerable at sea. Attempts to transport men and weapons from Milne Bay to Buna via the sea route relied on a disparate fleet of small naval supply ships as well as civilian vessels and crew, with neither the US nor the Australian Navy able to spare further ships and sailors.[14] On 16 November near Hariko, east of Cape Endaiadere, an attack by Japanese fighter planes on Allied vessels transporting US General Edwin Harding, personnel, guns and supplies resulted in the loss of men and equipment destined for the beachheads. Harding's subsequent attack on Buna did not succeed and he was replaced by Eichelberger. It is reasonable to argue that the lack of a large-scale Allied fleet in the area emboldened the Japanese to not only attack, but also successfully reinforce and resupply their own troops by sea well into December, when their strategy changed to one of withdrawal and evacuation.[15]

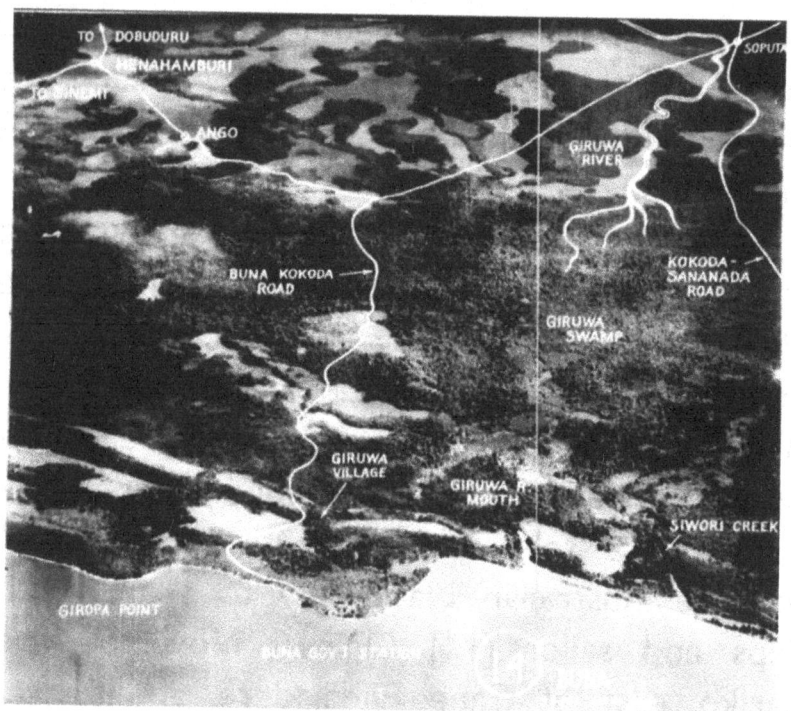

An October 1942 aerial reconnaissance photograph, taken over the Solomon Sea, of a section of the north-east coastline of Papua. Buna Government Station is front and centre, with Buna village slightly to the right (north). Sanananda and Gona (not shown) are further north from Buna. Note the location of Soputa on the banks of the Girua River, in the top right corner of the photograph (AWM 106525).

In mid-December, General MacArthur claimed that a series of 'mopping-up' operations was all that was needed to secure Allied victory in Papua.[16] As had been the case with MacArthur's premature declaration of victory at Milne Bay, this assessment underestimated the challenges remaining and devalued the many

Australian and American lives lost in these final weeks. The '"mopping up" campaigns ... had already raised some uncertainty in the minds of the troops and other more remote critics', especially in relation to the high price paid by the soldiers.[17] This was no 'mopping-up' exercise. Despite repeated attacks on all three fronts from 1 December, Gona did not fall to the Australians until 9 December—with only limited success achieved at Buna by this time. The Gona-Buna area did not fall to the Australians and Americans until 1 January 1943.[18] Resistance by the Japanese soldiers around Sanananda—men who General Blamey had vowed to 'liquidate gradually'—did not cease until 22 January 1943.[19]

MEDICAL SITUATION

The coastal terrain in which the beachhead battles were fought presented as many challenges for medical personnel as the Kokoda Track and the Owen Stanley Range. There was an unsettling sense of *déjà vu* that the faith placed in the aerial evacuation of casualties was far more than seemed warranted or wise. Such confidence was perhaps more understandable at this stage of the campaign, since some control of the skies had been gained, and the availability of Kokoda airstrip meant that medical supplies could now be 'landed, not thrown at us'.[20] The flight to Port Moresby from the northern coastal area took less than 40 minutes and it was expected that casualties from the fighting at the beachheads could be regularly evacuated from the new airstrips under construction at Popondetta and Soputa. However, the medical plans—like the military plans—ignored the lessons of the recent past, underestimated the challenges, and overestimated the Army's capabilities.

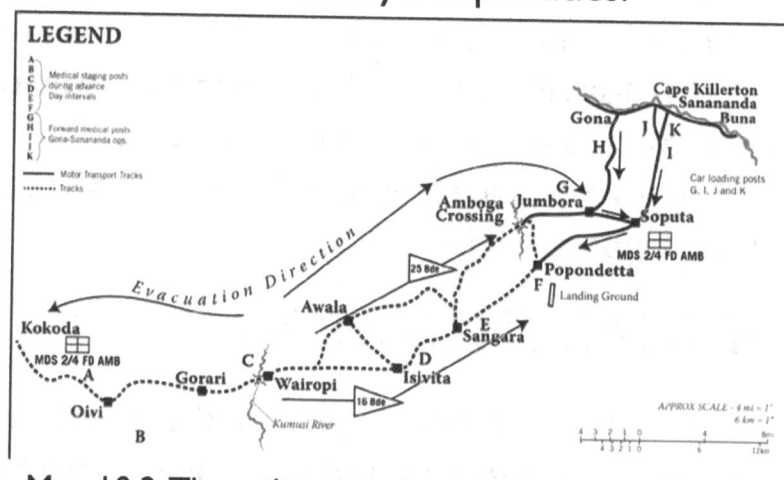

Map 10.2 The military and medical situation at the beachheads, November 1942. The arrows indicate that casualties south of Wairopi were evacuated back towards Kokoda, while those north of Wairopi were evacuated forward through Awala, Isivita, Sangara and Jumbora to the Soputa MDS. Casualties incurred in the beachhead area around Gona, Sanananda and Buna were treated at forward staging posts before being evacuated back to the Soputa MDS. They were then sent to the Popondetta staging post near the airstrip to await aerial evacuation (source: Walker,

Australia in the War of 1939-1945, Series 5, Vol.1, Clinical Problems of War, p.81).

To recap the medical situation: members of the 2/6th Field Ambulance remained marooned at Myola until late in December, while elements of the 14th were scattered back along the track towards the base area around Port Moresby. They were finally flown to Kokoda in mid-November to relieve the 2/4th Field Ambulance there. This in turn allowed the latter to move forward to Soputa—a place which came to represent both the zenith and the nadir of this unit's experience in Papua. Although small detachments of militia and AIF field ambulance units were present during various stages and at numerous locations as the beachhead battles unfolded, it was the stalwarts of the campaign thus far—the 14th, 2/6th and 2/4th field ambulances—that bore the brunt of the responsibility for saving the soldiers.[21] These three units continued to 'leapfrog' one another during the trek towards the beachheads, just as they had throughout the campaign thus far.

From a logistical perspective, the ability of three depleted field ambulance units to deliver an adequate level of front-line medical care for thousands of soldiers had still not been addressed at this stage of the campaign—they were neither relieved nor reinforced by fresh field ambulance units until most of the fighting had ended. While acknowledging the constraints on medical care presented by this extremely difficult terrain, it remains difficult to comprehend why so many of the same mistakes around planning, supply and evacuation that plagued the earlier stages were repeated in its final weeks. Innovations that had been instigated, pursued and refined by field ambulance personnel—such as forward surgery—saved lives during the beachheads phase. However, supply problems continued, evacuations faltered, medical posts overflowed, and men suffered due to the continued failure to prioritise medical care. With a tenacious enemy dug in on the beaches, personnel and patients stretched out along the jungle tracks, and an ever-increasing number of casualties piling up on the beaches, the challenges for the field ambulance units in this final phase remained virtually the same as those encountered during the fighting along the Kokoda Track and over the Owen Stanleys.

Despite the proven failure of a medical plan that relied on aircraft it did not have, to supply equipment it could not land, and evacuate casualties it could not access, the Allied military and medical hierarchy remained inexplicably optimistic into November, continuing to place their faith in aerial supply and evacuation. This is illustrated by an appreciation of the medical situation in Papua presented to Advanced Land Headquarters in Brisbane by DDMS Johnston on 11 November 1942. Johnston was confident that the medical situation would be much more manageable now that Kokoda and its airstrip had been regained. He was of the view that there was 'a gleam of light ahead ... and I hope to forward to L.H.Q. some sort of picture of the conditions and happenings up here before long.'[22]

Johnston noted that DGMS Burston's planned flight to Papua had been delayed and wondered at his current whereabouts, asking that Burston be given 'such extracts from this as you think would interest him, and also give him an idea of our doings here.'[23] Issues discussed included aerial evacuation, casualty statistics, assessments of the strengths and weaknesses of various medical personnel, and summaries of Johnston's recent visits to Myola and Kokoda MDS. Johnston mentioned he was in the process of writing another report—'Lessons Learned'—a title that suggested the medical situation in Papua was now under control and the campaign all but won.[24] Neither suggestion was true.

Away from the relative safety of Port Moresby, the work of the field ambulance units was far from finished. The 2/4th Field Ambulance handed over the Kokoda MDS to the 14th Field Ambulance on 16 November. Accompanied by 30 Papuan carriers, the unit continued along the muddy track to Oivi-Gorari and pushed onward towards the coast via villages such as Wairopi, Sangara Mission and Popondetta. The evidence of the heavy fighting that had taken place at Gorari assaulted their senses on arrival. The smell of the decomposing bodies of Japanese soldiers was overwhelming. Horses remained tied up and starving, others had been shot or bayoneted by the Japanese and left in nearby streams to contaminate the water, 'such were their tactics in their hasty retreat'.[25]

Although not directly exposed to the fighting, the overall health of medical personnel making their way north suffered as much as that of the soldiers. Hampered by sun, heat and humidity, each man of the unit carried his own pack, as well as medical and ordnance equipment from the 800 pounds (approximately 360 kilograms) of stores that Hobson had sent ahead from Kokoda by jeep. Hobson noted that 'the men did not travel well at all [and] in this climate the overloading of [medical] personnel is to be avoided if there is work to be done at the end of the day.'[26] Fresh fruit and vegetables were gathered by ANGAU staff, and foodstuffs such as bully beef and biscuits were dropped during these weeks. However, by this stage most of the field ambulance personnel were extremely sick, undernourished, and suffering from diarrhoea or dysentery. An advance detachment of the 2/4th Field Ambulance comprising Captain Alan Day and four medical personnel arrived at Wairopi and attempted to care for hundreds of patients, many of whom were also suffering from malaria. The whole situation here 'verged on the impossible' with sick, hungry and weary medical personnel attempting to tend to other wounded, ill and exhausted soldiers. The sight and smell of recently interred Japanese bodies that were now exposed by heavy rains added to their discomfort.[27]

NX473 Major Ian Firth Vickery, medical officer with the 2/4th Australian Field Ambulance at Sangara Mission on 18 November. The men were making their way to Soputa and had walked for three days from Kokoda, with only one

day's worth of rations. Vickery was killed nine days later at Soputa MDS (AWM P02423.036).

ADMS Norris selected locations for a number of small medical posts along the tracks in the area and advance parties of field ambulance units treated the casualties accumulating at these stations as they passed through. On arrival at each post, the main body of the 2/4th Field Ambulance was then called on to assist with the treatment of hundreds of sick and wounded soldiers. In between caring for the living, the men also reburied the Japanese dead.[28] By 19 November, the main party of the 2/4th had been ordered by Norris to make its way forward to Sangara Mission. A total of 19 medical staff under Captain Day was left behind at Wairopi to care for 265 casualties until B Company of the 14th Field Ambulance arrived from Kokoda five days later.[29]

In scenes again reminiscent of Myola and Kokoda, Day's small medical contingent, with its insufficient supplies and hundreds of patients, was destined to remain at Wairopi until late December. A request sent by Day to DDMS Johnston for 'special foods for sick men' instead resulted in an order to evacuate all patients to Kokoda as soon as possible.[30] One of the many problems with this instruction was the lack of Papuan carriers available to transport the patients. Carriers for three stretcher cases were found and, along with eight walking casualties, made their way to Kokoda. However, the situation at Wairopi remained fundamentally unchanged for almost a month, with Day reporting that 'during all this period messages to ADMS 7 Aust Div [Norris] received no reply.'[31] It was not until 13 December that 90 carriers arrived (without prior notice) and took the remaining patients to Popondetta for aerial evacuation, enabling personnel to close the Wairopi post and walk on to Soputa.

The ways in which the geography challenged the men seemed limitless. On leaving Captain Day at Wairopi, the main party of the 2/4th Field Ambulance crossed the Kumusi River, with 10 men at a time clinging to the hastily built makeshift bridge which 'swings about like a hammock but serve[s] the purpose well'.[32] Once across the river, the torrential rain that belted down through the night made for fitful sleep. Fatigue and hunger overtook many of the men the next day, as they made their way towards Sangara Mission and the promise of long-overdue food rations. Although the condition of the track improved the closer they moved to Sangara, the line of exhausted personnel had become increasingly strung out since leaving

Kokoda. Many Papuan carriers also fell by the wayside, so that by the evening of 18 November only two reported for duty.[33]

It was clear that resourcefulness and extemporisation would remain necessary for survival in this harsh country. Accordingly, the budding-off system that had been utilised throughout the campaign continued at Sangara Mission. Seven members of the 2/4th Field Ambulance remained to care for soldiers who were suffering so badly from malaria that they were unable to be moved. When the number of patients increased from eight to 40 by nightfall, Hobson arranged for them to receive rations as well as deliveries of fruit and vegetables. Despite these efforts to provide basic sustenance to the casualties, Hobson's 'cold, hungry and miserable' field ambulance personnel were forced to supplement their own diet by digging up potatoes from the Mission garden or scrounging for the green bananas, paw paws and wild chokos growing along the track.[34]

Aerial supply remained a major problem, though this does not seem to have been fully accounted for or acknowledged by senior medical officers. When the 2/4th Field Ambulance had set out from Kokoda, the men were told to take just one full day's food ration plus one emergency ration, as more would be available all along their route. The unit searched the low grey skies for supply drops which failed to materialise, before learning that they would not receive any food until they reached Soputa—still a day and a half's walk from Sangara Mission. The welcome sight of the 'biscuit bombers' (transport aircraft) that eventually dropped the much-anticipated rations of bully beef, biscuits, sugar, tea and powdered milk was tempered somewhat by the realisation that the cargo was falling perilously close to the medical station, forcing the men to take cover.[35]

Medical personnel were constantly confronted with the same shortages of personnel, rations, medical stores and shelter that had become the hallmark of their campaign thus far. The number and condition of the casualties encountered by the 2/4th Field Ambulance as the men made their way towards the coast was indicative of the poor health of the soldiers being sent into battle, the unrealistic expectations of the commanders, and the gross inadequacy of the medical treatment available. After carefully negotiating their way along the greasy, muddy track to Popondetta, the unit came across six field ambulance personnel under the command of Captain John Follent—a reinforcement medical officer for the 16th Brigade at Kokoda—who later accompanied the 2/4th Field Ambulance to Soputa. The group was caring for 70 soldiers, most of whom were suffering from malaria, with the number of casualties increasing to 120 by nightfall.[36]

This was the human cost of General MacArthur's unrealistic expectations. Hobson's observations as he made his way towards Soputa provide an insight into the physical state of the Australian soldiers advancing to take on the Japanese. He noted that 'in all villages en route we passed a large number of sick men, all waiting to get strong enough to proceed forward. Most were too weak to move, and as there were no bearers available we saw they had Quinine and rations, and left them with instructions to move forward when possible.'[37] The men of the depleted 25th Brigade, under Brigadier Ken Eather, were so sick and weak they could not cover the 40 miles (65 kilometres) of rough terrain to arrive at the Gona battle lines as scheduled. For similar reasons, the 16th Brigade, under the command of Brigadier John Lloyd, did not arrive at Sanananda in time for the launch of the attack. It was the Americans who first went into battle at Buna and Cape Endaiadere on 19 November 1942.[38]

At midday on 20 November, a small party from Lieutenant Colonel Hobson's 2/4th Field Ambulance was sent forward from Popondetta to Soputa under the command of Major Hew

McDonald. On arrival, McDonald's party established a medical post at Soputa and immediately commenced operating on the numerous battle casualties. At 9.00pm that night, Hobson received a signal from ADMS Norris relaying McDonald's request for urgent surgical assistance and another group from the 2/4th Field Ambulance was ordered by Hobson to 'get dressed and leave immediately for Soputa'.[39] They were told that a 'big attack' was planned at Gona the next day and that it was their task to assist McDonald's men in treating the casualties already at Soputa, as well as caring for the expected battle casualties from the fighting at Gona.[40] The party included the unit's dental officer, Captain Allan Watson, who was to administer anaesthetic for McDonald and the other surgeons. The men were tired, hungry and angry at Hobson, whose order caused them to forgo a much-needed overnight rest at Popondetta. Indeed, the men were so angry that some threatened desertion and were only placated with the promise of sandwiches to eat on the way, and a vehicle to transport them the six miles north-east to Soputa.[41]

Lieutenant Colonel Hobson clearly set out the chronology of these events in the unit diary:
Major MacDonald [sic] and advance party left Popondetta for Soputa at 1200

hrs to form a medical post. At 2100 hrs ADMS called with a signal from Maj MacDonald ... he was then holding 40 patients, 17 battle casualties, 2 perforated abdomens, and asking for surgical assistance. I sent Capt Gatenby, Capt Watson, Surgical orderlies, and 2 cooks with surgical gear and 50 rations forward at once on an old Chev utility, which had been found in a Jap workshop and reconditioned.[42]

These dying days of November had brought increasing numbers of soldiers and weapons into the area between Soputa and the coast, drawing attention from the Japanese on land as well as from the air, with constant surveillance and regular reconnaissance. The village of Soputa was approximately six miles inland from the coastal village of Buna and eight miles from Gona. Sanananda was situated between Buna and Gona. The proximity of Soputa to the front line coupled with the increased activity in response to General MacArthur's avowed intention to drive all columns through to the beachheads 'regardless of losses', placed the 2/4th Field Ambulance and its Soputa MDS at great risk.[43]

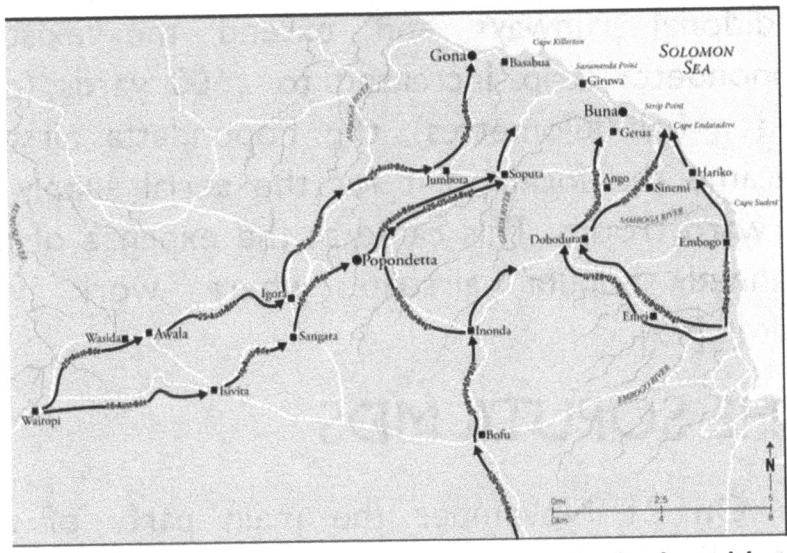

Map 10.3 Routes of Allied advance towards the beachheads from mid-November 1942

In the face of the unanticipated strength and determination of the Japanese resistance, Allied soldiers, weapons and ammunition continued to land in large numbers on Douglas and Dakota transport aircraft. Japanese pilots flew reconnaissance missions over Soputa and the surrounding area during the final weeks of November, as the build-up for the renewed Allied land offensive continued in and around the village. Work on Popondetta and Dobodura airstrips was hastened to enable ever more artillery and field guns, including disassembled 25-pounder guns, to be flown in.[44] The commander of the 7th Division, Major General George Vasey, was instructed to oversee the construction of additional runways and extend the existing Popondetta strip. Increased to 1600 yards (one and a half kilometres), the Popondetta airstrip became the focal point for the aerial supply of forward troops. This came at the expense of the planned Soputa airstrip, where work was halted.[45]

THE SOPUTA MDS

On 21 November the main party of the 2/4th Field Ambulance 'departed Poppindetta [sic] at 0845 hrs arriving Soputa 1400 hrs. Major MacDonald [sic] had set up his post on the west bank of the Girua River in a pleasant clearing.'[46] It is reasonable to assume that this was an area either chosen or approved by ADMS Norris, given that he had been responsible for overseeing the location and function of all medical facilities in Papua thus far in the campaign.

The 7th Division Headquarters arrived at Soputa from Popondetta an hour before the main group from the 2/4th Field Ambulance walked into the village.[47] The 16th Brigade, AIF, which had used up its 'last dregs of strength' in continued fighting against a determined enemy at Sanananda since 16 November, was reinforced by two battalions of the US 126th Infantry that same day.[48] On 25 November the 21st Brigade,

AIF (under General Dougherty), was flown in to Popondetta to reinforce the 25th Brigade attack on Gona, now scheduled for 29 November. MacArthur—keen to prove to a sceptical Blamey that the Americans could take Buna—also planned an escalation of the action at Buna on 30 November. Once landed at Popondetta, the soldiers and weapons 'moved up the track to Soputa where they went into action on the same day.'[49] This main transport route from the Popondetta airstrip to the front line at Sanananda passed alongside the Soputa MDS and the 7th Division Headquarters that was set up nearby. The track also skirted the US Clearing Station and Headquarters 16th Brigade, AIF, both located near the intersection with the track to Jumbora, north of Soputa.[50]

The 2/4th Field Ambulance personnel of six officers and 42 other ranks at the Soputa MDS were assisted by medical officers from the nearby US 126th Clearing Station. The influx of wounded continued unabated and the MDS held 200 patients by 6.00pm, with a further 50 casualties arriving just before midnight.[51] Hobson and Vickery worked through the night and into the early hours to clear the backlog of suffering, with all urgent operations completed by 5.00am on 22 November. Such a high number of casualties necessitated the construction of a second theatre that day to allow operations to be performed around the clock, with the first American battle casualties undergoing surgery in the Australian MDS later that evening.[52]

No medical supplies arrived for the 2/4th Field Ambulance at Soputa, despite increased Allied aerial activity in the skies above the village in preparation for the impending battles. Thousands of pounds of equipment and tents continued to arrive on aircraft at Popondetta. While the aircraft could land there to unload their cargo, supplies could only be dropped—not landed—at Soputa because work to construct the airstrip had been halted. It was a disheartened Hobson who recorded the 'usual acute shortage of medical and ordnance stores ... cooking gear and shelter.'[53] The loss of large amounts of medical equipment by the Papuan carriers while walking to Soputa and a lack of items such as blankets added to the difficulties. Conditions for medical personnel and their patients at Soputa remained 'desperate' until late on 23 November when five packages of medical supplies were dropped, further tents were erected, and an additional hut was constructed at the MDS.[54]

The shortage of supplies was not matched by a lack of patients. By 23 November, the Soputa MDS held more than 350 casualties, with

Hobson noting that 'the 2/4 Amb personnel have the care of from 750 to 800 cases, in posts between front line and Wairope [sic] inclusive.'[55] Private Kennedy's description of the personal toll taken by this Herculean task on the medical men suggests that it was a combination of dedication, altruism and optimism which got them through those dark and desperate days:

> Casualties are heavy here and our ambulance men are doing a great job. 36 hours sometimes and no sleep or just get an hour where possible, most of us are sick with malaria, some with dysentery, and a lot with both. But our wounded are suffering from this too as well as some of the ghastly wounds they have.
>
> The 2/4 Field Ambulance has wilted down in numbers and most of us have lost two or three stone [between 13 and 19 kilograms] over the past few weeks. Rations have been short and sometimes none, but we are still in hopes of something good turning up sooner or later. There is talk that 25 Brigade will be pulled out, as all the units are low in numbers now owing to the heavy casualties.[56]

In light of the increasing Japanese aerial reconnaissance and in anticipation of the battles and casualties to come, a small number of patients was transferred by jeep from Soputa MDS to Popondetta airstrip to await evacuation on 24 November. On 25 November an Australian jeep, travelling on the road that ran along the perimeter of the MDS, towed a 25-pounder gun into the grounds of the medical post while Japanese reconnaissance aircraft were overhead. The driver indicated that he intentionally did so because of the presence of the Japanese aircraft. The jeep stopped near the Red Cross ground flag that had been placed approximately 25 yards (23 metres) from the road.[57] The flag identified and protected the MDS in accordance with the Geneva Convention that stated in part 'the emblems indicating medical formations and establishments must be made clearly visible to the enemy's land, air and sea forces'.[58]

A surgical team from the US 5th Clearing Station as well as some 2/6th Field Ambulance personnel who had been stationed at Kokoda and another seven members of the 2/4th Field Ambulance arrived at Soputa and were much welcomed. The 2/4th detachment had been caring for any casualties still making their way to Soputa, until relieved by a detachment from the 14th Field Ambulance. More than 100 patients (79 battle casualties and 24 sick) were admitted to the Soputa MDS over the next few days. The

Americans assisted the Australians by supplying extra personnel and equipment.

The system of transporting patients from the Soputa MDS to Popondetta for aerial evacuation was made easier the next day when 300 Papuan carriers were allocated for the task. This, in conjunction with the arrival of more reinforcements from the 2/6th Field Ambulance and the establishment of the US clearing station, promised easier days ahead for the 2/4th Field Ambulance.[59] However, the improving situation was soon offset by an influx of 76 casualties. The Americans again came to the aid of the Australian doctors, providing medical officers to assist with surgery and distributing medical supplies including 'ether and dressings, and Pentothal, without which we couldn't have carried on.'[60] This welcome influx of men and materiel allowed Hobson to variously rest or relocate his medical officers, though he was acutely aware that the escalating military action posed an increased risk to the staff and patients of the MDS.

With this in mind, he sent the unit's dental officer (Watson) to Popondetta airstrip on 26 November with instructions 'to attempt to talk the pilots into taking off more patients each trip.'[61] The renewed urgency of clearing the MDS of patients before the offensive ramped up may well have influenced the decision to send a jeep full of captured Japanese equipment for use as a bartering tool in the 'squalid deal' to which Watson was a reluctant party at Popondetta.[62] Explaining the scale of the incentive-based payments, Watson later recalled that one Japanese helmet 'equalled' the evacuation of two sick or wounded Australians; one Japanese rifle could secure the transportation of between 10 and 12 casualties, while a rifle plus 20 rounds of ammunition bought aerial evacuation for up to 15 patients. He maintained that Australian pilots needed no incentive to evacuate casualties and did not take part in 'this awful degrading barter [that] went on from dawn to dusk with the result that all the 450 casualties were airlifted back to Port Moresby that day.'[63]

Watson's account of the system and the non-participation of Australian pilots was supported by another member of the 2/4th Field Ambulance, Warrant Officer Lorie Thompson, who recalled that American pilots had to be bribed to bring patients back. The Australian pilots loaded the planes to the hilt at Popondetta with patients, but the American pilots were not keen to do the same. The Australians traded Jap rifles and helmets with the US pilots to get them to take patients—they wanted souvenirs.[64]

'A BLACK DAY FOR THE 2/4th'

After five months of fighting in Papua, the aerial evacuation of Australian casualties from the 2/4th Field Ambulance MDS at Soputa had seemingly come down to the ability of medical personnel to barter for the lives of men. Perhaps the most tragic aspect of the humiliating trade in human life at Popondetta was that medical officers such as Hobson and Watson even found themselves in such a position—simply because no organised large-scale medical evacuation scheme had been put in place prior to the final beachheads offensive. As unpalatable as the bartering system was, it undoubtedly saved many lives. Warrant Officer Thompson reflected that it was 'lucky we had evacuated so many the day before as we knew they were planning a big attack on Gona [and] had to make room for the casualties. If we hadn't evacuated them it would have been much worse.'[65] Indeed.

The lives of thousands of Australian soldiers fighting at Gona, Buna and Sanananda depended on 90 medical personnel at the Soputa MDS: five officers and 50 other ranks of the 2/4th Field Ambulance; three officers and 27 other ranks of the 2/6th Field Ambulance, and five men from the 5th Clearing Station.[66] The MDS still held over 300 patients, despite Watson's bartering efforts. Evacuations continued throughout the night of 26 November and into the next day with 'jeeps carrying stores and ammunition from Poppindetta [sic] forward and back loading with patients.'[67] On the afternoon of 27 November, ADMS Norris convened a conference to discuss the medical plan that was to be implemented for the offensive. The meeting occurred at the Soputa MDS and concluded at 4.00pm, after which most of the medical officers made their way to the nearby kitchen. Lieutenant Colonel Hobson and DADMS Munro Alexander visited the dispensary and the quartermaster tent to discuss the medical stores situation when suddenly at 1630hrs Zeros appeared, and bombed and machine-gunned the MDS. Also 7 Div HQ and 126 US Combat Clearing Station. The raid lasted about 10 minutes, leaving 22 dead and a large number of wounded. Nearly all tents were holed and the Q store and dispensary were completely burned. Immediately after the raid all remaining personnel continued their jobs, wounded were collected, treated and evacuated, and the dead were put aside for burial ... all personnel behaved marvellously [names of dead and wounded are listed].[68]

Norris' recollections are more descriptive—and emotive:

> We were sitting on some coconut logs and discussing our plans over a mug of tea ... suddenly without warning there was a whirr of low planes, machine gun fire and bomb explosions nearby ... it was all over in a matter of seconds ... Fifteen men were dead and twenty-three wounded, huts set on fire with that nauseating odour of burning flesh ... victims of a savage, inhuman attack on a clearly marked medical post.[69]

A report from the US 107th Medical Battalion provides the American perspective, succinctly though graphically conveying the unexpected nature of the attack:

> A group of men volunteered to put up a ward tent next to the hospital shed. In the late afternoon, while erecting this, enemy dive bombers suddenly appeared and dropped two medium bombs into this group before they had any opportunity to seek cover [names and ranks listed] ... the five men, the first of the battalion to lose their lives in combat, were buried that evening in an open field near Soputa. Burial services were conducted by an Australian missionary present at the time.[70]

At Headquarters 7th Division, located 'within 100 yards' (90 metres) of the MDS, two soldiers were killed and three men were wounded. The event was noted in the routine military language common to official unit diaries: 'Adv HQ 7 Aust Div subjected to aerial dive bombing and strafing attack by 10 Jap planes. (Casualties – 2 ORs killed, 2 offrs and 1 OR wounded).'[71] ANGAU member Captain Herbert Kienzle was attached to 7th Division Headquarters, and was camped between the Australian and American medical posts at the time of the bombing. He reported that two of the Papuan carriers in his charge were killed and 14 wounded.[72]

As a young nursing orderly in the 2/4th Field Ambulance writing in his personal diary, Private Kennedy was not bound by the military formalities that stripped emotion from official reports. His words give a raw account that is more immediate and more personal:

> The 27th November is a black day for the 2/4, we come under heavy machine gun fire, and aerial bombardment, 36 are killed and 70 wounded. The O.C.[sic: CO] of our company is killed, Major Vickery, also Major McDonald. There is not much left here—dead, mangled bodies, blood, guts and mud. This is a day that none of the 2/4 will forget, and some great boys have paid the supreme sacrifice here.

Members of the 2/4th Australian Field Ambulance close to the wreckage of the unit's kitchen, which was destroyed in the Japanese air attack on the Soputa MDS, Headquarters 7th Division, AIF, and US Clearing Station on 27 November 1942 (AWM P02423.047).

Seven members of the 2/4th Field Ambulance were killed including those two 'handsome young men [Vickery and McDonald], whose appearance was matched only by their devotion and skill'.[73] Also among the dead was Lance Corporal Arthur Moodie, the multilingual 'lean and handsome Scot' who wrote loving letters home to his 'Tuppence'.[74] Many patients in the MDS sustained further wounds or were killed where they lay on stretchers—sick, wounded, unarmed and helpless. Surviving field ambulance personnel collected and treated the wounded—and prepared the dead for burial. Warrant Officer Thompson later wrote that the 'superb training as well as guts was telling, for instance, with Bill Kennedy, the nursing orderly who stayed in his tent-ward dressing the wounded as they were fired upon.'[75] Sergeant Bill Sweeting observed that 'the dead and wounded – including patients, members of the Field Ambulance, natives and visitors to the hospital lay everywhere.'[76]

The possibility of another attack and the need to quickly evacuate patients to safety, meant that all 'recording had to be temporarily ignored'.[77] This may go some way towards explaining the challenges of definitively identifying those patients killed as a result of the bombing and the discrepancies in the final casualty numbers. Approximately 27 Australians died in the broader Soputa area that day. Some of these were battle casualties, while others had been admitted as patients to the Soputa MDS in the days prior to 27 November and had not been discharged at the time of the attack. Two hundred casualties were in the Soputa MDS on the afternoon of 27 November 1942.[78]

The number and identity of all patients who died in the MDS as a result of the Japanese attack is unknown. Many have since been recorded as battle casualties, killed in action, or missing in action.[79] Personnel records show that at least four soldiers whose names are listed on the War Memorial to the Missing at Bomana War Cemetery were patients in the Soputa MDS at the time of the attack.[80] Fourteen of the 27 men who were killed in and around Soputa on 27 November were officially listed as 'Killed-In-Action as a result of enemy aircraft', and two of the soldiers were listed as 'presumed dead'.[81] The available evidence suggests that the Japanese aerial attack at Soputa resulted in the death or wounding of at least 60 Allied personnel.[82]

This photo, taken by the CO of the 2/4th Australian Field Ambulance, Lieutenant Colonel Arthur Hobson, shows the body of a soldier killed in the Japanese attack on the Soputa MDS on 27 November 1942. The soldier, suffering from malaria, was a patient in the MDS at the time of the attack (AWM P02424.143).

SOPUTA AFTERMATH

The harrowing attack at Soputa deeply affected those like Thompson and Kennedy who had witnessed its aftermath, but there was little time to grieve for lost mates as the continuing battles produced hundreds of casualties. On the morning after the bombing, the medical men picked up what remained of their shattered MDS piece by piece and relocated it a quarter of a mile back along the track in 'a belt of dense jungle' where the sun barely penetrated.[83] Those patients not transported to Popondetta for evacuation were transferred to this hastily established MDS, thereafter known at Soputa 2. By the time DDMS Johnston visited the area on 29 November, all patients had been relocated and the move completed. The monsoonal rains soon flooded the tents which were crowded with personnel and patients, many of whom, like Private Nick Kennedy, would have nervously looked skyward each night until exhaustion finally brought sleep:

> We have moved to a new position as we expect another blue that night. The moon makes everything as light as day. We wonder will Nip [the Japanese] send some planes over to drop some more bundles of death and destruction. Kit Gladhill and I

toss down together on our ground sheets, he thinks it is a good idea if we take it turnabout for a sleep but he is soon snoring and I follow suit.[84]

A sketch drawn by Kennedy many years after the attack showed the layout of the MDS, the areas where the bombs landed, the location of 2/4th Field Ambulance personnel when killed, and the original Soputa cemetery with 50 crosses contained within its perimeter. The sketch does not indicate the position of 7th Division Headquarters or the American medical post. The names of the seven men from Kennedy's unit who were killed and the horrific wounds that caused their deaths are graphically noted: 'disembowelled ... legs blown off at waist ... face blown off ... head blown off.'[85]

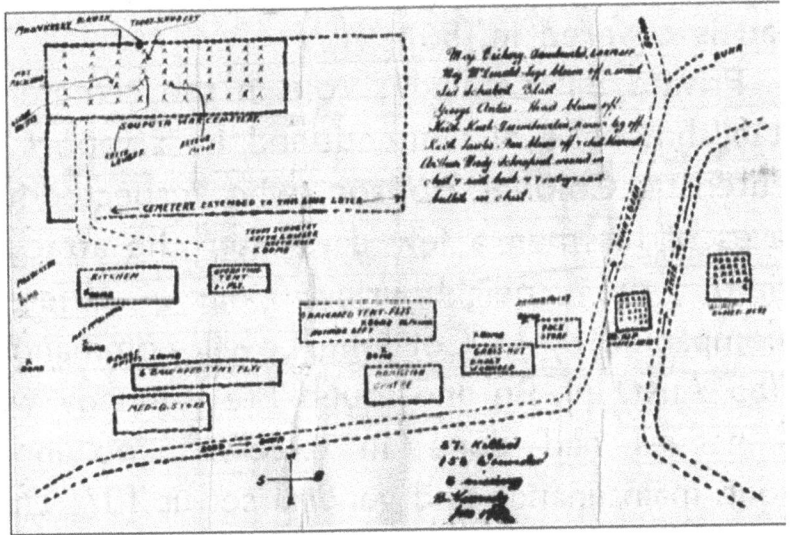

Sketch of the Soputa MDS site after the Japanese attack on 27 November 1942. The sketch was found among the belongings of Private Lawrence Nicholis (Nick) Kennedy, nursing orderly in Headquarters Company, 2/4th Australian Field Ambulance. Kennedy passed away in 1976. The smudged writing at the bottom of the page makes it difficult to determine exactly when the sketch was drawn, however, the type of paper indicates that it may have been many years after the event (author image).

As well as assisting any understanding of the attack at Soputa, the Kennedy diary and sketch contribute to the history of the original Soputa cemetery. His drawing shows the location of the graves of those killed and indicates the extent to which the cemetery was later expanded to cope with the mounting death toll. Kennedy's diary entry describing the attack also noted the role played by his brother: 'Bill buries most of our dead. It is midnight before the last of the dead is covered in.'[86]

Private Bill Kennedy's role in the cemetery's establishment is also mentioned in a report by Lieutenant Colonel Hobson, who inspected the graves of his men a few days after the attack: 'I visited the neighbouring war cemetery, accompanied by Lt Col John Lovell, commanding 53/55 Aust. Inf. Bn and found Pte Kennedy with his natives had done an excellent job in its layout, maintenance and general set-up.'[87] Little more is known of the establishment and maintenance of the Soputa cemetery where, by war's end, the bodies of 1728 servicemen were interred. It subsequently became the first war cemetery in Papua to be maintained by the Commonwealth War Graves Commission.[88]

Two additional burial sites beyond the cemetery perimeter are shown on the sketch, with crosses indicating the graves of a further 43 AIF soldiers. It is not known whether these deaths occurred as a result of the Soputa attack, or the battles around Gona, Buna and Sanananda. One site, marked with 22 crosses, is situated between the Sanananda Road and the Girua River, while the other (21 crosses) is located on the northern riverbank.[89] The bodies from various graves and small cemeteries across Papua were later disinterred and reburied by the Australian Army Graves Service in the Bomana War Cemetery near Port Moresby. Whether those buried outside the perimeter of the Soputa cemetery were later relocated to Bomana is unknown.

THE WEBB INQUIRY

Events surrounding the Japanese attack on the 2/4th Field Ambulance MDS at Soputa were examined in the first of three commissions conducted by the Chief Justice of Queensland, Sir William Webb, between 1943 and 1945.[90]

Webb heard evidence in various locations across Australia, Papua and New Guinea. The overarching remit of the Commission of Inquiry, which was conducted 'with the approval of General McArthur [sic] and General Blamey and by direction of the Government of the Commonwealth of Australia', was to determine whether any personnel on active service against the Japanese in 'or in the neighbourhood of New Guinea' had reliable information on four matters—whether the Japanese fired on the Red Cross, either at hospitals or elsewhere; whether the Japanese fired on doctors or medical detachment or aid personnel of any kind; whether the Japanese had committed treacherous or atrocious acts against Allied personnel or the natives; and whether the Japanese were guilty of acts of cannibalism.

Any person stating that such acts had occurred was required to produce full details (when, where, under what circumstances), identify witnesses to the event, and state what evidence the witnesses could provide. If, after examining the evidence, 'the opinion is formed that in the main the Japanese have honourably conducted the war according to the laws and usages of warfare' an officer was obliged to sign a statement to that effect. If it was determined that the Japanese 'have not so conducted the war', those personnel who could produce the evidence to prove this must testify before Justice Webb, who would then decide whether the matter should be referred to the United Nations Commission for the Investigation of War Crimes.[91]

The investigation into the bombing of the Soputa MDS was underpinned by Exhibit 95 Copy of General Routine Orders: Identification of Medical and Other Personnel Protected under Geneva Convention (Red Cross Convention), which set out the relevant sections of the Convention as they appeared in the Australian edition of the *Manual of Military Law*.[92] There was no ambiguity surrounding the circumstances in which protection from enemy attack would be lost: 'the privileges cease if these formations and establishments are made use of to commit acts harmful to the enemy'.[93] However, it seems there was some initial confusion as to the international application of the Convention, with Justice Webb calling for clarification:

> Will you please find out if there is at Newcastle or Sydney some officer who will give us authoritative evidence stating precisely ... what rules are there in the US Army about brassards [armbands] ... what are the Jap rules ... and is there any known Jap army rule about treating all who do not

wear distinctive Red Cross markings as combatant troops?[94]

The decision as to which Australian and American personnel would be called on to provide further evidence was based on answers to a questionnaire comprising 14 questions. The responses varied markedly in terms of the level of detail provided. The three questions most relevant to the Soputa attack were:

> 10 (a) Can you give any information regarding attacks by Japs. On Medical or Red Cross, or Aid personnel or installations?
>
> 11. Did the Medical, Red Cross or Aid personnel wear the prescribed distinguishing insignia?
>
> 12. If not, for what reason, and on whose instruction?

Webb concentrated on three main issues: the proximity of military installations and activities to the MDS, the actions of medical and military personnel in and around the MDS, and the Red Cross markings displayed by the MDS. He then assessed whether any of these factors contributed to the Japanese attack on 27 November 1942. Exhibits tabled before Webb included sworn testimonies, correspondence, photographs, technical reports and diary extracts. Extensively detailed written testimony was submitted by some personnel—including senior medical officers.

LOCATION OF MDS AND DIVISIONAL HEADQUARTERS

The fact that the MDS was located very close to the road transporting men and weapons between Popondetta airstrip and the Sanananda front line was one of the few issues on which the majority of witnesses agreed—though exactly *how* close remained debatable. The road was variously described as running through the grounds of the MDS and as close as 30 feet (10 metres) to the medical facility.[95]

It was far more difficult for Webb to ascertain the exact locations of the medical and military establishments—both in terms of their proximity to each other, and the natural environment in which they were situated. This information was crucial to Webb's assessment of whether the Japanese could have clearly identified the Australian (and American) medical posts and differentiated them from legitimate military targets.

Estimates of the distance between 7th Division Headquarters and the 2/4th Field Ambulance MDS varied widely. Sergeant Jack Clark placed 7th Division Headquarters at 'half a mile [800 metres] from the MDS at the furthest part, but may have come up to the hospital clearing', speculating that 'they [the Japanese] may have been having a shot at Div. H.Q.'[96] Warrant Officer Harry Edwards, however, recalled the MDS as being considerably closer to Divisional Headquarters, explaining that the Extreme end of the Divisional area was 200yds [182 metres] from the MDS buildings; the first bomb landed in the Divisional area and was obviously aimed at buildings there, because the planes were so low ... other planes dropped their bombs in the Divisional area and finished up by dropping them on the MDS.[97]

Evidence presented included sketches of the area by ADMS Brigadier Frank Norris and Private Reginald Balfour. Both sketches showed the location of the MDS, Divisional Headquarters and the American medical post.[98] The locations of the facilities, however, differed markedly, with Balfour's sketch also including 16th Brigade Headquarters close to the American medical post. Both agreed that the three facilities were located alongside the main road to Sanananda, and that the US 107th Clearing Station was situated furthest north. Norris situated 7th Division Headquarters between the US and Australian medical facilities, clearly stipulating that it was 500 yards south of the US facility and 400 yards north of the 2/4th MDS.[99] Balfour's drawing also differed from Norris' in showing the 2/4th

MDS situated *between* the US 107th Clearing Station and the Australian 7th Division Headquarters.[100]

ADMS Norris described the Soputa MDS as being in an exposed setting in a 'kind of clearing'. He explained that Divisional Headquarters was 'also in a relative clearing'—though not in the same clearing. According to Norris, there was jungle between the two establishments—both located in 'definite clearings'—and that the effect of this was that the hospital did not appear as though it was part of the headquarters.[101] When asked if there was jungle between the hospital and 7th Division Headquarters, Warrant Officer Ralph Albanese explained that it was 'not actually jungle but it was lightly timbered'.[102] The CO of the 2/16th Battalion, Lieutenant Colonel Frank Sublet, agreed with Norris that Divisional Headquarters was in a separate clearing, 'but I think it could have been mistaken at the time for Divisional Headquarters because Divisional Headquarters was straight up the track on the same side of the road, about 700 or 800 yards away.'[103] Private David Windsor testified that Divisional Headquarters was 'about 700 or 800 yards away in same clearing as hospital'.[104] The testimony of Lieutenant Colonel Sidney Smith when asked about legitimate military targets at

Soputa was unambiguous: 'Yes, I must admit that HQ 7 Div was adjoining the hospital.'[105]

WEAPONS, IDENTIFICATION, PROTECTION

Reports that a 25-pounder gun had been towed onto the site of the Soputa MDS in the days before the attack were carefully considered by Webb as such action could have legitimised the Japanese attack.[106] It was the evidence of Private Reginald Balfour that Webb found most persuasive on this matter, prompting him to call for further witnesses. Balfour testified that While Japanese reconnaissance planes were over on the 25th November, 1942, two days before the bombing took place, and were presumably taking photographs, a 25-pounder was driven into the hospital grounds within 25 yards of the red cross on the ground, and that the driver of the jeep conveying the gun intimated that he knew the planes were Japanese and for that reason took the gun there.[107]

The testimony of Lance Sergeant Lawrence Thompson most closely aligned with that of Balfour. Thompson stated that, on the evening of 25 November, he saw 10 Japanese Zero aircraft flying at various altitudes over the MDS and that a 25-pounder gun was passing at the time on the road, which went along the grounds of the MDS within 30ft [less than 10 metres] of the cross; the gun stopped for a few minutes; there was a flagpole with an Australian flag and a red cross; the gun was drawn by a jeep; the jeep driver did not drive into the MDS but stayed on the road about 15yds [13 metres] from the red cross.[108]

This photo, taken by the CO of the 2/4th Australian Field Ambulance, Lieutenant Colonel Arthur Hobson, shows the proximity of the Soputa MDS to the Sanananda Track, along which troops and weapons were transported to the front line. The jeep is being used to transport sick and wounded soldiers to the MDS. Note that there is a Red Cross flag on the other end of the pole displaying the Australian flag (attached to the trunk of a palm tree). These flags identify the MDS as a medical facility (AWM P02423.044).

Private William Kennedy and Corporal Roy Hargreaves saw jeeps and 25-pounder guns passing either 'through', 'not exactly through', or 'close to' the MDS when Japanese aircraft were undertaking reconnaissance in the days leading up to the bombing.[109] Signalman Horatio Sinclair, Corporal Sydney Gribble and Lance Corporal Arthur Green, however, saw no jeeps in the hospital area and 'did not see any guns about' when the Japanese reconnaissance aircraft flew over.[110] Signalman Ronald Miles stated that jeeps 'were passing up and down [the road] all the time, but not with troops or guns'.[111]

The degree to which these key issues examined by Webb—the location of the medical and military facilities, and the presence of weapons in the grounds of the MDS—contributed to the Japanese attack at Soputa was considered in relation to one overarching question: did the 2/4th Australian Field Ambulance MDS and its personnel comply with the requirements of the Identification of Medical and Other Personnel Protected under Geneva Convention as set out in the Australian Army's *Manual of Military Law*?

Testimonies regarding the location and size of the Red Cross flag on the grounds of the medical posts—and the degree to which this would have been visible to the Japanese pilots—differed. Witness estimates of the size of the flag at the Australian MDS ranged from four metres square to one measuring approximately five by six metres, and located between one and 30 metres from the road.[112] ADMS Norris stated that the Soputa MDS was the only medical post in Papua that was situated in an exposed location and that, throughout the entire campaign, only forward staging posts were identified with a Red Cross flag. Regarding the visibility of the ground flag from the air, Norris testified that at Soputa the 'Red Cross would be distinguishable about 3,000ft up, but the ground sheet is visible from 10,000ft [3000 metres]'—admitting in further questioning that he had never verified this from an aircraft.[113]

The ground flag displayed at the American clearing station that was also bombed at Soputa was described by US Sergeant Schloff as 'improvised out of a parachute'.[114] Captain Charles Lawrence, the CO of the 107th Medical Battalion, explained that 'the station was then marked with white cross [made from] 8ft long strips [and] 3ft wide'.[115] Lawrence told the inquiry that this white cross was removed on the morning of the bombing because American pilots mistook it as identifying a drop zone, and so dropped supplies on the medical post.[116] ADMS Norris, who was responsible for all Australian and American medical establishments in the area, stated that he was aware that the flag displayed by the Americans did not comply with that required by the Geneva Convention, stating 'I gave an instruction that they would use their ground sheet – and they produced a thing in white and black – I don't know where they got it from.'[117]

Many of the testimonies from Australian and American medical personnel stated that they did not wear the prescribed armbands or carry their identification cards while caring for casualties. US Captain Lawrence answered 'no ... not in the forward area'.[118] When asked who had instructed the men not to wear the armbands (and why), Lawrence replied 'Combat Commander. Red Cross would be a good mark.'[119] This was supported by US Corporal Charles Grant, who said the men were 'told not to [wear them] on grounds that the wearer is too good a target'.[120] Private Dole explained that the men had worn the insignia occasionally in Papua but 'took it off because it would be too good a target. 128th Infantry wore them and lost a few men.'[121]

The testimony of Norris—the most senior medical officer in Papua—regarding the wearing of identification insignias is candid, forthright and unapologetic. His testimony also reveals that medical personnel of all ranks regularly carried weapons with his knowledge and approval and that of senior military officers. When asked if he wore Red Cross brassards when working in a medical capacity, Norris replied that none of the men wore them. When asked if he wore anything that would distinguish him from an ordinary soldier while performing medical tasks, he replied 'No'. Norris' statement that it was a divisional matter as to whether medical units displayed 'any signs at all' was later altered to read 'operational' matter:

> It was my practice as senior medical officer to ask whether we wanted to display Geneva signs and they may say "No, we do not want to disclose, or give any marks at all." I personally always carried grenades and declined any protection whatever. I would leave my identity card behind. Every medical officer is entitled to an identity card. I always left mine behind and carried grenades ... you cannot have it both ways. I will not claim protection and then kill a Jap.[122]

Norris was invited to clarify whether he carried arms in Papua purely for defensive purposes, to which he replied:

> Yes, that is laid down [in the Geneva Convention]. Many AMC personnel carried arms ... I have asked for a ruling and a direction from Army personnel and no one has faced the responsibility for giving such a ruling. I have been quite definite in my instruction that you cannot have it both ways. You either go armed in the jungle, which is advisable, on which occasions, if you are armed, I have given instructions that all forms of protection will be discarded, such as brassards and identity cards. You either do one thing or the other.[123]

Justice Webb concluded that the 2/4th Australian Field Ambulance MDS at Soputa 'was clearly marked in the conventional way' and that there was not enough evidence to conclusively prove that the 25-pounder gun was brought onto the MDS site.[124] However, the proximity of 7th Division Headquarters to the MDS proved to be the crucial factor in Webb's final decision:

> Some witnesses appear to have assumed that as 7 Div. H.Q. was hidden among the trees the Japanese were not aware of its existence. I would not care to press this

case on such an assumption of Japanese ignorance.[125]

Having reviewed all available evidence regarding the Japanese attack on the 2/4th Field Ambulance MDS at Soputa, Webb decided not to refer the incident to the United Nations Commission for the Investigation of War Crimes. In situating the 7th Division Headquarters so close to the MDS, the protection afforded the medical facility under the Geneva Convention was lost and it was effectively legitimised as an enemy target.

CHAPTER 11

THE BEACHHEAD BATTLES AND VICTORY

'There are a lot under wooden crosses not coming back with us this trip'

NEW DDMS, OLD CHALLENGES

The day after the Japanese attack at Soputa, reinforcements from Brigadier Ivan Dougherty's 21st Brigade were flown to nearby Popondetta to strengthen Eather's 25th Brigade for the Australian attack on Gona, to the north-west. Brigadier William Johnston was replaced as DDMS on the same day (28 November). The new DDMS, Lieutenant Colonel Clive Disher, took charge of medical arrangements in Papua thereafter, with Johnston later assuming Disher's previous role of DDMS II Corps. The arrival of DDMS Disher brought renewed vigour, enthusiasm and determination to overcome the problems that had plagued the medical units in Papua. His was a more 'hands on' approach than that of his predecessor—one which was undoubtedly easier to implement at this time because of the slowly improving military situation. The unrelentingly dire nature of the medical situation in Papua since July clearly necessitated a change in leadership at some level. The Japanese attack on the medical facilities at Soputa coupled with Johnston's acknowledged delay in communicating details of the events to DGMS Burston may have added to the urgency for change.

Johnston was 55 years old and there was some speculation that the intensity of the Papuan campaign had affected his health. However, concerns over his well-being were not the primary reasons for Johnston's return to Australia.[1] While certainly weary from the many months spent in Papua, Johnston had recently flown from Port Moresby to Soputa and Popondetta after the attack on the MDS, spent a few days assessing the medical situation there, and returned to Moresby looking quite well. Disher stated that Johnston was in better condition than many other medical officers who remained in Papua.[2] In fact, he was well enough to stay on in Papua until mid-December and accompany Disher on visits to medical facilities in Port Moresby and surrounding areas, familiarising him with the locations. Before returning to Australia, Johnston reported to DGMS Burston that 'the brunt of the work is being borne by 2/4 Fd Amb ... Norris is full of praise of the extraordinarily good work done by the Field Ambulance for many weeks past.'[3]

It is important to note that Disher's appointment as DDMS was made by Advance NGF, which 'took over control of the Popondetta area' from the 7th Division, AIF—and not by DGMS Burston, whose location around the time of the Soputa attack is difficult to ascertain.[4] This is relevant in terms of issues associated with leadership and decision-making. Correspondence from Advanced Land Headquarters in Brisbane noted that DGMS Burston returned from 'New Guinea' on 24 November 1942 and left Brisbane for Sydney by aircraft on the afternoon of 26 November—the day before the Soputa attack. This seems to be supported by newspaper reports that Burston was in Sydney inspecting the first group of nursing graduates at the New South Wales VAD (Voluntary Aid Detachments) Training School on 28 November—the day after the Soputa bombing.[5] Yet an amended copy of Burston's Officer's Record of Service has him in Papua until 29 November.[6]

While the reports of DGMS Burston's trip to Port Moresby are inconsistent, by his own account Burston was neither aware of, nor involved in, the decision to replace Johnston as DDMS. On 9 December, Burston wrote to Johnston to thank him for the updates regarding the medical situation, acknowledge the difficulties the DDMS had faced in Papua, and reiterate his gratitude for his good work. Burston discussed the timing of Johnston's removal from the role of DDMS stating 'I found to my surprise when I got back, that a signal had come from New Guinea Force asking for Disher to go as soon as possible to relieve you.'[7] Burston explained that 'action had been taken on the signal and Clive [Disher] was on the move by the time I reached Melbourne.'[8]

Disher, like Johnston, was an experienced medical officer and well-respected World War I veteran. More recently, he had served as ADMS for the 6th Division in the Middle East and North Africa campaigns, before being appointed DDMS of II Corps in Australia.[9] Disher spent his first few weeks in Papua gathering information from Johnston and other medical personnel, familiarising himself with various medical facilities and generally assessing the current medical situation.[10] His willingness to travel to front-line medical facilities at Jumbora, Popondetta and Soputa to discuss the challenges with the medical personnel not only earned him the respect of the men, but enabled him to gain a true picture of the situation and to push for measures aimed at warding off further crises of care.

Disher's immediate challenges centred on relieving the front-line field ambulance units and dealing more effectively with the huge number of casualties now suffering from sickness—primarily malaria. Changes were instigated to accelerate the evacuation of the desperately ill. These soldiers were now 'passed straight through' the Soputa MDS to the staging post at Popondetta and on to Port Moresby by aircraft, primarily because the 2/4th Field Ambulance personnel were themselves too ill with the disease to care for the hundreds of malaria casualties.[11] This situation was compounded by the lack of beds in the MDS and at the Popondetta medical post, meaning that 'though men with malaria were not supposed to be sent back to the base area unless their condition warranted it ... simply, they could not be held.'[12]

A December 1942 report by the RMO 2/3rd Battalion, Captain Lynn Joseph, highlighted the suffering wrought by malaria and other diseases by this stage of the Papuan campaign. Joseph not only argued that the infantry soldiers were unfit for front-line duty, but added that 'extremely few will ever be fit for front-line service again, while the remainder will only be fit after prolonged rest in a temperate climate out of this country.'[13] He praised the troops for their courage and endurance, stating that 'no-one but the men themselves will ever know what they withstood.'[14] Joseph further argued that any move to the front line by the soldiers was not only 'futile but dangerous', adding that if they were to go into battle, neither they nor their COs could be held responsible for any failure that ensued. The men were ordered to the front line the following day.[15]

The need for battle casualties to undergo surgery as soon as possible and the continuing problems of casualty transportation and evacuation pushed the field ambulance units ever closer to the front line throughout November and December. Even the most naïve of men could see that medical personnel and patients were at increased risk of attack from deliberate or accidental fire the closer they were to the fighting, and the longer they remained there. On 6 December more than 25 Japanese aircraft bombed Popondetta with the aim of destroying a damaged Allied aircraft that had been on the airstrip for the past two days. Whether by fortune or design, no Japanese bombs landed on the nearby medical post, which held at least 400 patients.[16] Nevertheless, the need for the reinforcement of, and improvements to, front-line medical care in conjunction with the regular evacuation of casualties could no longer be ignored.

STRUGGLING ON AT SOPUTA

The 2/4th Field Ambulance continued to shoulder the bulk of the medical work at the front. At the end of November, most of the unit's personnel were based at the newly established Soputa 2 MDS: Captain John Follett and a small party were at the ADS at Popondetta, with Captain Robert Dunn at the Jumbora ADS, to the west of Soputa.[17] The Japanese attack at Soputa on 27 November had demonstrated that the risk to unarmed medical personnel and the casualties in their care was all too real. It was subsequently recommended that RAPs and other medical stations be located at greater distances from the front-line fighting than had been the case thus far. Discussions with surgeons at medical posts close to Soputa reached the somewhat unsurprising conclusion that performing operations at posts situated between Allied troops with 25-pounder guns on one side and Japanese soldiers who returned fire from the other, placed them in 'a very uncomfortable position' and did not allow them to do their best work.[18] Despite acknowledging the proximity of Divisional Headquarters to the Soputa MDS and the role this played in the Japanese attack, Johnston's report on the incident contained no recommendation that military installations should be located away from medical facilities.[19]

The Soputa 2 MDS after monsoon rains, December 1942 (AWM P02423.057).

All medical personnel continued to be overwhelmed and under-resourced, despite Disher's efforts to improve their situation. After moving into the jungle and establishing the Soputa 2 MDS, the 2/4th Field Ambulance continued its work there well into December. A more organised approach to medical care was put in place early in the month with Major Stanley McDonnell, the Deputy Assistant Director of Hygiene, stationed at Soputa to act as coordinator and medical representative of NGF. This was a much-needed development, but did not address the key question of personnel numbers that was of most concern to the unit. Similarly, the procurement of a converted car to serve as a motor ambulance was a welcome, if simplistic, solution to a complex problem. A maximum of five patients (four lying and one sitting) could be transported at a time.[20]

On 1 December, Hobson reported that his 2/4th Field Ambulance at Soputa was struggling to cope due to '9 ORs [other ranks] sick with malaria and most of the others tending to run temperatures, thus making it difficult to provide sufficient personnel for the duties.'[21] Nineteen members of the 14th Field Ambulance arrived the next day. Their CO, Lieutenant Colonel Malcolm Earlam, observed that the majority of 2/4th personnel were suffering from inadequately suppressed malaria, despite taking 20 grains of quinine per day—the usual suppressive dose was half this amount.[22]

The latest policy laid down by ADMS Norris in relation to malaria was that infantry soldiers suffering from Pyrexia [fever] of Unknown Origin (PUO) and those who could not return to their unit within a day were to be evacuated to Port Moresby, while divisional and corps soldiers such as field ambulance personnel were to remain in their lines and be given a full course of anti-malarial treatment.[23] When 16 members of the 2/4th Field Ambulance were suffering from malaria in early December, Hobson cited the Army's policy of maintaining troops in the field as the reason he was 'compelled to start courses of treatment and get my AAMC personnel back to duty as soon as possible so as to cope with the influx of sick and wounded until relief or reinforcements arrive.'[24]

Private Nick Kennedy and his brother, Bill, had survived the Japanese attack at Soputa and both men continued to care for casualties at Soputa 2. Nick's diary entries during this time suggest a medical unit pushed well beyond its limits:

> Where we are at present there is mud six inches deep. There have been heavy storms every night, this black mud has a hell of a stench. Everything goes blue mouldy, and matches are hard to strike. A terrific storm breaks one night at midnight. We are all washed out, a b....... [sic]of a place, no doubt. The rations have been a little better of late and we are getting some smokes. Most of us are down with malaria. Our R.S.M.[Regimental Sergeant Major] is extra crook, just skin and bone, the same

as most of us, mentally and physically buggered.[25]

A wounded V125229 Private Ronald Weakley of the 39th Battalion arrives on a stretcher at the Soputa 2 MDS, December 1942 (AWM 013926).

The men had no choice but to endure, as sick and wounded soldiers continued to stream into the MDS. On 4 December, the US 126th Clearing Station—also hit during the Japanese attack at Soputa—was relocated to Dobodura. A US Portable Hospital would take over its former site in the Soputa area, but this had yet to be established. Recently arrived American troops were heavily engaged in the fighting despite the lack of their own medical facilities, and so it was the Australians who initially carried this burden. Forty-two Americans suffering various wounds and illnesses walked into the 2/4th MDS at Soputa 2 on 4 December. The first American death in the facility occurred that same day, when a wounded soldier succumbed to peritonitis. It was also on this day that ADMS Norris called a conference to organise relief at the Popondetta staging post and begin arrangements for 14th Field Ambulance personnel to proceed to Soputa, with a view to finally relieving the 2/4th Field Ambulance.

The arrival of the Americans both helped and hindered the work of the Australians. Their medical staff provided valuable assistance and equipment in those first frantic days at Soputa in late November. However, the fact that the US medical facilities were not fully established, staffed and utilised until early December meant that many of their sick and wounded soldiers were treated in Australian facilities. Military activity around Gona, Buna and along the Sanananda Track was increasing during this period as more men and weapons were thrown into the battles. Allied attacks on Japanese positions had failed to break through thus far, with only small gains made and any real progress effectively stalled. By 6.00pm on 4 December, Soputa 2 MDS held over 300 patients (eight Australian and 27 American battle casualties as well as 251 Australian and 38 American sick). A further 146 casualties had been evacuated.[26] Surgery continued the following day as two Australian and 54 US battle casualties were admitted.

Within a few days it became necessary for Lieutenant Colonel Hobson to establish a second operating theatre due to the 'record influx' of battle casualties, most of whom were Americans. By 9.00pm on 7 December, Hobson reported that 'every available shelter was occupied ... there is not an empty stretcher ... high sick rate among 2/4 and 2/6 Fd Amb personnel with malaria. I have only had 42 all ranks available for work from these units.'[27] Hobson must have welcomed the establishment of the 17th US Portable Hospital on 8 December, especially given that 30 of the 2/4th Field Ambulance personnel, 26 members of the 2/6th Field Ambulance detachment, and four personnel from the 14th Field Ambulance were incapacitated by malaria. The decision was made to continue treating all medical personnel with daily quinine with the aim of suppressing the symptoms of malaria and so 'keep them on their feet'.[28] Gona finally fell to the Australians the following day.

American soldiers transporting casualties to an ADS at Buna, December 1942. Note that the soldiers are not wearing Red Cross armbands and are carrying weapons (AWM 013991).

The incumbent Australian DDMS, Johnston, and his successor, Disher, visited Colonel Blank of the US Medical Combined Operations Service Command to discuss the urgent need to move American medical units forward in response to the push on Buna and Sanananda. Disher inspected the US Portable Hospital at Soputa on 10 December. This facility was acting as a clearing hospital, but still lacked many vital medical supplies. The Portable Hospital had been set up in the open and was devoid of cover—despite the recent attacks on Australian and American medical units at Soputa. Disher advised that it should be moved into nearby jungle as a precaution.

DDMS Disher travelled to Dobodura by air the following day to meet with American Generals Eichelberger and Beyers and inspect the medical facilities of the 32nd US Division Headquarters. Disher noted that both generals 'seemed anxious for help and advice regarding medical matters', which indicated to him the level of unpreparedness and lack of understanding of what was required medically.[29] The attitude of the CO of the 2nd US Field Hospital seemed to support this conclusion—this officer was upset that his hospital was holding 165 patients, when it had been established to hold 160. Disher patiently explained to him that 'our MDS had held over 600 on one night and last night over 300, but it didn't seem to register.'[30]

There were other notable differences between Australian and American attitudes. Discussions revealed that some US medical officers thought they were positioned too far forward and felt they would be better placed two or three miles back from the front, so they could work without being exposed to constant machine-gun and mortar fire. Disher generally agreed with this assertion, while also commenting that they were being overcautious in some matters. He observed that they were 'all inclined to be a bit jumpy as a result of bombing, and go to earth on the slightest alarm ... could not convince them that they needn't be quite so serious about such things.'[31] In hindsight, many of the fears seem justified given the locations in which some US medical personnel found themselves. Echoing DDMS Johnston's observations, Disher noted that the US 19th Portable Hospital near Gona had initially been located 'in between some of our 25 pounders [and] ensuing fire from the Japs put them in a very uncomfortable position and they had moved back.' The 17th Portable Hospital was also sited close to the 25-pounders, with one surgeon expressing the opinion that better work could be done if they were sited a little further back from the fighting.[32]

SOME RELIEF

Disher's inspections of Australian and American medical facilities at the front and in the base area appear to mark the first time that this important task was undertaken to this extent in Papua. Such visits enabled the formulation of a more comprehensive plan for future medical care. He worked closely with ADMS Norris and others to improve aspects of the medical plans identified as major concerns—including evacuation and the regular supply of anti-malarial treatment. When he returned to Port Moresby and reported on the state of the American medical units at the front, he would surely have been disappointed with the ambivalent reaction to much of his advice. The US Corps surgeon, Merhee, initially agreed with Disher's suggestion, but later reconsidered and decided in favour of the hospital units bringing their service forward to the troops, rather than requiring casualties to be brought further back to the hospital. Disher essentially dismissed this approach on the basis that the American was inexperienced and had not yet been to the front. On updating US Colonel Blank regarding the American medical situation at the front, Disher was similarly underwhelmed by his response, stating that '[I] doubt if a word sank in as he never seems to concentrate for more than one second on anything.'[33]

The Australian situation at Soputa and nearby Popondetta was closely monitored by Disher and

ADMS Norris throughout December. Unforeseen problems included the grounded aircraft on the Popondetta airstrip that had attracted the attention of the Japanese, and flooding rain, which conspired to hamper treatment and evacuation. Improvements to the supply of medical stores, a gradual slowing of battle casualties, increased evacuations, and the arrival by air of additional 14th Field Ambulance personnel finally brought some relief for those struggling on at Soputa. It did not come a moment too soon. From a total of 83 men in November, the effective strength of the 2/4th Field Ambulance was reduced to two officers and 33 other ranks by 14 December. The 2/6th detachment could muster just one officer and 12 other ranks from a total of 35 men.[34]

There was a limited pool from which to draw experienced medical personnel. The 2/5th Field Ambulance had laboriously made its way by land and sea to Buna from Milne Bay in support of the 18th Brigade. The bulk of this unit, however, remained at Waigani in Milne Bay.[35] That the decision to add a 'small surgical kit' to the equipment of the CO, Major John Lavarack, was not made until final instructions were received on the morning of the detachment's departure gives some indication of the degree to which the intensity of the beachhead battles was underestimated. Within 30 minutes of the attack by the 2/9th Infantry Battalion at 7.00am on 18 December, battle casualties began arriving at Lavarack's RAP, which had been hastily set up between Cape Endaiadere and Hariko. Within the first 12 hours of establishing the facility, 110 battle casualties were treated, with most suffering from 'small perforating wounds of chest, abdomen and limbs'.[36] Due to the failure of additional medical personnel to arrive prior to the fighting, the most seriously wounded Australians had to be evacuated from Lavarack's RAP to the nearby US Portable Hospital for surgery. Approximately 10 Australians were operated on here, with four later dying.[37]

A group of 'walking wounded' soldiers waiting at the Soputa 2 MDS for a jeep to transport them to Popondetta airstrip for evacuation to Port Moresby (AWM P02423.062).

Lavarack's account vindicated the views expressed to Disher by the American surgeon, Merhee—that it was better to take the hospital to the soldiers rather than move badly wounded soldiers back to the hospital:

> The Americans found that patients took at least 24 hours to get to Moresby at the best. They hoped, by having good surgical teams forward, to save abdomens and shock cases which might not survive a trip to base. Our nearest surgery was at Moresby and it seemed worth while [sic] trying to do selected cases here, evacuating the bulk.[38]

The light sections from the 2/5th Field Ambulance (under Captains Scott and Edelman) that were sent from Milne Bay to assist Lavarack and his men at Buna finally arrived on 19 December. Another small group of 2/5th Field Ambulance personnel set out from Waigani to join them on 20 December.[39]

In some ways, and in some locations, the medical situation in Papua slowly improved in the final month of 1942. For example, the most rapid aerial evacuation and treatment of a casualty to date occurred on 16 December when a soldier wounded in the fighting at 8.00am underwent surgery at the Soputa MDS at 9.00am and arrived at the 2/9th AGH at Port Moresby at 2.00pm, just six hours after being wounded. ADMS Norris noted that this coincided with the last casualty being evacuated from the Myola MDS, nine weeks after being wounded—wryly commenting 'such are the incongruities of war'.[40]

That it had taken five months to reach the point where prompt medical evacuation from the front line was possible, and more than two months to evacuate casualties from Myola was as bittersweet as it was incongruous. Seventy-five field ambulance personnel wracked by malaria made their way to Popondetta airstrip from Soputa two days later to await aerial evacuation to Port Moresby. This sorry scene in the northern sector also saw those members of the 2/6th Field Ambulance who had been at Myola since October finally close their MDS on 19 December and make their way—on foot—down the Kokoda Track towards Ilolo, for a period of rest and rehabilitation. 'Thus', mused Colonel Chenhall, 'the final curtain falls on the MDS Myola after a period of two months.'[41]

Although an end to their own ordeal was now in sight, Lieutenant Colonel Hobson and many of his 2/4th Field Ambulance remained at Soputa until Christmas Eve 1942. They joined medical personnel and casualties still waiting at Popondetta for aerial evacuation, only to find themselves spending Christmas Day beside the airstrip. It was not until 29 December that the last of the 2/4th Field Ambulance personnel were flown back to Port Moresby.

Private Kennedy's writings during these final few days provide an insight into the emotions of the field ambulance personnel—the 'ordinary ranks' who had undertaken such an extraordinary mission in their country's name. Kennedy's words encapsulated the exhaustion, the sadness, the loss, the frustration, and the dangers encountered throughout three long months of administering medical care in Papua:

> We never want to see or hear of this part of New Guinea again. There are a lot under wooden crosses not coming back with us this trip. We arrive at Popinditta [sic] air strip at 12p.m. We are camped on the end of the strip. They say there may be planes in to take us out any day. We think where we camped is the world's worst. If they bomb the strip and miss it, they are sure to collect us. Every day we think that we may get away, but no planes. We are all worn out, sick with fever, and getting cranky with one another.
>
> Every night there is nuisance raids, so that one seems to be in and out of a trench most of the night. A full moon now

which makes things more unpleasant. Xmas Eve comes, a great b...... of a place to spend Xmas everyone thinks. Well it could have been worse, we could have been back along the track under one of those wooden crosses.

Xmas eve night is anything but pleasant. Nip planes are over from about 9pm to 4am. Just get out of a hole, and lay down for a while and the b...... are over again. It is daylight before we get much sleep. Xmas Eve 42 has not been a real happy one. We have a bully beef stew for Xmas day. Well we curse everything possible, and call ourselves silly b......... for ever joining this army.[42] [original punctuation]

COMPLAINTS AT POPONDETTA

With the evacuation of the 2/4th Field Ambulance from Soputa, the situation was such that the 14th Field Ambulance 'now held the medical position in their hands on the Australian Gona-Sanananda front.'[43] Small detachments of medical personnel remained dotted along the Kokoda Track and dispersed among facilities in the forward areas throughout December and into January 1943.[44] The presence of American medical personnel and facilities was crucial to the provision of care throughout this period, with statistics showing that hundreds of Australians were treated in US facilities.[45] A small group of 14th Field Ambulance personnel ran the staging post at Popondetta from late November until 93 members of the 10th Field Ambulance took over, allowing the 14th to move to Soputa 2 MDS and relieve the 2/4th Field Ambulance on 18 December. The 14th Field Ambulance was finally flown to Port Moresby when the 10th Field Ambulance took over in the forward area on 25 January 1943. During that five-week period (18 December–25 January), the 14th Field Ambulance cared for almost 700 battle casualties and 3000 sick.[46]

The 14th Field Ambulance, a militia unit, had been in Papua since June 1942—well before the Japanese landing. This was the unit that had provided the only medical care available to the 39th Battalion during the Australian advance from July until September. Members of the 14th Field Ambulance had reinforced medical posts at Myola, Kokoda and Soputa, along the Kokoda Track, and in the base area around Port Moresby during both the Australian withdrawal and advance. In short, this unit provided medical care to militia and AIF soldiers during every stage of the Papuan campaign. Little wonder then that complaints regarding their work at the Popondetta staging post—which encompassed everything from ill-discipline and inadequate food to poor treatment and the evacuation process—were so passionately and empathically refuted by the same officer who had led them throughout the entire Papuan campaign, Lieutenant Colonel Malcolm Earlam.

The official complaint was lodged on 17 December—the day before the 14th Field Ambulance left Popondetta to relieve the 2/4th Field Ambulance at Soputa. It was signed by Major Andrew Buckley of the 2/2nd AIF Infantry Battalion and counter-signed by four other officers who had been patients at Popondetta in December. The minutiae of the complaints, as much as the complaints themselves, reveal a lack of comprehension regarding the conditions under which the medical personnel in Papua had laboured for months. The complaints can be divided into those primarily concerned with medical treatment, and those centred on issues of discipline.

Those regarding medical treatment included the lack of thorough, regular medical inspections and sick parades, the failure to ensure that patients took their malaria medications, a severe lack of hygiene measures, and no discernible system of evacuation. One of the more serious issues raised was the suggestion that the death of a patient evacuated to the 2/9th AGH in Port Moresby could have been avoided had he received prompt treatment at the Popondetta post.[47] The officers also maintained that there was no system of evacuation for fever cases, stating that it was basically a case of 'survival of the fittest', with those who could walk reaching the aircraft before those who were too sick to leave their tents. It was noted too that, despite earlier aerial attacks on medical posts and headquarters, 'a number of white tents were placed on the edge of the strip, with no attempt to camouflage them or move them to under the trees ... at one time there were approximately 400 personnel in an area 150yds x 50yds [135 metres by 45 metres].'[48]

Historical tensions between the AIF and CMF (militia) can be discerned in some of the non-medical matters raised by the AIF officers concerning the behaviour of the 'chocos' of the 14th Field Ambulance.[49] They were appalled by the ill-disciplined and shirtless nursing orderlies who showed no respect for rank and frequently referred to officers as 'Sport' or 'Dig' (Digger). Buckley stated that the field ambulance men continually complained and squabbled and 'showed themselves most proficient in the use of bad language ...[They] could more than hold their own with AIF troops.'[50]

Food was also a contentious issue, with complaints ranged from the failure to offer patients a cup of tea on arrival and the lack of eating utensils, to rations that were of a poor quality for patients (bully beef, rice and very few vegetables) but much better for medical personnel (sausages, meat and vegetables, jam). The lack of a good cup of tea seemed to have especially rankled Buckley, who observed a seemingly hierarchical dispensing system that was not to his liking. He noted that the tea often ran out despite ample supplies of water and wood for heating (as well as 'natives' to fetch both) 'but there was always a Dixie left for staff ... patients asking for tea were told that it was for the staff NOT the patients.'[51]

Official responses to the complaints varied. DDMS Disher wrote to the ADMS 6th Division, Colonel George Maitland, and to Major General Frank Norris, ADMS 7th Division. Interestingly, Disher's note to Maitland was more strongly worded than that written to Norris, under whose command the 14th Field Ambulance had served for most of the campaign.[52] However, Maitland was aware of the issues as it was he who had suggested that Buckley lodge his complaints in writing.[53] Norris expressed complete confidence in Major Eben Hipsley, the officer in charge at Popondetta. The ADMS also carefully noted that, at the time of the complaint, Popondetta was not under his (Norris') administration, but that of Advance NGF. This seemed to be a case of 'splitting hairs'—while the report was certainly lodged after Norris ceased administering the area, the incidents that formed the basis of the complaint occurred on his watch.[54] Disher explained that he was personally acquainted with Major Buckley and felt his word could be relied on. He suggested that the 14th Field Ambulance unit as a whole be given 'a good kick in the pants' and its staff reminded that they were there to give service 'and service 24 hours on end'.[55] That officers like Disher, Maitland and Norris, who had all seen the medical situation first-hand, could distance themselves from the reality of administering medical care in Papua is surprising. The readiness with which they apportioned blame must have been disappointing for the CO of the 14th Field Ambulance, Earlam, especially given the unit's indefatigable service in Papua since June. Earlam's response was comprehensive and uncompromisingly candid, letting the facts speak for themselves.

Earlam explained that severe shortages of men and equipment had meant that just 25 members of the 14th Field Ambulance arrived at

Popondetta in response to a request by then DDMS, Johnston, on 21 November. This small group was not told of the nature of the task before arriving. The party consisted mainly of stretcher-bearers, with just one corporal assigned to nursing duties. These men were assisted by six Papuan carriers. On average, three field ambulance personnel were unavailable for work at Popondetta at any one time, due to either malaria or exhaustion. The duties required to be undertaken by such a small number of staff day and night meant they were always hopelessly overstretched. For example, five men were allocated to ward duties, one to the orderly room and two worked in hygiene and sanitation. The reception and admission of patients, the unloading of jeeps, loading of aircraft, and general duties such as cleaning, cooking and feeding were completed by a group of just seven men.[56]

Earlam drew on extracts from the unit's war diary entries to illustrate the extreme conditions confronting his men at Popondetta. These included an influx of casualties in the lead-up to the planned military push towards the beaches, an aircraft crash on the airstrip which prevented evacuations, and the aftermath of the attack on the nearby Soputa MDS. He pointed out that on the day prior to the arrival of Major Buckley, there were already 140 patients at the

Popondetta post. By 5 December there were almost 400 casualties and no available beds, groundsheets or blankets. Two days later, there were 450 patients, some of whom were debilitated by typhus or malaria, as well as an acute shortage of nursing orderlies and no evacuations. Hundreds more casualties were being held in the open area near the airstrip. Apart from medical stores and a minimal amount of eating utensils, the group had been supplied with a total of seven tents, 18 stretchers, 40 groundsheets, 50 blankets and the same number of mosquito nets. Those in authority were aware of the situation: 'DADMS has been notified of the position here. Major Denville of "Q" Corps H.Q. has also been notified. Unless more transport is available a holding policy with the staff to do it must be formulated for this area.'[57]

Earlam worked his way through each complaint methodically and addressed every criticism. Many of the complaints regarding the distribution of food rations and tea, cleanliness and hygiene standards, were either disputed outright or explained in the context of the shortage of personnel available to undertake such tasks. The lack of camouflage for tents set up near the airstrip was attributed to the Papuan carriers, who had erected the tents to give shelter to the casualties without the knowledge or authority of officers. Once constructed, they could not be moved immediately due to the shortage of personnel to perform the task.

Earlam admitted and acknowledged failings where appropriate, while also explaining the context in which such deficiencies occurred:

> The medical inspection in most cases was certainly brief, and necessarily so; ... Officers were certainly not segregated from O.R.'s [other ranks]. I have never before encountered Officers who expected it in a Fd Amb; ... Complaints by orderlies about the amount of work were quite justified. Four hours night duty immediately following 12 hours day shift was quite unreasonable but had to be done ... Complaint about the staff being improperly dressed would appear to have been included in order that nothing possible might be left out. I regard it as entirely frivolous.[58]

Complaints about medical treatment were similarly addressed. Earlam stated that patients were issued with six quinine tablets (not two as stated) and all battle casualties received 10 grains of quinine nightly. A daily sick parade was held, which involved examinations of outpatients, new admissions and those awaiting evacuation. Every man reporting as sick was given adequate doses of quinine, aspirin or other treatment as required—a task that took two medical officers a day to complete. Earlam admitted that the sheer number of casualties meant that it was difficult to give adequate attention to all, pointing out that Hipsley (the medical officer in charge) made regular rounds and examined those brought to his attention. Hipsley told Earlam that he did recall seeing the sick soldier who later died in hospital (Private Dunn) after being requested to do so by an orderly, but that he could not find Dunn when he again attempted to check on his condition.[59]

Earlam was adamant that casualty evacuation procedures had existed and were followed at Popondetta. Battle casualties were initially given priority for evacuation over sick soldiers until the new system instigated by ADMS Norris prioritised medical casualties in response to the overwhelming number of malaria cases at the front. Earlam's reply to the allegation that the evacuation system was nonexistent and relied on a 'survival of the fittest' approach was caustic and scathing:

> The statement that fit patients reached plane first while the really sick remained in their tent is in at least one instance correct as on one occasion two Officers, both medical cases, and neither really sick, walked

on to the landing strip without authority, with the apparent intention of boarding a plane, and were sent back to their lines.[60]

It is not clear whether Earlam was implying that the two officers who attempted to board the aircraft were signatories to the complaint. It is known, however, that Major Buckley was admitted to Popondetta with malaria and was evacuated in early December.[61] Earlam made no secret of his opinion of Buckley and his failure to follow correct procedure by initially complaining in person to Hipsley, the officer in charge at Popondetta. Earlam concluded his report by expressing admiration for his small detachment of field ambulance personnel at Popondetta who had

> succeeded with almost hopelessly inadequate resources in carrying out an almost impossible task which by virtue of operational necessity had to be given it [and] reflects the greatest credit on all the Officers and men concerned.[62]

VICTORY IN PAPUA

That the Japanese continued to mount such a determined defence of the coastline well into January 1943 despite being 'reduced in numbers, short of ammunition, food and supplies ... weak in artillery ... attacked by our Air Force and artillery and [with] no adequate counter-measures' confounded some Allied commanders.[63] However, Norris later wrote that some officers, such as Brigadier George Wootten, felt it was just a matter of time until the enemy was beaten: 'They'll break, said George, they'll break.'[64] In response to the intense fighting and in anticipation of a final push towards the coast, a detachment of 36 medical personnel was formed by fusing together three groups of 2/5th Field Ambulance personnel that had been sent from Milne Bay. This unit was to replace the recently evacuated 2/4th Field Ambulance in the forward area throughout January 1943. The group was required to be 'elastic' so as to undertake the wide range of tasks now assigned to them.[65] Medical personnel capable of undertaking a full range of duties, rather than those with specialist training, had been included in the unit. They were variously responsible for the ADS at Buna, the evacuation of casualties to Dobodura airstrip, manning the advanced operating theatre in conjunction with the 10th Field Ambulance, working with the 14th Field Ambulance at the Soputa MDS, and providing light sections on the Sanananda Road and Killerton Track.[66]

The issue of protection for medical posts situated so near to the front line continued to present problems: 'the tracks behind the infantry, as they move forward, are almost no man's land ... the ambulance is left to bridge the gap so left and must look after itself in its own perimeter in the case of forward posts.'[67] For example, the forward ADS at Cape Killerton (to the west of Sanananda) was beyond the limits of the jeeps. Battle casualties were instead evacuated from the ADS by field ambulance bearers and then handed over to Papuan carriers, who walked up to two miles 'through atrocious country', often under sniper fire.[68] The possibility of medical personnel coming under enemy attack was further increased when some medical posts were sited near reserve companies of soldiers, and the stretcher-bearers moved forward with armed parties, including ammunition units.

Field ambulance stretcher-bearers and Papuan carriers were sometimes required to carry patients through the mangroves and jungles for 10 miles or more. It was a case of weighing up the risks to the field ambulance personnel and patients against the realities of casualty care in an environment such as this. The CO of the 2/5th Field Ambulance, Major Lavarack, reasoned that 'it is difficult to see how one can avoid arming bearers for their own protection in the conditions. One felt that an ambulance might have its own armed protection. Infantry battalions can hardly be asked to spare men.'[69] It should be noted that casualty evacuation during this period was also heavily reliant on American medical posts and personnel in the area.

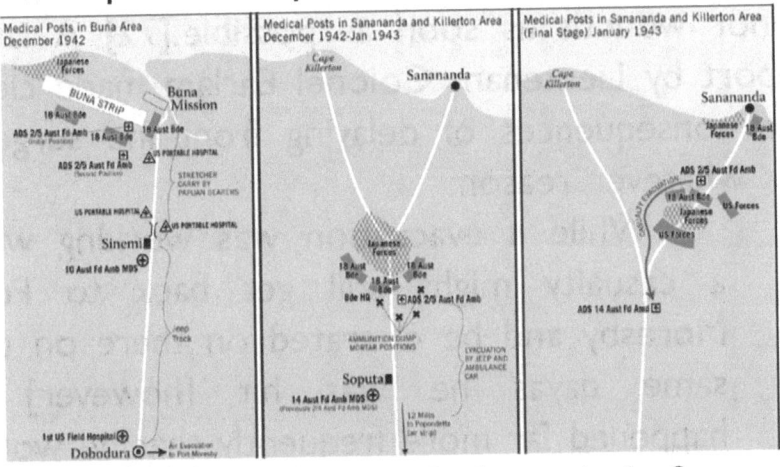

Map 11.1 Australian and US medical posts in the Sanananda area, January 1943

On 1 January 1943, General MacArthur anticipated an imminent and 'decisive victory' in the 'bitter and desperate' Papuan campaign.[70] The fight against the Japanese was accordingly ramped up in an effort to finally drive the Allied forces through to the sea. Giropa Point fell that day, while Buna Mission, Buna and Cape Endaiadere all fell in relatively quick succession in early January.[71] Medical personnel adapted to the shifting military situation. Consultant surgeon at Soputa, Lieutenant Colonel Charles Littlejohn, had influenced ADMS Norris in the decision to bring forward four surgical teams to operate at the MDS during December and January. This was prompted by Littlejohn's witnessing the suffering and delayed recovery that resulted from the failure to operate on relatively minor wounds as soon as possible.[72] A later report by Lieutenant Colonel Earlam made clear the consequences of delaying front-line surgery for whatever reason:

> While if evacuation was working well, a casualty might still get back to Port Moresby and be operated on there on the same day as he was hit [however] it happened far more frequently that he would have to wait at Popondetta, on occasions for some days, until planes landed. This factor naturally prolonged convalescence to a considerable degree.[73]

Forward surgical teams were moved to the area around Sanananda and Soputa after the fall of Buna on 3 January.[74] These initially performed only those operations deemed critical to save the patient's life before evacuation—such as abdominal surgery. Eventually, the arrival of extra personnel and equipment meant that most necessary operations could be performed before patients were evacuated by jeep or bearer to the airstrip and on to Port Moresby for further care. Operations undertaken by these front-line surgical teams included all head, chest and abdominal wounds, as well as compound fractures and haemorrhages. The steady stream of sick soldiers—as many as 170 admissions on a single day—added to the workload of the MDS.[75]

Surgeons and medical personnel readied themselves for the next wave of casualties expected from the planned advance of the Australian 18th Brigade (sent from Milne Bay in December) and the US 163rd Regiment on Sanananda.[76] After a short respite, the medical units were once again overwhelmed by battle casualties when the attack was launched on 12 January 1943. The Soputa MDS was already holding over 100 patients and almost 300 casualties remained at Popondetta. Shifts of surgical teams at Soputa worked day and night to cope with the newly arrived casualties—operating on all fractures, head and chest wounds. Although the wounded were treated swiftly, the challenges of aerial evacuation regularly hampered efforts to quickly move patients through the MDS and on to hospital at Port Moresby. When the Japanese began to evacuate the area around Sanananda on 13 January, further offensive Allied action 'was not contemplated as little ground had been gained and casualties were extremely heavy.'[77]

Aerial reconnaissance photograph of coastline between Sanananda and Gona, 14 January 1943. The Sanananda–Soputa road is in the foreground (AWM 106527).

This decision was no doubt welcomed by medical personnel at Popondetta where 'saturation point had been reached; blankets and food were scarce ... the strip organisation could carry on one more day without further air-lift, but after that patients would have to be taken to Dobodura by native carriers.'[78] The arrival of fine weather after days of flooding rain allowed the aerial evacuation of 400 patients from Popondetta that same day. This also eased the strain at the Soputa MDS, where the number of casualties had been slowly increasing given the inability to evacuate to Popondetta due to the rain. The arrival of DDMS Disher at the front must have lifted spirits as he visited medical posts in the area, moving medical and surgical staff between facilities to plug the gaps in personnel. Casualties increased again during the week of 17 January 1943, as first Killerton and then Sanananda were definitively claimed by the Allies. In a rousing, hyperbolic speech that evening, General Blamey declared to the Australian public that the Enemy had been defeated and his army in Papua destroyed by the superior quality of the Allied troops, who had shown the proud Asiatic that he was an inferior creature to the product of Western civilisation. They had out-marched him, they had out fought him, they had inflicted casualties far heavier than they themselves suffered.[79]

Organised Japanese resistance at Sanananda ended on 22 January 1943, with the Allied victory in Papua officially declared the following day.[80] The final week of fighting had seen over 200 battle casualties treated at Soputa and the declaration of victory did not put an end to the work of the field ambulance units. On the night that victory was declared, two surgical teams completed 39 operations across two makeshift theatres—one under blackout conditions, the other in the open. Those in the open theatre ceased work only during the periods when enemy aircraft, which were still flying over the area, were directly overhead.[81]

Though the organised fighting had ceased, the evacuation of soldiers who remained sick and wounded among the swamps and mangroves continued to present significant challenges. Plans to utilise jeeps for the task faltered when these vehicles were unable to negotiate the boggy terrain and thick jungle. Armed Australian stretcher-bearers did much of the initial work on foot until Papuans carrying supplies forward were back-loaded with patients. In a statement that encapsulates the attitudes of the Allies to the local Papuan men, in terms of their value to the campaign, the CO of the 10th Field Ambulance, Lieutenant Colonel Edward Palmer, prosaically explained that, in circumstances such as those at Buna and Sanananda, 'the native carrier is best considered as an Ambulance Waggon ... he cannot be used where he is liable to be fired on.'[82]

The 14th Field Ambulance was finally relieved on 25 January 1943, with Earlam's weary men arriving back in Port Moresby by air a week later. Statistics for the Soputa 2 MDS show that the pressure on the 14th Field Ambulance in the five weeks since 18 December was intense and sustained. Of 694 battle casualties admitted to the medical post, 336 underwent operations and

651 were eventually evacuated. Just nine of the 694 were returned to their units after treatment and 34 soldiers died. The sick made up the bulk of casualties treated by the unit, with 2902 admissions, 2590 evacuations, 311 returned to their units and one death.[83] Sickness also took a heavy toll on the medical personnel. Like the 2/4th Field Ambulance it had relieved, the 14th Field Ambulance was devastated by disease throughout the campaign. Yet just 31 of 156 personnel were evacuated. A further 102 men were treated for malaria and other illnesses in the line and continued working. One member of the unit died. Some 20% (31) of the men suffered dysentery, while a staggering 75% (117) of 14th Field Ambulance personnel were diagnosed with malaria—most contracting the disease north of Kokoda.[84]

Major Lavarack's 2/5th Field Ambulance detachment, sent to Buna from Milne Bay in December and January, remained in the area until it was flown back to Port Moresby on 15 February 1943. Two members had earlier been evacuated due to illness and one (Private Joseph Rhodes) was killed on 2 January while evacuating casualties from the RAP at Buna.[85] Casualties who remained in the forward area after victory was declared were flown out when the Popondetta medical post closed on 7 February

1943. Members of the 10th Field Ambulance remained at Soputa MDS until it closed shortly after Popondetta.[86] Medical responsibility for the Australians who were still in the northern areas was then transferred to the Americans—any soldier needing treatment or evacuation after this time was held in American medical facilities and evacuated from Dobodura Drome if necessary. Towards the end of February, disparate Australian medical personnel in the forward area made their way to the camp hospital at Oro Bay, 15 miles south-east of Buna, and were consolidated as a unit under Lieutenant Colonel Palmer of the 10th Field Ambulance.[87] Australian field ambulance personnel had been involved in every stage of the medical care of Australian soldiers in Papua since July 1942.

CHAPTER 12

YEAR'S END AT PORT MORESBY

'The lack of an effective system'

COSC AND CASUALTY EVACUATIONS

Balancing the experiences of the forward field ambulance units with the challenges that confronted medical personnel in the base area around Port Moresby during the final weeks of the campaign provides a comprehensive understanding of the medical situation in Papua. Such an overview also provides an insight into what was waiting for the casualties and field ambulance men once they were finally evacuated from the northern battlefields of Gona, Buna and Sanananda. The fact that no large-scale program of medical evacuation from Papua to Australia had yet been implemented meant that these casualties from the beachheads, who now swamped the basic Australian medical facilities in and around Port Moresby, could go no further.[1]

Responsibility for the impasse rested with instructions given by General Thomas Blamey, with the implicit acquiescence of DGMS Samuel Burston. The military imperative drove Blamey's decision to hold thousands of casualties in Papua for the duration of the campaign, with little regard for the inevitable medical consequences:

> Evacuation to the mainland was a possible means of relief [of the medical situation], but not one in accordance with military policy, for since Blamey's ruling on this important question, all efforts had been made to keep men in New Guinea who were considered fit to return to duty after a course of treatment for malaria.[2]

The rate at which the soldiers in Papua continued to fall ill from malaria led medical officers to conclude that 'if all Malarial patients were retained on the Island, existing Medical Units would not be able to cope with the position.'[3] As a result, the two key concerns for the medical facilities in the base area during the final weeks of the fighting centred on the evacuation of casualties and the provision of hospital beds.

Burston was regularly apprised of the medical situation in Papua, though it is doubtful that its dire nature was accurately conveyed to him. In his reports, Brigadier William Johnston (who had been DDMS in Papua until replaced by Disher in December 1942) represented the evacuation process from the front line to the base area at this time as a relatively seamless operation, interrupted only by the vagaries of nature. The organised way that casualties were unloaded from the aircraft at Ward's Drome near Port Moresby, transferred to motor ambulances, passed through the 5th Clearing Station and dispersed to appropriate medical facilities in the base area was described by Johnston as 'smashing'.[4] Months earlier, he had given Burston an overview of conditions at the Myola MDS that was overly optimistic in light of Colonel Chenhall's frantic communiqués—explaining that, while the hundreds of casualties there were not lying on a 'bed of roses' the situation was not really too bad.[5] Neither of Johnston's accounts accurately conveyed the suffering that resulted from the inadequacies of the casualty evacuation system—both from the front line to the base, and from Port Moresby to Australia.[6]

On 31 December 1942, the Minister for the Army, Frank Forde, wrote to General Blamey in response to a newspaper article in which the Australian Comforts Fund Commissioner, Major Gibbons, declared that 'no soldier should be stationed in New Guinea longer than three or four months at a time ... Allied troops in New

Guinea were fighting under worse conditions than had been experienced in any other war.'[7] In his response, Forde expressed his concerns over the casualty situation in Papua and urged Blamey to organise the relief of the Australian soldiers as soon as strategically possible. He specifically asked for a report on 'the progress that is being made in relieving the men who have been the spearhead of attack for some time.'[8]

The Combined Operational Service Command (COSC), a joint American-Australian body responsible for the coordination of the service branches of both forces in Papua, was formed in October 1942. Its areas of responsibility encompassed construction, supply, transport, ordnance, small ships, some ANGAU activities, and medical services. Aspects of the medical services in the base areas of Port Moresby and Milne Bay for which COSC was responsible extended to the siting of hospitals, the coordination of the mutual use of hospital beds by American and Australian soldiers, the supervision of activities in hospitals and convalescent depots, and 'evacuations by Hospital Ship and Air'.[9] The medical facilities for which COSC was responsible in the Port Moresby area comprised the 2/9th AGH, the 2/5th AGH (which arrived in January 1943), the 46th Camp Hospital, the 113th Australian Convalescent Depot and the Advance Depot Medical Stores. The 2/3rd Convalescent Depot at Milne Bay was also the responsibility of COSC.[10]

ADMS Lieutenant Colonel Roderick Macdonald of the Australian Army worked with US Colonel Julius Blank to oversee the coordination of casualty evacuation.[11] On 29 November 1942, Macdonald travelled to Port Moresby to discuss the current hospital situation there and consider suggestions on how best to coordinate the large-scale aerial evacuation of stretcher cases to Australia.[12] The ADMS 7th Division, Colonel Norris, advised Macdonald that sufficient aircraft should be made available for the daily evacuation of 50 stretcher cases from Port Moresby, and that each aircraft should be accompanied by a medical orderly from Australia. Further, he recommended that a higher priority should be given to transporting another 600-bed hospital from Australia to Port Moresby. Taking a holistic approach to the issue, Norris also recommended that a 'pool' of AAMC orderlies should be established in Townsville to process the patients on their arrival in Australia.[13] The two priorities identified by Macdonald as a result of the discussions were the allocation of medical orderlies and six transport aircraft, as well as the provision of three flying boats (amphibious aircraft)—each fitted out to carry 25 stretcher cases.[14] It was only now that the Army's previously vague intentions to transport thousands of Australian casualties from Papua to Australia as part of regular, organised and ongoing operations were finally translated into action.[15]

Between 1 and 24 December, approximately 1500 Australians were evacuated from Milne Bay and just over 2000 from Port Moresby. Almost all of those from Milne Bay, and 'a high percentage' of those sent from Moresby, were suffering from malaria. COSC estimated that it would become necessary to evacuate almost 2000 Allied casualties—700 from Milne Bay and 1200 from Port Moresby—each week to ease the burden on personnel and facilities in both places. Sound medical policy also demanded that all malaria patients be cared for in fully equipped beds in the AGH and given an appropriate level of nursing attention, rather than treated in basic aid posts or dressing stations. All medical facilities around Port Moresby continued to buckle under the sheer weight of casualties, with more than 3000 patients languishing in medical establishments across Papua on Christmas Eve and a further 1000 recovering in convalescent facilities.[16]

Many of the challenges presented by the evacuation of Australian casualties throughout the Papuan campaign were the result of ill-conceived strategies as much as geography. Unnecessary and prolonged suffering resulted from the Army's failure to either implement an effective long-term evacuation plan or organise adequate medical personnel and facilities to care for those who were not evacuated. That the simultaneous implementation of both solutions was possible did not seem to have been considered. While it could be argued that the medical situation in Papua eventually improved simply because 'sheer numbers emphasised the need for a wider employment of both sea and air transport', the reality is more complex.[17] The changing military situation, the fight for air supremacy, the influx of American troops to the front line, the effects of disease on the capabilities of the fighting soldiers, and the dogged persistence of front-line medical personnel in pushing for better conditions were all contributing factors.

Since the start of the Papuan campaign in July 1942, any thoughts of large-scale casualty evacuation to Australia had been focused on the sea. The August medical plans did consider the use of aerial evacuation to the mainland 'when necessary', yet also acknowledged that 'definite arrangements for such a service are in course of preparation and instructions will be issued in due course.'[18] DDMS Disher later judged the lack of suitable aircraft from the outset to be a great handicap in regard to rendering adequate

Medical Service to the fighting troops. Much more could have been done if more facilities had been available. The allotment of even two **suitable** Red Cross Ambulance planes would have without doubt been the means of providing much more adequate service and the means of saving more lives.[19] [original punctuation]

This absence of air ambulances staffed by trained medical personnel meant that ships formed the basis for the evacuation of casualties from Port Moresby to Australia. Ideally, this should have seen sick and wounded men transferred onto well-resourced and well-staffed hospital ships that had been specifically fitted out for carrying patients. Transportation by sea ambulance transport (SAT) staffed by qualified medical personnel was another possible means of evacuation. However, the lack of hospital ships, SAT vessels, and medical personnel rendered this an evacuation plan in theory only. The converted passenger ship HT (Hospital Transport) *Manunda*, which had survived Japanese attacks while anchored in Darwin Harbour and at Milne Bay in February and September 1942 respectively, was the primary means by which casualties were transported from Port Moresby to Australia. SAT vessels—*Katoomba, Taroona, Charon, Gorgon* and *Centaur*—were more often used at Milne Bay. The need for *Manunda* to call at Milne Bay was not as great because, while there were large numbers of malaria patients, there were far fewer battle casualties awaiting evacuation.

The lack of specially equipped and staffed ambulance aircraft seriously affected the level of care provided for any casualties evacuated by air. There were only two types of craft available for the task, both of which could carry only a minimal number of stretcher cases unless specially fitted out. The unconverted flying boats had space for nine such cases and no room for any other personnel, while the land planes (Roadsters) could carry just three stretcher cases each trip. It was estimated that, if appropriately fitted out, they could transport up to 40 casualties between them.[20] The RAAF had established the No.1 Air Ambulance Unit in 1942, with No.2 Air Ambulance Unit commencing service the following year.[21] Neither of these units served in Papua, and it was not until later in 1943 that medical evacuation was handed over to the Allied air forces, with the large military transport aircraft of the Americans eventually responsible for all medical evacuations within (and from) New Guinea.[22] The aerial evacuation of thousands of patients over the Owen Stanley Range to Port Moresby was accomplished by Australian and American transport planes without benefit of medical personnel. Although various official reports noted the lack of an effective system of air evacuation from New Guinea, no basic change took place until the arrival of the 804th Medical Air Evacuation Transport Squadron in June 1943.[23]

The Australian hospital ship Manunda. The ship was anchored in Milne Bay when the Japanese successfully evacuated thousands of their troops by sea on 6 and 7 September 1942. The fact that the Japanese did not attack Manunda meant that it could evacuate thousands of Australian soldiers from Port Moresby and Milne Bay over subsequent months (AWM 006727).

The fall of Buna and the declaration of victory at Sanananda in January 1943 understandably reduced the demand for—and workload of—the front-line medical units, especially in terms of battle casualties. Casualty evacuations from the base area continued with 'the remnants of the fighting troops of 7 Div and 32 US Div ... being returned by sea to the mainland.'[24] Throughout the month, 264 casualties were evacuated by air and almost 1000 by SAT. *Manunda* made three visits to Papua, transporting a total of 770 Australian and 195 American casualties (as well as three Japanese prisoners of war) to Australia. More than 1000 casualties were evacuated from Milne Bay during this period—the majority on SATs. Evacuations continued into February, with more than 600 returning to Australia from Port Moresby and almost 200 from Milne Bay.[25]

MORE CHALLENGES FOR THE FIELD AMBULANCE

Field ambulance personnel who returned to the base area from the beachheads during December and January confronted challenges both similar—and markedly different—to those faced on the Kokoda Track and the beachheads. The CO of the 2/6th Australian Field Ambulance, Colonel Fred Chenhall, had finally returned with his unit to Ilolo, near the southern end of the Kokoda Track, in late December 1942. His unit was then instructed to move to the nearby Donadabu Rest and Training Camp on the southern bank of the Laloki River. The men had been caring for casualties in Papua since August—along the Kokoda Track, and in the MDS at Myola and Soputa. They were now tasked with establishing a medical post to assist in the care of patients in the base area. When Chenhall inspected the proposed site, he found it to be 'in a shocking condition having only just recently been occupied by horses. The whole area was fouled ... a letter was sent to the ADMS 6 Aust Div informing him of the findings and pointing out the area in its present state was unsuitable for any unit and certainly for a Medical unit.'[26] Echoes of earlier issues and previous terse correspondence regarding conditions at Myola must have reverberated with both Chenhall and his superiors.

Chenhall asked permission to select another site for his unit. Permission was denied on the basis that, in the five weeks since the horses had been corralled there, the effects of both sun and rain had cleansed the area. Chenhall disagreed with this assessment, responding in the same forthright style used in his earlier correspondence regarding Myola. He pointed out that 'considerable numbers' of flies continued to breed in the area and that the horses had remained there until very recently.[27] There were numerous other reasons he considered the area unsuitable for a medical unit, including a lack of roads accessible by any vehicle other than a four-wheel drive, the geographical features which made future expansion impossible, and the presence of the malaria vector: the Anopheles mosquito.

Chenhall argued that a move to this location would compromise the health of his men who, despite their 'trying time' along the Kokoda Track and on the northern beaches, had so far managed to escape the ravages of disease. He resented the fact that they were now expected to locate 'alongside a large human reservoir of uncontrolled malaria'.[28] That 'reservoir' included over 1000 soldiers from the 16th and 25th AIF brigades who had recently arrived from the beachheads after fighting the Japanese since September. These troops were now either camped in the base area around Donadabu or were recovering in the 2/9th AGH.[29] The site of another unit had recently been condemned and the men forced to move some distance from a 'native' hospital to reduce the risk of contracting disease. Well aware that it was the risk of malaria that prompted this action and keen to make his point, Chenhall seized on the incident to ask the ADMS 'of what is he frightened – leprosy?'[30]

Further inspections of the proposed site by Chenhall and fellow officers confirmed that it remained filthy, flyblown, and generally inaccessible. A compromise was reached when he agreed to move his men to the site once it was cleaned up and the large amount of rubbish which littered the area was removed. Chenhall initially refused to admit patients to any medical facilities established there—a stand from which he later retreated. On 27 December, he dryly recorded 'Unit HQ opens in the horse lines Donadabu Camp'.[31] His men began making the site as clean and hygienic as possible, working hard to transform the area. When the 2/4th Field Ambulance arrived there from Soputa two days later, there was no reference to horses, filth or flies. A relieved Lieutenant Colonel Hobson noted that the post was 'comfortable ... close to water and the [2/4th] unit has no duties whatever.'[32]

Chenhall's summary of the issues highlighted by these events at Donadabu underscored that which should have been obvious to all by this stage of the campaign:

> It is just beginning to dawn on some people that this war will not be lost by our splendid fighting troops but can [be lost] if more attention is not paid to two aspects: 1) supply 2) preventative medicine. Regarding the latter, I submit the voice of knowledgeable medicine has been far too silent in which case Commanders have not

had a chance to grasp its true significance.[33]

Chenhall's comment emphasised the need for a proactive, rather than reactive, Army medical service and was reminiscent of the succinct assessment given to DGMS Burston by Director of Pathology, Lieutenant Colonel Esmond Keogh, that many of the medical problems in Papua arose largely because 'knowledge was not translated into action'.[34] The failure of the military and medical leadership to act on reports by experts such as Keogh and his colleagues Mackerras, Fairley and Holmes cost the soldiers dearly.[35] It would seem that the disconnect between the front-line medical units and the medical hierarchy continued, even away from the fighting.

THE 2/9th AGH

In line with General Blamey's instructions on casualty evacuation, the original Australian Army Medical Service plan for the Papuan campaign centred on holding and treating most of the casualties in Papua. It seemed self-evident that, for this plan to work, there needed to be an adequate number of appropriately equipped and staffed beds in that country. Yet the total number of hospital beds in Papua could accommodate just 5% of the Australian soldiers. By comparison, the number of hospital beds for the Australians in the Middle East equated to 8%. The size of NGF increased from three infantry brigades in July to nine by October, with no corresponding increase in the number of hospital beds.[36] At the end of November, there were 700 beds available to Allied casualties across the base area. Of these, just 37 were vacant—and none was in the 2/9th AGH.[37]

In contrast to the Australian plan to hold most of the casualties in Papua, the Americans focused on maintaining a minimal number of hospital beds there and evacuating most of their casualties to Australia for treatment. Of the total 5811 equipped hospital beds available to American soldiers, 1650 were in Papua. Most of these were consolidated at Port Moresby in the No.10 Evacuation Hospital with a further 900 beds split between two surgical and station hospitals in the Port Moresby area.[38] The possibility of expanding the bed numbers in Papua to 2000 had been factored into initial plans and mooted as early as October, but there were no immediate plans to do so. Conversely, there were plans to withdraw two companies of the US 135th Medical Regiment from Papua and leave behind their 'equipment, tents and so on, to be operated by medical personnel already there'.[39]

The aim of this 1942 Australian Army poster depicting Mars, the Roman God of War, was to improve levels of hygiene among the soldiers. Mars is stirring a pot of blood and bones. The 'menu' highlights the number of lives lost to diseases, such as dysentery, typhus and malaria, over centuries of war (AWM ARTV02482).

An inspection of the 2/9th AGH was undertaken by the new DDMS, Brigadier Clive Disher, in December. The hospital's CO, Colonel Arthur Green, was overseeing the care of thousands of casualties in a facility originally intended for 600 patients. Expansion of the hospital to 1200 beds on 18 November had proved inadequate, with more than 1500 patients admitted by early December.[40] The 46th Camp Hospital at King's Hollow, 21 miles from Port Moresby, was the original 'base' hospital. As offshoots had already been developed at Rouna and Koitaki to serve as convalescent posts, the King's Hollow site was regarded as unsuitable for further expansion. The rudimentary facilities of the 3rd Field Ambulance were also considered unsuitable for use as hospital accommodation, especially for serious surgical cases.[41] Disher's predecessor, DDMS Johnston, had already expressed his concerns over the hospital situation to DGMS Burston—referencing Blamey's orders regarding the holding of casualties in Papua:

> I don't like hospitalization at all in this country but unless we can be cleared to the mainland there is no other alternative, and in the mean time we live from day to day and have to send people back to their units marked for light duties. No good. All wrong. I don't like it.[42]

Ultimately it would be malaria, the *bête noire* of medical men in Papua, which finally impelled those in command to act on the issue of casualty care and evacuation from Port Moresby.[43] While there had been an increased number of battle casualties admitted to the hospital since the final push around Gona, Buna and Sanananda, the key reason for the rapid increase in hospital admissions was the high rate of malaria among the soldiers.[44] On 10 December it was agreed that the bed numbers in the 2/9th AGH should be increased from 1200 to 1600, despite no official approval for such an expansion. Within three days even this proved inadequate. Patient numbers continued to climb so that, by Christmas Day, there were more than 2000 patients in this hospital originally built to hold 600.[45] Green noted that the daily admission rate had increased by over 450% in three months:

> during the period 5 September 1942 to 18 December 1942, the daily admission rate has increased from 45.1 to 211.5 ... the average daily admission rate of 120 keeps 2400 beds continually occupied ... if this is exceeded the hospital ceases to function as such and patients fail to receive adequate treatment.[46]

Colonel Green posited just two possible courses of action: increased casualty evacuation to Australia or increased hospital accommodation in Papua.[47] The already desperate medical situation around Port Moresby would continue to deteriorate unless issues of overcrowding and understaffing were addressed holistically. The overarching question of casualty evacuation needed to be considered by taking a coordinated approach to the two distinct sectors affected by the fighting in Papua—the soldiers requiring evacuation from the northern beachheads to Port Moresby, and those needing evacuation from Port Moresby to Australia. It was obvious that any increased rate of evacuation from the front line without corresponding increases in evacuations to Australia would be a double-edged sword, given that the AGH at Port Moresby was already at breaking point.

Increased evacuation alone would not solve all of the issues and may even have added to the problems. Discharging casualties before they had fully recovered or completed their course of treatment increased the risks to their health, and to their fellow soldiers. Green noted that 'beds are only made available by the evacuation and discharge of patients before they are suitable for either' and was not convinced that increased evacuation was necessarily helpful or warranted.[48] He knew that sending patients back to Australia presented its own problems, outlining four key concerns that lend a different perspective to the issue. He reiterated that the primary duty of the medical services was not to return patients home, but to return soldiers to their units as quickly as possible and so 'maintain the fighting forces'.[49]

Green argued that some soldiers evacuated to Australia would have been fit to return to the front line, had they been able to access courses of treatment for conditions such as malaria while in Papua. He explained that the increasing demand on hospital staff in preparing the patients for evacuation decreased the hospital's efficiency. Green also noted the loss of personnel, pointing out that those who accompanied patients to Australia were slow to return, with some never seen in Papua again. It was, however, acknowledged that the return of personnel from the mainland to Papua was largely dependent on the availability of transport.[50]

The effects of the return of casualties to Australia on the morale of those still in Papua was perhaps Green's most controversial argument. His questioning of the character and integrity of the casualties left behind presents an image of the Australian soldier that contrasts markedly with more traditional representations. Indeed, Green's soldiers have more in common with the 'malingerers' on the Kokoda Track identified by Lieutenant Colonel Earlam in the early weeks of the campaign, or those accused of suffering self-inflicted wounds at medical posts in the Owen Stanleys:[51]

Evacuation to the mainland lowers morale of troops ... the incentive for a case to get better is removed, as by not improving, he has more opportunity of returning to the mainland. Cases are reported where treatment was evaded when the Hospital ship was reported as arriving ... letters censored at 5 C.C.S. have commented that had they reached 2/9 Aust Gen Hosp instead they would have been more fortunate in being returned to the mainland.

When it comes known in the front line that cases of sickness, normally retained in New Guinea, are evacuated, patients report sick more readily and will not 'hang on' as tirelessly as usual. The attitude of the soldier is "Give it a fly. If I get to the hospital, I might be returned to Australia, and Australia is home" ... it is reported that once in Australia they report sick in order to prolong their stay.[52]

Colonel Green's concerns over the adverse consequences of evacuation to Australia—expressed in the face of the seemingly insurmountable problems he faced in the 2/9th AGH—can perhaps best be understood through the lens of the AAMC remit to return sick and wounded soldiers to the fighting. He articulated many of the less obvious issues that the large-scale evacuation of casualties might bring for the patients themselves, for the fighting forces, and for the medical units in Papua. His words portray the sick and wounded soldiers, not as fearless warriors prepared to sacrifice their lives, but desperate and exhausted men keen to get home to family and friends—by any means possible. Such observations invite a very different interpretation of the Australian soldier and afford a better understanding of Green's own conflicted role as a medical officer serving two masters—the homogenous and impersonal military machine of the Australian Army, and the soldiers in his care.

GOING HOME

For the sick, wounded and weary Australians who had survived the ordeal that was the Papuan campaign, victory simply meant going home. After spending Christmas Day 1942 waiting near the Popondetta airstrip with his fellow 2/4th Field Ambulance personnel, Private Nick Kennedy finally left the fighting behind a few days later:

> Xmas day 42 passes like all other days in these parts here. We have been given orders that we have got to be ready to move at daylight on the 29th [December].

Douglas transport planes will arrive shortly after daylight to take us to Port Moresby ... It is a full moon and before the first light of dawn in the east, we have had a billy of tea and bully beef snack and are ready to move off. There are battle casualties to be flown out too, so they of course go before us. There is only four out of our unit [who] get away. George Smart, Reg Gladhill and Major Love and myself.

It is my first trip in a plane. I always said I would never get in one but I am pleased to hop into this one. It is a great feeling as she races down the strip ... we are soon soaring over the mountain tops ... it is quite cold and misty over the range. We certainly bless that pilot, the plane and her motors for this trip ... at last we touch down on Jackson's Drome at Port Moresby. The trip takes forty minutes. If we had to walk back it would have taken us sixteen days to have crossed the Owen Stanley Range again.[53]

By mid-January 1943, the remaining members of the 2/4th Field Ambulance had joined Kennedy at Donadabu Rest Camp. The men took comfort from the simple things they had missed for so long, with their first meal of meat stew, bread and jam, tasting 'like a meal from the Gods'.[54]

They slept in dry tents and rested their heads on straw pillows: 'the first night for a long time that we have been able to lay down and sleep in peace'.[55] Along with the 14th and the 2/6th Australian Field Ambulance units, the 2/4th had cared for the Australian soldiers along the Kokoda Track, across the Owen Stanleys, and on the northern beaches of Papua for more than three months.

Members of the 2/4th Australian Field Ambulance at Popondetta on 28 December 1942. The men are about to board the US Army Air Force aircraft that will take them back to Port Moresby after five months of caring for Australian front-line soldiers on the Kokoda Track and at the beachheads (AWM P02424.149).

By January, the Kennedy brothers—Nick and Bill—were both sick and weak after contracting malignant tertian malaria, the most severe strain of the disease, 'but no-one wants to report sick and be sent to hospital as we think we may miss the boat to Australia.'[56] Bill Kennedy had spent five days as a patient in the Soputa 2 MDS and Nick was treated 'in lines' at Donadabu Camp in January. The two were with their mates from the 2/4th Field Ambulance as they sailed for home four months to the day since arriving in Port Moresby:

> We leave our camp at 1am on the 17th January 1943, Sunday, to embark on the Duntroon [troopship]. We sail at 12pm, most of us have bunks. As we sail out of Port Moresby we take a last glimpse as we think of the rugged mountains of New Guinea.[57]

The man who had led the 2/4th Field Ambulance, Lieutenant Colonel Arthur Hobson, later reflected on the medical campaign in Papua and those who did not return to Australia with their mates:

> It was only natural on sighting Australia once again, that our thoughts should turn to those members of the unit no longer in our midst. We recalled that nightmare journey across the Owen Stanley Range ... most of all we remembered that dreadful day at Soputa on the 27 Nov 42, the utterly helpless feeling we had as the Japs

dive-bombed and strafed the unit personnel and the patients who were under our care ... we felt rather proud that the occasion had not found us wanting.[58]

CHAPTER 13

'ONE WONDERS WHY ALL THIS STRIFE SHOULD BE'

THE SHAPE OF VICTORY

Shortly after arriving in Australia in March 1942—and prior to his appointment as Supreme Commander SWPA—US General Douglas MacArthur inspired an anxious Australian public when he proclaimed 'We shall win or we shall die, and to this end I pledge the full resources of all the mighty power of my country and all the blood of my countrymen.'[1] With operational control of the war in the south-west Pacific soon to be in MacArthur's hands, the Australian government under Prime Minister Curtin had little choice but to follow suit.[2] The Papuan campaign provided ample opportunity for both countries to honour MacArthur's pledge to win or die. For many fighting soldiers though, it was a third scenario that came to pass: they would both win *and* die.

Victory is rarely a straightforward concept—there is much room for nuance. General MacArthur claimed a military victory at Milne Bay against enemy forces that subsequently evacuated most of their troops by ship, successfully and largely unopposed. His declaration came before the fighting had ceased, before further Australians were killed and wounded in action, and before the only Victoria Cross of the Milne Bay campaign was won. Similarly, Lieutenant Colonel Arnold claimed a military victory when Drake Force achieved its stated mission of 'eliminating' the Japanese from Goodenough Island and denying its use to the enemy, yet this claim belies the litany of military and medical failures that beset the operation.[3]

Victory in Papua was declared on 23 January 1943 after six months of fighting. And while MacArthur and the Commander-in Chief of the Australian Military Forces, General Thomas Blamey, had their win, triumph looked very different to that envisaged the previous year. Both the enemy and the environment had stood resolutely in the way of any swift and decisive victory in Papua. MacArthur's avowed intention to drive the land forces through to the beaches at Gona and Buna in the final months of the campaign 'regardless of losses' produced further unnecessary suffering, sickness and death.[4] The declaration could be seen to exemplify the determination of a strong leader focused on absolute victory. It might also simply signify a reckless disregard for young lives. Whatever the rationale, there was no doubt that seasoned military leaders such as MacArthur and Blamey were very much aware of the sacrifice needed to triumph here.

Generals Thomas Blamey and Douglas MacArthur with Prime Minister John Curtin, March 1942 (AWM 042766).

THE NATURE OF LEADERSHIP

It was often the case in Papua that the nature and quality of leadership varied according to the officer's proximity to the front line—a point not lost on Major General Frank Kingsley

Norris. Medical officers like Magarey, Earlam, Chenhall and Hobson led from the front on the Kokoda Track, while Maitland, Wall and Crakanthorp did likewise at Milne Bay. As ADMS for the 7th Division, Norris questioned why it was that the military and medical leadership had failed to foresee the dire ramifications of a medical plan based on unfulfilled promises and untested scenarios. He suggested that a better result might have been achieved if those ultimately responsible for the medical decisions in Papua took the opportunity to visit the front line:

> Australian troops have been continuously in action for the first time in jungle warfare accessible within a day's flight of the mainland ... it is recommended that in future, such an instructive opportunity of appreciating the end results of their activities under forward operational conditions be NOT denied personally to those who are responsible for them.[5]

Yet he too must take some responsibility for the formulation of medical plans that relied so heavily on aerial evacuation. Though effectively hamstrung by seemingly endless difficulties, Norris had experienced the perils of the Kokoda Track first-hand during the Australian withdrawal; he had witnessed the problems associated with moving casualties forward towards Myola and Kokoda in anticipation of aerial evacuation; he had seen the suffering when this plan failed and casualties were forced to walk or crawl their way back along the track towards Port Moresby.

The GOC Milne Force, General Cyril Clowes, was evacuated by sea in December 1942 after contracting malignant tertian malaria. Out of favour with both Blamey and MacArthur by this time, Clowes was sent back to Milne Bay on his recovery and was 'left languishing' there until October 1943.[6] In a stark representation of the confluence of military and medical experiences in Papua, the malaria situation at Milne Bay was later used against him. That Clowes was effectively hoisted on his own petard by an inquiry which held him, as GOC, primarily responsible for the high rates of the disease within Milne Force seems as specious as the lack of consideration given to the many factors that both contributed to the epidemic and hastened its end.[7] There is also an obvious failure to hold to account those military and medical officers further up the chain of command.

The DDMS, Brigadier William Johnston, wrote a summary of 'some of the problems associated with the Medical Administration of I Aust Corps' in Papua. Johnston noted the problems of casualty evacuation that beset the campaign from the start—the lack of suitable ships, aircraft, and trained personnel as well as complex administrative and organisational processes that 'came to be regarded as a veritable nightmare'.[8] He summarised the supply problems, especially the difficulties with aerial supply such as flight delays and mistakes in ordering, packaging, labelling, dropping. Johnston added that 'it must be admitted that a great proportion of the medical supplies requested ... never reached their destination'—highlighting issues with the supply of urgently needed quinine, which 'found its way back to the Depot' instead of being delivered to Kokoda.[9] Further problems associated with anti-malaria measures were discussed: 'for months, there was no anti-malarial equipment to work with and one saw the anomalous position of anti-malarial units ready to work but without the wherewithal.'[10]

Johnston's comments on the problems faced by Chenhall and the 2/6th Field Ambulance at Myola included one simple sentence that summed up the unfathomable level of faith placed in aerial evacuation: 'Unfortunately, when the possibilities of evacuating patients by plane were considered, all these practical difficulties [short runway, challenging topography, no suitable aircraft] were not at first realised and the belief became fixed that planes would be able to accomplish the task satisfactorily.'[11] The crux of the evacuation crisis, however, was Commander-in-Chief Blamey's directive that all malaria patients and most of the sick and wounded were to be held in Papua and not evacuated back to Australia for treatment. This instruction could not have been issued or enforced without the support of senior medical officers, including Johnston and the man ultimately responsible for the Australian Army Medical Service, Major General Samuel Burston.

The fact that, by mid-1941, Major General Rupert Downes was no longer DGMS, influenced the way in which the 1942 medical campaign in Papua was conducted. To speculate on what course this might have taken with either Downes or his immediate successor, Major General Frederick Maguire, in charge serves no real purpose—except by way of comparison with the man who did eventually oversee the campaign. DGMS Burston was appointed to the most senior position in the Australian Army Medical Service in controversial circumstances. Unlike his predecessors, he served in the Middle East in 1941—an experience that allowed him to accrue important first-hand knowledge on the administration of battlefield medicine. However, the timing of his return to Australia and subsequent promotion to the position of DGMS in April 1942 meant he did not have a full appreciation of the medical situation on the mainland and in the SWPA, nor any real opportunity to gain that understanding before the Papuan campaign commenced in July. Thus, Burston was promoted to the most senior position within the AAMC at arguably the most crucial time in its short history. Downes and Maguire had both been moved aside to make way for Burston, taking with them their knowledge and experience.

Burston's responsibilities as DGMS, like those of his predecessors, were many and varied. He, like them, came up against an entrenched intransigence in the upper echelons of the Australian Army that could be both obstructive and destructive towards the medical services. This should not serve as an excuse for the medical situation in Papua. Nevertheless, it seems that history has respected the recommendation of Johnston, who was unwilling to ascribe blame for the failings of the medical campaign to his colleague and friend, Burston:

> One feels that when the history of this campaign is written, the fact should be made plain that where the ideal medical objective was not always attained, no charge lies against the D.G.M.S. and his staff at the Medical Directorate L.H.Q.[12]

Not everyone was as keen to relieve the most senior officers of their responsibilities. The months spent caring for sick, wounded and dying soldiers along the Kokoda Track and at the Myola MDS left Lieutenant Colonel Fred Chenhall unwilling to excuse the 'Crimean mentality' exhibited by those in charge of the medical campaign in Papua. Indeed, Chenhall called on a much higher power to grant such men absolution: 'God forgive the blind stupid people who are responsible for such a state of affairs.'[13]

While it is true that Burston alone cannot be held responsible for all that had gone before—nor all that went wrong—in Papua, it is equally true that devolution of responsibility and delegation of duty do not absolve the ultimate leader of his ultimate responsibility. Although many factors contributed to the medical difficulties in Papua, it was Burston's core responsibility as DGMS to identify and overcome the logistical challenges.

THE COST OF VICTORY

During the final months of fighting in the malarial morass of the north coast of Papua, the military commanders threw everything into defeating the Japanese. Despite the harsh lessons of the previous months, however, that same level of commitment to winning the medical campaign was not evident. Medical men such as Private Nick Kennedy witnessed the cost of such failures first-hand:

> One wonders why all this strife should be. These men in the prime of their life 'cut down like flowers' ... There are a few mounds here now with little wooden crosses over them ... their troubles are over and a nice and better world awaits them.[14]

Casualty Registers of Australian servicemen killed and wounded during the Papuan campaign (author image).

The names of the dead, wounded and missing Australian soldiers from the six-month Papuan campaign can be found in two large, tattered and stained volumes held at the Australian National Archives—the Casualty Registers of Australian

Servicemen.[15] Casualties from disease or illness are not mentioned, unless to reconcile the men's fate—a missing soldier may have been later located as a patient in an MDS, for example. The soldier's service number, name and unit, as well as the place, date and 'nature of casualty' are recorded. The fate of the men is categorised and summarised in the succinct language of the military—killed in action; killed in action as a result of enemy aircraft; died of wounds; accidently wounded; missing; missing believed killed; for official purposes presumed dead. Such details are listed for 1380 Australians killed in action and 307 who died from wounds received in Papua. Headings such as 'additions', 'deletions', 'nett total', 'progressive total' remind the reader that these registers of young lives saved or lost must be balanced. It is the sight of so many pages and so many names that bring home the high price paid for victory in Papua.

There are inherent difficulties in ascertaining definitive statistics for the casualties of war.[16] The total casualties of a whole campaign may be given, or the killed and wounded might be listed according to their brigades, battalions, battles or campaign stages. The official military historian of the Papuan campaign, Dudley McCarthy, estimated that at least 13,000 of more than 20,000 Japanese troops who were engaged across all stages and fronts in Papua died, and that Allied casualties (killed and wounded) totalled 8546.[17] The official medical historian, Allan S. Walker, included further details in his summary of Allied casualties. He recorded 7752 total battle casualties, of whom over 6000 were Australian. Walker notes too that, of the 37,360 Allied servicemen who suffered from tropical diseases, almost 30,000 were Australian. Casualties from malaria warranted a separate column, with 21,600 Australians and 6292 American soldiers contracting the disease.[18] Other sources estimate that almost 4000 Papuans were killed or wounded over the course of the Papuan campaign.[19]

Page from Casualty Register showing names of soldiers killed in action, including VX24147 Private Kuch and VX14704 Major McDonald of the 2/4th Field Ambulance (author image).

LONG SHADOWS

The iconic image of Papuan carriers carefully assisting Australian sick and wounded soldiers on the Kokoda Track has become synonymous with medical care during the Papuan campaign. This ubiquitous representation has had unintended consequences, overshadowing the contributions of the Australian medical men in Papua. History has room for both. An examination of the experiences of the front-line Australian medical units—the field ambulances—goes some way to more fully understanding the campaign and deconstructing the myths. Viewing the military campaign through the lens of the medical campaign invites new interpretations of a history most Australians feel they know well.

The popular representation of the Australian soldiers who fought along the Kokoda Track, at Milne Bay, and in the beachhead battles tends to be an idealised one. It is possible for the accounts of medical personnel to humanise that image. Diary writings by medical men such as Private Kennedy, who witnessed the cost of war and victory, allow some insight into the experiences of a soldier whose orders were not to take life, but to save it. Kennedy's raw and unpolished account provides history's first draft of one man's medical campaign in Papua.

Entry in Kennedy diary describing Japanese attack on Soputa MDS (author image).

Examining the Papuan campaign through the lens of the medical units shines a light on the bold, the heroic and the admirable—while also reminding us that clearly delineated heroes and villains are rare and that most men exhibit traits of both. For all the examples of courage, mateship, endurance and sacrifice in Papua, there was desperation, fear, selfishness, weakness and cowardice that occasionally manifested as self-inflicted wounds, malingering, and a longing for home. The men of the field ambulances bore witness to the best and the worst of the campaign. To separate those experiences is to render them less meaningful. The passage of time and the capricious nature of history have brushed away many of the harsh realities of the medical campaign in Papua, leaving behind a more comfortable version of the truth. Acknowledgement of this can help to shape the one-dimensional myth of 'Kokoda' into a more complex and multi-dimensional narrative of the entire Papuan campaign—one that puts flesh on the bones of heroes, angels, soldiers, and men.

APPENDIX I

AIF AND AAMC FIELD AMBULANCE UNITS

Structure, Size and Allocation in World War II

> **I Australian Corps** (30,000+)
> 6th, 7th, 8th, 9th divisions (10,000-20,000)
> Three brigades to each division (2500-5000)
> Three battalions to each brigade (550-1000)
> Four companies to each battalion (100-225)
> Three platoons to each company (30-60)
> Sections (various)

> **Field Ambulance**
> (c.12 officers and 225 other ranks)
> Three field ambulance units to each division
> One field ambulance unit to each brigade
> Three companies to each field ambulance
> Headquarters (Main Dressing Station)

A Company (Advance Dressing Station/Bearers)
B Company (Advance Dressing Station/Bearers)

6th Division AIF
2/1st, 2/2nd, 2/7th field ambulances
7th Division AIF
2/4th, 2/5th, 2/6th field ambulances
8th Division AIF
2/9th, 2/10th, 2/12th field ambulances
9th Division AIF
2/3rd, 2/8th, 2/11th field ambulances

APPENDIX 2

CMF/MILITIA

Field Ambulance units and overseas service in WWII

UNIT	LOCATION
2nd	New Britain
3rd*	Port Moresby
4th	Goodenough Island, Huon Peninsula, Madang, New Britain
6th	Huon Peninsula, New Britain
7th	Bougainville, Huon Peninsula, Wau-Salamaua
8th	Bougainville
9th	Markham and Ramu Valleys, Wau-Salamaua
10th	Borneo, Gona-Buna-Sanananda, Huon Peninsula
11th	Bougainville, Milne Bay
14th	Gona-Buna-Sanananda, Kokoda Track, Port Moresby
15th	Bougainville, Madang, Markham and Ramu Valleys, Saidor, Wau-Salamaua
17th	Bougainville and outer islands
18th	Huon Peninsula
19th	Bougainville

*Amalgamated with the 14th in September 1943 to form 3/14th Field Ambulance

APPENDIX 3

Casualties evacuated from Kokoda area by No.2 Light Section 14th Field Ambulance in 24 hours to midnight 9 September 1942

NATURE OF CASUALTY (TOTAL = 66)	BATTALION	STRETCHER
Angina of effort	53	No
Angio-neurotic oedema	2/27	No
Blistered feet	39	No
Chronic Otitis Media	2/27	No
Compound fracture and GSW left ankle	2/14	Yes
Diarrhoea	2/16	No
Diarrhoea, exhaustion, Pyrexia Unknown Origin (PUO)	39	No
Dysentery	3	No
Gun Shot Wound (GSW) both hands	2/16	No
GSW left and right lower legs	2/14	Yes
GSW left ankle and foot	53rd	Yes
GSW left ankle, probable fracture	2/14	Yes
GSW left chest and arm	2/16	Yes
GSW left foot, left buttock	53	Yes
GSW left head, left shoulder	2/14	Yes
GSW left knee	53	Yes
GSW left knee – queried fracture	39	Yes

GSW left knee/GSW right lower leg	2/14	Yes
GSW left leg, compound fracture	2/16	Yes
GSW left shin	2/16	No
GSW left thigh, tangent wound right buttock	2/16	No
GSW lower back	39	Yes
GSW lower leg	39	Yes
GSW right chest, dysentery	2/14	No
GSW right femur	2/14	Yes
GSW right hand	53	No
GSW right leg, compound fracture left tibia & fibular	53	Yes
GSW right lower leg	53	Yes
GSW right neck, shoulder and back	2/14	Yes
GSW right thigh	2/16	No
GSW right thigh	2/14	Yes
GSW right thigh	2/16	Yes
GSW right thigh and leg	2/4	No
GSW right thigh, left hip	2/16	Yes
GSW right thigh, left leg	39	Yes
GSW right thigh, lower femur, queried fracture	2/14	Yes
GSW right thigh, scrotum, left thigh (large)	2/14	Yes
Infected abrasions both hands and legs	53	No
Infected abrasions to feet	39	No

Infected knees	2/16	No
Infected sores in foot and malaria	39	No
Lumbar Fibrositis	53	No
Malaria	39	No
Malaria	53	No
Malaria	39	No
Malaria	39	Yes
Measles	39	Yes
Not yet diagnosed – queried malaria	39	Yes
Perforating GSW right groin	2/14	Yes
Perforating GSW left thigh, left groin	2/14	Yes
Perforating wound left knee, creased right knee	2/16	Yes
Pneumonia, infected middle finger	39	Yes
PUO – queried malaria	39	Yes
PUO – queried scrub typhus	2/14 RAE	No
Queried hernia	3	No
Queried infected tinea. Diarrhoea	39	No
Queried malaria	53	No
Scabies	39	No
Shrapnel wound behind left knee	53rd	Yes
Shrapnel wound right cheek, infected orbit	2/16	Yes
Synovitis left knee debilitating	39	No
Toothache	53	No
Traumatic pleurisy	2/16	No

Upper Respiratory Tract Infection	39	Yes
Varicocele strain of abdominal muscles	53	No
Varicose Veins	2/16	No

APPENDIX 4

2/6th FIELD AMBULANCE MDS MYOLA 2

SUMMARY OF CASUALTIES OCTOBER – DECEMBER 1942

TOTAL CASES ADMITTED	BATTLE CASUALTIES	SICK & ACCIDENTALLY WOUNDED
576*	250	326**

*Includes 120 cases transferred from 2/4th Australian Field Ambulance MDS at Myola 1.
**Approximately 11 of the sick cases were accidentally wounded

TYPES OF BATTLE CASUALTIES TREATED

COMPOUND FRACTURES	96
Carpus or Metacarpus	17
Clavicle	1
Face (and injuries to eye)	13
Femur	7

Fore arm bones	5
Humerus	13
Involving Joints	15
Knee	8
Elbow	4
Wrist	3
Sacrum	1
Skull	7
Tarsus or Metatarsus	10
Tibia and/or Fibula	7

PERFORATIONS	16
Abdomen	3
Thorax	13

OPERATIONS PERFORMED

PRIMARY	128
SECONDARY	61

BATTLE CASUALTY DEATHS IN MDS

DEATHS	4
Compound fracture to skull (after admission)	1
Compound fracture to face (after operation)	1

Perforated thorax (complications)	1
Amputation right leg at thigh (on operating table)	1

SICK (Malaria, Scrub Typhus, Dysentery, skin disorders)

DEATHS	3
Scrub Typhus	1
Scrub Typhus, dysentery, peritonitis, ruptured colon	1
Suspected Cerebral Malaria	1

EVACUATION – ALL PATIENTS

MODE	TOTAL = 576
Air	43
Dead on Arrival	1
Died	7
Papuan Carrier to Kokoda	46
Returned to Unit	237
Walked to Ilolo	242

APPENDIX 5

OVERVIEW OF MEDICAL UNITS AND FACILITIES IN PAPUAN CAMPAIGN 1942

Unit	Location	Notes
2/4 Advanced Depot Medical Stores	Port Moresby	See Depot Medical Stores.
2/1 Casualty Clearing Station	Milne Bay	Arrived 6 September on Manunda, with a detachment of 2/2 Anti Malaria Control Unit (8 AMCU arrived later).
2/2 Casualty Clearing Station	Port Moresby Owen Stanleys	Arrived 2 October and established in annexe at Koitaki.
5 Casualty Clearing Station	Port Moresby	Expanded scope to assist other units cope e.g. with dysentery patients. A mobile bacteriological laboratory was attached to 5 CCS.
110 (10) Casualty Clearing Station	Milne Bay	Arrived on 21 August and functioned as a hospital. The unit remained at Milne Bay until March 1943. No AGH was sent. The unit also took on the duties of an Advanced Depot Medical Stores as none was sent to Milne Bay.
8 Convalescent Unit	Milne Bay	Arrived 6 September on Manunda. Stores were on board Anshun when it was sunk in Japanese naval attack.

113 Convalescent Depot	Murray Barracks	Moved from Sogeri Valley to Murray Barracks. Returned to Sogeri 7 October.
Convalescent Home (Red Cross)	Rouna	This Red Cross site later became an offshoot of 46 Camp Hospital Convalescent Unit.
2/3 Convalescent Depot	Milne Bay	Opened convalescent depot in Waigani area in December.
256 Dental Unit	Port Moresby	Arrived September. Note that dental officers at Milne Bay formed a mobile dental centre
Depot Medical Stores	New Guinea District	This originated from dispensary of 46 Camp Hospital. It was absorbed into 2/4 Advanced Depot Medical Stores on arrival of 1 Australian Corps.
2/1 Field Ambulance	Port Moresby	Arrived early October with 16 Brigade (6 Division). Established small medical posts and an ADS and MDS near Bomana airfield. Unit set up medical wards which functioned as malaria hospital and held over 400 patients.
2/2 Field Ambulance	Milne Bay	Arrived October.

2/4 Field Ambulance	Owen Stanleys Gona-Buna-Sanananda	Arrived 17 September and provided medical care during Australian advance (Owen Stanley and beachhead campaigns). When 2/6 Field Ambulance was forced to remain at Myola in October, 2/4 Field Ambulance provided the only medical support for two brigades (2/16 and 2/25) until detachment of 14 Field Ambulance arrived at Kokoda by aircraft mid-November. At one stage was responsible for all medical care in forward area.
2/5 Field Ambulance	Milne Bay Goodenough Island Gona-Buna-Sanananda	The unit was based at Milne Bay, with an advance party arriving with 18 Brigade, 7 Division, AIF, on 13 August. In October, detachments of the unit accompanied soldiers of 2/12 Battalion, 18 Brigade (Drake Force), during Operation Drake on Goodenough Island. In mid-December a detachment was formed and sent to Buna under Major Lavarack. Numbers were boosted as other parties arrived. The unit established and manned ADS and MDS in Buna-Endaiadere area. Personnel also worked at Soputa MDS in January 1943. During November and December detachments also supported various forces across Milne Bay at places such as Wedau-Taupota. The Milne Bay component did not leave for Australia until 9 March 1943.

2/6 Field Ambulance	Owen Stanleys Gona-Buna-Sanananda Port Moresby area	Arrived 14 August and provided medical care during initial Australian advance and subsequent withdrawal. Proceeded forward again in conjunction with 2/4 Field Ambulance during October. Most of unit remained at Myola MDS until December. Small detachments moved forward to Soputa to assist 2/4 Field Ambulance in late November.
3 Field Ambulance	Port Moresby	Arrived Murray Barracks 3 January and established basic medical facilities. The unit effectively became static and treated medical and infectious patients. Later set up MDS at Bomana and ADS near Seven Mile Drome. The unit provided all medical care for all defence force troops in area until May, despite lack of staff and equipment.
4 Field Ambulance	Goodenough Island	B Company of the unit arrived in early 1943.
10 Field Ambulance	Gona-Buna-Sanananda	Arrived Port Moresby 28 November to work with 2/9 AGH. Detachment flew to Dobodura on 17 December to establish medical posts and undertake surgical work in Buna-Endaiadere area. Relieved 14 Field Ambulance at Soputa in January 1943.
11 Field Ambulance	Milne Bay	Advance party arrived on 13 July and established an MDS and ADS, with the rest of the unit at Milne Bay by the end of the month.

14 Field Ambulance	Port Moresby Owen Stanleys Gona-Buna-Sanananda	Arrived 3 June to assist 3 Field Ambulance. In support of 30 Brigade. Detachment from this unit comprised first medical personnel to cross Owen Stanleys in support of 39 Battalion in July. Further detachments provided the only medical care on the Kokoda Track until arrival of 2/6 Field Ambulance in August. Both units then supported troops during withdrawal. Remainder of unit provided medical support in Port Moresby area. Relieved 2/4 and 2/6 Field Ambulance posts as these units advanced during October-November. Detachments flown to Kokoda on 15 November to assist 2/4 Field Ambulance. Further detachments filled other vacancies in northern area. On 16 December a detachment took over the MDS at Soputa and was not relieved until 25 January 1943 (10 Field Ambulance).
2/2 Field Hygiene Section	Owen Stanleys	Moved to Koitaki after arrival of 25 Brigade in September. Was previously on mainland in process of being disbanded due to introduction of new hygiene system.
16 Field Hygiene Section	Port Moresby	Unit primarily responsible for establishment and maintenance of hygiene facilities and adherence to procedures around Port Moresby area during initial stages.

Base Hospital	Port Moresby	Transferred to King's Hollow in March. Later became 46 Camp Hospital.
46 Camp Hospital	Port Moresby	Formed from Base Hospital. Developed two convalescent sections (Rouna and Koitaki).
2/5 General Hospital	Port Moresby	Arrived in Port Moresby January 1943 and began receiving patients within the month.
2/9 General Hospital	Port Moresby	Arrived 23 August with poor water supply and sanitation, unsuitable site, lack of equipment and no nurses. Opened in September with 600 beds. Permission granted to expand to 800 beds later in month (had requested 1200 plus further 600-bed hospital from Australia). AANS members posted to the hospital from October. Delays in completion of the operating theatre meant major surgery was not undertaken until 25 October.
Malaria Control Units	Milne Bay	Malaria squads initially formed from infantry units and trained by 8 Malaria Control Unit. 2/2 Malaria Control Unit arrived in mid-December.
1 Mobile Entomological Unit	Milne Bay	Arrived in September to assist 8 Malaria Control Unit.

Regimental Aid Posts	Owen Stanleys Gona-Buna-Sanananda	Located at various points along Kokoda Track and in beachheads area. Staffed by RMO, corporal and three orderlies. Supported by rear aid post staffed by sergeant, chaplain, orderlies and carriers.
Regimental Medical Officers	Owen Stanleys Gona-Buna-Sanananda	Officer in forward units responsible for establishment and command of RAPs during all stages of campaign.
Rest Camp	Port Moresby	Located at Donadabu.
Rest House	Owen Stanleys Located at Isurava.	
Staging Posts	Owen Stanleys	Located at various points along Kokoda Track and in beachheads area.
Surgical Teams	Owen Stanleys Gona Buna-Sanananda	Small surgical unit was set up by 14 Field Ambulance detachment at Eora Creek in August but was forced to withdraw to Templeton's Crossing. No further surgery possible during withdrawal. Surgical teams sent forward with 2/4 and 2/6 Field Ambulance during second advance September-October. First surgery at Myola performed in mid-October. Detachments flown to Kokoda in mid-November to undertake surgery during fighting north of Kokoda.

ENDNOTES

Notes on Terminology

[1] The quotation is from D. McCarthy, 'Kokoda Re-visited', p.1, AWM 67, item 13/73 cited in K. James, 'The Track: A historical desktop study of the Kokoda Track', Military History Section, Australian War Memorial Canberra, 2009, p.24. Available at https://www.environment.gov.au/system/files/resources/3a7f218a-d2d6-49fd-b6f6-240a55058ed2/files/awm-kokoda-report.pdf

[2] See Administrator (later Lieutenant Governor), 'Annual Report on British New Guinea', Government Printer, Brisbane, 1888–1906. See also B. James, *Field Guide to the Kokoda Track*, Kokoda Press, Australia, 2006, p.40.

[3] James, ibid., p.40; James, 'The Track', p.56.

[4] Private L.N. Kennedy used the term 'Track' on 31 occasions. There are just four references to 'Trail' in the diary. Note too that the official organisation in Papua New Guinea responsible for protecting the Kokoda Track's 'intrinsic

and historic value' is the Kokoda Track Authority. See http://www.kokodatracka uthority.org

Introduction

[1] Allan S. Walker, *Australia in the War of 1939-1945*, Series 5, Vol.3, *The Island Campaigns*, Australian War Memorial, Canberra, 1957, p.121.

[2] See Department of Veterans' Affairs website 'Commemorations, memorials and war graves'.

[3] Paul Hasluck, *Australia in the War of 1939-1945*, Series 4, Vol.1, *The Government and the People 1942–1945*, Australian War Memorial, Canberra, 1970, p.70.

[4] Ibid.; Appreciations by Australian Chiefs of Staff Jan–April 1942, Advisory War Council Minute, War Cabinet Agendum No.159/1942, Canberra, 18 March 1942, in NAA Series A5954, Item 563/1, Summary of the views of the Advisory War Council (point 12) states: 'it was affirmed that Darwin and Port Moresby should be defended to the fullest possible extent and that every endeavour should be made to provide the forces

required to ensure the adequate defence of these localities'.

[5] The Singapore Strategy dominated Australia's defence strategy during the inter-war years. It relied on a strong British naval presence in Singapore to deter Japanese aggression in the Far East and Pacific regions. A myriad of current and potential problems failed to 'discourage a willingness on the part of Australian leaders to accept the basic premises of the Singapore Strategy'. See Peter Dennis, Jeffrey Grey, Robin Prior and Jean Bou (eds), *The Oxford Companion to Australian Military History* (2nd edn), Oxford University Press, South Melbourne, 2008, p.495.

[6] See David Horner, 'Defending Australia in 1942' in *War and Society* 11(1), May 1993, pp.1–20; Frank Sublet, *Kokoda to the Sea*, Slouch Hat Publications, Victoria, 2000; Appreciation on Defence of Australia and Anzac Area, in NAA Series A2684, Item 905.

[7] Entry on page headed Canberra, 22 Nov 44, in AWM67, Item 1/7, Records of Gavin Long (1944–1945), hereafter, Long Diary.

[8] Long Diary.

[9] Butler quoted in Long Diary.
[10] Ibid.
[11] Bean quoted in Long Diary.

Chapter One

[1] See Australian War Memorial website, 'War History – Sudan (New South Wales Contingent) March-June 1885'.

[2] Craig Wilcox in Dennis et al. (eds), *The Oxford Companion to Australian Military History*, pp.93–97. Lieutenant Neville Howse of the NSW Medical Corps was awarded Australia's first Victoria Cross in 1901 for rescuing a wounded man from the battlefield at Vredefort while under fire (see also p.266).

[3] The Corps acquired its 'Royal' prefix in 1948. See A.G. Butler (ed.), *The Australian Army Medical Services in the War of 1914-1918*, Vol.1, *Gallipoli, Palestine and New Guinea*, Australian War Memorial, Melbourne, 1938, Chapter 1; Michael Tyquin, *Little by Little: A Centenary History of the Royal Australian Army Medical Corps*, Australian Military History Publications, Loftus, NSW, 2003.

[4] Jennifer Gurner, *The Origins of The Royal Australian Army Medical Corps*, Hawthorn

Press, Melbourne, 1970, p.50 (original emphasis). Williams served as Director General of Medical Services from 1902 to 1916.

[5] A.J. Hill, 'Williams, Sir William Daniel Campbell (1856-1919)', *Australian Dictionary of Biography (ADB)*, Melbourne University Press (MUP), 1990; see also Gurner, *The Origins of The Royal Australian Army Medical Corps*; Michael Tyquin, 'Sir William "Mo" Williams, KCMG, CB, KStj, Creator of Australia's Army Medical Services – Maligned or Misunderstood' in *Journal of the Royal Australian Historical Society* 84, 1998, pp.68–81.

[6] Butler, *The Australian Army Medical Services in the War of 1914-1918*, Vol.1, *Gallipoli, Palestine and New Guinea*; G.B. Barton (ed.), *The Story of South Africa*, vol. II, World Publishing Company, Sydney, 1903; Tyquin, 'Sir William "Mo" Williams, p.70.

[7] 'Reports of the Commandants 1901' in Butler, *The Australian Army Medical Services in the War of 1914-1918*, Vol.1, *Gallipoli, Palestine and New Guinea*, p.3.

[8] The Australian Army Service Corps was created in 1903. It was responsible for

supply and transport, taking over this role from various colonial organisations. See Dennis et al. (eds), *The Oxford Companion to Australian Military History*, p.463.

[9] Albert Palazzo, *The Australian Army – A History of its Organization 1901–2001*, Oxford University Press, South Melbourne, 2001, pp.17–18. See also Jeffrey Grey, *The Australian Centenary History of Defence*, Vol.1, *The Australian Army*, Oxford University Press, South Melbourne, 2001, pp.5–35.

[10] Dennis et al. (eds), *The Oxford Companion to Australian Military History*, p.353. General Routine Order No.115, 21 July 1902 'published an extract of the Commonwealth of Australia Gazette No.34 which provisionally appointed Colonel William Daniel Campbell Williams CB to be Director General of Medical Services effective 1 April 1902.' General Routine Order No.123, 30 July 1902 promulgated that 'the existing Medical Services of the various states should be organized on one similar basis and should be reconstructed and organized so as to form one Corps, the Australian Army

Medical Corps, to take effect on and from 1 July 1902.'

[11] Butler, *The Australian Army Medical Services in the War of 1914-1918*, Vol.1, *Gallipoli, Palestine and New Guinea*, pp.4–5; RAAMC Association website.

[12] Butler, ibid., pp.5–9.

[13] Australian Government, Department of Defence website, 'Royal Australian Army Medical Corps (RAAMC)'.

[14] See Butler, *The Australian Army Medical Services in the War of 1914-1918*, Vol.1, *Gallipoli, Palestine and New Guinea*; Walker, *Australia in the War of 1939-1945*, Series 5, Vol.3, *The Island Campaigns*.

[15] Butler, ibid., pp.9–16.

[16] Ibid., p.21; Hill, 'Williams, Sir William Daniel Campbell (1856-1919)'. The DGMS in Australia for the duration of the conflict was Major General Richard Fetherston.

[17] A.G. Butler (ed.), *The Australian Army Medical Services in the War of 1914-1918*, Vol.3, *Special Problems and Services*, Australian War Memorial, Canberra, 1943, pp.220, 228–29.

[18] Ibid., p.221.

[19] Henri Dunant, author of *Un Souvenir de Solferino* (1862), helped to establish the First Geneva Convention and the International Committee for Relief to the Wounded, later the International Red Cross. See International Committee of the Red Cross website, 'Henri Dunant (1828-1910)'.

[20] For background, see Robert Linke, 'The influence of German surveying on the development of Papua New Guinea' presented at 'Shaping the Change', XXIII FIG Conference, Munich, 8–13 October 2006.

[21] Cited in B. Jinks, P. Biskup and H. Nelson (eds), *Readings in New Guinea History*, Angus & Robertson, Sydney, 1973, p.2.

[22] John Moresby in Jinks et al. (eds), ibid., pp.8–11; Francis West, 'Stanley, Owen (1811–1850)', *ADB*, National Centre of Biography, Australian National University, accessed 31 August 2012. See also Jinks et al. (eds), pp.2–5; 'Australasian Islands (from the Colonial Magazine)', Sydney *Herald*, 23 March 1841.

[23] Similarly, a French nobleman, the Marquis de Rays, oversaw the

colonisation of the 'miasmal eldorado' of Port Breton on nearby New Ireland. Over 1000 French, Belgian, Spanish and Italians emigrated to Port Breton between 1879 and 1882, and most died there. Jinks et al. (eds), *Readings in New Guinea History*, pp.11–12.

[24] H.J. Gibbney, 'Hocking, Sidney Edwin (1859–1935)', *ADB*, Vol.9, MUP, 1983; Powerhouse Museum website, 'Guide to the Lawrence Hargrave Archive 1994'.

[25] Marjorie G. Jacobs, 'Bismarck and the Annexation of New Guinea' in *Historical Studies: Australia and New Zealand* 5 (17), 1951, pp.14–26.

[26] In 1883, the Premier of Queensland unsuccessfully attempted to annex New Guinea in the name of Britain.

[27] Hank Nelson, *Taim Bilong Masta: the Australian involvement with Papua New Guinea*, Australian Broadcasting Commission, Sydney, 1982, p.11. See also Hank Nelson, *Black, White and Gold: Goldmining in Papua New Guinea 1878-1930*, Australian National University Press, Canberra, 1976.

[28] Bill James, *Field Guide to the Kokoda Track*, Kokoda Press, Lane Cove, NSW, 2006, pp.33–37.

[29] British New Guinea Annual Report of 1889/90, p.19 in Jinks et al. (eds), *Readings in New Guinea History*, p.65.

[30] Medical Reports and Arrangements Milne Bay area-Medical Experiences at Milne Bay, Lieutenant Colonel F.L. Wall, July 1943 (hereafter Wall Report) in AWM Series 54, Item 481/12/220. See also Jinks et al. (eds), *Readings in New Guinea History*.

[31] F.A. Maguire in Butler, *The Australian Army Medical Services in the War of 1914-1918*, Vol.1, *Gallipoli, Palestine and New Guinea*, p.782; Ian Cope, 'F.A. Maguire – A Man of Many Parts, 1888-1953, First Chairman, Australian Regional Council, Royal College of Obstetricians and Gynaecologists' in *Australian and New Zealand Journal of Obstetrics and Gynaecology*, 37 (3), 1997, pp.325–28.

[32] Maguire in Butler, ibid., pp.782–86. Surgeon General Richard Fetherston served as DGMS from 1914 to 1918.

[33] Ibid.; Cope, 'F.A. Maguire – A Man of Many Parts'.

[34] *Berrima* was 'hastily fitted up in dock to act as a troop-transport ... well suited for the purpose'. Maguire states that the health record for the voyage was 'excellent'. F.A. Maguire and R.W. Cilento in Butler, *The Australian Army Medical Services in the War of 1914-1918,* Vol.1, *Gallipoli, Palestine and New Guinea,* pp.782–92.

[35] Maguire in Butler, ibid., p.787.

[36] Ibid.

[37] The volunteer force comprised eight infantry companies and six companies of the Royal Australian Naval Reserve. Royal Australian Navy website 'Australian naval and military expeditionary force'.

[38] Maguire replaced Rupert Downes as DGMS in 1941. Howse served as DGMS from July 1921 to November 1922. Maguire was DGMS between March 1941 and November 1942. See Hill, A.J., 'Howse, Sir Neville Reginald (1863-1930), *ADB,* Vol.9. MUP, 1983.

[39] Seven Australians were killed during this encounter on 11 September 1914. On 14 September, an Australian submarine patrolling near Rabaul disappeared with 35 men on board.

See Chris Coulthard-Clarke, *Where Australians Fought: The Encyclopaedia of Australia's Battles*, Allen & Unwin, St Leonards, NSW, 1998, p.97.

[40] Brian Pockley was killed in action on Rabaul on 11 September 1914 after giving his Red Cross brassard to Kember, the medical orderly who was caring for a wounded soldier. Pockley's brassard was later forwarded to his mother by the Australian War Memorial, along with a citation that stated he was 'the first Australian to die in the great cause of the world's liberty'. See NSW State Archive MLMSS 1092, Item 1 Brian Colden Antill Pockley papers, 1910-1917 and Item 5 Pockley family photographs ca 1866-1918. See also MLMSS 15, Box 2, Folder 1 General William Holmes telegrams and cables, September-October 1914.

[41] Maguire in Butler, *The Australian Army Medical Services in the War of 1914-1918*, Vol.1, *Gallipoli, Palestine and New Guinea*, p.782; Cope, 'F.A. Maguire – A Man of Many Parts', p.325.

[42] Maguire in Butler, ibid., pp.782–92.

[43] Enquiry re looting at Rabaul by Australian Naval & Military Expeditionary Force-Memorandum from Government House, Rabaul to The Minister of State for Defence, Melbourne 19th February 1915; Decodes or Copies of Wires despatched to Defence, Melbourne since 1st February 1915, A.50 February 11th stated, 'Private James Morgan, "C" Company, died malaria at Angerum, New Guinea, 19th January.' NAA Series MP367/1, Item 580/2/3346.

[44] Ibid.

[45] Ibid.

[46] Cilento in Butler, *The Australian Army Medical Services in the War of 1914-1918*, Vol.1, *Gallipoli, Palestine and New Guinea*, p.798.

[47] Western Samoa was mandated to New Zealand, while Bougainville and the Bismarck Archipelago were mandated to Australia. Nauru was mandated to Australia, New Zealand and the United Kingdom. See 'The South Pacific', *The Advertiser*, 16 December 1919, p.6; 'The Ex-German Pacific Islands', *The Mercury*, 21 February 1919, p.5; 'Samoa – New Zealand Mandate', *The Examiner*, 4

November 1919, p.5; 'Control of Nauru – British Empire Mandate', *Sydney Morning Herald*, 12 July 1919, p.17.

[48] The Marshall and Caroline islands are part of Micronesia. Japan was awarded a Class C mandate over all except two Micronesian islands. The Gilbert Islands were administered by Britain, while Guam (part of the Mariana Islands) was administered by the US.

[49] W.M. Hughes in 'The Peace Treaty Submitted to Parliament – Mr Hughes Reviews Provisions', *Argus*, Melbourne, 11 September 1919, pp.7–8.

[50] See League of Nations Mandate for the Territory of New Guinea, 17 December 1920 in *Official Year Book of the Commonwealth of Australia No 31 – 1938*.

[51] 'History of World War II (Volume III): War in the South Seas, and Peril Approaches Australia', *Argus*, Melbourne, 6 February 1943, p.4.

[52] Cook cited in Jinks et al. (eds), *Readings in New Guinea History*, p.295.

[53] Jinks et al. (eds), ibid., p.296.

[54] Felix M. Keesing, 'Atoms of Empire' in *Far Eastern Survey*, 10 (5), March 1941, p.54.

[55] *Cairns Post*, 16 February 1939, p.14. The Covenant of the League of Nations (Paragraph Three, Article One) states that: 'Any Member of the League may, after two years' notice of its intention so to do, withdraw from the League, provided that all its international obligations and all its obligations under this Covenant shall have been fulfilled at the time of its withdrawal.' Germany withdrew from the League on 23 October 1933.

[56] Article 4 of the New Guinea Mandate stated that 'the military training of the natives, otherwise than for purposes of internal police and the local defence of the territory, shall be prohibited. Furthermore, no military or naval bases shall be established or fortifications erected in the territory.' See League of Nations Mandate for the Territory of New Guinea.

[57] See Thomas Wilds, 'How Japan Fortified the Mandates' in *US Naval Proceedings* 626, April 1955, pp.401–07; Dirk Anthony Ballendorf, 'Secrets

Without Substance' in *The Journal of Pacific History*, 19 (2), 1984, pp.83–99.

[58] Until 1909, Rabaul was known as Simpsonshafen. In 1910, it replaced Herbertshöhe as the capital of Kaiser Wilhelmsland (German New Guinea). Rabaul remained the capital after the AN&MEF took control of German New Guinea in 1914.

[59] The Lieutenant Governor of Papua, Hubert Murray, was one who initially pushed for the amalgamation of the two territories—with Murray as the head of the administration. He later changed his views, fearing 'less humane control'. See H.N. Nelson, 'Murray, Sir John Hubert Plunkett (1861–1940)', *ADB*, Vol.10, MUP, 1986. The amalgamation of Papua and New Guinea did not occur until 1949.

[60] Harrison quoted in 'Papua and New Guinea', *Tweed Daily*, 30 November 1938, p.4.

[61] 'Capital Site – Rabaul Protest', *Argus*, Melbourne, 26 August 1938, p.2. Locations inspected included Madang, Salamaua, Wau and Upper Ramu.

[62] See 'New Guinea and Papua – Merger Problem: Administrator's Views', *Sydney*

Morning Herald, 6 December 1938, p.12.

[63] 'Legendary Monkey Men in New Guinea: Mr Hughes Twitted in House', Advertiser, Adelaide, 19 May 1938. In 1910, the same newspaper had published "'Queer People of Papua: Dwarfs and 'Men with Tails'", which was an account of the original report by Judge Murray, Lieutenant Governor of Papua.

[64] Advertiser, Adelaide, p.6.

[65] Cairns Post, p.14.

[66] 6 John Coates, An Atlas of Australia's Wars, Oxford University Press, Melbourne, 2001, p.228.

[67] Cairns Post, p.14; 'Papuan Fortifications', Argus, Melbourne, 23 February 1939.

[68] Downes, Personal Diaries 1939–45: Rough Diary 1939, Notes on Canberra Visit. NAA Series DRL No 2184 (3rd Series)—(file number is given as AWM 417/20/28 with note 'wrong file number'). Downes was appointed DGMS in August 1934.

[69] Walker, Australia in the War of 1939-1945, Series 5, Vol.3, The Island Campaigns, pp.1–3.

[70] *Commonwealth of Australia Year Book 1938*, pp.264–65. Diseases prevalent in the area around Port Moresby included malaria, scrub typhus and beriberi. See Walker, ibid., p.2. Yaws is a tropical infection of the skin, bones and joints.

[71] See 'The Man Who Tamed Papua', *Courier-Mail*, Brisbane, 29 February 1940, p.4; Nelson, 'Murray, Sir John Hubert Plunkett (1861–1940)'.

[72] A.J. Hill, 'Downes, Rupert Major (1885–1945)', *ADB*, Vol.8, MUP, 1981. Downes also wrote Part II of Butler's *The Australian Army Medical Services in the War of 1914-1918*, Vol.1, *Gallipoli, Palestine and New Guinea*.

[73] Ian Howie-Willis, *Surgeon and General: A Life of Major General Rupert Downes*, Australian Military History Publications, Loftus, NSW, 2008, p.264.

[74] 'Notes on Canberra Visit 4/12/39' in NAA series DRL No 2184.

[75] Walker, *Australia in the War of 1939-1945*, Series 5, Vol.3, *The Island Campaigns*, p.1. See also collection of primary source documents related to administrative, economic and social issues of Papua and New Guinea,

1768–1970s in Jinks et al. (eds), *Readings in New Guinea History*.

Chapter Two

[1]   The British Army commissioned its first motorised ambulances in 1905 and they were used by all nations during World War I. See John S. Haller, *Farmcarts to Fords: a history of the military ambulance 1790-1925*, Southern Illinois University Press, Carbondale, 1992.

[2]   Butler, *The Australian Army Medical Services in the War of 1914-1918*, Vol.3, *Special Problems and Services*, p.234. See also Michael B. Tyquin, *Gallipoli: The Medical War – the Australian Army medical services in the Dardanelles campaign of 1915*, University of New South Wales Press, Kensington, NSW, 1993. The term 'long nineteenth century' refers to the period between the French Revolution in 1789 and World War I in 1914.

[3]   In World War I, an Australian Army infantry division numbered approximately 18,000, with five infantry divisions and two mounted divisions fielded during this conflict. Dennis et al. (eds), *The Oxford Companion to Australian Military History*,

p.187. See also Grey, *The Australian Centenary History of Defence*, Vol.1, *The Australian Army*; Australian War Memorial website, 'Military organisation and structure'.

[4] International Committee of the Red Cross website 'Rules: Rule 25. Medical Personnel'.

[5] A.J. Sweeting, 'The 2/4th Field Ambulance A.I.F. during the Owen Stanleys Campaign 1942: Memories of Sgt A.J. (Bill) Sweeting M.B.E.' (no date); letter to author from Bill Sweeting, 8 February 2009.

[6] Downes was not sent overseas until March 1939. He was tasked with investigating the organisation, requirements, supply and allocation of medical equipment for Australia if war occurred. See Allan S. Walker, *Australia in the War of 1939–1945*, Series 5, Vol.2, *Middle East and Far East*, Australian War Memorial, Canberra, 1953, p.20.

[7] For an overview of these committees, see Ian Howie-Willis, *A Medical Emergency: Major-General 'Ginger' Burston and the Army Medical Service in World War II*, Big Sky Publishing, Sydney, 2012, pp.135–36.

[8] See also Jan McLeod, 'The House That Jack Built: DGMS Rupert Downes and Australian Army Medical Preparations for World War II' in *Health and History* 19 (1), 2017, pp.80–101.

[9] Dennis et al. (eds), *The Oxford Companion to Australian Military History*, pp.90–93. Blamey was described by the British General, William Birdwood, as having 'by no means a pleasing personality'.

[10] Howie-Willis, *A Medical Emergency*, p.128.

[11] For assessments of Blamey's leadership, see Gavin Long, *Australia in the War of 1939–1945*, Series I, Army, Vol. I, *To Benghazi*, Australian War Memorial, Canberra, 1961, various chapters; David Horner concluded that 'it would be difficult to think of another Australian general with the prestige, personality or grasp of politics necessary to lead the Army in its greatest trials.' David Horner, Blamey, Sir Thomas Albert (1884–1951), *ADB*, Vol.13, MUP, 1993.

[12] Long, ibid., pp.88–89.

[13] Palazzo, *The Australian Army*, p.182.

[14] See Howie-Willis, *A Medical Emergency*, pp.118–23.

[15] Quoted in Howie-Willis, *Surgeon and General*, p.292.

[16] Howie-Willis, *A Medical Emergency*, pp.125, 220.

[17] See Walker, *Australia in the War of 1939–1945*, Series 5, Vol.2, *Middle East and Far East*, Chapter 1, for full details.

[18] See Observations on the Administration of the Army Medical Service in the first 4 ½ months of the War – 1940, AWM Series 54, Item 481/2/40, for Downes' account of the shortcomings and influence of the British Army; see also McLeod, 'The House That Jack Built', pp.80–101.

[19] AWM Series 54, Item 481/2/40. In terms of what was expected from civilian medical practitioners, the National Security Act of September 1939 required all medical personnel to 'practise or place their services at the disposal of the Commonwealth in places and for periods specified'. Walker, *Australia in the War of 1939–1945*, Series 5, Vol.2, *Middle East and Far East*, p.51.

[20] 'Australian youth has made a magnificent response' to the call for volunteers of 1939, *Argus* Melbourne, 19 September 1939. The *Argus*, Melbourne, 14 September 1939 included a report 'The Spirit of Anzac' which told of 'recruiting offices overflowing with applicants'.
[21] AWM Series 54, Item 481/2/40.
[22] Ibid.
[23] 'Canberra Air Disaster', National Archives Fact Sheet No. 142.
[24] Prime Minister Robert Menzies described the crash as 'a shocking calamity ... the full effect of which even yet is not fully realised'. *Canberra Times*, 14–15 August 1940.
[25] AWM Series DRL 2184 (3rd Series), Item 417/20/28 DGMS Downes Personal Diaries 1939–45.
[26] Ibid. See entry for 11 December 1939: 'Street told me to see him at once if blocked [regarding] equipment, Obstructions then in being.'
[27] Ibid., entry for 11 October 1939 recorded 'Street to dinner – discussed need of medical service and delays (S. told me to see him at once if blocked), dental, independence of

M.S.[Medical Service] and recent obstruction'; see also AWM Series 54, Item 481/2/40.

[28] AWM Series 54, Item 481/2/40.
[29] AWM 292 MED 40/76, Personal Letters to DGMS Burston 1939–1943, letter from Burston to Colonel Clive Disher, 2 April 1940.
[30] VX2 Burston, S.R., Army Service Record, p.24 in NAA Series B663; Howie-Willis, *A Medical Emergency*, pp.121–22, 131.
[31] Howie-Willis, ibid., pp.118–20, 129–30.
[32] Burston, S.R. to Downes, R.M., 16 December 1940 in Howie-Willis, ibid., p.138; Walker, *Australia in the War of 1939–1945*, Series 5, Vol.2, *Middle East and Far East*, p.338.
[33] See Howie-Willis, ibid., pp.101–03; Howie-Willis, *Surgeon and General*, p.130; Butler, *The Australian Army Medical Services in the War of 1914-1918*, Vol.1, *Gallipoli, Palestine and New Guinea*, pp.1–16 for an explanation of AAMC hierarchy in World War I and the role of Howse.
[34] Howie-Willis, *A Medical Emergency*, pp.138–39.
[35] Ibid., p.138.

[36] Serial No 24, 27 December 1940 in AWM Series 54, Item 481/1/8 (Downes Papers).
[37] Letter to Colonel W.W.S. Johnston, 19 March 1941, in AWM Series 54, Item 481/1/8.
[38] Ibid.
[39] Ibid.
[40] Serial No 24, 27 December 1940 in AWM Series 54, Item 481/1/8.
[41] See Walker, *Australia in the War of 1939–1945*, Series 5, Vol.2, *Middle East and Far East*; Howie-Willis, *A Medical Emergency*. Downes was later appointed DMS of Second Army—created by Blamey in April 1942 for the defence of NSW, Victoria, South Australia and Tasmania.
[42] In a letter to 'Coops'[Lieutenant Colonel Eric Leonard Cooper] dated 26 March 1941, Downes wrote 'the A.-G. informed me that it was political, and that the Army had never been consulted. The two appointments are temporary, of course, as I have a fixed job until August 1943.' AWM Series 54, Item 481/1/8.
[43] Correspondence on appointment of DGMS, D.M.S. and Inspector-General

Medical Services 1941-Extract from letter from DGMS Downes to D.M.S. Burston, 2 March 1941 in AWM Series 54, Item 481/1/8 Part 3.

[44] In the Australian Army, three divisions form one corps. A division numbers 8000 to 10,000 men. Three brigades form one division. A brigade comprises 1800 to 2500 men. The 6th Division originally had four brigades but was reorganised into three once in the Middle East, in line with the British Army organisation. For a detailed explanation of all aspects of the Australian Army including the 'two army' system of AIF and CMF (militia), see Grey, *The Australian Centenary History of Defence*, Vol.1, *The Australian Army*.

[45] Hierarchical structure of the Army: corps, division, brigade, battalion (or unit), company platoon, section. See Dennis et al. (eds), *The Oxford Companion to Australian Military History*, pp. xvi-xx. For organisational details, see Grey, *The Australian Centenary History of Defence*, Vol.1, *The Australian Army*, pp.133–48 (especially Figure 5.1, Tables 5.1 and 5.3); Long, *Australia in*

the War of 1939–1945, Vol. I, To Benghazi, Chapter 4.

[46] The Australian Comfort Fund was established in 1916 to supply soldiers with so-called luxury items. It was largely run by female volunteers. Items sent overseas included socks, razor blades, toothbrushes and reading materials. See Museums Victoria Collections 'Australian Comforts Fund, World War II, 1939-1946'.

[47] Unit Diary 2/1 Battalion, 6th Division AIF-Voyage Report No 1, Lieutenant-Colonel K. Eather, 3 January 1940 in AWM Series 52, Item 8/3/1. Appendix III of the diary shows symbols to be used for labelling the various boxes of equipment: a round label with Red Cross for medical stores; inverted red triangle with diagonal lines for veterinary supplies; round red label with diagonal lines for AASC stores.

[48] Voyage Report No.1, 2 and 3, January–February 1940 in AWM Series 52, Item 8/3/1.

[49] The fate of the soldier is unknown. AWM Series 52, Item 8/3/2, Unit Diary 2/2 Battalion, 6th Division AIF,

Lieutenant-Colonel Wooten (Officer Commanding Troops), January–February 1940. Note: 'HMT' refers to 'Hired Military Transport'. Civilian passenger ships were converted for use by the Navy as troopships during war. Originally named SS *Ortranto*, the ship was built in England in 1929.

[50] AWM Series 52, Item 8/3/2, Unit Diary 2/2 Battalion, 6th Division AIF.

[51] Walker, *Australia in the War of 1939–1945*, Series 5, Vol.2, *Middle East and Far East*, p.63.

[52] 6th Division: 2/1, 2/2, 2/7 field ambulances; 7th Division: 2/4, 2/5, 2/6 field ambulances; 9th Division: 2/3, 2/8, 2/11 field ambulances. See Howie-Willis, *A Medical Emergency*, pp.129–30.

[53] Howie-Willis, ibid., pp.128–29, 236.

[54] Bryan Egan, 'Disher, Harold Clive (1891–1976)', *ADB*, MUP, Vol.14, 1996. Disher's correspondence is held in the University of Melbourne Archives, 'Strathfield Estate'; Walker, *Australia in the War of 1939–1945*, Series 5, Vol.2, *Middle East and Far East*, p.86.

[55] Walker, ibid., pp.90–91.

[56] Ibid., p.96.

[57] Ibid., Chapter 5. The initial Australian medical units were the 2/1st AGH, 2/1st Field Ambulance, 2/1st Field Hygiene Section and 2/1st Convalescent Depot.

[58] Money donated by Australians was not specifically allocated to supplementing supplies for Australian soldiers. See 'Gift of Ambulance', Launceston *Examiner*, 3 July 1940.

[59] 'Services For Soldiers', Camperdown *Chronicle* (Victoria), 13 August 1940.

[60] 'Red Cross Appeal: 15 Ambulances for Overseas', *Sydney Morning Herald*, 4 October 1940.

[61] Just 20% of the 16th Brigade were deemed dentally fit and the brigade's dental health remained poor during 1940. For example, the 2/5th Battalion required 1200 fillings and 120 sets of dentures in that year. The demand for dental care was so high, and equipment levels so inadequate, that the British Army's DDMS in Palestine 'presented to the AIF four out of six dental trailers captured from the Italians'. Walker, *Australia in the War of 1939–1945*, Series 5, Vol.2, *Middle East and Far East*, p.98; Mark Harrison,

Medicine and Victory: British Military Medicine in World War II, Oxford University Press, New York, 2004, p.46.

[62] Howie-Willis, *A Medical Emergency*, p.120.

[63] Letters from Colonel H.C. Disher, 1940–41, in Burston World War II correspondence, quoted in Howie-Willis, ibid., Chapter 6. For a summary of relevant aspects regarding medical organisation and supply 1940–41, see Walker, *Australia in the War of 1939–1945*, Series 5, Vol.2, *Middle East and Far East*, Chapter 15.

[64] See Grey, *The Australian Centenary History of Defence*, Vol.1, *The Australian Army*, pp.124, 133; Dennis et al. (eds), *The Oxford Companion to Australian Military History*, pp.530–32; Long, *Australia in the War of 1939–1945*, Vol. I, *To Benghazi*, Chapters 9–11.

[65] For background on the Crete campaign see entry by John Coates in Dennis et al. (eds), ibid., pp.166–70.

[66] Howie-Willis, *A Medical Emergency*, p.170; Long, *Australia in the War of 1939–1945*, Vol. I, *To Benghazi*, Chapter 10.

[67] Walker, *Australia in the War of 1939–1945*, Series 5, Vol.2, *Middle East and Far East*, p.277.

[68] Ibid.

[69] Howie-Willis, *A Medical Emergency*, p.172.

[70] There were 6486 AIF troops in Crete prior to the German attack. Of the approximately 3500 who were unable to be evacuated and so remained on the island during the fighting, more than 3000 were taken prisoner and almost 300 died. Walker, *Australia in the War of 1939–1945*, Series 5, Vol.2, *Middle East and Far East*, Appendix I: Numbers of A.I.F. Troops in Crete, p.295.

[71] Howie-Willis, *A Medical Emergency*, p.177. Howie-Willis cites Michael Tyquin's observation that 'Burston and his staff were railroaded into a full commitment by a tragically overconfident general staff.'

[72] Summary of Medical Plan 7th Australian Division Syrian Campaign; Progress Report Nos 2 and 3 ADMS Australian Division "Exporter"; Commission of Control Syria – Interim Report of Committee No 11 (Medical), Jun-Jul

	1941 in AWM Series 54, Item 531/1/4; Notes on a Field Ambulance, Lieutenant Colonel G.G.B. Maitland DSO, DGM, January 1942 in AWM Series 54, Item 19/7/18.
[73]	Progress Reports Nos 2 & 3, ADMS Aust Div "Exporter"; Commission of Control Syria Interim Report of Committee No 11 (Medical) 24 July 1941, Colonel Norris in AWM Series 54, Item 531/1/4.
[74]	Harrison, *Medicine and Victory*, p.63. For example, Colonel Large had difficulty keeping track of the locations of medical units in the Greece and Crete campaigns and recognised that the CCS was 'too cumbersome' for mobile warfare.
[75]	Introduction by British DGAMS (Director General Army Medical Services) Alexander Hood in Re-organization of Medical Services in the Field, 3 November 1942 in PRO Series WO, Item 22/89 quoted in Harrison, *Medicine and Victory*, p.113.
[76]	Field Ambulance Report, p.2 in AWM Series 54, Item 531/1/4.
[77]	Ibid.

[78] Field Ambulance Report, p.4 in AWM Series 54, Item 531/1/4.
[79] Ibid.
[80] Ibid.
[81] Ibid. For details of the Libyan campaign and siege of Tobruk see Dennis et al. (eds), *The Oxford Companion to Australian Military History*, pp.316–17, 530–32.
[82] Field Ambulance Report, p.4.
[83] Field Ambulance Report, p.5 in AWM Series 54, Item 531/1/4. Disher's discussion of aspects of the dental service such as duties, transport and command indicate there were some tensions regarding these issues. For example, he stated that 'a man of the branches of the combatant forces has often to perform duties other than those of his particular branch.' He also pointed out that it is 'just as logical to say that Medical Officers should not do other than doctoring as it is to say that dental personnel should only do dental work.'
[84] Diary of NX 21854 Private L.N. Kennedy, 2/4th Field Ambulance, 7th Division, AIF (hereafter Kennedy Diary).

[85] Ibid., January 1941.
[86] Ibid., April 1941.
[87] Ibid., January, February, April 1941.
[88] Ibid., June 1941.
[89] Ibid., July 1941.
[90] Ibid., 1 January 1942.

Chapter Three

[1] Joan Beaumont, *Australia's War 1939–45*, Allen & Unwin, St Leonards, NSW, 1996, p.27; the 6th Division was not at full strength for most of 1940, while the 7th and 9th divisions had a 'fluid composition' during 1941, interchanging battalions and brigades. See Adrian Threlfall, *Jungle Warriors: From Tobruk to Kokoda and beyond*, Allen & Unwin, Sydney, 2014, chapters 1–2, p.17.

[2] See relevant entries in Dennis et al. (eds), *The Oxford Companion to Australian Military History*, for information on the Coral Sea and Midway battles.

[3] Walker, *Australia in the War of 1939–1945*, Series 5, Vol.3, *The Island Campaigns*, p.15.

[4] The Japanese 'planned offensive was assisted ... by intelligence failures at the headquarters of General Douglas

MacArthur, which played down the likelihood of an early renewal of Japanese activity.' See Dennis et al. (eds), *The Oxford Companion to Australian Military History*, pp.300, 384.

[5] Peter Dean (ed.), *Australia 1942: in the shadow of war*, Cambridge University Press, Melbourne, 2013, pp.11–29. The Central Pacific Area encompassed the Palau, Caroline, Mariana, Marshall, Midway and Hawaiian islands, as well as Truk, Guam and Iwo Jima.

[6] Army Chief of Staff, Sugiyama, 11 July 1942 in Steven Bullard (trans), *Japanese Army Operations in the South Pacific Area*, Australian War Memorial, Canberra, 2007, p.151.

[7] 'Moresby – nothing sent up there? Have Air Force sent anything up', Notes on Conference, 21 October 1940 in AWM Series 54, Item 481/1/27.

[8] Notes on Conference-Report by DGMS Downes (Hospitals), 11 September 1940. See also Report by Colonel Evans (Hospitals), 24 February 1941 in AWM Series 54, Item 481/1/27. Downes' assessment that the Darwin situation had eased was based on the availability of Bagot Compound for use as a medical

facility, which reduced the size of the hospital planned for Darwin. After Darwin was bombed in February 1941, this situation was deemed unsatisfactory as plans for the hospital were incomplete, no tenders had been received and troops were being sent there in response to the Japanese attack.

[9] Report by Colonel Holmes, 25 November 1940 in AWM Series 54, Item 481/1/27.
[10] Ibid.
[11] Ibid.
[12] Report by Colonel Evans (Hospitals) presented at weekly conference, 24 February 1941. This assessment appears to refer to the situation in Port Moresby since there is a separate subheading of 'Darwin' which specifically discusses the inadequacy of the hospital situation there. See AWM Series 54, Item 481/1/27.
[13] Dudley McCarthy, *Australia in the War of 1939-1945*, Series 1, Army, vol. V, *South-West Pacific Area – First Year Kokoda to Wau*, Australian War Memorial, Canberra, 1959, p.42. Note that many women, including missionaries and nurses, remained in

New Guinea and other islands such as New Britain. See Australian War Memorial, 'Australian-Japanese Research Project: Remembering the war in New Guinea – Women and war in New Guinea'.

[14] 'Amazed at Australians' Casualness to War', Camperdown *Chronicle*, 3 March 1942, p.1; 'Evacuees from New Guinea and Papua – more than 2,000 in Australia', Singleton *Argus*, 11 March 1942, p.1; 'Last White Woman out of Moresby', Brisbane *Courier-Mail*, 18 April 1942, p.1.

[15] Walker, *Australia in the War of 1939–1945*, Series 5, Vol.3, *The Island Campaigns*, p.1.

[16] Ibid. See also Lionel Wigmore, *Australia in the War of 1939-1945*, Series 1, Army, vol. IV, *The Japanese Thrust*, Australian War Memorial, Canberra, 1957, pp.393–94. The Singapore Conference in February led to further discussions and the decision to send a battalion to Rabaul. The 2/22nd Battalion, 23rd Brigade, arrived during March and April 1941. Other units included coastal defence and an anti-tank battery.

[17] Walker, *Australia in the War of 1939–1945*, Series 5, Vol.3, *The Island Campaigns*, p.4.

[18] Report by Colonel Holmes, 10 March 1941 in AWM Series 54, Item 481/2/27.

[19] Ibid.

[20] Report by Miss Wood (Australian Army Nursing Service) presented at weekly conference, 17 March 1941. Wood also reported that four sisters had been sent to Alice Springs and that 24 reinforcements and 12 ambulance transports were ready for deployment. AWM Series 54, Item 481/2/27.

[21] Notes on conference 14 March 1941, 5.15pm: 'The duties of the appointment of Inspector-General would be inspecting and reporting on all Medical Services, whether in Australia or Overseas; reports to be made to the Military Board' in AWM Series 54, Item 481/1/27. Downes was to 'carry out inspections and report to the Military Board on any matters affecting ... the organisation, interior economy, efficiency, location, equipment and transport of the medical service and

	medical units and establishment of the AMF and AIF [and] the health, morale and general well-being of the troops, or in the maintenance of the physical efficiency of the Army.' Duties of IGMS, 27th March 1941 in AWM Series 54, Item 481/12/166 cited in Howie-Willis, *Surgeon and General*, p.316.
[22]	Letter from Rupert Downes to 'Coop' (Lieutenant Colonel Eric Leonard Cooper), 26 March 1941 in AWM Series 54, Item 481/2/27.
[23]	Sequence of Conferences and Visits to Medical Establishments and Reports arising there from (various documents) in AWM Series 54, Item 481/1/27.
[24]	Appreciation of Port Moresby, R. Downes, May 1941 in AWM Series 54, Item 481/1/27.
[25]	Ibid.
[26]	Ibid.
[27]	Forde was appointed to the portfolios as part of the Labor ministry under the newly elected Prime Minister John Curtin and was sworn in on 7 October 1941.
[28]	Notes on three-quarters of an hour interview with the Minister (Mr Forde),

	R. Downes, 23rd October 1941 in AWM Series 54, Item 481/1/27.
[29]	Ibid.
[30]	Ibid.
[31]	Ibid.
[32]	Ibid.
[33]	Ibid.
[34]	Arrangements for Dealing with Australia's Sick and Wounded Overseas. The Minute was forwarded via tele-printer by Minister F.M. Forde to Inspector-General of Medical Services and the Secretary, Military Board for the DGMS. It was signed by Forde on 11 February and forwarded on 12 February 1942, three days before the fall of Singapore. See AWM Series 54, Item 481/12/245.
[35]	Arrangements for Dealing with Australia's Sick and Wounded Overseas in AWM Series 54, Item 481/12/245.
[36]	Transcript of report from Mr Blackburn to Minister Forde—Arrangements for Sick and Wounded Overseas in AWM Series 54, Item 481/12/245. The fall of Rabaul and the fate of the Australian soldiers is discussed in Wigmore, *Australia in the War of 1939-1945*, Series I, Army,

vol. IV, *The Japanese Thrust*, Chapter 18.

[37] Diary entry, 17 February 1942 in AWM Series 54, Item 481/1/27.

[38] Arrangements for Dealing with Australia's Sick and Wounded Overseas in AWM Series 54, Item 481/12/245.

[39] Diary Entry, 20 February 1942 in AWM Series 54, Item 481/1/27.

[40] Summary of report, February 20 to 22nd 1942, Lieutenant-Colonel D. Galbraith in AWM Series 54, Item 481/12/245. The units stationed at Port Moresby were the 3rd Field Ambulance, 16th Field Hygiene Section, 210th Camp Hospital, Red Cross Convalescent Home, Army Convalescent Depot and four independent dental units.

[41] AANS members were among the dead and wounded when the 2/1st Australian Hospital Ship, *Manunda*, was hit during Japanese air raids on Darwin Harbour. The attack was deemed by some to be a violation of the Geneva Conventions. Others argued that the ship was accidentally hit and the real target was two American destroyers anchored nearby. See Jan Bassett, *Guns*

	and Brooches: Australian Army Nursing from the Boer War to the Gulf War, Oxford University Press, South Melbourne, 1992, pp.153–61.
[42]	Summary of report in AWM Series 54, Item 481/12/245.
[43]	A total of 68 AANS arrived on *Manunda* on 24 October. For an account of nurses' experiences in Papua, see Joan Crouch, '2/9th Australian General Hospital New Guinea August 1942 – January 1943' in *The Defence Force Journal* 57, March/April 1986, pp.32–37.
[44]	Summary of report in AWM Series 54, Item 481/12/245.
[45]	Ibid.
[46]	Notes regarding Reports 11 and 12, R. Downes, March 1942 in AWM Series 54, Item 481/1/27.
[47]	Diary entry, 21 February 1942 in AWM Series 54, Item 481/1/27. Salamaua is located on the north-east coast of what was then the Territory of New Guinea.
[48]	Diary entries, 21 and 22 February 1942 in AWM Series 54, Item 481/1/27.

[49]	Points from Port Moresby, 22 February 1942 in AWM Series 54, Item 481/1/27.
[50]	Ibid.
[51]	Ibid.
[52]	In November 1942, Koitaki was the site of General Blamey's infamous 'Rabbits' address to the 21st Brigade. See James, *Field Guide to the Kokoda Track*, pp.132–36; Paul Ham, *Kokoda*, HarperCollins, Pymble, NSW, 2004, pp.260, 281–83.
[53]	Summary of Report on Visit to Port Moresby in AWM Series 54, Item 481/12/245.

Chapter Four

[1]	Diary entry 21 February 1942 in AWM Series 54, Item 481/1/27.
[2]	Signal from Major General Sydney Rowell, Deputy Chief of the General Staff, to Major General Basil Morris, 8th Military District, 3 February 1942 in McCarthy, *Australia in the War of 1939-1945*, vol. V, Series 1, *South-West Pacific Area – First Year Kokoda to Wau*, p.111. Japanese troops landed unopposed at Salamaua and Lae in March 1942.

[3] McCarthy, ibid., p.114.

[4] Information on the landing location and the composition of the Japanese Army in Papua varies. See. for example: Department of Veterans' Affairs website 'The Kokoda Track'; Karl James, 'The Track', a historical desktop study of the Kokoda Track, Canberra, 2009 published online; Peter Williams, *The Kokoda Campaign 1942: myth and reality*, Cambridge University Press, Port Melbourne, 2012.

[5] Operational orders from the *17th Army, No 2* in Bullard (trans), *Japanese Army Operations in the South Pacific Area*, pp.120–21.

[6] McCarthy, *Australia in the War of 1939-1945*, vol. V, Series 1, *South-West Pacific Area – First Year Kokoda to Wau*, pp.114, 122–23.

[7] Bullard (trans), *Japanese Army Operations in the South Pacific Area*, p.112. In March 1941, Major Toyofuku Tetsuo arrived in Port Moresby disguised as a crew member of a Japanese ship. He photographed the local area, established that there was no vehicular road from Port Moresby north over the Owen Stanleys, and noted the various foot

tracks in existence. This information, as well as information gathered by the Japanese Consulate in Australia, was later included in Toyofuku's intelligence report for the Japanese Army. The report included Australian maps of the tracks over the Papuan mountains. See Australian Government Kokoda Commemoration website, 'The Kokoda Track – Japanese Intelligence'.

[8] See Australian Government Kokoda Commemoration website, 'The Kokoda Track-Japanese landing and advance to Kokoda'.

[9] Bullard (trans), *Japanese Army Operations in the South Pacific Area*, pp.120–22.

[10] Ibid., pp.1–2.

[11] Ibid.

[12] See Robyn Kienzle, *The Architect of Kokoda: Bert Kienzle – the man who made the Kokoda Trail*, Hachette Australia, Sydney, 2011, for exploration, mining and plantation life in this area and a history of the Kokoda Trail.

[13] Walker, *Australia in the War of 1939–1945*, Vol.3, Series 5, *The Island Campaigns*, p.16.

[14] Bullard (trans), *Japanese Army Operations in the South Pacific Area*, p.159.

[15] Morris' reply cited in Bullard, ibid.
[16] Allied ground forces: 1098 AIF, 12,273 militia and 2208 US soldiers. Walker, *Australia in the War of 1939–1945*, Vol.3, Series 5, *The Island Campaigns*, pp.17–18.
[17] James, 'The Track', p.8.
[18] Porter was an AIF officer who had commanded the 2/31st Battalion in Syria. Peter Brune, *A Bastard Of A Place: The Australians in Papua*, Allen & Unwin, Sydney, 2003, pp.92–93.
[19] Report on Operations 14 Aust Fd Amb – Papua, Chronological Account of Incidents B: Advance to Awala and Withdrawal to Ioribiawa, Lieutenant-Colonel M.M.S. Earlam, Commanding Officer, 14th Australian Field Ambulance, p.3 (hereafter, Report on Operations) in AWM Series 54, Item 19/7/17.
[20] Report on Operations, p.3 in AWM Series 54, Item 19/7/17. The Papuan Infantry Battalion was formed in 1940 and was led by a New Zealander, Major William Watson. Its officers were Australian, its privates and non-commissioned officers were Papuans. See Australian Government,

Department of Veterans' Affairs website 'Four Peoples at War: The New Guineans'. For a list of principal units and commanders, see AWM Series 54, Item 557/6/9 Officers commanding Aust units which were engaged in the Owen Stanley-Gona-Sanananda Campaign.

[21] Frank Kingsley Norris, *No Memory For Pain*, Heinemann, Melbourne, 1970, p.145.

[22] Sublet, *Kokoda to the Sea*, p.91. For discussion of the 'Brisbane Line' controversy, see detailed footnote in McCarthy, *Australia in the War of 1939-1945*, vol. V, Series 1, *South-West Pacific Area – First Year Kokoda to Wau*, p.112.

[23] See Howie-Willis, *Surgeon and General*, chapters 9 and 10; 'Military Hospitals', Gippsland *Times*, 2 March 1939; 'Report on Military Hospitals', *Age*, 6 April 1940; 'All Camps Will Have Hospitals', *The Sun*, 21 July 1940; 'Hospitals For The Forces', *Age*, 11 December 1942.

[24] See Australian War Memorial website, 'The Australian-Japanese Research Project'.

[25] While a 100-bed American station hospital had been set up at Milne Bay since June, US medical units did not arrive at Port Moresby until much later. The 11th Australian Field Ambulance arrived at Milne Bay in mid-July 1942. See AWM Series 52, Item 11/1/1 Units in New Guinea List in Branch AG 7 Army Headquarters, Melbourne, Director General Medical Services, Land Headquarters (whole diary—13 items) December 1941-November 1945.

[26] Walker, *Australia in the War of 1939–1945*, Vol.3, Series 5, *The Island Campaigns*, p.18. NGF commanded the Australian and US Army, Navy and Air Forces of the SWPA. The commander of NGF 'was to exercise operational control over NGF and such other troops as might thereafter be assigned thereto.' GHQ Operations Instructions N. 15 cited in NAA Series B6121, Item 74L, Establishment of New Guinea Force and Miscellaneous GHQ Correspondence Relative to NGF, p.1.

[27] Review of Production of War Material. General MacArthur's Statement of

Priorities in NAA Series A816, Item 42/301/279.

[28] Report on Operations 2/6 Australian Field Ambulance New Guinea, Major J.R. Magarey, 26-29 August 1942 in AWM Series 54, Item 481/12/67 (hereafter, Report on Operations).

[29] Report on Operations in AWM Series 54, Item 19/7/17. At this stage, the militia 14th Australian Infantry Brigade comprised the 3rd, 36th and 55th battalions.

[30] Report on Operations in AWM Series 54, Item 19/7/17.

[31] Ibid.

[32] Bullard (trans), *Japanese Army Operations in the South Pacific Area*, pp.159–60.

[33] PX11 Warrant Officer Class 2 John Dobell Wilkinson of ANGAU was Mentioned in Despatches (July 1945) for distinguished service in the SWPA.

[34] James, 'The Track', p.9.

[35] See Wilkinson's description of Vernon's arrival at Deniki on 29 July in Peter Brune, *Those Ragged Bloody Heroes*, Allen & Unwin, Sydney, 1991, p.43; Walker, *Australia in the War of 1939–1945*, Vol.3, Series 5, *The Island Campaigns*, pp.17–18.

[36] Vernon's diary cited in Brune, ibid., p.104. The official medical historian described Owen as 'mortally wounded' and did not mention that he was left behind. The official military historian stated he was 'unconscious ... with only a few minutes to live [as] the Australians were falling back'. See Walker, *Australia in the War of 1939–1945*, Vol.3, Series 5, *The Island Campaigns*, p.19; McCarthy, *Australia in the War of 1939-1945*, vol. V, Series 1, *South-West Pacific Area – First Year Kokoda to Wau*, p.129.

[37] Walker, ibid., p.19.

[38] NAA Series B883 Personnel Record of VX45223 Owen, William Taylor. It was later reported that Owen's body was buried 'in vicinity of Grahams House Kokoda'. The two reports of the burial are dated 13 January and 12 August 1943. The January listing notes also that Owen's body was reburied in Kokoda War Cemetery. The acronym 'NDG' (presumably, 'no date given') is listed in the Date of Casualty column, pp.10, 13.

[39] Norris, *No Memory For Pain*, p.145.

[40] Report on Operations, p.3 in AWM Series 54, Item 19/7/17. On 25 July, Lieutenant Colonel Brennan was replaced as ADMS of New Guinea Force due to illness and Lieutenant Colonel Gunning became Acting ADMS. See Walker, *Australia in the War of 1939–1945*, Vol.3, Series 5, *The Island Campaigns*, p.18.

[41] Report on Operations in AWM Series 54, Item 19/7/17. Note that Earlam's account refers to Eora Creek as Euro Creek throughout; Walker, ibid., p.19.

[42] Report on Operations in AWM Series 54, Item 19/7/17.

[43] Ibid.; Walker, *Australia in the War of 1939–1945*, Vol.3, Series 5, *The Island Campaigns*, pp.21–22.

[44] Report on Operations, p.4 in AWM Series 54, Item 19/7/17.

[45] Report on Operations, p.3 in AWM Series 54, Item 19/7/17. From mid-August until 8 September this detachment at Ilolo treated almost 500 patients, of whom 179 suffered gunshot wounds and over 300 suffered illnesses including malaria, diarrhoea and exhaustion. See analysis of patients passing through staging post up till [sic]

	8 Sept 42, p.6 in AWM Series 54, Item 19/7/17.
[46]	Report on Operations, p.4 in AWM Series 54, Item 19/7/17.
[47]	Ibid.
[48]	Walker, *Australia in the War of 1939–1945*, Vol.3, Series 5, *The Island Campaigns*, p.18. The 21st Brigade comprised the 2/14th, 2/16th and 2/27th infantry battalions. The 7th Brigade (9th, 25th and 61st battalions), 18th Brigade, AIF (2/9th, 2/10th and 2/12th battalions), and 9th Battery, 2/5th Field Regiment, were sent to Milne Bay on the eastern tip of New Guinea in August 1942. Medical aspects of the Milne Bay campaign are examined in later chapters of this book.
[49]	Walker, ibid., pp.23–24.
[50]	Signal from Morris quoted in McCarthy, *Australia in the War of 1939-1945*, vol. V, Series 1, *South-West Pacific Area – First Year Kokoda to Wau*, p.140.
[51]	Walker, *Australia in the War of 1939–1945*, Vol.3, Series 5, *The Island Campaigns*, p.24
[52]	Ibid., pp.23–24.

[53] Rowell was concerned about 'the effect on discipline and on the men's viewpoint if a differentiation were made.' Milne Force Medical Arrangements – Medical Layout – Suppressive Quinine, DDMS, NGF Brigadier W.W.S. Johnston, 3 September 1942, pp.4–5 in AWM Series 54, Item 481/12/220 (Dr Walker's Records Medical Reports & Arrangements, Milne Bay Area).

[54] Report on Operations in AWM Series 54, Item 19/7/17.

[55] Report on Operations, p.3 in AWM Series 54, Item 19/7/17.

[56] The Myola situation will be discussed in detail in following chapters.

[57] Report on Operations, p.5 in AWM Series 54, Item 19/7/17.

[58] Ibid. Sulphaguanidine is an anti-infective agent and was used to treat bacillary dysentery in both World Wars. The Australian Army was the first to adopt sulphaguanidine to treat dysentery. See Australian Science and Technology Heritage Centre, University of Melbourne, website, 'Technology in Australia 1788-1988'. Magnesium Sulphate was used to treat infected

battle wounds in both conflicts. It is also the basis of Epsom Salt, which was commonly used for centuries as a laxative. See Albert E. Morrison, 'The Treatment of Infected War Wounds by Magnesium Sulphate' in *The British Medical Journal* 1, 1918, p.342.

[59] Report on Operations in AWM Series 54, Item 19/7/17.

[60] International Committee of the Red Cross website 'Convention for the Amelioration of the Wounded and Sick of Armies in the Field, Geneva, 27 July 1929'. See Chapter VI: the distinctive emblem, Articles 19–24.

[61] Report on Operations, p.9 in AWM Series 54, Item 19/7/17.

[62] National Security (Inquiries) Regulations Inquiry by Sir William Webb, 2 August 1943. See, for example, testimony by Frank Kingsley Norris, p.377 in NAA Series A6237.

[63] International Committee of the Red Cross website, 'Customary International Humanitarian Law, Rule 25. Medical Personnel'; Geneva Convention, Chapter VI: the distinctive emblem, Articles 19–24.

[64] Report on Operations, p.27 in AWM Series 54, Item 19/7/17.
[65] Ibid.
[66] Report on Operations, p.9 in AWM Series 54, Item 19/7/17. The military term 'picquet' refers to the placing of soldiers forward of a position to warn of enemy approach.
[67] Report on Operations, pp.8–9 in AWM Series 54, Item 19/7/17.
[68] Ibid.
[69] Ibid.
[70] Ibid.
[71] Ibid.
[72] Walker, *Australia in the War of 1939–1945*, Series 5, Vol.1, *Clinical Problems of War*, p.321.
[73] Report on Operations in AWM Series 54, Item 19/7/17.
[74] Ibid.
[75] Walker, *Australia in the War of 1939–1945*, Series 5, Vol.1, *Clinical Problems of War*, p.323.
[76] Ibid. The Vitamin B deficiency was treated with Marmite and nicotinic acid (Niacin). Symptoms of Pellagra are wide-ranging and can affect the skin, the digestive and nervous systems as well as brain function.

[77] Walker, *Australia in the War of 1939–1945*, Series 5, Vol.1, *Clinical Problems of War*, p.320.

[78] Appendix 26F in AWM Series 52, Item 1/10/1 cited in E. Rogerson, 'The "Fuzzy Wuzzy Angels": looking beyond the myth', Australian War Memorial, SVSS paper, 2012, published online, p.11.

[79] Rogerson, ibid., pp.11–16.

[80] O. White, *Parliament of a thousand tribes*, p.129, cited in Rogerson, ibid., p.12.

[81] Report on Operations, p.7 in AWM Series 54, Item 19/7/17.

[82] Ibid.

[83] Ibid.

[84] Ibid.

[85] Walker, *Australia in the War of 1939–1945*, Vol.3, Series 5, *The Island Campaigns*, p. xv; Report on Operations, p.7 in AWM Series 54, Item 19/7/17.

[86] Report on Operations, p.7 in AWM Series 54, Item 19/7/17.

[87] Report on Operations, p.8 in AWM Series 54, Item 19/7/17.

[88] Ibid.

[89] Ibid.

[90]   Ibid.
[91]   Ibid.
[92]   Ibid.
[93]   Walker, *Australia in the War of 1939–1945*, Vol.3, Series 5, *The Island Campaigns*, p.35.

Chapter Five

[1]   Norris, *No Memory For Pain*, p.145.
[2]   Norris is referring to Lieutenant Colonel F.A. Chenhall who was appointed CO of the 2/6th Field Ambulance on 8 August, but did not arrive in Papua until 20 August. See AWM Series 54, Item 481/12/13 (Medical Service 7 Aust Division During Papuan Campaign, F. Kingsley Norris, Colonel ADMS 7 Aust. Div, January 1943).
[3]   Brief account of the activities of the 7th Australian Division – Medical Services during the six months campaign in Papua, p.7 in AWM Series 54, Item 481/12/13.
[4]   Norris, *No Memory For Pain*, p.150. See also 'Notes on Medical Service N.G.F. HQ – Mid Aug to Mid Dec '42, Medical Reports & Arrangements Milne Bay Area (unsigned, but presumably by DDMS

	Johnston), p.1 in AWM Series 54, Item 481/12/220. The 16th Field Hygiene Section was in the Port Moresby area in mid-August 1942 as was a Medical Stores Depot.
[5]	Diary entry, 26 March 1942 in AWM Series 52, Item 11/12/15, 2/6th Field Ambulance Diary.
[6]	Report on Bde Exercise by O.C. 'B' Coy, 2/6 Aust. Fd. Amb, Conclusions, 1. For example, 'This excercise [sic] was of little if any practical training value to most of the AAMC personnel … A "Cab-rank" for collection and evac would not be practicable without escort, and with escort, would violate Geneva Convention … Little attention was paid to the protection of the ADS … Notification of moves involving medical personnel were not forthcoming … the password system rendered travel by night an arduous business since the passwords were not given to ambulance personnel' in AWM Series 52, Item 11/12/15, 2/6th Field Ambulance Diary.
[7]	Owers' Corner marks the southern end of the Kokoda Track. It is located approximately 60 kilometres north-east of Port Moresby.

[8] Notes on Medical Service N.G.F. HQ in AWM Series 54, Item 481/12/220.
[9] Diary entries for August and September 1942 in AWM Series 52, Item 11/12/15.
[10] Colonel A.H. Green, 25 December 1942, Medical-Reports: SWPA (Various)-Appreciation of the situation at 2/9 Australian General Hospital by Col Green in AWM Series 54, Item 481/12/247. The 2/9th AGH was established as a 600-bed hospital in South Australia in 1940 and operated as a hospital in the Middle East during 1941.
[11] See Walker, *Australia in the War of 1939–1945*, Vol.3, Series 5, *The Island Campaigns*, pp.38–40 for the medical situation in the Port Moresby, Ilolo, Koitaki, Owers' Corner areas. See James, *Field Guide to the Kokoda Track*, for photographs, directions and maps, especially Part One: Port Moresby to Owers' Corner, Medical Units, pp.122–38.
[12] Appreciation of situation, Colonel Green in AWM Series 54, Item 481/12/247.
[13] Ibid. Green's report noted that the operating theatre did not open until

November 1942 and that cases admitted during September and October were medical, those requiring minor surgery, and convalescent cases who had been transferred from other medical facilities. The original Base Hospital was relocated to King's Hollow (21 miles from Moresby) in March 1942. It later evolved into the 46th Camp Hospital and developed two offshoots for those patients requiring or undergoing convalescence. One was located at Rouna. The other facility at Koitaki was pulled back to Port Moresby in July due to the Japanese threat. See Walker, *Australia in the War of 1939–1945,* Vol.3, Series 5, *The Island Campaigns,* pp.5, 40, 42, 87.

[14] Appreciation of situation, Appendix B in AWM Series 54, Item 481/12/247.

[15] Magarey's daughter, Professor Susan Magarey AM, FASSA, PhD, confirmed that her father was generally known by his second name, Rupert, or as 'Bob' by his family and school friends.

[16] Walker, *Australia in the War of 1939–1945,* Vol.3, Series 5, *The Island Campaigns,* pp.22–23; Norris, *No*

Memory For Pain, p.150. The unit diary refers to Magarey's appointment to this position. See entry 12 September 1942 in AWM Series 52, Item 11/12/15. See also NAA Series B883, Service Record of SX3668 Magarey, James Rupert.

[17] Diary entry, 17 August 1942 in AWM Series 52, Item 11/12/15.

[18] Norris, *No Memory For Pain*, p.151. See also Walker, *Australia in the War of 1939–1945*, Vol.3, Series 5, *The Island Campaigns*, p.23. Magarey sent orderlies from the 2/6th Field Ambulance to establish staging posts at Uberi, Ioribaiwa, Nauro, Menari and Efogi.

[19] Report on Operations, p.2 in AWM Series 54, Item 481/12/67.

[20] Report on Operations, p.3 in AWM Series 54, Item 481/12/67.

[21] See Osmar White, *Green Armour*, Angus & Robertson, Sydney, 1945, p.172, for description of the ADS at Eora Creek where 'the wounded had been like clots of flies round the dressing station.'

[22] Report on Operations, pp.2–3 in AWM Series 54, Item 481/12/67.

[23] Report on Operations, p.5 in AWM Series 54, Item 481/12/67.
[24] Ibid.
[25] Vernon's diary cited in Brune, *Those Ragged Bloody Heroes*, p.104.
[26] Vernon's unpublished memoirs quoted in James, *Field Guide to the Kokoda Track*, p.298.
[27] Report on Operations, p.6 in AWM Series 54, Item 481/12/67.
[28] Ibid.
[29] Ibid.
[30] Ibid. In a chapter on abdominal wounds during World War II, the official medical historian wrote that there were some who were too gravely ill for surgery and so 'a realistic view was necessary with these patients for whom morphine alone remained.' Allan S. Walker, *Australia in the War of 1939-1945*, Series 5, Vol.1, *Clinical Problems of War*, Australian War Memorial, Canberra, 1952, p.545.
[31] Morphine syringes (syrettes) supplied to some members of the US armed forces in World War I contained '1/2 grain per 1.5 cc.' World War II US Medical Research Centre website, Medical Kits & Contents: Class 9

Items: Drugs, Chemicals and Biological Stains Morphine Tartrate, illustration of Item No.9775700.

[32] Susan Buchholz and Grace Henke, *Henke's Med-Math: Dosage Calculation, Preparation and Administration*, Lippincott Williams & Wilkins, Philadelphia, 2009, p.55.

[33] Report on Operations, p.6 in AWM Series 54, Item 481/12/67.

[34] Ibid. 'Moribund' is defined as being at the point of death, or in terminal decline.

[35] Entry for 31 August, Report on Operations in AWM Series 54, Item 481/12/67 (original punctuation). The 'morphia gr V' refers to the five grains of morphine administered. When discussing the incident 45 years later, Magarey referred to the hut being located at Templeton's Crossing. AWM S02366 Oral History recording, Magarey, Major J.R. Interview with Peter Brune 10 June 1987, Part 2 [37:50 minutes].

[36] Papua New Guinea Association of Australia Library website, 'Recollections of ANGAU' (no date). Note too that Magarey's 1987 recollection differs

from Grahams law's account and from Magarey's original report: 'the next morning ... one of the doctors told me that he'd, I think he said they'd all been alive the night before ... so I went down to this hut ... one was dead, one died while I was there, and the third one looked up at me and said "Hey doc, I thought you were going to take me out last night when you put me on the stretcher"'. AWM S02366 Oral History recording, Magarey, Major J.R. Interview with Peter Brune 10 June 1987, Part 2 [37:50 minutes].

[37] Conclusion 5: Treatment of Wounded and Sick (a) Wounded, p.3, Report on Operations in AWM Series 54, Item 481/12/67.

[38] General Conclusions of a Report by Capt. W.W. McLaren, 14 Aust Fd Amb on the Kokoda Area from 24 July – 8 Sept, Appendix A Medical Notes, New Guinea Campaign – Brig W.W.S. Johnson [sic] D.D.M.S. New Guinea Force in AWM Series 54, Item 481/12/48.

[39] Message from ADMS Norris detailed in Report on Operations, p.6 in AWM Series 54, Item 481/12/67.
[40] Norris, *No Memory For Pain*, p.150.
[41] Bert Kienzle to Brigadier Porter, 21 August 1942, in Kienzle, *The Architect of Kokoda*, p.148.
[42] See RAAF aircraft 1935–1963 at Australian Government RAAF Museum Point Cook website.
[43] Entry for 1 September 1942, p.8, Report on Operations in AWM Series 54, Item 481/12/67. For military aspects see also Brune, *A Bastard Of A Place*, Chapter 10.
[44] Report by Bert Kienzle, September 1942 in Kienzle, *The Architect of Kokoda*, p.151.
[45] See, for example, Brune, *A Bastard Of A Place*, p.190: 'the whole supply debacle was quite simply a tragic case of far too little when it mattered most, and almost too much when all seemed lost between Myola and Kokoda.'
[46] Report on Operations, p.8 in AWM Series 54, Item 481/12/67.
[47] Ibid.
[48] Ibid.

[49]	Spelling: 'Priess' in Report on Operations, AWM Series 54, Item 481/12/67; 'Preece' in Walker, *Australia in the War of 1939–1945*, Vol.3, Series 5, *The Island Campaigns*, p.27.
[50]	Report on Operations, pp.8–9 in AWM Series 54, Item 481/12/67.
[51]	Report on Operations, p.10 in AWM Series 54, Item 481/12/67.
[52]	Ibid.
[53]	Ian Howie-Willis, *An Unending War: the Australian Army's struggle against malaria 1885-2015*, Big Sky Publishing, Newport, NSW, 2016, p.132. See also graph 'Hospital admissions for malaria, Australia and New Guinea, 1942-1943' in Walker, *Australia in the War of 1939-1945*, Vol.1, Series 5, *Clinical Problems of War*, p.82.
[54]	Report of ADMS 7 Aust Division of January 1943 on medical services during the Papuan Campaign – notes on medical services – N.G.F. HQ mid-August to mid December 1942, p.3 in AWM Series 54, Item 481/12/220 (Dr Walker's Records).
[55]	Walker, *Australia in the War of 1939–1945*, Vol.3, Series 5, *The Island Campaigns*, p.83.

[56] Supply of Quinine to 7 Aust Div New Guinea Campaign 1942/43: extracts from a letter to Brigadier Johnston ... from Major F. Matyear, O.C. NGF Depot Med Stores written on 16th April 1943 in AWM Series 54, Item 481/12/220. Matyear reported that at least one consignment of 60,000 quinine tablets 'lay at Kokoda for some time' before being found and returned to depot stores unopened a few months later.

[57] Report of ADMS 7 Aust Division of January 1943 on medical services during the Papuan Campaign – notes on medical services, p.3 in AWM Series 54, Item 481/12/220.

[58] Report on Operations, p.11 in AWM Series 54, Item 481/12/67.

[59] Ibid.

[60] Battles fought at Efogi Ridge became known as the Battle for Brigade Hill. Over 60 Australians were killed, including Captain Nye of the 2/14th Battalion and Captain Langridge of the 2/16th Battalion. See Australian Army website, 'Brigade Hill – Papua New Guinea'; 'The Battle for Brigade Hill'.

[61] NAA Series B883, Service Record of NX446 Humphery, Ronald James. See also AWM Roll of Honour; *Sydney Morning Herald*, 21 July 1945, p.4.

[62] Conclusion, Report on Operations in AWM Series 54, Item 481/12/67.

[63] Recommendations, Report on Operations in AWM Series 54, Item 481/12/67.

[64] Conclusion; Recommendations, Report on Operations in AWM Series 54, Item 481/12/67.

[65] See previous chapter. Report on Operations, Lieutenant Colonel Earlam, p.8, 14 Aust Field Ambulance Papua NAA: AWM54, 19/7/17; Conclusion, 3, Report on Operations in AWM Series 54, Item 481/12/67.

[66] Conclusion, Report on Operations in AWM Series 54, Item 481/12/67.

[67] Ibid. In the 1987 interview, Magarey states that the big toe or the fingers is the most common site of self-inflicted wounds and stressed that 'it happened not only in New Guinea, it happened all over the place. Man's got a rifle and he doesn't like what's happening, so he puts it on his toe and shoots it. Well okay, he's shot it.

Now he may take all sorts of punishment as a result of that, but he's not in the war any more.' AWM S02366 Oral History recording, Magarey, Major J.R. Interview with Peter Brune 10 June 1987, Part 2 [1hr:03].

[68] Ibid.

[69] Appendix A, General Conclusions of a Report by Capt. W.W. McLaren, 14 Aust Fd Amb on the Kokoda Area From 24.7.42 to 8.9.42, Medical Notes, New Guinea Campaign-Brig W.W.S. Johnson [sic] D.D.M.S. New Guinea Force November 1942 in AWM Series 54, Item 481/12/48.

[70] Recommendations, Report on Operations in AWM Series 54, Item 481/12/67.

[71] Appendix A, Medical Notes, New Guinea Campaign-Brig W.W.S. Johnson [sic], November 1942 in AWM Series 54, Item 481/12/48.

[72] Appendix A, General Conclusions by Captain McLaren in AWM Series 54, Item 481/12/48.

[73] Ibid. McLaren reported that medical supplies were lost when the main forward supply dump at Eora Creek

had to be abandoned. He argued that if supplies were kept further back, they could be 'rushed up by native carriers in a few hours.'

[74] Conclusion, Report on Operations in AWM Series 54, Item 481/12/67.

[75] Ibid.

[76] Report on Operations in AWM Series 54, Item 481/12/67. 'Chopping down' refers to decisions made at the base medical stores on which requested supplies would be sent forward to the field ambulance units and which would be held back.

[77] Conclusion, Report on Operations in AWM Series 54, Item 481/12/67.

[78] Ibid. Magarey explained that, since bayonets were the only equipment available with which the soldiers could dig latrines, the toilet facilities were 'not good'.

[79] Conclusion, Recommendations, Report on Operations in AWM Series 54, Item 481/12/67.

[80] Conclusion, Report on Operations in AWM Series 54, Item 481/12/67.

[81] Ibid.

[82] Appendix A, General Conclusions by Captain McLaren in AWM Series 54, Item 481/12/48.

[83] Conclusion, Report on Operations in AWM Series 54, Item 481/12/67.

[84] Recommendations, p.8, Report on Operations in AWM Series 54, Item 481/12/67.

[85] Appendix A, General Conclusions by Captain McLaren in AWM Series 54, Item 481/12/48.

[86] Magarey interview 10 June 1987 cited in Brune, *A Bastard Of A Place*, p.186. Magarey's comment in full: 'If you got an abdominal wound on the Kokoda Trail you might as well give up. We never told the troops that but we knew bloody well that that was what would happen [Interviewer comments]. Well to deal with an abdominal wound you have to have an operating theatre, an anaesthetist, a surgeon, possible an assistant surgeon and a good deal of gear [Interviewer comments]. Didn't have any of those things, just couldn't do it. So, you gave them a shot of morphine like I gave that chap at Templeton's Crossing. Wasn't anything to do, anything else to do. What else

could you do?'. AWM S02366 Oral History recording, Magarey, Major J.R. Interview with Peter Brune 10 June 1987, Part 2 [52:00 minutes].

Chapter Six

[1] Reinforcements were landed a few days later. Estimates of Japanese troop numbers vary up to 2800. The figure cited is taken from a 1943 report by the CO of 110th CCS, Lieutenant Colonel Wall, p.4 in AWM Series 54, Item 481/12/220 (hereafter Wall Report). Note that the GOC Milne Force, Major General Cyril Clowes, cited 'direct evidence' that up to 1600 Japanese landed in the original force and stated there was 'no direct evidence' regarding the landing of any reinforcements. Clowes added that it 'appears ... some were landed, probably up to 600 in number.' See Appendix 1, p.15 in AWM Series 213, Item 293 (Forde Report).

[2] Australian War Memorial website, 'Battle of Milne Bay'; Richard Reid, *Milne Bay 1942*, Department of Veterans' Affairs, Canberra, 2007, p.13. The quotation is from Medical Reports and Arrangements

	Milne Bay area-Medical Experiences at Milne Bay, Lieutenant Colonel F.L. Wall, July 1943 p.4 (Wall Report) in AWM Series 54, Item 481/12/220.
[3]	Reid, ibid., pp.3–5.
[4]	Wall Report, p.2 in AWM Series 54, Item 481/12/220.
[5]	Karl James, 'General Clowes of Milne Bay' Bay' in *Wartime Magazine* 59, 2012, pp.16–21.
[6]	War Diary, Appendix A, 11 Australian Field Ambulance Unit Diary, Major J.J. Ryan, O/C Advance Party in AWM Series 54, Item 11/12/35.
[7]	See extracts from A.50, Kittyhawk – No 76 Squadron Milne Bay in NAA Series A9695, Item 927.
[8]	The Japanese force that left Rabaul for Milne Bay totalled nine ships and included destroyers and submarine chasers. See G. Hermon Gill, *Australia in the War of 1939-1945*, Series 2, Navy, vol. II, *Royal Australian Navy, 1942-1945*, Australian War Memorial, Canberra, 1968, p.166.
[9]	Appendix 1 'Report by Commander Milne Force on Operations between 25 Aug and 7 Sep 42', p.2, AWM Series 213, Item 293.

[10] Reid, *Milne Bay 1942*, p.6.
[11] James, 'General Clowes of Milne Bay'.
[12] HMAS *Arunta*, the 'only naval vessel of any consequence' in the area had been ordered from Gili Gili to Port Moresby when the Japanese fleet was first sighted heading towards Milne Bay. See Gill, *Australia in the War of 1939-1945, Series 2, Navy, vol. II, Royal Australian Navy, 1942-1945*.
[13] William Slim quoted in McCarthy, *Australia in the War of 1939-1945, Series 1, Army, vol. V, South-West Pacific Area – First Year Kokoda to Wau*, p.187. See also, Slim quoted in 'Why Milne Bay is part of Kokoda's legend', *The Age*, 3 August 2002: 'We were greatly cheered by the news of the Australian victory at Milne Bay. This was the first-ever defeat of the Japanese on land. If the Australians had done it, so could we.'
[14] 'This is a day to remember–Twelve years ago at Milne Bay Australia won a famous victory', *The Courier Mail*, 25 August 1954, p.2.
[15] 'Slashing Australian Victory over Japs at Milne Bay', *The Manning River Times and Advocate for the Northern Coast*

Districts of New South Wales, 2 September 1942, p.2. See also, 'Japs Trapped and Heavily Defeated at Milne Bay', *The News*, 31 August 1942, p.1; 'Leaders' Comments On Milne Bay Victory', *Northern Star*, 1 September 1942, p.1; 'Mopping Up Milne Bay', *The Sun*, 1 September 1942, p.1.

[16] See Anthony Staunton, 'French, John Alexander (Jack) (1914–1942)', *ADB*, Vol.14, MUP, 1996.

[17] See Reid, *Milne Bay 1942*, p.13. Reid cites Clowes' figures as '353, of whom 161 were killed or missing'.

[18] The AWM website gives the duration of the battle as 25 August–7 September. See James, 'General Clowes of Milne Bay'.

[19] Milne Force Medical Arrangements, Medical Reports and Arrangements Milne Bay Area, Brigadier Johnston, DDMS NGF, 3 September 1942, p.1 in AWM Series 54, Item 481/12/220. See J.R. McAlpine and G. Keig, *Climate of Papua New Guinea*, ANU Press, Canberra, 1983.

[20] Appendix 1, p.17 in AWM Series 213, Item 293 (Forde Report).

[21] Ibid.

[22] Ibid.
[23] AWM Series 213, Item 293 Forde Report, p.25.
[24] Appendix I, p.17 in AWM Series 213, Item 293 Forde Report.
[25] AWM Series 213, Item 293, Forde Report, pp.23–24.
[26] Walker, *Australia in the War of 1939-1945*, Series 5, Vol.1, *Clinical Problems of War*, p.90.
[27] Ibid. Lieutenant Colonel Edward Ford, Assistant Director of Pathology to New Guinea Force, was also its unofficial malariologist (see Walker, *Australia in the War of 1939-1945*, Series 5, Vol.1, *Clinical Problems of War*, p.91, note 7).
[28] Walker, *Australia in the War of 1939-1945*, Series 5, Vol.1, *Clinical Problems of War*, p.92. The order has generally been attributed to General Blamey. Walker does not state when this order was issued, though it is referred to in the context of the improved malaria situation at Milne Bay in early 1943.
[29] Recollections of Lt-Col Blair 11 Fd Amb Milne Bay, p.1 in AWM Series 54, Item 481/12/220; Walker, *Australia*

in the War of 1939–1945, Series 5, Vol.3, *The Island Campaigns*, p.116.

[30] Letter from Dr McQueen, Department of Public Health Adelaide 24 September 1953, p.1, Letters to Dr A.S. Walker in reply to his request for comments on criticism of draft copy of "Milne Bay" for Medical War History, vol. III in AWM Series 54, Item 481/1/7 Pt 8.

[31] Walker, *Australia in the War of 1939-1945*, Series 5, Vol.1, *Clinical Problems of War*, p.90.

[32] The School of Public Health and Tropical Medicine at the University of Sydney conducted surveys in the areas around Port Moresby in 1935 and in the Milne Bay District in 1938–39. See Howie-Willis, *An Unending War*, p.85.

[33] Appendix B, Dawkins Report, p.1 in AWM Series 54, Item 481/12/220.

[34] See Medical Technical Instruction No.1 – Suppressive Treatment of Malaria: 'Treatment will commence within seven days of landing for all ranks', 11th Australian Field Ambulance (June and July) in AWM Series 54, Item 11/12/35.

[35] Notes on Medical Service – N.G.F. HQ Mid Aug to Mid Dec 42: Milne

Force, p.20, Medical Reports and Arrangements Milne Bay area in AWM Series 54, Item 481/12/220.

[36] For explanation of malaria and malariology, see Howie-Willis, *An Unending War,* Chapter 1.

[37] Comment on Appendix B. of Col. Dawkins' Letter, Major E. Ford, 18 August 1942 in AWM Series 54 Item 481/12/220.

[38] Notes of conference held on 16th, 17th and 18th [December 1942] D.G.M.S., D.D.G.M.S. and A.D.G.M.S. Landops – attached document in AWM Series 52, Item 11/1/1 (Official War Diaries of DGMS).

[39] Milne Force-Medical Situation Report 5 Nov 1942 in AWM Series 54, Item 481/12/220; Entry 30 November, 11 Australian Field Ambulance Unit Diary, AWM Series 54, Item 11/12/35.

[40] Report for week ending 1200 hrs Saturday 7 November and 21 November 'Daily details of new sick' in AWM Series 54, Item 11/12/35, 11 Australian Field Ambulance Unit Diary. The strength of the unit is shown as 12 officers and 226 other ranks/12 officers and 229 other ranks,

respectively and includes attached personnel. 'Sick Parade' is the morning report to the medical officer by all sick patients.

[41]	Appendix F, 2/5 Field Ambulance Unit Diary, January 1943 in AWM Series 52, Item 11/12/14.
[42]	Ibid.
[43]	Report on Malaria by Lieutenant-Colonel Keogh, 18 December 1942, AWM Series 52, Item 11/1/1.
[44]	Letter from Colonel Maitland, p.1 in AWM Series 54, Item 481/1/7. The minimum number of soldiers in a battalion was approximately 550.
[45]	Milne Force – Admissions to Medical Units December 1942, AWM Series 54, Item 481/12/220.
[46]	Wall Report, p.7 in AWM Series 54, Item 481/12/220.
[47]	Letter from G.B.G. Maitland 28 June 1953 in AWM Series 54, Item 481/1/7 Pt 8.
[48]	Letter to Johnston from DGMS Burston, 9 December 1942, AWM Series 292 Med 40/76 (Personal Letters to DGMS 27 December 1939 – 12 May 1943).

[49] Ibid.
[50] Letter to Disher from DGMS Burston, 31 December 1942, AWM Series 292 Med 40/76.
[51] Ibid.
[52] Wall Report, p.7 in AWM Series 54, Item 481/12/220.
[53] Entries November and December 1942, 11 Field Ambulance Unit Diary, AWM Series 54, Item 11/12/35.
[54] Entries November and December 1942, 11 Australian Field Ambulance Unit Diary, AWM Series 54, Item 11/12/35. See also Appendix C 'Toxic Effect of Plasmoquine from HQ 11 Aust. Fd Amb to ADMS Milne Force, 9 December 1942.
[55] Toxic Effect of Plasmoquine, AWM Series 54, Item 11/12/35.
[56] Entries November and December 1942, 11 Australian Field Ambulance Unit Diary, AWM Series 54, Item 11/12/35. See also Appendix C 'Toxic Effect of Plasmoquine from HQ 11 Aust. Fd Amb to ADMS Milne Force, 9 December 1942.
[57] See, for example Nominal Rolls 28 October, 7 November, 15 November, 26 November in AWM Series 54, Item

11/12/35, 11 Australian Field Ambulance.

[58] Notes of conference held on 16th, 17th and 18th [December 1942] D.G.M.S., D.D.G.M.S. and A.D.G.M.S. Landops – attached document in AWM Series 52, Item 11/1/1.

[59] Report of visit by Minister for the Army (Hon. F.M. Forde) 1st to 4th October 1942, pp.17–18 in AWM Series 213, Item 293.

[60] The war establishment refers to the level of equipment and manpower required by an army in wartime.

[61] Report of visit by Minister for the Army (Hon. F.M. Forde) 1st to 4th October 1942, p.7 in AWM Series 213, Item 293.

[62] Walker recorded 200 killed and wounded in the six days before *Manunda* sailed from Milne Bay on 7 September. Total battle casualties are given as 373, including 24 officers. See Walker, *Australia in the War of 1939-1945*, Series 5, Vol.3, *The Island Campaigns*.

[63] Report of visit by Minister for the Army (Hon. F.M. Forde) 1st to 4th

	October 1942, pp. 2, 17, 19 in AWM Series 213, Item 293.
[64]	Report of visit by Minister for the Army (Hon. F.M. Forde) 1st to 4th October 1942, p.19 in AWM Series 213, Item 293.
[65]	On this occasion, the Japanese observed the Articles of the Geneva Convention relating to the respect for, and protection of, medical personnel. Despite having an easy target and ample opportunity when evacuating their troops from Milne Bay in September, the Japanese ships did not fire on the clearly marked and brightly illuminated Australian hospital ship, *Manunda*, which was at anchor in Milne Bay. Indeed, 'no hostile gesture was made to the Manunda' despite repeated shelling in the direction of the No.1 Airstrip. See Walker, *Australia in the War of 1939–1945*, Series 5, Vol.3, *The Island Campaigns*, p.57; Reid, *Milne Bay 1942*, p.12; Gill, *Australia in the War of 1939-1945*, Series 2, Navy, vol. II, *Royal Australian Navy, 1942-1945*, p.172.
[66]	Report of visit by Minister for the Army (Hon. F.M. Forde) 1st to 4th

October 1942, p.20 in AWM Series 213, Item 293.

[67] Observations of the GOC Milne Force [Clowes] p.3 in AWM Series 213, Item 293.

[68] Report of visit by Minister for the Army (Hon. F.M. Forde) 1st to 4th October 1942, p.20 in AWM Series 213, Item 293.

[69] Report of visit by Minister for the Army (Hon. F.M. Forde) 1st to 4th October 1942, pp.20–21 in AWM Series 213, Item 293.

[70] Report of visit by Minister for the Army (Hon. F.M. Forde) 1st to 4th October 1942, p.21 in AWM Series 213, Item 293.

[71] Summary of Operations – Para. 39 – New appreciation required, p.29 in AWM Series 213, Item 293.

[72] Report of visit by Minister for the Army (Hon. F.M. Forde) 1st to 4th October 1942, p.19 in AWM Series 213, Item 293.

[73] Ibid.

[74] Pharmacy, Appendix M: Facts relating to consignment showing most loss, AWM Series 54, Item 483/9/24.

[75] Report on the sufficiency of standing orders for the Aust. Army Medical Services in relation to the control of poisons and dangerous drugs in military establishments-Report of inspection visit to Moresby and Milne Bay by Major R. Townley A.M.D.3., p.2 in AWM Series 54, Item 483/9/24.

[76] Pharmacy, Appendix E: Mainland stores' methods adversely affecting medical supplies to New Guinea in AWM Series 54, Item 483/9/24.

[77] Report of visit by Minister for the Army (Hon. F.M. Forde) 1st to 4th October 1942, pp.28–30 in AWM Series 213, Item 293.

[78] Letter from the Prime Minister to the Hon. F.M. Forde, M.P., 15 October 1942 in AWM Series 213, Item 293.

Chapter Seven

[1] Comment on Appendix B of Col. Dawkins' Letter [by Major E. Ford], 18 August 1942, p.1 in AWM Series 54 481/12/220. The population was estimated at 25,000. Yaws is an infection that attacks skin, bone and cartilage leading to disfigurement and disability.

Filaria (also known as elephantiasis) is transmitted by mosquitoes carrying the parasite. It produces painful and disfiguring swellings leading to disability and disfigurement. Leprosy is a bacterial infection that causes deformity, disability and progressive damage to skin, nerves, limbs and eyes.

[2] McCarthy, *Australia in the War of 1939-1945, Series 1, Army, vol. V, South-West Pacific Area – First Year Kokoda to Wau*, pp.158, 161, 185.

[3] 'Bombers sink Jap Destroyer', *Army News*, Darwin, 13 September, p.1; P.S. Dull, *A Battle History of the Imperial Japanese Navy 1941–1945*, Naval Institute Press, Annapolis, 1978, pp.177–78.

[4] Entry 24 September 1942, 2/5 Australian Field Ambulance Unit Diary in AWM Series 52, Item 11/12/14. Interrogation reports on prisoners of war Sakaki and Moriyama are cited in Clowes' report on Milne Bay. There were eight wounded among these prisoners of war. See Report by Commander Milne Force on Operations between 25 Aug 42 and 7 Sep 42, pp.13–14 in AWM5 Series 4, Item 481/12/220.

[5] See also section of summary medical report entitled Japanese Treatment of Wounded: 'The Japanese make every endeavour to move their own dead and wounded'. Medical Reports and Arrangements Milne Bay Area in AWM Series 54, Item 481/12/220.

[6] See McCarthy, *Australia in the War of 1939-1945, Series I, Army, vol. V, South-West Pacific Area – First Year Kokoda to Wau*, pp.173–75.

[7] Operations Goodenough Island – 22–26 Oct 42: Lessons from Operations – No.4, p.1, Medical Reports and Arrangements Milne Bay Area, AWM Series 54, Item 481/12/220.

[8] Ibid.

[9] See also Goodenough Island 22-27 October 1942 Battle Casualties, Battle Casualties Milne Bay Area, Goodenough Island, Australian Military Forces 25th August 1942 – 7th September 1942, showing total of 26 killed and wounded, AWM Series 54, Item 171/2/23.

[10] Operations Goodenough Island – 22–26 Oct 42: Lessons from Operations – No.4, p.1, Medical Reports and Arrangements Milne Bay

Area, pp.1-2 in AWM Series 54, Item 481/12/220.

[11] Operations Goodenough Island – 22-26 Oct 42: Lessons from Operations – No.4, p.1, Medical Reports and Arrangements Milne Bay Area, pp.1-5 in AWM Series 54, Item 481/12/220. See also result of close recce by 1 B25 of Goodenough Island, Messages and Reports, AWM Series 54, Item 585/6/1 which reported that low altitude aerial reconnaissance on 26 October did not see any signs of hostile troops.

[12] A message from Milne Force to NGF on 28 October reported that reconnaissance of Fergusson Island the previous day failed to locate tents or 'anything unusual'. See Messages and Reports Operations Goodenough Island 1942, in Message 8170/0910/29, AWM Series 54, Item 585/6/1.

[13] McCarthy, *Australia in the War of 1939-1945*, Series 1, Army, vol. V, *South-West Pacific Area – First Year Kokoda to Wau*, p.349. The CO of Taleba Force, Gategood, reported that 'two large launches carrying about 200 Japs were observed to land on

southern tip of Ferguson [sic] Island (Bwaida Peninsular)' in 'A' Beach Force CO K.A.J. Gategood – Goodenough Island Area, 25 October, AWM Series 54, Item 585/7/2.

[14] The two detachments from the 2/5th Field Ambulance to Drake Force were A – one medical officer, four stretcher-bearers and two nursing orderlies and B – one medical officer, 12 stretcher-bearers and four nursing orderlies. See Appendix C, AWM Series 52, Item 11/12/14.

[15] Appendix D, Report of Medical Services attached to Drake Force, Captain J Scott, AWM Series 52, Item 11/12/14, 2/5 Australian Field Ambulance.

[16] Ibid.

[17] Appendix E, Report on Activity of "B" Coy Personnel Attached to Drake Force, Captain R. Holmes, p.1, AWM Series 52, Item 11/12/14, 2/5 Australian Field Ambulance. Note: It is not clear from reports whether this 'ketch' is *Maclaren King* or another vessel. The CO of Taleba Force, Gategood, refers to 'the small cutter' being fired on by 'two MMGs'[medium machine-guns] and

withdrawing to Taleba Bay 'without taking wounded'. See Reports on Operation at Goodenough Island, 'A' Beach Force C O KAJ Gategood, p.1 in AWM Series 54, Item 585/7/2.

[18] See for example, 'The Convention for the Amelioration of the Condition of the Wounded and Sick in Armies in the Field', Geneva, 27 July 1929, Chapter IV Article 22; Chapter II Article 7 International Committee of the Red Cross website.

[19] See Jervis Bay Maritime Museum Blog 'Launch of the Maclaren King 1923'.

[20] See AWM collection, photographs 151002, 013500.

[21] Appendix D, Report of Medical Services attached to Drake Force, Captain J Scott, AWM Series 52, Item 11/12/14, 2/5 Australian Field Ambulance.

[22] Appendix E, Report on Activity of "B" Coy Personnel Attached to Drake Force, Captain R. Holmes, p.1, AWM Series 52, Item 11/12/14, 2/5 Australian Field Ambulance.

[23] Ibid.

[24] Ibid. Note that the 2/5th Field Ambulance Unit Diary records Miles as 'missing'.

[25] Entries 8–25 October, 2/5th Field Ambulance Unit Diary 1942, AWM Series 52, Item 11/12/14.

[26] Appendix D, Report of Medical Services attached to Drake Force, Captain J Scott, AWM Series 52, Item 11/12/14, 2/5 Australian Field Ambulance. See Chapter III Article 9 of the Geneva Convention (1929): 'the personnel engaged exclusively in the collection, transport and treatment of the wounded and sick ... shall be respected and protected under all circumstances.'

[27] 'The protected status of medical personnel does not cease if they are equipped with light individual weapons solely to defend their patients or themselves against acts of violence ... If they use such weapons in combat against enemy forces acting in conformity with the laws of war ... they forfeit their protection.' Geneva Convention Rule 25: Medical Personnel – Equipment of medical personnel with light individual weapons.

[28] Appendix D, Report of Medical Services attached to Drake Force, Captain J Scott, AWM Series 52, Item 11/12/14, 2/5 Australian Field Ambulance.
[29] Ibid.
[30] Appendix E, Report on Activity of "B" Coy Personnel Attached to Drake Force, Captain R. Holmes, p.1, AWM Series 52, Item 11/12/14, 2/5 Australian Field Ambulance.
[31] NAA Series B883, VX20960 Private R Marriott Service Record, Recommendation for DCM, Signed by Major-General C.A. Clowes, Commander Milne Force, Received 6 December 1942.
[32] Appendix D, Report of Medical Services attached to Drake Force, Captain J Scott, AWM Series 52, Item 11/12/14, 2/5 Australian Field Ambulance.
[33] Ibid.
[34] Ibid.
[35] Appendix E, Report on Activity of "B" Coy Personnel Attached to Drake Force, Captain R. Holmes, p.1, AWM Series 52, Item 11/12/14, 2/5 Australian Field Ambulance.

[36] Report on Operation at Goodenough Island by Lt-Col Arnold C.O. 2/12 Aust. Infantry Bn 22–26 October 1942, p.2 in AWM Series 54, Item 422/7/8.

[37] Battle Casualties Milne Bay Area, Goodenough Island Australian Military Forces 25th August 1942 – 7th September 1942, p.3 in AWM Series 54, Item 171/2/23. See McCarthy, *Australia in the War of 1939-1945*, Series 1, Army, vol. V, *South-West Pacific Area – First Year Kokoda to Wau*, p.349; Walker, *Australia in the War of 1939–1945*, Series 5, Vol.3, *The Island Campaigns*, p.120. Making no distinction between the fighting soldiers and the AAMC personnel, McCarthy gives the total Australian casualties as 13 killed with one officer and 18 men wounded. Walker states that there were 27 battle casualties, including 13 killed.

[38] Report on Operation at Goodenough Island by Lt-Col Arnold C.O. 2/12 Aust. Infantry Bn 22–26 October 1942, p.2 in AWM Series 54, Item 422/7/8.

[39] Letter to DDMS Johnston from DGMS Burston, 9 December 1942 in AWM Series 292 MED 40/76 Personal letters

to DGMS 27 December 1939 – 12 May 1943.

[40] See letter to MacArthur from Blamey, 10 December and MacArthur's reply in AWM Series 54, Item 585/3/2 Correspondence between General Sir Thomas Blamey and General Douglas MacArthur on aerodrome construction on Goodenough Island, December 1942.

[41] Medical care on Goodenough in 1943 was initially provided by B Company of the 4th Field Ambulance and the RMO of the 47th Infantry Battalion. The RAAF also stationed medical personnel and facilities on Goodenough. See AWM Series 54, Item 585/3/1 Operation Hackney Goodenough Island Deception Scheme. See Walker, *Australia in the War of 1939–1945*, Series 5, Vol.3, *The Island Campaigns*, pp.119–20.

[42] Report – Lt Sec 2/5 Aust Fd Amb Attached Drake Force 4 December 1942 in AWM Series 52, Item 11/12/14, 2/5 Field Ambulance Unit Diary.

[43] Report – Lt Sec 2/5 Aust Fd Amb Attached Drake Force, 13 December

1942 in AWM Series 52, Item 11/12/14, 2/5 Field Ambulance Unit Diary.

[44] Appendix B, Drake Force 26 November 1942 in AWM Series 52, Item 11/12/14, 2/5 Field Ambulance Unit Diary.

[45] Milne Force numbers increased from 10,617 to 13,296. See Appendices A and B for distribution of troops and numbers in Milne Bay Area as at 23 October 1942 in AWM Series 52, Item 11/12/14, 2/5 Field Ambulance Unit Diary.

[46] Medical Reports and Arrangements Milne Bay Area, Medical Experiences at Milne Bay (F.L.W. written July 1943), pp.5–6 in AWM Series 54, Item 481/12/220.

[47] Ibid.

[48] Walker, *Australia in the War of 1939–1945*, Series 5, Vol.3, *The Island Campaigns*, pp.111–12.

[49] Blood typing involved taking a sample of blood and mixing this with antibodies, which indicated how the subject's immune system would react to a blood transfusion.

[50]	See Entries, October–December 1942 in AWM Series 52, Item 11/12/35, 11 Australian Field Ambulance Unit Diary; Entry 8 December 1942 in AWM Series 52, Item 11/12/14, 2/5 Australian Field Ambulance Unit Diary. See Report on activities of detachment 2/5 Field Ambulance – Medical Service with "Hammer" Forces in Buna-Sanananda Areas 12 Dec–15 Feb 1942/1943 in AWM Series 54, Item 19/7/6. Note that research indicates that Hanson Force (2/5th Field Ambulance detachments sent in support) refers to the 2/10th Australian Infantry Battalion stationed at Wanigela and Porlock, Milne Bay—and sent to Buna, arriving 17 December.
[51]	Appendix A, Preliminary Medical Report – Wedau Det, Captain H.J. Edelman, 16 October 1942 in AWM Series 52, Item 11/12/14, 2/5 Australian Field Ambulance Unit Diary.
[52]	Ibid.
[53]	Appendix A, Preliminary Medical Report – Wedau Det, Captain H.J. Edelman, 4 December 1942 in AWM Series 52, Item 11/12/14, 2/5 Australian Field Ambulance Unit Diary.

[54] Ibid.
[55] Ibid.
[56] Ibid.
[57] Correspondence from HQ 2/5 Aust Fd Amb to Captain Scott, Hanson Force, 10 December 1942 in AWM Series 52, Item 11/12/14, 2/5 Australian Field Ambulance Unit Diary.
[58] Appendix A, Preliminary Medical Report – Wedau Det, Captain H.J. Edelman in AWM Series 52, Item 11/12/14, 2/5 Australian Field Ambulance Unit Diary.
[59] Ibid.
[60] Routine Orders Part 1, Lt-Col Blair 26 October 1942 in AWM Series 52, Item 11/12/35, 11 Australian Field Ambulance Unit Diary.
[61] Appendix A, AWM Series 52, Item 11/12/14, 2/5 Australian Field Ambulance Unit Diary.
[62] Communique from HQ 2/5 Aust Fd Amb to Capt. Edelman, Hat Force, 10 December 1942 in AWM Series 52, Item 11/12/14, 2/5 Australian Field Ambulance Unit Diary. Hat Force, mostly soldiers from the 2/10th Battalion, led the advance along the north-east coast from Milne Bay to

[63] Giruwa. See Williams, *The Kokoda Campaign 1942: myth and reality*, p.203. See report on activities of detachment 2/5 Field Ambulance – Medical Service with "Hammer" Forces in Buna-Sanananda Areas 12 Dec – 15 Feb 1942/1943, AWM Series 54, Item 19/7/6.

[64] John Moremon, *Battle of the Beachheads 1942-1943*, Department of Veterans' Affairs, Canberra, 2002, p.3.

[65] Appendix E Report on Hanson Force by Major Lavarack, p.1 in AWM Series 52, Item 11/12/14, 2/5 Australian Field Ambulance Unit Diary.

[66] Medical Reports and Arrangements Milne Bay Area, Medical Experiences at Milne Bay (F.L.W. written July 1943), p.7 in AWM Series 54, Item 481/12/220.

[67] Ibid.

[68] AWM Series 54, Item 481/12/220 Dr Walker's Records; Medical Reports and Arrangements Milne Bay Area, Medical Experiences at Milne Bay (F.L.W. written July 1943), p.6 in AWM Series 54, Item 481/12/220; Entry 31 December 1942, AWM Series 54, Item 11/12/35, 11 Australian Field

Ambulance Unit Diary; December – Medical Statistics for 1942 in AWM Series 52, Item 11/12/14, 2/5 Australian Field Ambulance Unit Diary.

[69] December – Medical Statistics for 1942 in AWM Series 52, Item 11/12/14, 2/5 Australian Field Ambulance Unit Diary: Admissions to MDS. Thirty-one patients were diagnosed with typhus and 457 with 'other' illnesses. Figures did not include those 'passing through' and being treated at ADS, light sections, on transports or at sea.

[70] Medical Reports and Arrangements Milne Bay Area, Medical Experiences at Milne Bay (F.L.W. written July 1943), p.9 in AWM Series 54, Item 481/12/220.

[71] Official War Diaries of DGMS, Medical Units – New Guinea Force, AWM Series 52, Item 11/1/1.

Chapter Eight

[1] Barry Reed, 'Endurance, Courage and Care: the Kokoda Campaign of Captain Alan Watson and the 2/4 Field Ambulance' in *Journal of Military and*

Veterans' Health 19 (2), August 2011, pp.32–40.

[2] Summary for March 1942, AWM Series 52, Item 11/12/13, 2/4 Field Ambulance Diary [whole diary-27 items] May 1940–May1946.

[3] Sweeting, 'The 2/4th Field Ambulance A.I.F. during the Owen Stanleys Campaign 1942', p.

[4] Entry, 3 September 1942 in AWM Series 52, Item 11/12/13, 2/4 Field Ambulance Diary.

[5] Sweeting, 'The 2/4th Field Ambulance A.I.F. during the Owen Stanleys Campaign 1942', pp.3–4.

[6] Ibid.

[7] Ibid., pp.1–4.

[8] Ibid., pp.3–4.

[9] Ibid., p.4.

[10] NAA Series B883 Personnel Records of VX14704 Temporary Major Hew Fancourt Graham McDonald; NX473 Major Ian Firth Vickery; NX25177 Lance Corporal Arthur Mowbray Moodie.

[11] See AWM Series 52, Item 11/12/13, 2/4 Field Ambulance Diary.

[12] Entry July 1942, AWM Series 52, Item 11/12/13, 2/4 Field Ambulance Diary.

[13] Entry 14 July 1942, AWM Series 52, Item 11/12/13, 2/4 Field Ambulance Diary.

[14] Entry 27 August 1942, AWM Series 52, Item 11/12/13, 2/4 Field Ambulance Diary.

[15] Entries 17–27 August 1942, AWM Series 52, Item 11/12/13, 2/4 Field Ambulance Diary.

[16] Sweeting, 'The 2/4th Field Ambulance A.I.F. during the Owen Stanleys Campaign 1942', p.5. SS *Jasper Lea* was launched in June 1942 and renamed *Jason Lee*. Liberty ships were cargo ships built by the US under lend-lease arrangements with Britain.

[17] See Entries August 1942 in AWM Series 52, Item 11/12/13, 2/4 Field Ambulance Diary. Personnel had variously left or joined the unit since its return to Australia. For example, in August there were 178 members (seven officers, 135 other ranks and 36 reinforcements).

[18] Casualties Evacuated From Maroubra: Movement Fd Amb Under Comd 25 Aust Inf Bde Gp, 16 September 1942 in AWM Series 52, Item 11/12/15, 2/6

	Field Ambulance [whole diary—29 items] May 1940–Dec 1945.
[19]	Entry Thursday 17 September 1942, Kennedy Diary.
[20]	Ibid.
[21]	Sweeting, 'The 2/4th Field Ambulance A.I.F. during the Owen Stanleys Campaign 1942', p.5.
[22]	Bullard (trans), *Japanese Army Operations in the South Pacific Area*, pp.182–85; Entry 17 September 1942, AWM Series 52, Item 11/12/13, 2/4 Field Ambulance Diary.
[23]	Deployment Policy, Point 3 in Bullard, ibid., p.184. Point 1 stated that the current objective (Ioribaiwa) should be captured if possible and used to defend the front line. Point 2 discussed the deployment of soldiers to the Mawai district 'to appropriate all food from native villages'.
[24]	Norris, *No Memory For Pain*, p.160. The 14th Field Regiment bombarded the Japanese from Owers' Corner between 21 and 24 September 1942. Australian patrols were conducted around Imita Ridge. An attack on Ioribaiwa was planned for 28 September, but met no

	opposition. See Reid, *Milne Bay 1942*, p.9.
[25]	Three battalions of the 21st Brigade, AIF (2/14th, 2/16th and 2/27th), withdrew to Ioribaiwa from Menari and were 'pulled back' on 17 September. See Reid, ibid., pp.7–8.
[26]	McCarthy, *Australia in the War of 1939-1945, Series I, Army, vol. V, South-West Pacific Area – First Year Kokoda to Wau*, pp.229–33.
[27]	Bullard (trans), *Japanese Army Operations in the South Pacific Area*, p.166.
[28]	Ibid. The original report is not cited.
[29]	McCarthy, *Australia in the War of 1939-1945, Series I, Army, vol. V, South-West Pacific Area – First Year Kokoda to Wau*, p.233.
[30]	See Australian War Memorial website, 'Imita Ridge Operations'. The 16th Brigade had been detached from the 6th Division, AIF.
[31]	Entry 30 September 1942, AWM Series 52, Item 11/12/15, 2/6 Field Ambulance Diary.
[32]	September 1942, AWM Series 52, Item 11/12/15, 2/6 Field Ambulance Diary.

[33] Entry 27 September 1942, AWM Series 52, Item 11/12/15, 2/6 Field Ambulance Diary.

[34] Proposed Medical Evacuation Plan Uberi – Ilolo, Lt Col F. Chenhall, 6 September 1942 in AWM Series 52, Item 11/12/15, 2/6 Field Ambulance Diary.

[35] Proposed Medical Evacuation Plan Uberi – Ilolo, Lt Col F. Chenhall, 6 September 1942; Entries 8–10 September 1942, in AWM Series 52, Item 11/12/15, 2/6 Field Ambulance Diary.

[36] Entry 12 September 1942 in AWM Series 52, Item 11/12/15, 2/6 Field Ambulance Diary; Report on Operations 2/6 Field Ambulance 26–29 August 1942, Major J.R. Magarey in AWM Series 54, Item 481/12/67.

[37] Entry 12 September 1942 in AWM Series 52, Item 11/12/15, 2/6 Field Ambulance Diary.

[38] Entry 11 September 1942 in AWM Series 52, Item 11/12/15, 2/6 Field Ambulance Diary.

[39] Entry 19 September 1942 in AWM Series 52, Item 11/12/15, 2/6 Field Ambulance Diary.

[40] Ibid. Chenhall commented that 'it seems a shame that this cannot be stopped by more drastic control.'

[41] Letter from DGMS Burston to DDMS Johnston, 3 September 1942, Directorate of Medical Services in AWM Series 376 (Alternative Series AWM292 Med 40/76) Personal Letters to DGMS 27 December 1939-12 May 1943.

[42] Ibid. See also James, *Field Guide to the Kokoda Track*, p.106. The 'undulating bushland setting' known as 17-Mile was also the site for the 2/4th Advanced Depot Medical Stores with the 166th American Clearing Station located nearby.

[43] Letter from DGMS Burston to DDMS Johnston, 3 September 1942, Directorate of Medical Services in AWM Series 376 (Alternative Series AWM292 Med 40/76).

[44] Ibid.

[45] Ibid. Johnston wrote 'we will miss 2/1 C.C.S.... I expect Dawkins will tell you something of the story.' The decision to send the CCS to Milne Bay was seen by some as more practical than sending a field ambulance unit, which

was regarded as only 'a temporary expedient'. However, this decision presented logistical difficulties due to the extra equipment and personnel required by the CCS. See Walker, *Australia in the War of 1939–1945*, Series 5, Vol.3, *The Island Campaigns*, p.108.

[46] Nick Anderson, *To Kokoda*, Big Sky Publishing, Sydney, 2017, p.126.

[47] Appreciation of the situation at 2/9 Australian General Hospital by Colonel A.H. Green, 25 December 1942 in AWM Series 54, Item 407/7/7.

[48] These terms are used throughout the unit diaries and reports.

[49] Entries 17–30 September 1942 and CO Summary for September 1942 in AWM Series 52, Item 11/12/13, 2/4 Field Ambulance Diary; See Walker, *Australia in the War of 1939–1945*, Series 5, Vol.3, *The Island Campaigns*, pp.58–60.

[50] Sweeting, 'The 2/4th Field Ambulance A.I.F. during the Owen Stanleys Campaign 1942', p.5.

[51] Ibid., p.6.

[52] Entry October 1942, Kennedy Diary.

[53] Sweeting, 'The 2/4th Field Ambulance A.I.F. during the Owen Stanleys Campaign 1942', p.7.

[54] Entry October 1942, Nauro, Kennedy Diary.

[55] Entry 21 September 1942 in AWM Series 52, Item 11/12/15, 2/6 Field Ambulance Diary.

[56] Entry 27 September 1942 in AWM Series 52, Item 11/12/15, 2/6 Field Ambulance Diary.

[57] D.R. Leslie quoted in R. Grogan, 'The Operation of Forward Surgical Teams in the Kokoda-Buna Campaigns' in *Australian and New Zealand Journal of Surgery* 68 (1), January 1998, p.69.

[58] Notes on Operations (Earlier Stages) Owen Stanleys – Buna Areas, Brigadier Johnston DDMS, New Guinea Force, April 1943 in AWM Series 54, Item 481/12/224 Medical Notes on Operations Owen Stanley Area – Papuan Campaign.

[59] Entry 10 October 1942 in AWM Series 52, Item 11/12/13, 2/4 Field Ambulance Diary. See photographs of surgical operations at Myola (P02423.012 and P02424.063) at Australian War Memorial website.

[60] Walker, *Australia in the War of 1939–1945*, Series 5, Vol.3, *The Island Campaigns*, p.75; Entry at Uberi 31 October 1942 in AWM Series 52, Item 11/12/15, 2/6 Field Ambulance Diary. Captain McLaren (14th Field Ambulance) arrived at Uberi on 30 October with instructions to take over all medical posts between Uberi and Efogi. This instruction had not been received by the Headquarters of 2/6th Field Ambulance and rear 7th Division Headquarters knew nothing of it. It was noted that such miscommunication showed 'a total lack of co-ordination by 1st Aust Corps HQ.'

[61] Entries October 1942 at Menari, South Efogi, North Efogi in Kennedy Diary.

[62] On 28 October Allen was relieved of his command of the 7th Division. The commander of the 6th Division in Papua, Major General Vasey, then assumed command of the 7th Division. David Horner, 'Vasey, George Alan (1895–1945)', *ADB*, Vol.16, MUP, 2002.

[63] Entry October 1942 at North Efogi, Kennedy Diary; entries for October 1942 in AWM Series 52, Item

	11/12/13, 2/4th Field Ambulance unit diary.
[64]	Sweeting, 'The 2/4th Field Ambulance A.I.F. during the Owen Stanleys Campaign 1942', p.8.
[65]	Walker, *Australia in the War of 1939–1945*, Series 5, Vol.3, *The Island Campaigns*, p.75.
[66]	Kienzle, *The Architect of Kokoda*, p.148.
[67]	Entries 14–18 October 1942, AWM Series 52, Item 11/12/13, 2/4 Field Ambulance Diary; entry 18 October 1942, AWM Series 52, Item 11/12/13, 2/6 Field Ambulance Diary.
[68]	Sweeting, 'The 2/4th Field Ambulance A.I.F. during the Owen Stanleys Campaign 1942', p.8.
[69]	Entries 14–16 October 1942, AWM Series 52, Item 11/12/13, 2/4 Field Ambulance Diary.
[70]	Sweeting, 'The 2/4th Field Ambulance A.I.F. during the Owen Stanleys Campaign 1942', p.8; entry 17 October 1942, AWM Series 52, Item 11/12/13, 2/4 Field Ambulance Diary.
[71]	Entry 17 October 1942, AWM Series 52, Item 11/12/13, 2/4 Field Ambulance Diary.

[72] Entry October 1942 at Myola, Kennedy Diary.
[73] Entries 17 October 1942, AWM Series 52, Item 11/12/13, 2/4 Field Ambulance Diary. This account by Lieutenant Colonel Hobson (CO) differs from that of the official medical historian who wrote that 'Chenhall with five officers and sixty-eight O. Rs was moving up there to staff an MDS ... The 2/6 MDS was established at Myola 2 on the 24th.' See Walker, *Australia in the War of 1939–1945*, Series 5, Vol.3, *The Island Campaigns*, p.75.
[74] Entry 20 October 1942, AWM Series 52, Item 11/12/13, 2/4 Field Ambulance Diary.
[75] Entry 20 October 1942, Kennedy Diary.
[76] Entry 20 October 1942, AWM Series 52, Item 11/12/13, 2/4 Field Ambulance Diary.
[77] See Walker, *Australia in the War of 1939–1945*, Series 5, Vol.3, *The Island Campaigns*, pp.75–76: 'from the point of view of planning Myola seemed ideal ... it was then [16 October] doubtful if evacuation from Myola could be arranged or not ... even before Myola

came into use as a medical and surgical centre the difficulties attending air transport of sick and wounded were apparent.'

[78] Entry 17 October 1942, AWM Series 52, Item 11/12/15, 2/6 Field Ambulance Diary.

[79] Walker, *Australia in the War of 1939–1945*, Series 5, Vol.3, *The Island Campaigns*, p.76.

[80] Entries October 1942, AWM Series 52, Item 11/12/15, 2/6 Field Ambulance Diary.

[81] Ibid.
[82] Ibid.
[83] Ibid.
[84] Entries 27–31 October 1942 at Myola, AWM Series 52, Item 11/12/15, 2/6 Field Ambulance Diary; Sweeting, 'The 2/4th Field Ambulance A.I.F. during the Owen Stanleys Campaign 1942', p.9.

[85] Brief account of activities, ADMS Norris in AWM Series 54, Item 481/12/13.

[86] Ibid.
[87] Walker, *Australia in the War of 1939–1945*, Series 5, Vol.3, *The Island Campaigns*, p.76.

[88] Message to LHQ for Consulting Surgeon Repeated DDMS NGF, ADMS 7 Aust Div from 2/6 Aust Fd Amb in AWM Series 54, Item 19/7/23. Note that original punctuation and abbreviations have been altered for clarity. Chenhall referred to the 'drastic signal' in AWM Series 52, Item 11/12/15, 2/6 Field Ambulance Diary.

[89] Addendum to Letter from DDMS Johnston to DGMS Burston, 30 October 1942 in AWM Series 376 MED 40/76.

[90] Ibid.

[91] Entries 27-31 October 1942 at Myola in AWM Series 52, Item 11/12/15, 2/6 Field Ambulance Diary; Sweeting, 'The 2/4th Field Ambulance A.I.F. during the Owen Stanleys Campaign 1942', p.8.

[92] Addendum to Letter from Johnston to Burston, 30 October 1942 in AWM Series 376 MED 40/76. Edmund Herring replaced Rowell as Commander NGF in September after Rowell was removed from the position by General Blamey.

[93] Letter from Johnston to Burston, 30 October 1942 in AWM Series 376 MED 40/76.

[94] See Letter from DDMS Johnston to DGMS Burston, 3 November 1942 in AWM Series 376 MED 40/76. Johnston explained that the three-engine Stinson sent from Australia proved unsuitable and the single-engine Stinson could make a maximum of three trips daily due to weather conditions—and could only evacuate one sitting patient each time.

[95] Letter from DDMS Johnston to DGMS Burston, 3 November 1942, p.1 in AWM Series 376 MED 40/76.

[96] Ibid.

[97] Letter from Johnston to Burston, 30 October 1942, p.2 in AWM Series 376 MED 40/76.

[98] Complaints by Commanding Officer 2/6th Field Ambulance, Donadabu, on selection of camp site and his subsequent reposting to the Mainland, Copy of Message, Broadbent to Divisional Commander, in response to Chenhall message, 3 November 1942, no date [note that Vasey replaced Allen as Commander 7th Division on 27 October] in AWM Series 54, Item 19/7/23. Chenhall's complaint

	regarding Donadabu is discussed later in this book.
[99]	Copy of Message to NGF from NANI, W. Tredinnick 8 November 1942 in AWM Series 54, Item 19/7/23. The message states 'DDMS for comments and recommendations please. Who is to replace Chenhall if he is transferred to a Hospital appointment?' Note that VX108101 Lieutenant William Hamilton Tredinnick is listed in the Roll of Officers of The Australian Army Legal Department and The Australian Army Legal Corps. See B. Oswald and J. Waddell (eds), *Justice in Arms: Military Lawyers in The Australian Army's First Hundred Years*, Big Sky Publishing, Newport, NSW, 2014, Appendix 8.
[100]	Confidential Correspondence regarding Lt Col Chenhall, 18 December 1942 from W.W.S. Johnston, DDMS N G Force in AWM Series 54, Item 19/7/23.
[101]	Extract of Letter from Col F.A. Chenhall, 2/6 Aust Fd Amb to Dr W. Chenhall (reproduced in correspondence from Major-General V.A.H. Stantke, Adjutant-General to Allied Land Forces HQ Victoria

Barracks Melbourne), 23 December 1942, Complaints by Commanding Officer 2/6th Field Ambulance, Donadabu, on selection of campsite and his subsequent reposting to the Mainland in AWM Series 54, Item 19/7/23.

[102] Extract of Letter from Col F.A. Chenhall letter in AWM Series 54, Item 19/7/23.

[103] Stantke correspondence, Victoria Barracks Melbourne, 23 December 1942, point 2 in AWM Series 54, Item 19/7/23.

[104] Entry 5 January 1943, Donadabu, in AWM Series 52, Item 11/12/15, 2/6 Field Ambulance Unit Diary.

Chapter Nine

[1] Dennis et al. (eds), *The Oxford Companion to Australian Military History*, p.428.

[2] Ibid., p.22.

[3] Conversation as reported by John Hetherington, 'The Blamey Papers No 11: Full story of the clash with Rowell', *Argus*, Melbourne, 10 December 1953. Blamey was referring to the decision by

Winston Churchill in August 1942 to remove British field marshal and Commander-in-Chief Auchinleck after the First Battle of El Alamein.

[4] Notes of Secraphone conversation between the Prime Minister and the Commander-in-Chief SWPA, 17 September 1942, 1, Higher Army Direction of Operations in New Guinea in NAA Series A5954, 266/1.

[5] Letter Blamey to Rowell via Captain R. Porter quoted in Hetherington, Blamey Papers, Argus; NAA: A5954, Item 266/1 Correspondence from Blamey to Rowell, 26 September 1942.

[6] Hetherington, 'The Blamey Papers No 11: Full story of the clash with Rowell', *Argus*, Melbourne, 10 December 1953. Hopkins later became Rowell's Chief of Staff.

[7] Howie-Willis, *A Medical Emergency*, pp.270–71.

[8] 'Burston who wished to inspect medical units in New Guinea, suggested he should accompany Blamey. Blamey agreed.' Hetherington, 'The Blamey Papers', *Argus*, Melbourne, 10 December 1953.

[9] Cablegram from Blamey to Prime Minister Curtin, 28 September 1942 in NAA Series A5954, Item 266/1.

[10] Hetherington, 'The Blamey Papers No 11: Full story of the clash with Rowell', *Argus*, Melbourne, 10 December 1953.

[11] Burston to Rowell, quoted in Howie-Willis, *A Medical Emergency*, p.271.

[12] Howie-Willis, *A Medical Emergency*, p.271.

[13] John Hetherington, 'Blamey won in a clash of personalities', *Courier-Mail*, Brisbane, 7 December 1953, p.7.

[14] Cablegram from Blamey to Curtin and MacArthur, 28 September 1942; Cablegram from Blamey to Minister of Defence, 12 November 1942, Higher Army Direction of Operations in New Guinea in NAA Series A5954, Item 266/1.

[15] NAA Series B883, Personnel Record of VX2 Burston, Samuel Roy. See 'Pacific Star: Approval by C-in-C: VX 2, Maj-Gen S.R. Burston, H.Q., A.M.F., 5 December 1945' showing periods spent in the prescribed operational area.

[16] Walker, *Australia in the War of 1939-1945*, Series 5, Vol.1, *Clinical Problems of War*, p.95.

[17] Report on Operations – 14 Aust Field Ambulance – Papua: Colonel N. Hamilton Fairley and Major I.M. Mackerras, Malaria in Papua Report, 6 [Handwritten note 'Report made after visit, 26/6/42'] in AWM Series 54, Item 19/7/17. For details of the Australian Army's campaign against malaria in Palestine, Australia, Papua and the Pacific during World War II see Walker, *Australia in the War of 1939-1945*, Series 5, Vol.1, *Clinical Problems of War*, Chapter 7.

[18] Atebrin was known as mepacrine in Britain after 1941. In America, it was known as quinacrine and marketed there as atabrine. For details regarding research into malaria and the development of synthetic drug treatments see Tony Sweeney, *Malaria Frontline: Australian Army research during World War II*, Melbourne University Press, Melbourne, 2003; Howie-Willis, *An Unending War*; D. Greenwood, *Antimicrobial Drugs: Chronicle of a*

Twentieth Century Triumph, Oxford University Press, UK, 2008.

[19] Report on Malaria in Papua by Fairley and Mackerras, p.3 in AWM Series 54, Item 19/7/17.

[20] Ibid. The men tested were from the 3rd Australian Field Ambulance. Splenomegaly (enlarged spleen) is one of the typical indications of malaria. It was noted that some who tested positive for malaria did not have enlarged spleens, while some with enlarged spleens did not test positive for the malaria parasite. See Walker, *Australia in the War of 1939 1945*, Series 5, Vol.1, *Clinical Problems of War*, p.81.

[21] Report on Malaria in Papua by Fairley and Mackerras, p.6 in AWM Series 54, Item 19/7/17.

[22] Report on Malaria in Papua by Fairley and Mackerras, p.7 in AWM Series 54, Item 19/7/17.

[23] The other members of the Anti-Malaria Advisory Committee were Colonel Turnbull, Lieutenant Colonel Ross and Captain Ratcliffe.

[24] Anti-Malarial Advisory Committee, Minutes of first meeting held at 2200

[25] hrs on 18th August 1942 in AWM Series 52, Item 11/1/1 (DGMS Diary). Anti-Malarial Advisory Committee, Minutes of 2nd Meeting Held at 1430 hrs on 8th September in AWM Series 52, Item 11/1/1. Note that the netting was afforded a B6 priority.
[26] Ibid.
[27] Walker, *Australia in the War of 1939-1945*, Series 5, Vol.1, *Clinical Problems of War*, p.84.
[28] Correspondence from Burston to Blamey, 10 December 1942, NAA: SWM 3DRL/6643 cited in Howie-Willis, *An Unending War*, p.153.
[29] Walker, *Australia in the War of 1939-1945*, Series 5, Vol.1, *Clinical Problems of War*, p.84; Burston, S.R. to Blamey, T.A., 18 December 1942, Official War Diary of DGMS, November and December 1942 quoted in Howie-Willis, *A Medical Emergency*, p.270.
[30] Report on Malaria to DGMS from Lieutenant-Colonel Keogh, 18 December 1942, AWM Series 52, Item 11/1/1.
[31] Ibid.
[32] Ibid [original emphasis].

[33]   Correspondence DGMS Burston to Blamey, 18th December 1942, AWM Series 52, Item11/1/1.
[34]   Report on Malaria, Keogh, 18 December 1942, AWM Series 52, Item 11/1/1.
[35]   Ibid.
[36]   Supply of Drugs and Medical Equipment correspondence to Secretary, Department of the Army from Adjutant-General, 29 December 1942, AWM Series 52, Item 11/1/1.
[37]   Report on Operations, Colonel F.K. Norris, ADMS 7 Aust Div, Wastage 7 Aust Div, 27 September 1942 in AWM Series 54, Item 19/7/17; Norris, *No Memory For Pain*, p.146.
[38]   Norris, ibid., p.172.
[39]   Letter from DGMS Burston to DDMS Disher, 17 December 1942 in AWM Series 356 Med 40/76.
[40]   Note on medical services, p.3 in AWM Series 54, Item 481/12/220.
[41]   Minutes Daily Staff Conference Adv LHQ, 2 November 1942, p.2 in AWM Series 52, Item 1/2/1/5 Advance Headquarters Australian Military Forces G Branch.
[42]   Norris, *No Memory For Pain*, pp.172–73.

[43] Letter from Johnston to Burston, 2 December 1942, p.2 in AWM Series 356 Med 40/76.
[44] Letter DGMS Burston to DDMS Johnston, 9 November 1942 in AWM Series 356 Med 40/76.
[45] Letter from DDMS Johnston to Advanced Land Headquarters, 11 November 1942 in AWM Series 356 Med 40/76.
[46] Ibid.
[47] Ibid.
[48] Walker, *Australia in the War of 1939-1945*, Series 5, Vol.3, *The Island Campaigns*, p.77: 'Groups of walking patients both medical and surgical were sent on to Ilolo; from the 25th to the end of the month forty-two patients were able to make the journey under their own power.'
[49] L.C. Thompson, 'Blitzed Ambulance: the story of an AIF field medical unit by WO/2 L.C. Thompson [sic], NX15734' in *Salt* 7, 29 March 1943, p.29.
[50] Kokoda Track Memorial Walkway website, Oral Histories, Jim Bell, 'Wounded and back to Myola then on to Moresby.'

[51] Ibid.
[52] Thompson, 'Blitzed Ambulance: the story of an AIF field medical unit by WO/2 L.C. Thompson [sic], NX15734', pp.28–29.
[53] Kokoda Track Memorial Walkway website, Oral Histories, Jim Bell, 'Wounded and back to Myola then on to Moresby.'
[54] Ibid.
[55] Ibid.
[56] Entry November 1942, Kennedy Diary.
[57] Ibid.
[58] A. Watson, 'Kokoda War Diary 1942-1943: The Recollections and Photographs of Dr Alan Watson A.M.' (videocassette), Blackmore-Gocking Production, 1991.
[59] Letter from DDMS Johnston, 11 November 1942, p.3 in AWM Series 356 Med 40/76.
[60] Entry 5 November 1942, AWM Series 52, Item 11/12/13, 2/4th Field Ambulance Unit Diary.
[61] Entry for November, Hobson in AWM Series 52, Item 11/12/13, 2/4th Field Ambulance Unit Diary; Entry November 1942 in Kennedy Diary; Walker, *Australia in the War of*

1939-1945, Series 5, Vol.3, *The Island Campaigns*, p.72.

[62] Walker, *Australia in the War of 1939-1945*, Series 5, Vol.3, *The Island Campaign s*, p.72.

[63] Entries 2–12 November 1942, AWM Series 52, Item 11/12/13, 2/4th Field Ambulance Unit Diary.

[64] Letter from DDMS Johnston, 11 November 1942, p.3 in AWM Series 356 Med 40/76.

[65] Entry November 1942, AWM Series 52, Item 11/12/13, 2/4th Field Ambulance Unit Diary. Ward's Drome (also known as Ward's Strip and 5-Mile Drome) was located west of Jackson's Field near Port Moresby. It was primarily used for cargo and large aircraft. See James, *Field Guide to the Kokoda Track*, p.85

[66] Chronological Account of Incidents, Section D: Advance from Kokoda, pp.12–13, Colonel Earlam, Report on Operations in AWM Series 54, Item 19/7/17.

[67] Ibid.
[68] Ibid.
[69] Ibid.

[70] Chronological Account of Incidents, Section D: Advance from Kokoda, p.14, Colonel Earlam, Report on Operations in AWM Series 54, Item 19/7/1714. Presumably, 'foul ground' refers to human waste, or excreta.

[71] A 'flying fox' is a gravity-propelled system of cables and pulleys used for transporting items or people.

[72] Chronological Account of Incidents, Section D: Advance from Kokoda, pp.13–14, Colonel Earlam, Report on Operations in AWM Series 54, Item 19/7/1714.

[73] Ibid.

[74] Ibid.

[75] Analysis of patients who passed through MDS, p.14-Chronological Account of Incidents, Section D: Advance from Kokoda, Colonel Earlam, Report on Operations in AWM Series 54, Item 19/7/1714.

[76] Entry 5 December 1942, AWM Series 52, Item 11/12/15, 2/6 Field Ambulance Diary.

[77] Entry 15 December 1942, AWM Series 52, Item 11/12/15, 2/6 Field Ambulance Diary.

[78] AWM Series 52, Item 11/12/15, 2/6 Field Ambulance Diary.
[79] Report on Malaria, Keogh, 18 December 1942, AWM Series 52, Item 11/1/1.

Chapter Ten

[1] Mite-borne (scrub) typhus caused severe and debilitating symptoms in men whose resistance was already weakened by exhaustion, poor diet and other diseases. Symptoms included rash, cough, bloody sputum, severe headache, fever, and delirium. Prompt access to hospital care was vital. Almost 10% of 626 men admitted to the 2/9th AGH from the beachheads fighting died. The overall mortality rate in Papua at this stage was less than 7%. See Walker, *Australia in the War of 1939-1945*, Series 5, Vol.1, *Clinical Problems of War*, pp.177–202.
[2] Blamey to Shedden, 30 November 1942 cited in Ham, *Kokoda*, p.412.
[3] Moremon, *Battle of the Beachheads 1942-1943*, p.2; Karl James (ed.), *Kokoda: Beyond the Legend*, Cambridge University Press, Port Melbourne, 2017, pp.94–108.

[4] Australian War Memorial website, 'Battle of Gorari'.

[5] See McCarthy, *Australia in the War of 1939-1945*, Series I, Army, vol. V, *South-West Pacific Area – First Year Kokoda to Wau*, chapters 10 and 11.

[6] The 32nd Division under General Edwin Harding was an under-strength National Guard unit from Michigan and Wisconsin comprising National Guardsmen, Reserve officers and draftees. The division included the 126th, 127th and 128th infantry regiments and the 107th Medical Battalion. Buna Mission consisted of three houses and a series of native huts and was the seat of pre-war government administration in the area.

[7] Bullard (trans), *Japanese Army Operations in the South Pacific Area*, pp.203–04; Moremon, *Battle of the Beachheads 1942-1943*, pp.2–3.

[8] Elements of the 2nd Battalion, 126th Infantry, supported by detachments of A and D companies of the US 107th Medical Battalion crossed the Owen Stanley Range on foot during October. See After Action Report – Buna (Papuan) Campaign – 107th Medical Battalion 32nd Inf Div 21 Sept 42 – 1

March 43, 'Company A: New Guinea Campaign' US Archives 332.Med-0.3. The Kapa Kapa Trail runs from Kapa Kapa (Gabagaba) on the south coast to Jaure in the north. See James Campbell, *The Ghost Mountain Boys: Their Epic March and the Terrifying Battle for New Guinea – The Forgotten War of the South Pacific*, Crown Publishing, New York, 2007.

[9] Moremon, *Battle of the Beachheads 1942-1943*, pp.2–3.

[10] Peter J. Dean, 'Grinding out a victory: Australian and American commanders during the beachhead battles', address presented at 'Kokoda: Beyond the Legend' Conference, Australian War Memorial, Canberra, 7 September 2012; James (ed.), *Kokoda: Beyond the Legend*, pp.164–87.

[11] Moremon, *Battle of the Beachheads 1942-1943*, p.2.

[12] For detailed accounts of the land battles see Brune, *A Bastard Of A Place*, chapters 20–27; McCarthy, *Australia in the War of 1939-1945*, Series I, Army, vol. V, *South-West Pacific Area – First Year Kokoda to Wau*, chapters 11–18. For information on the Allied air forces see Douglas Gillison, *Australia*

in the *War of 1939–1945*, Series 3, Air, vol.1, *Royal Australian Air Force, 1939–1942*, Australian War Memorial, Canberra, 1962, Chapter 31.

[13] For example, Gillison records that on the morning of 21 November an Allied aerial attack comprising American-manned Bostons and Mitchells killed four American soldiers and wounded two. Later that same day the 'unfortunate incident ... was repeated' killing six and wounding 12. See Gillison, ibid., p.659.

[14] Moremon, *Battle of the Beachheads 1942-1943*, p.3.

[15] Ibid., p.4; Bullard (trans), *Japanese Army Operations in the South Pacific Area*, p.212.

[16] See communiques and reports from 1 December quoted in 'Gains at Buna,' *Central Queensland Herald*, 10 December 1942.

[17] Walker, *Australia in the War of 1939-1945*, Series 5, vol.1, *Clinical Problems of War*, pp.704–05.

[18] See Department of Veterans' Affairs, The Anzac Portal, 'The Battle of the Beachheads (November, December, January)'.

[19] 'Papuan Campaign: Difficulties Overcome, Enemy Menace – Sir T. Blamey's Address', *West Australian*, 18 January 1943, p.2.

[20] Norris, *No Memory For Pain*, p.172.

[21] The field ambulance units deployed at various stages to the beachheads were the 2/4th, 14th, 2/6th, 2/5th and 10th. See Walker, *Australia in the War of 1939-1945*, Series 5, vol.1, *Clinical Problems of War*, index; see also p.79: 'Only two field ambulances had been available to the force on the range, the 2/4th and 2/6th, with assisting detachments of the 14th Field Ambulance which was stationed in the upper Moresby area.'

[22] Letter from Johnston to Advanced Land Headquarters, p.6 in AWM Series 376, MED 40/76.

[23] Ibid.

[24] Ibid.

[25] Entry 16 November 1942, Kennedy Diary.

[26] Entry 16 November 1942, AWM Series 52, Item 11/12/13, 2/4 Field Ambulance Unit Diary.

[27] Walker, *Australia in the War of 1939-1945*, Series 5, vol.1, *Clinical*

	Problems of War, p.73; Entry 17 November 1942, Kennedy Diary.
[28]	Entry 17 November 1942, Kennedy Diary: 'We completed the job of burying them to break down the odour that was rising from these.'
[29]	Entry 17 November 1942, Kennedy Diary; for details of the circumstances that led to this situation, see Note interposed by Captain Day to elucidate Wairope [sic] position, 18 November 1942, AWM Series 52, Items 11/12/13 2/4 Field Ambulance Diary; Walker, *Australia in the War of 1939-1945*, Series 5, vol.1, *Clinical Problems of War*, pp.73–74.
[30]	Day's report on his arrival at Soputa as written by Hobson, 18 December 1942 in AWM Series 52, Items 11/12/13, 2/4 Field Ambulance Diary.
[31]	Entry 8 December 1942 in AWM Series 52, Items 11/12/13, 2/4 Field Ambulance Diary.
[32]	Entry 18 November 1942, Kennedy Diary.
[33]	Entry 18 November 1942, AWM Series 52, Items 11/12/13, 2/4 Field Ambulance Diary.

[34] Entry November 1942, AWM Series 52, Items 11/12/13, 2/4 Field Ambulance Diary; Entry November 1942, Kennedy Diary; Watson, 'Kokoda War Diary 1942-1943', Chapter 10.

[35] Entry November 1942 in AWM Series 52, Items 11/12/13, 2/4 Field Ambulance Diary; Entry November 1942, Kennedy Diary.

[36] Entry November 1942, Kennedy Diary. The greasy, slippery track in this area was peppered with 'patches of mud like a quagmire' and littered with abandoned Japanese trucks, bicycles, and equipment.

[37] Entry 19 November 1942, AWM Series 52, Items 11/12/13, 2/4 Field Ambulance Diary.

[38] Moremon, *Battle of the Beachheads 1942-1943*, pp.5–7.

[39] Watson, 'Kokoda War Diary 1942-1943', Chapter 10.

[40] Ibid.

[41] Ibid.

[42] Entry 20 November 1942 in AWM Series 52, Items 11/12/13, 2/4 Field Ambulance Diary.

[43] General D. MacArthur to General T. Blamey 20 November 1942 quoted in

McCarthy, *Australia in the War of 1939-1945*, Series I, Army, vol. V, *South-West Pacific Area — First Year Kokoda to Wau*, p.359.

[44] 25-pounder guns were produced in Australia from late 1940 and sent overseas. The guns were hauled along the Kokoda Track by the soldiers and used in the beachhead battles.

[45] McCarthy, *Australia in the War of 1939-1945*, Series I, Army, vol. V, *South-West Pacific Area — First Year Kokoda to Wau*, p.398.

[46] Entry 21 November 1942 in AWM Series 52, Items 11/12/13, 2/4 Field Ambulance Diary.

[47] Ibid. See Entry 0800 hours 21 November 1942 in AWM Series 52, Item 8/2/25/15 November – December 1942 where Brigadier Eather recorded that 'HQ 7 Div closes Popondetta and reopens Soputa 1300hrs'.

[48] Moremon, *Battle of the Beachheads*, p.10. Refer to McCarthy, *Australia in the War of 1939 1945*, Series I, Army, vol. V, *South-West Pacific Area — First Year Kokoda to Wau*, and other military histories of the Papuan campaign for details. The 16th Brigade was also

reinforced by the Australian 30th Brigade in early December.

[49] Gillison, *Australia in the War of 1939–1945*, Series 3, Air, vol.1, *Royal Australian Air Force, 1939–1942*, p.661.

[50] Exhibits 16 and 35, Rough drawn sketches of front line by F. Kingsley Norris and Private Reginald Murray Balfour in NAA Series A6237 National Security Inquiry by Sir William Webb, 2 August 1943.

[51] Entry 21 November 1942 in AWM Series 52, Items 11/12/13, 2/4 Field Ambulance Diary.

[52] Entries 21–22 November 1942 in AWM Series 52, Items 11/12/13, 2/4 Field Ambulance Diary.

[53] McCarthy, *Australia in the War of 1939-1945*, Series 1, Army, vol. V, *South-West Pacific Area – First Year Kokoda to Wau*, pp.394–96; Entry 22 November 1942 in AWM Series 52, Items 11/12/13, 2/4 Field Ambulance Diary.

[54] Entry 23 November 1942 in AWM Series 52, Items 11/12/13, 2/4 Field Ambulance Diary.

[55] Ibid.

[56] Entry November 1942, Soputa, Kennedy Diary.

[57] See Justice Webb's Decision, p.79; see also witness accounts, pp.78–86; Summary of further evidence, Reference 185 in AWM Series 54, Item1010/9/129 A Report on War Crimes Against Australians Committed by Individual Members of the Armed Forces of the Enemy By Sir William Webb K.T.

[58] Exhibit 95 Identification of Medical and Other Personnel Protected Under Geneva Convention (Red Cross Convention) NAA Series A6237 National Security Inquiry by Sir William Webb, 2 August 1943.

[59] Watson, 'Kokoda War Diary 1942-1943', Chapter 10. The US 32nd Division medical units included the 2nd Battalion Aid Station, which moved forward from Soputa on 22 November. The 3rd Battalion Aid Station and 17th Portable Hospital were later established at Soputa in support of the 3rd Battalion, 126th Infantry Combat Team, fighting at Sanananda. See US Army Medical Department, Office of Medical History (2014).

[60] Entries 22 and 23 November 1942 in AWM Series 52, Items 11/12/13, 2/4 Field Ambulance Diary. Sodium Pentothal was used as an anaesthetic.
[61] Entry 26 November 1942 in AWM Series 52, Items 11/12/13, 2/4 Field Ambulance Diary.
[62] Watson, 'Kokoda War Diary 1942-1943', Chapter 12.
[63] Ibid.
[64] Telephone conversation between author and Lorie Thompson, 30 June 2009. A transcript of the conversation was approved by Thompson.
[65] Ibid.
[66] Entries 26 and 27 November 1942 in AWM Series 52, Items 11/12/13, 2/4 Field Ambulance Diary.
[67] Ibid.
[68] Entry 27 November 1942 in AWM Series 52, Items 11/12/13, 2/4 Field Ambulance Diary.
[69] Norris, *No Memory For Pain*, pp.179–80.
[70] After Action Report – Buna (Papuan) Campaign – 107th Medical Battalion 32nd Inf Div 21 Sept 42 – 1 March 43, 'Company A: New Guinea Campaign' p.2 in US Archives 332.

Med-0.3. See also US Army Medical Department website, Buna Campaign.

[71] Entry 27 November, Soputa, AWM Series 52, Item 1/5/15 War Diary, 7 Australian Division Adjutant and Quartermaster General Branch (7 Aust Div AQ Branch). See also Walker, *Australia in the War of 1939-1945*, Series 5, vol.1, *Clinical Problems of War*, p.82. Note that Walker states the MDS was within 100 yards of divisional headquarters.

[72] Evidence given by Captain Kienzle in NAA Series A6237 National Security Inquiry by Sir William Webb, 2 August 1943.

[73] Sweeting, 'The 2/4th Field Ambulance A.I.F. during the Owen Stanleys Campaign 1942', p.4.

[74] Ibid.

[75] Thompson, 'Blitzed Ambulance: the story of an AIF field medical unit by WO/2 L.C. Thompson, NX15734', p.25.

[76] Sweeting, 'The 2/4th Field Ambulance A.I.F. during the Owen Stanleys Campaign 1942', p.12.

[77] Entry 27 November 1942 in AWM Series 52, Items 11/12/13, 2/4 Field Ambulance Diary.

[78] These numbers were attained by cross-referencing the AWM Roll of Honour with personnel service records, the 2/4th Field Ambulance Diary, Commonwealth War Graves information, and the Casualty Registers for the Papuan campaign.

[79] See, for example, casualty lists in James, *Field Guide to the Kokoda Track*, p.420; 440ff.

[80] See NAA Series B883 Personnel records; AWM Roll of Honour; NAA Series MP 917/2, Control 7 and 8, Casualty Registers, Australian servicemen: Papua, for all States (Deaths and Wounded in Action).

[81] NAA Series MP 917/2, Control 7 and 8.

[82] Casualties are recorded as 22 dead and 50 wounded by the official military historian. See McCarthy, *Australia in the War of 1939-1945*, Series I, Army, vol. V, *South-West Pacific Area – First Year Kokoda to Wau*, p.399.

[83]	Entry 1 December 1942 AWM Series 52, Items 11/12/13, 2/4 Field Ambulance Diary.
[84]	Entry 27 November 1942, Kennedy Diary.
[85]	Members of the 2/4 Field Ambulance killed and ages: Major Ian Vickery, 28; Temporary Major Hew McDonald, 30; Privates George Antees, 21; Keith Kuch, 23; Keith Lawler, 23; Lance Corporal Arthur Moodie (or Moody), 31; Private Edmund Schubert, 34. Private Gordon Pugh, aged 25, suffered severe head wounds and died from complications in Australia on 31 December 1942. Two soldiers who were attached to the 2/4th Field Ambulance at the time of the attack, Sig. George Dean (7th Division Signals) and Sapper Horace Thomas (Field Park Company, RAE) were also killed. See NAA Series MP 917/2, Control 7 and 8, Casualty Registers; Kennedy sketch of Soputa MDS site after the attack; AWM Series 52, Items 11/12/13, 2/4 Field Ambulance Diary; James, *Field Guide to the Kokoda Track*, p.420.
[86]	Entry 27 November 1942, Kennedy Diary.

[87]   Entry 5 December 1942 in AWM Series 52, Items 11/12/13, 2/4 Field Ambulance Diary. See also photograph P02423.053 in AWM Collection. The photograph was taken by Lieutenant Colonel Hobson and shows the graves of Majors Vickery and McDonald. The unidentified grave is that of Private George Antees, 2/4 Field Ambulance.

[88]   Email correspondence with Commonwealth War Graves Commission, 26 August 2007; G.H. Cranswick, 'The Diocese of New Guinea in 1946'.

[89]   Kennedy sketch of Soputa MDS site after the attack.

[90]   See National Archives of Australia, Fact Sheet 61 – World War II Crimes: The inquiries of Sir William Webb.

[91]   NAA Series A3439 Commission of Inquiry into Conduct of Japanese, p.202.

[92]   Exhibit 95 Identification of Medical and Other Personnel Protected Under Geneva Convention (Red Cross Convention) NAA Series A6237 National Security Inquiry by Sir William Webb.

[93]   Ibid.

[94] Question from Justice Webb to Mr Sexton, NAA Series A6237 National Security Inquiry by Sir William Webb.

[95] Webb Inquiry, Summary of further evidence. See, for example, testimonies of Lance Corporal Arthur Green; Private William Kennedy; Warrant Officer Frank Lingham; Private Herbert Wray; Signalman John Sorbie MacKenzie; Corporal Malcolm Laurie Hill in AWM Series 54, Item 1010/9/129.

[96] Webb Inquiry, Summary of further evidence, Jack Clark, Sergeant H.Q. Company 2/27th Australian Infantry Battalion in AWM Series 54, Item 1010/9/129.

[97] Webb Inquiry, Summary of further evidence, Harry Edwards Warrant Officer II, 2/2 Supply Depot in AWM Series 54, Item 1010/9/129.

[98] Exhibit 16 and Exhibit 35, NAA Series A6237.

[99] Ibid.

[100] Exhibit 35, NAA Series A6237.

[101] Transcript of sworn testimony given at Yungaburra, Atherton Tablelands, Frank Kingsley Norris, 2 August 1943, NAA Series A6236.

[102] Testimony of Warrant Officer Ralph Albanese, A Company 2/1st Australian Infantry, NAA Series A6236.

[103] Testimony of Lieutenant Colonel Frank Henry Sublet, HQ 7 Australian Division Moresby Area 1 September 1943, NAA Series A6236.

[104] Questionnaire completed by Private David Windsor, A Company 2/2nd Australian Infantry Battalion, NAA Series A3439.

[105] Testimony of Lieutenant Colonel Sidney Eliot Smith, ANGAU, Port Moresby 28 August 1943, NAA Series A6236.

[106] Article 24(1) of the 1923 Hague Rules of Air Warfare provides: 'Aerial bombardment is legitimate only when directed at a military objective, that is to say, an object of which the destruction or injury would constitute a distinct military advantage to the belligerent.' Article 2 of the 1907 Hague Convention (IX) allows the bombardment of '[m]ilitary works, military or naval establishments, depots of arms or war *matériel,* workshops or plant which could be

utilized for the needs of the hostile fleet or army, and the ships of war in the harbour.' See International Committee of the Red Cross: Practice Relating to Rule 8 Definition of Military Objectives.

[107] Report on Soputa (Medical Dressing Station) Bombing, p.78 in AWM Series 54, Item 1010/9/129.

[108] Summary of further evidence Lance Sergeant Lawrence Charles Thompson, 2/4th Australian Field Ambulance, AWM Series 54, Item 1010/9/129.

[109] Summary of further evidence, Private William Claude Kennedy, 2/4th Australian Field Ambulance; Corporal Roy Alton Hargreaves, 7 Australian Division Provost Corps, in AWM Series 54, Item 1010/9/129.

[110] Summary of further evidence, Signalman Horatio William Sinclair, 7th Division Signals, Corporal Sydney Frederick Gribble, 2/4th Australian Field Ambulance; Lance Corporal Arthur Vincent Green, 2/4th Australian Field Ambulance, in AWM Series 54, Item 1010/9/129.

[111] Summary of further evidence, Ronald David Miles, signalman, 7 Australian Division, in AWM Series 54, Item 1010/9/129.

[112] Summary of further evidence, for example, testimony of Lance Sergeant Lawrence Thompson; Private William Kennedy; Corporal Sydney Gribble; Warrant Officer Lingham, in AWM Series 54, Item 1010/9/129.

[113] Transcript of sworn testimony given at Yungaburra, Atherton Tablelands, Frank Kingsley Norris, 2 August 1943 in NAA Series A6236.

[114] Testimony of Sgt James Edward Schloff, Medical Detachment, 126 Infantry in NAA Series A6236.

[115] Summary of further evidence, Questionnaire of Captain Charles Lawrence in AWM Series 54, Item 1010/9/129.

[116] Ibid.

[117] Transcript of sworn testimony given at Yungaburra, Atherton Tablelands, Frank Kingsley Norris, 2 August 1943 in NAA Series A6236.

[118] Questionnaire of Captain Charles Lawrence in NAA Series A6236.

[119] Ibid.

[120] Questionnaire of Corporal Technician Charles J. Grant, Medical Detachment, US 126 Infantry, 20 July 1943 in NAA Series A6236.

[121] Questionnaire of Private First-Class L. Dale [unclear-Dole?] in NAA Series A6236.

[12]2 Transcript of sworn testimony given at Yungaburra, Atherton Tablelands, Frank Kingsley Norris, 2 August 1943, p.380 in NAA Series A6236.

[123] Transcript of sworn testimony given at Yungaburra, Atherton Tablelands, Frank Kingsley Norris, 2 August 1943, p.381 in NAA Series A6236.

[124] Reference to finding on page 163 of 'Japanese Atrocity Report' in AWM Series 54, Item 1010/9/129.

[125] Report on Soputa (Medical Dressing Station) Bombing, p.79 in AWM Series 54, Item 1010/9/129.

Chapter Eleven

[1] 'It was good to see Clive Disher again. He had taken over from Bill Johnston, relieved only when he became desperately sick.' Norris, *No Memory For Pain*, p.184.

[2] Handwritten letter from Disher to Burston [no date] in AWM Series 356 Med 40/76.
[3] Report on Operations by DDMS, 10 December 1942 in NAA: AWM356, Med 40/76.
[4] Walker, *Australia in the War of 1939–1945*, Series 5, vol.3, *The Island Campaigns*, p.84.
[5] 'Training V.A.s', *Sydney Morning Herald*, Monday 30 November 1942, p.4.
[6] Adv LHQ Information Letter No 42, 26 November stated that 'DGMS LHQ arrived Adv LHQ from NG on 24 Nov 1942. An Adv LHQ Information Letter No 43, 29 Nov 1942 stated that 'DGMS departed by plane for Sydney on the afternoon of 26 Nov.' AWM Series 52, Item 1/2/5. This is at odds with the handwritten entry on Burston's Officer's Record of Service regarding 'emplaned' in New Guinea and 'deplaned' in Australia. The original date has been written over and appears to read '29-11-42.' Another entry has been typed on a separate piece of paper and glued to a separate record of service sheet. This entry clearly reads 'Emplaned N.G. Deplaned Aust 29/11/42. See NAA

Series B883, VX2 Service Record Burston Samuel Roy, pp.33, 38.

[7] Letter from Burston to Johnston, 9 December 1942, AWM Series 356 Med 40/76.
[8] Ibid.
[9] Bryan Egan, 'Disher, Harold Clive (1891–1976)', *ADB*, vol.14, MUP, 1996.
[10] Timeline 28 Nov–13 Dec 1942, Report on Operations in AWM Series 54, Item 19/7/17.
[11] Walker, *Australia in the War of 1939–1945*, Series 5, vol.3, *The Island Campaigns*, p.84.
[12] Ibid.
[13] Observations on medical aspects: Owen Stanleys – Buna Areas: Fitness of the 2/3 Inf Bn for Front Line Service, Captain Joseph, Medical Notes on Operations Owen Stanley Area – Papuan Campaign in AWM Series 54, Item 481/12/224 Observations on medical aspects by Captain L. Joseph A.A.M.C.
[14] Ibid.
[15] Ibid.
[16] Walker, *Australia in the War of 1939–1945*, Series 5, vol.3, *The Island Campaigns*, p.84.

[17] See Report on Operations: Gona – Amboga River Ops, Earlam in AWM Series 54, Item19/7/17; Walker, *Australia in the War of 1939–1945*, Series 5, vol.3, *The Island Campaigns*, p.79.

[18] Report on Operations by Brigadier W.W.S. Johnston, 10 December 1942 in AWM Series 54, Item 19/7/17.

[19] Report by DDMS Johnston to DGMS Burston, 10 December 1942, Medical notes on operations in the Owen Stanley area, Papuan Campaign, in AWM Series 54, Item 481/12/224.

[20] Walker, *Australia in the War of 1939–1945*, Series 5, vol.3, *The Island Campaigns*, p.84.

[21] Entry 1 December 1942, AWM Series 52, Item 11/12/13, 2/4 Field Ambulance Diary.

[22] Report on Operations – Sanananda Operations, Earlam in AWM Series 54, Item 19/7/17.

[23] Report on Operations – Policy Regarding Evacuation, Earlam in AWM Series 54, Item 19/7/17.

[24] Entry 3 December 1942, AWM Series 52, Item 11/12/13, 2/4 Field Ambulance Diary.

[25] Entry December 1942, Kennedy Diary. See also NAA: B883 NX21554 Kennedy Lawrence Nicholis, Service and Casualty Form in Service Record showing admission to MDS suffering PUO 18–22 December; NAA: B883 NX17737 Private Kennedy William Claude which shows admission 29 November – 2 December for PUO and admission 15-20 December for Malaria MT. Also see Commanding Officer's Summary for months of October, November, December, Lieutenant Colonel Hobson, AWM Series 52, Item 11/12/13, 2/4th Field Ambulance Unit Diary, noting 'malaria towards the latter part of the campaign, affected almost 100% of personnel.'

[26] Entry 4 December 1942, AWM Series 52, Item 11/12/13, 2/4th Field Ambulance Unit Diary shows that those evacuated comprised four Australian and 21 American battle casualties, 85 Australian and 36 American sick.

[27] Entries 6-8 December 1942, AWM Series 52, Item 11/12/13, 2/4th Field Ambulance Unit Diary. Walker,

Australia in the War of 1939–1945, Series 5, vol.3, *The Island Campaigns*, p.83 states that an American hospital could take casualties on 6 December 1942. This differs from Hobson's account.

[28] Entry 8 December 1942, AWM Series 52, Item 11/12/13, 2/4th Field Ambulance Unit Diary.

[29] Timeline 28 Nov–13 Dec 1942, Report on Operations in AWM Series 54, Item 19/7/17.

[30] Ibid.

[31] Ibid.

[32] Maps showing positions of units and CCS, 1942 in AWM Series 54, Item 581/7/33 Report on Operations Buna Gona Sanananda Medical Positions – Work of 2/4 Field Ambulance.

[33] Timeline 28 Nov–13 Dec 1942, Report on Operations in AWM Series 54, Item 19/7/17.

[34] AWM Series 52, 11/12/13, 2/4 Field Ambulance Diary; AWM Series 52, 11/12/15, 2/6 Field Ambulance Diary.

[35] A detachment of the 2/5th Field Ambulance had arrived at Buna from Milne Bay (under Major Lavarack) in December 1942. They later set up an

ADS near Cape Endaiadere before moving to Soputa and Sanananda in January 1943. See Walker, *Australia in the War of 1939–1945*, Series 5, vol.3, *The Island Campaigns*, pp.89–94.

[36] Appendix E, AWM Series 52, Item 11/12/14, 2/5 Australian Field Ambulance Unit Diary.

[37] Ibid.

[38] Ibid.

[39] For Lavarack's detailed account of the work of the detachment at Buna see Report on activities of detachment 2/5 Field Ambulance – Medical Service with "Hammer" Forces in Buna-Sanananda Areas 12 Dec–15 Feb 1942/1943 in AWM Series 54, Item 19/7/6 and Appendix E, AWM Series 52, Item 11/12/14, 2/5 Australian Field Ambulance Unit Diary.

[40] Brief Account of the activities of the 7th Australian Division – Medical Services during six months campaign in Papua 1943, Colonel F.K. Norris, AWM Series 54, Item 481/12/13.

[41] Entry 19 December 1942, Lieutenant Colonel Chenhall, AWM Series 52, Items 11/12/15, 2/6 Field Ambulance Diary.

[42] Entry December 1942, Kennedy Diary (original spelling and punctuation).

[43] Walker, *Australia in the War of 1939–1945*, Series 5, vol.3, *The Island Campaigns*, p.87.

[44] For example, a small party of AASC personnel acted as stretcher-bearers for the 30th Brigade on the Sanananda Track, stretcher-bearers were despatched to RAPs at Sanananda Point, small surgical teams were at Jumbora and Soputa. Many of the stretcher-bearers were armed.

[45] For example: the US 23rd Portable Hospital treated 47 Australians; the 18th in conjunction with the 22nd Portable Hospital at Hariko treated 62 sick, 292 battle casualties and five wounded Australians between 24 November and 14 December 1942; the 14th Portable Hospital treated 41 Australian sick and 150 Australian battle casualties. See Records of the Adjutant General's Office WWII Operations Reports 1940-48 32nd Infantry Division Box 7944 Entry 427, US Archives 332-26 Medical Narrative History – Papuan Campaign New

[46] Guinea, Office of the Div Surgeons 32 Division 15 Sept 1942–17 March 1943. Entries December 1942, AWM Series 52, Items 11/12/13, 2/4 Field Ambulance Diary. A 10th Field Ambulance detachment of 28 other ranks, attached surgical team and two aircraft loads of equipment arrived at Dobodura and proceeded to Cape Endaiadere where they combined with the 2/5th Field Ambulance detachment manning a dressing station there. The 10th performed surgery while the 2/5th cared for the sick. See Walker, *Australia in the War of 1939–1945*, Series 5, vol.3, *The Island Campaigns*, pp.91, 98.

[47] Report on Conditions and Complaints at 14th Field Ambulance Popondetta December 1942, AWM Series 54, Item 9/7/22, Report on 14 Aust Fd Amb, Major Buckley.

[48] Ibid.

[49] Geographical restrictions on where CMF soldiers could serve (in defence of Australia and its territories) contributed to the attitudes of some AIF soldiers. The derogatory term 'chocolate soldiers' or 'chocos' implied

the militia men would melt in the heat of battle. See Australian Army website 'Army – Our History – The offending 'M' – WW2 Army service numbers'.

[50] Report on Conditions and Complaints at 14th Field Ambulance Popondetta December 1942, AWM Series 54, Item 9/7/22 Report on charges made by Major Buckley and other officers against 14 Aust Fd Amb, Lieutenant Colonel Earlam, 28 December 1942.

[51] Ibid.

[52] Communique to ADMS 7 Aust Div from Brigadier Disher-Report on 14 Aust Fd Amb 25 December 1942; Communique to ADMS 6 Aust Div-Report on 24 Aust Fd Amb, 28 December 1942 in AWM Series 54, Item 19/7/22.

[53] Report on Conditions and Complaints at 14th Field Ambulance Popondetta December 1942, AWM Series 54, Item 9/7/22.

[54] Communique to DDMS NGF from Colonel Norris, Report on 14 Aust Fd Amb, 29 December 1942, AWM Series 54, Item 9/7/22. See also Report on Operations 14 Aust Field Ambulance – Papua, Colonel Earlam. Earlam wrote

[55]	that 'on 7 December it was decided that as staging post was about 12 miles in rear of Adv HQ 7 Aust Div it should be administered from Adv HQ NGF' in AWM Series 54, Item19/7/17. Communique to ADMS 6 Aust Div from Colonel Disher, 28 December 1942, AWM Series 54, Item 9/7/22.
[56]	AWM Series 54, Item 9/7/22 Report on charges made by Major Buckley and other officers against 14 Aust Fd Amb, Lieutenant Colonel Earlam, 28 December 1942.
[57]	Ibid.
[58]	Ibid.
[59]	Ibid.
[60]	Ibid.
[61]	'Vale NX321 Andrew Adrian Buckley, 2/2nd Infantry Battalion ... From 21 November 1942 Major Buckley led the battalion in the battles on the Sanananda Track. In early December while acting CO Major Buckley contracted malaria and was evacuated.' *In Support*, magazine of the friends of the 2nd Infantry Battalions, 2008, p.13.
[62]	AWM Series 54, Item 9/7/22 Report on charges made by Major Buckley and other officers against 14 Aust Fd Amb,

Lieutenant Colonel Earlam, 28 December 1942.

[63] Appreciation by Lieutenant General Herring cited in McCarthy, *Australia in the War of 1939-1945*, Series I, Army, vol. V, *South-West Pacific Area – First Year Kokoda to Wau*, p.510.

[64] Norris, *No Memory For Pain*, p.185.

[65] Medical Service with 'Hammer' forces in Buna-Gona-Sanananda Areas 12 Dec-15 Feb 1942/43, AWM Series 54, Item 19/7/6 Report on Activities of Detachment 2/5 Aust. Fd. Ambulance; Entries January and February 1943; Report on Personnel by Major Lavarack, 13 January 1943; Activities of Maj Lavarack's detachment with appended maps in AWM Series 52, Item 11/12/14, 2/5 Field Ambulance Unit Diary.

[66] Report on Activities of Detachment 2/5 Aust. Fd. Ambulance in AWM Series 54, Item 19/7/6.

[67] Ibid.

[68] Ibid.

[69] Ibid.

[70] 'Hopes For Victory In Papua', *Sydney Morning Herald*, 1 January 1943, p.4.

[71] See McCarthy, *Australia in the War of 1939-1945*, Series 1, Army, vol. V, *South-West Pacific Area – First Year Kokoda to Wau*; Moremon, *Battle of the Beachheads 1942-1943*; Brune, *A Bastard Of A Place*; Threlfall, *Jungle Warriors: From Tobruk to Kokoda and beyond*, for battle details.

[72] Colonel C.W.B. Littlejohn later served as consultant surgeon to Land Headquarters.

[73] Report on Operations – Sanananda, AWM Series 54, Item 19/7/17.

[74] Report on Activities of Detachment 2/5 Aust. Fd. Ambulance, AWM Series 54, Item 19/7/6.

[75] Report – Sanananda Operations, Lieutenant Colonel Earlam, AWM series 54, Item 19/7/17.

[76] Walker, *Australia in the War of 1939–1945*, Series 5, vol.3, *The Island Campaigns*, p.94; Report on Activities of Detachment 2/5 Aust Fd Ambulance, AWM Series 54, Item 19/7/6.

[77] Report on Operations – Sanananda, AWM Series 54, Item 19/7/17.

[78] Walker, *Australia in the War of 1939–1945*, Series 5, vol.3, *The Island Campaigns*, p.96.

[79] 'Victory in Papua – Leader's Tribute and Warning', *The Age*, 18 January, p.3.

[80] Report on Operations – Sanananda, AWM Series 54, Item 19/7/17; NAA: AWM54, 19/7/6, Report on Activities of Detachment 2/5 Aust. Fd. Ambulance, AWM Series 54, Item 19/7/6.

[81] Report on Operations – Sanananda, AWM Series 54, Item 19/7/17.

[82] Strength of medical detachments at Buna by Lt-Col Palmer, CO 10th Australian Field Ambulance, AWM Series 54, Item 19/7/11, Report on 10 Australian Field Ambulance Buna Campaign December 1942 – February 1943.

[83] Analysis of patients admitted to Soputa from 18 Dec 42 til 25 Jan 43 – Report on Operations 14 Field Ambulance, AWM Series 54, Item 19/7/17.

[84] Statistical Data: analysis of malarial incidence in the unit-Report on Operations 14 Field Ambulance, AWM Series 54, Item 19/7/17.

[85] Report on Personnel, Major Lavarack, 13 January 1943, AWM 52, Item

	11/12/14, 2/5 Field Ambulance Unit Diary.
[86]	The 10th Field Ambulance had been temporarily stationed at the 2/9th AGH in Port Moresby since 28 November. A detachment of the unit, including a surgical team, was flown to Dobodura on 17 December.
[87]	Walker, *Australia in the War of 1939–1945*, Series 5, vol.3, *The Island Campaigns*, pp.94–99.

Chapter Twelve

[1]	Walker, *Australia in the War of 1939–1945*, Series 5, vol.3, *The Island Campaigns*, p.102 states 'The Australian sick and wounded owed a great deal to the American air transports.' Medical evacuation from Papua is not mentioned in the official history of the RAAF. See Gillison, *Australia in the War of 1939–1945*, Series 3, Air, vol.1, *Royal Australian Air Force, 1939–1942*, Index.
[2]	Walker, ibid., p.121.
[3]	Evacuation of Patients from New Guinea, ADMS COSC, 29 December 1942 [original punctuation], AWM Series 54, Item 481/12/247.

[4] Report by Brigadier Johnston, AWM Series 54, Item 19/7/17. Johnston described the system instigated by Colonel Fisher and Major Humphery whereby the pilot waved a coloured piece of cloth from the cockpit; the colour varied according to the number of Australian and American ambulances required. He also noted that the insufficient number of available AAMC personnel meant that combat troops assisted with the unloading of patients.

[5] DDMS Johnston to DGMS Burston, 30 October 1942 in AWM Series 376 MED 40/76.

[6] Report by Brigadier Johnston, AWM Series 54, Item 19/7/17.

[7] Minute Paper – Relief of Soldiers in New Guinea, Minister F. Forde, 31 December 1942 in NAA Series MP742/1, Item 259/2/502.

[8] Ibid.

[9] Establishment of an operational service command in New Guinea, Brigadier General Dwight F. Johns US Army, 14 October 1942; O.O.B. – COSC – AMF Moresby Sub Area & Milne Bay Sub Area, AWM Series 52 Item 1/11/1 Australian Military Forces, Army

Headquarters, formation and unit diaries 1939-1945, Miscellaneous – Combined Operational Services Command (COSC) October 1942 – March 1943.
[10] Ibid.
[11] AWM Series 52, Item 1/11/1 COSC Unit Diary.
[12] Entry 29 November 1942, AWM Series 52, Item 1/11/1 COSC Unit Diary.
[13] Memo on the subject of evacuation, AWM Series 54, Item 277/4/2.
[14] Correspondence from Brigadier Johns, Commander COSC to HQ New Guinea Force, 29 November 1942 in AWM Series 52, Item 1/11/1 COSC Unit Diary.
[15] Evacuation of Patients from New Guinea, 29 December 1942, AWM Series 54, Item 481/12/247 Headquarters, C.O.S.C, [Medical – Reports:] SWPA (Various).
[16] Walker, *Australia in the War of 1939–1945*, Series 5, vol.3, *The Island Campaigns*, p.121.
[17] Ibid., p.41.
[18] 'Appendix A: Medical Arrangements – Milne Bay' 7 August 1942, Report from Allied Land Forces Southwest Pacific Area Advanced Headquarters to DGMS

LHQ, 11 August 1942, AWM Series 54, Item 481/12/220 Dr Walker's Records – Medical Reports and Arrangements Milne Bay area.

[19] Report on Owen Stanleys and Buna Medical Notes on Operations, AWM Series 54, Item 481/12/224.

[20] Movement of Medical Cases By Air, ADMS Macdonald, 29 November 1942, AWM Series 52, Item 1/11/1.

[21] See Allan S. Walker, *Australia in the War of 1939-1945, Series 5, vol.4, Medical Services of the R.A.N. and R.A.A.F.*, Australian War Memorial, Canberra, 1961, p.358. No.1 Air Ambulance comprised three de Havillands (DH86) which saw service in the Middle East until 1943. During this time, they transported approximately 9000 patients to medical care; No.2 Air Ambulance was based in Canberra and served in Australia in 1942 and New Guinea in 1943; see also The Royal Australian Air Force website.

[22] No.804 Squadron was part of 54 Group Carrier Wing, 5th Air Force, USAAF. At the time of its entry into the war, the US was similarly

unprepared for large-scale casualty evacuations by air. Although an average of 21 patients per month were evacuated by air from the Pacific region, large-scale evacuations did not begin until late November 1943. See U.S. Medical Research Centre, World War Two website; Air Force News website.

[23] U.S. Army Medical Department, Office of Medical History, Chapter 10-The South West Pacific Area, p.437.

[24] Entry 18 January 1943, AWM Series 52, Item 1/11/1 COSC Unit Diary.

[25] Summary for January 1943, AWM Series 52, Item 1/11/1 COSC Unit Diary.

[26] Colonel Chenhall, 22 December 1942, AWM Series 52, Item 11/12/15, 2/6 Field Ambulance Diary.

[27] Medical Appreciation – Proposed Donadabu Camp, December 1942, Colonel Chenhall, AWM Series 52, Item 11/12/15, 2/6 Field Ambulance Diary.

[28] Ibid.

[29] The 16th and 25th AIF brigades at Donadabu wanted to use the area for their transport vehicles. See also AWM

Series 54, Item 481/12/13 Report by ADMS Norris, [Medical-Reports:] Brief account of the activities of the 7 Australian Division – Medical services during the six months campaign in Papua (Jan 1943). Norris described the high casualty rate across these brigades as 'woeful'.

[30] Medical Appreciation – Proposed Donadabu Camp, December 1942, Colonel Chenhall, AWM Series 52, Item 11/12/15, 2/6 Field Ambulance Diary.

[31] Entry 27 December 1942, AWM Series 52, Item 11/12/15, 2/6 Field Ambulance Diary.

[32] Entry for 29 December 1942, AWM Series 52, Item 11/12/13, 2/4 Field Ambulance Diary.

[33] Medical Appreciation – Proposed Donadabu Camp, December 1942, Colonel Chenhall, AWM Series 52, Item 11/12/15, 2/6 Field Ambulance Diary.

[34] Report on Malaria, Keogh, 18 December 1942, AWM Series 52, Item 11/1/1.

[35] Mackerras was in charge of entomology during 1942 and was appointed

Director of Entomology in 1943; Fairley was Director of Medicine, Land Headquarters; Holmes was Director of Pathology and Hygiene.

[36] Walker, *Australia in the War of 1939–1945*, Series 5, vol.3, *The Island Campaigns*, p.39.

[37] Evacuation of Casualties from New Guinea, ADMS Macdonald 29 November 1942 AWM Series 52, Item 11/1/1.

[38] See M. Condon-Rall and A. Cowdrey, *United States Army in World War II: The Technical Services,The Medical Department: Medical Service in the War Against Japan*, Center of Military History, United States Army, Washington D.C., 1998, pp.127–47.

[39] Report on American Hospitalization, AWM Series 54, Item 403/1/16.

[40] Appreciation of the situation at 2/9 Australian General Hospital, by Col Green, AWM Series 54, Item 481/12/247 Medical Reports SWPA (Various).

[41] Memo on the subject of evacuation, AWM Series 54, Item 277/4/2; Walker, *Australia in the War of 1939–1945*,

	Series 5, vol.3, *The Island Campaigns*, pp.5, 40.
[42]	Letter from Johnston to Burston, 8 December 1942, AWM Series 356 MED 40/76.
[43]	The French term '*bête noire*' translates as 'black beast' and is used to describe something especially disliked or feared.
[44]	Appreciation of the situation at 2/9 Australian General Hospital, by Col Green, AWM Series 54, Item 481/12/247.
[45]	Ibid.
[46]	Ibid. All statistics and quotations in this paragraph are from this document.
[47]	Ibid.
[48]	Ibid.
[49]	Ibid.
[50]	Ibid.
[51]	Report on Operations, 14th Field Ambulance, AWM Series 54, Item 19/7/17.
[52]	Appreciation of the situation at 2/9 Australian General Hospital, by Col Green, AWM Series 54, Item 481/12/247.
[53]	Entry December 1942, Kennedy Diary.
[54]	Ibid.
[55]	Ibid.

[56] Entry January 1943, Kennedy Diary.
[57] Ibid.
[58] Commanding Officer's Review for month of January 1943, Lieutenant-Colonel Hobson, AWM Series 52, Item 11/12/13, 2/4 Field Ambulance Unit Diary.

Chapter Thirteen

[1] 'Canberra Visit: MacArthur's Pledge', *Sydney Morning Herald*, 27 March 1942, p.4.
[2] 'Editorial-MacArthur's Pledge And Ours', *Courier-Mail*, 28 March 1942, p.4.
[3] Report on Operation at Goodenough Island by Lt-Col Arnold C.O. 2/12 Aust. Infantry Bn 22–26 October 1942, pp.1–8 in AWM Series 54, Item 422/7/8.
[4] General D. MacArthur to General T. Blamey 20 November 1942 cited in McCarthy, *Australia in the War of 1939-1945*, Series 1, Army, vol. V, *South-West Pacific Area – First Year Kokoda to Wau*, p.359.
[5] Medical Service 7 Aust Div. During Papuan Campaign, ADMS Norris, January 1943, p.13 [original emphasis] in AWM Series 54, Item 481/12/13.

[6] See James, 'General Clowes of Milne Bay'. It is speculated that Clowes' long-standing friendship with Rowell (who had been relieved of command of NGF by Blamey) contributed to this situation. See Dennis et al. (eds), *The Oxford Companion to Australian Military History*, p.135.

[7] Brune, *A Bastard Of A Place*, pp.396–97.

[8] Medical Reports and Arrangements Milne Bay Area, Notes on Medical Service – N.G.F. Mid Aug to Mid Dec 42 in AWM Series 54, Item 481/12/220. Note that the report is not signed, however, a note on page 19 refers to 'the foregoing notes ... as seen by DDMS N.G.F.' William Johnston held this position until replaced by Clive Disher in mid-December 1942.

[9] Medical Reports and Arrangements Milne Bay Area, Notes on Medical Service – N.G.F. Mid Aug to Mid Dec 42, p.10 in AWM Series 54, Item 481/12/220.

[10] Medical Reports and Arrangements Milne Bay Area, Notes on Medical Service – N.G.F. Mid Aug to Mid Dec 42, p.6 in AWM Series 54, Item 481/12/220.

[11] Medical Reports and Arrangements Milne Bay Area, Notes on Medical Service – N.G.F. Mid Aug to Mid Dec 42, p.11 in AWM Series 54, Item 481/12/220.

[12] Medical Reports and Arrangements Milne Bay Area, Notes on Medical Service – N.G.F. Mid Aug to Mid Dec 42 in AWM Series 54, Item 481/12/220.

[13] Entry 27 September 1942, AWM Series 52, Item 11/12/15; Extract of Chenhall letter in AWM Series 54, Item 19/7/23.

[14] Entries November and December 1942 at Myola and Popondetta, Kennedy Diary.

[15] National Archives Series MP 917/2, Controls 7 and 8, Casualty Registers, Australian servicemen: Papua, for all States (Deaths and Wounded in Action).

[16] 'During the whole Papuan campaign (including the mountain, Milne Bay and beach phases) ... about 22,000 Australian troops served in combat or support roles. Of these, 2165 were killed, 3500 wounded and 15,575 received treatment for disease.' Ham, *Kokoda*, p.518. See Butler, *The*

Australian Army Medical Services in the War of 1914-1918, vol.1, *Gallipoli, Palestine and New Guinea*, Chapter XVII for discussion of compilation of statistics. Recent publications regarding statistical discrepancies include David Noonan, *Those we forget: recounting Australian casualties of the First World War*, Melbourne University Press, Victoria, 2014.

[17] See McCarthy, *Australia in the War of 1939-1945*, Series I, Army, vol. V, *South-West Pacific Area – First Year Kokoda to Wau*, Chapter 17 – Allied and Enemy Casualties, pp.527–31. Note that some historians have questioned the accepted casualty figures, particularly in relation to the Kokoda phase of the Papuan campaign. Historians such as Williams have argued that 'Australian post-battle estimates of huge Japanese losses have often been accepted and decades on have become cemented into the Kokoda myth.' Williams, *The Kokoda Campaign 1942*, p.235.

[18] Walker, *Australia in the War of 1939–1945*, Series 5, vol.3, *The Island Campaigns*, p.121.

[19] PIB and Royal Papuan Constabulary – 14 killed in action; four died on active service; 38 wounded in action. 'Other New Guineans' – 140 died while serving with Allies; 1200 died while serving with Japanese. The Australian Government Department of Veterans' Affairs, 'The Kokoda Track-List of casualties for Kokoda, Milne Bay and Buna-Gona.'

BIBLIOGRAPHY

Official records

Australian War Memorial

AWM 54 Written Records, 1939-45 War

AWM 213 Operations in New Guinea

AWM 292 Med 40/76 Personal letters to DGMS 27 December 1939 – 12 May 1943

AWM 376 (Alternative Series AWM 292), Med 40/76

AWM 52 2nd AIF and CMF unit war diaries, 1939 – 45 War

AWM 67 Records of Gavin Long

AWM 25 Written Records 1914–18 War

AWM 75 Official History, 1939–45 War, Series 5 (Medical): Records of Allan S. Walker

B883 Second Australian Imperial Force personnel dossiers 1939–1947

B6121 Establishment of New Guinea Force and Miscellaneous GHQ Correspondence Relative to NGF

DRL No 2184 3rd Series, DGMS Downes Personal Diaries 1939–45

National Archives of Australia

A2684 Advisory War Council Minute Files

A3439 Commission of Inquiry into Conduct of Japanese

A5954 The Shedden Collection

A6236 Transcript of the hearings of the Commission of Inquiry into Japanese Forces Atrocities

A6237 National Security (Inquiries) Regulations Inquiry by Sir William Webb, 2 August 1943

A816 Correspondence Files

A9695 Folders of historical documents World War II, RAAF Series 1

MP 917/2 Control 7 and 8, Casualty Registers, Australian servicemen: Papua, for all States (Deaths and Wounded in Action)

MP 367/1 General Correspondence files (1917–1929)

MP 508/1 General correspondence files, multiple number series

MP 742/1 General and civil staff correspondence files and Army personnel files, multiple number series

MP 917 Casualty Registers Australian Servicemen Papua for all states

State Archives (NSW)

MLMSS 1092/Item 1 Brian Colden Antill Pockley papers, 1910-1917

MLMSS 1092/Item 5 Pockley family photographs ca 1866-1918

MLMSS 15/Box 2/Folder 1 General William Holmes telegrams and cables, September-October 1914

MLMSS 15/Box 2/Folder 1 General William Holmes telegrams and cables, September-October 1914

National Archives and Records Administration (United States)

332 Med 0.1 History – 107th Medical Battalion – 32nd Infantry Division 15 Oct 1940 – 1 March 1943

332 Med 0.3 After Action Report – Buna (Papuan) Campaign – 107th Medical Battalion 32nd Infantry Division 21 Sept 1942 – 1 March 1943

332-26 Medical Narrative History – Papuan Campaign New Guinea, Office of the Div Surgeons 32 Division 15 Sept 1942-17 March 1943

Books

Anderson, Nicholas, *To Kokoda*, Big Sky Publishing, Sydney, 2017.

Barton, G.B. (ed.), *The Story of South Africa*, vol. II, World Publishing Company, Sydney, 1903.

Bassett, Jan, *Guns and Brooches: Australian Army Nursing from the Boer War to the Gulf War*, Oxford University Press, South Melbourne, 1992.

Beaumont, Joan, *Australia's War 1939–45*, Allen & Unwin, St Leonards, NSW, 1996.

Brune, P., *Those Ragged Bloody Heroes*, Allen & Unwin, Sydney, 1991.

———, *A Bastard Of A Place: The Australians in Papua*, Allen & Unwin, Sydney, 2003.

Buchholz, Susan and Henke, Grace, *Henke's Med-Math: Dosage Calculation, Preparation and Administration*, Lippincott Williams & Wilkins, Philadelphia, 2009.

Bullard, Stephen (trans), *Japanese Army Operations in the South Pacific Area*, Australian War Memorial, Canberra, 2007.

Butler, A.G. (ed.), *The Australian Army Medical Services in the War of 1914-1918*, vol.1, Gallipoli,

Palestine and New Guinea, Australian War Memorial, Melbourne, 1938.

_____, *The Australian Army Medical Services in the War of 1914-1918*, vol.3, *Special Problems and Services*, Australian War Memorial, Canberra, 1943.

Campbell, James, *The Ghost Mountain Boys: Their Epic March and the Terrifying Battle for New Guinea – The Forgotten War of the South Pacific*, Crown Publishing, New York, 2007.

Coates, John, *An Atlas of Australia's Wars*, Oxford University Press, Melbourne, 2001. Condon-Rall, M. and Cowdrey, A., *The United States Army in World War II: The Technical Services, The Medical Department: Medical Service in the War Against Japan*, Center of Military History United States Army, Washington D.C., 1998.

Coulthard-Clark, Chris, *Where Australians Fought: The Encyclopaedia of Australia's Battles*, Allen & Unwin, St Leonards, NSW, 1998.

_____, *Australia's Military Map Makers*, Oxford University Press, South Melbourne, 2000.

Dean, Peter J. (ed.), *Australia 1942: in the shadow of war*, Cambridge University Press, Melbourne, 2013.

Dennis, Peter, Grey, Jeffery, Morris, Ewan, Prior, Robin and Bou, Jean (eds), *The Oxford Companion to Australian Military History*, Oxford University Press, South Melbourne, 2008.

Dull, P.S., *A Battle History of the Imperial Japanese Navy 1941–1945*, Naval Institute Press, Annapolis, 1978.

Fitzpatrick, Georgina, McCormack, Tim and Morris, Narrelle (eds), *Australia's War Crimes Trials 1945-51*, Brill Nijhoff, Leiden, 2016.

Gill, G. Hermon, *Australia in the War of 1939-1945*, Series 2, Navy, vol. II, *Royal Australian Navy, 1942-1945*, Australian War Memorial, Canberra, 1968.

Gillison, Douglas, *Australia in the War of 1939–1945*, Series 3, Air, vol. I, *Royal Australian Air Force, 1939–1942*, Australian War Memorial, Canberra, 1962.

Greenwood, D., *Antimicrobial Drugs: Chronicle of a Twentieth Century Triumph*, Oxford University Press, UK, 2008.

Grey, Jeffrey, *The Australian Centenary History of Defence*, vol.1, *The Australian Army*, Oxford University Press, South Melbourne, 2001.

Gurner, Jennifer, *The Origins of The Royal Australian Army Medical Corps*, Hawthorn Press, Melbourne, 1970.

Haller, John S., *Farmcarts to Fords: a history of the military ambulance 1790-1925*, Southern Illinois University Press, Carbondale, 1992.

Ham, Paul, *Kokoda*, HarperCollins, Pymble, NSW, 2004.

Harrison, Mark, *Medicine and Victory: British Military Medicine in World War II*, Oxford University Press, New York, 2004.

Hasluck, Paul, *Australia in the War of 1939–1945*, Series 4, vol.1, *The Government and the People 1942–1945*, Australian War Memorial, Canberra, 1970.

Hayashi, Saburo, *Kogun: the Japanese army in the Pacific war*, Marine Corps Association, Quantico, US, 1959.

Howie-Willis, Ian, *Surgeon and General: A Life of Major General Rupert Downes*, Australian Military History Publications, Loftus, NSW, 2008.

_____, *A Medical Emergency: Major-General 'Ginger' Burston and the Army Medical Service in World War II*, Big Sky Publishing, Newport, 2012.

_____, *An Unending War: the Australian Army's struggle against malaria 1885-2015*, Big Sky Publishing, Newport, NSW, 2016.

James, Bill, *Field Guide to the Kokoda Track*, Kokoda Press, Lane Cove, NSW, 2006.

James, Karl (ed.), *Kokoda: Beyond the Legend*, Cambridge University Press, Port Melbourne, 2017.

Jinks, B., Biskup, P. and Nelson, H. (eds), *Readings in New Guinea History*, Angus & Robertson, Sydney, 1973.

Johnston, George, *War Diary 1942*, Collins, Sydney, 1984.

Johnston, Mark, *At the Front Line: Experiences of Australian Soldiers in World War II*, Cambridge University Press, Cambridge, 1996.

Kienzle, Robyn, *The Architect of Kokoda: Bert Kienzle – the man who made the Kokoda Trail*, Hachette Australia, Sydney, 2011.

Le Souef, Leslie, *To War without a Gun*, Artlook, Perth, 1980.

Long, Gavin, *Australia in the War of 1939–1945*, Series I, Army, vol. I, *To Benghazi*, Australian War Memorial, Canberra, 1961.

Mayo, Lida, *Bloody Buna*, Doubleday, New York, 1974.

McCarthy, Dudley, *Australia in the War of 1939-1945*, Series I, Army, vol. V, *South-West Pacific Area – First Year Kokoda to Wau*, Australian War Memorial, Canberra, 1959.

McCarthy, Len, *Medics at war: an abridged history and anecdotes of the 2/13th Field Ambulance (A.I.F.), 1940-1945*, NAM Publications, Fremantle, 1995.

Moremon, J., *Battle of the Beachheads 1942-1943*, Department of Veterans' Affairs, Canberra, 2002.

Nelson, Hank, *Black, White and Gold: Goldmining in Papua New Guinea 1878 1930*, Australian National University Press, Canberra, 1976.

_____, *Taim Bilong Masta: the Australian involvement with Papua New Guinea*, Australian Broadcasting Commission, Sydney, 1982.

Nicholls, T.B., *Organisation, Strategy and Tactics of the Army Medical Service in War*, Tindall & Cox, London, 1937.

Noonan, David, *Those we forget: recounting Australian casualties of the First World War*, Melbourne University Press, Victoria, 2014.

Norris, Kingsley, *No Memory For Pain*, Heinemann, Melbourne, 1970.

Oswald, B. and Waddell, J. (eds), *Justice in Arms: Military Lawyers in The Australian Army's First Hundred Years*, Big Sky Publishing, Newport, NSW, 2014.

Palazzo, Albert, *The Australian Army – A History of its Organisation 1901–2001*, Oxford University Press, South Melbourne, 2001.

Pearn, John, *Arms and Aesculapius: Military Medicine in Pre-Federation Queensland*, Amphion Press, Brisbane, 1996.

Reid, Richard, *Milne Bay 1942*, Department of Veterans' Affairs, Canberra, 2007.

Robinson, Neville K., *Villagers at War: Some Papua New Guinean Experiences in World War II*, Australian National University, Canberra, 1979.

Sublet, Frank, *Kokoda to the Sea*, Slouch Hat Publications, Victoria, 2000.

Sweeney, Tony, *Malaria Frontline: Australian Army research during World War II*, Melbourne University Press, Melbourne, 2003.

Tan, Lloyd, *Unit History: 2/5th Australian Field Ambulance 1940-1945*, 2/5th Australian Field Ambulance Association, 1987.

Threlfall, Adrian, *Jungle Warriors: From Tobruk to Kokoda and beyond*, Allen & Unwin, Sydney, 2014.

Tyquin, Michael B., *Gallipoli: The Medical War – the Australian Army medical services in the Dardanelles campaign of 1915*, New South Wales University Press, Kensington, NSW, 1993.

———, *Little by Little: A Centenary History of the Royal Australian Army Medical Corps*, Australian Military History Publications, Loftus, NSW, 2003.

Walker, Allan S., *Australia in the War of 1939-1945*, Series 5, vol.1, *Clinical Problems of War*, Australian War Memorial, Canberra, 1952.

———, *Australia in the War of 1939–1945*, Series 5, vol.2, *Middle East and Far East*, Australian War Memorial, Canberra, 1953.

———, *Australia in the War of 1939–1945*, Series 5, vol.3, *The Island Campaigns*, Australian War Memorial, Canberra, 1957.

———, *Australia in the War of 1939-1945*, Series 5, vol.4, *Medical Services of the R.A.N. and R.A.A.F.*, Australian War Memorial, Canberra, 1961.

White, Osmar, *Green Armour*, Angus & Robertson, Sydney, 1945.

Wigmore, Lionel, *Australia in the War of 1939-1945*, Series I, Army, vol. IV, *The Japanese Thrust*, Australian War Memorial, Canberra, 1957

Williams, Peter, *The Kokoda Campaign 1942: myth and reality*, Cambridge University Press, Port Melbourne, 2012.

Wise, Brian, *History 2/6 Australian Field Ambulance, Australian Imperial Force, World War II 1939-1945*, 2/6 Australian Field Ambulance Social Club, Adelaide, 1989.

Journal Articles

Ballendorf, Dirk Anthony, 'Secrets Without Substance' in *The Journal of Pacific History* 19 (2), 1984.

Bullard, Steven, 'The Great Enemy of Humanity – Malaria and the Japanese Medical Corps in Papua 1942-43' in *The Journal of Pacific History* 39 (2), 2004.

Cope, Ian, 'F.A. Maguire – A Man of Many Parts, 1888-1953, First Chairman, Australian Regional Council, Royal College of Obstetricians and Gynaecologists' in *Australian and New Zealand Journal of Obstetrics and Gynaecology* 37 (3), 1997.

Crouch, Joan, '2/9th Australian General Hospital New Guinea August 1942 – January 1943' in *The Defence Force Journal* 57, March/April 1986.

Daley, Paul, 'Anzac: Endurance, Truth, Courage and Mythology' in *Meanjin* 69 (3), 2010.

Graves, Matthew and Rechniewski, Liz, 'Australian war memorialism and the politics of remembrance: from Gallipoli to Long Tan' in *Cultures of the Commonwealth* 14, Winter 2007–2008.

Grogan, R., 'The Operation of Forward Surgical Teams in the Kokoda-Buna Campaigns' in *Australian and New Zealand Journal of Surgery* 68 (1), January 1998.

Horner, D., 'Defending Australia in 1942' in *War and Society* 11(1), May 1993.

Hostnik, L.B. and Rury, J., 'Michigan medics in action: the 107th Medical Battalion in World War II' in *Michigan History* 72 (1), 1988.

Jacobs, Marjorie G., 'Bismarck and the Annexation of New Guinea' in *Historical Studies: Australia and New Zealand* 5 (17), 1951.

James, Karl, 'General Clowes of Milne Bay' in *Wartime Magazine* 59, 2012.

Leslie, Douglas R., 'A Surgeon on the Kokoda Trail' in *Medical Journal of Australia* 155, 11–12, December 1991.

Keesing, Felix M., 'Atoms of Empire' in *Far Eastern Survey* 10 (5), March 1941.

McLeod, Jan, 'The House That Jack Built: DGMS Rupert Downes and Australian Army Medical Preparations for World War II' in *Health and History* 19 (1), 2017.

Morrison, Albert E., 'The Treatment of Infected War Wounds by Magnesium Sulphate' in *The British Medical Journal* 1, 1918.

Nelson, Hank, 'Gallipoli, Kokoda and the Making of National Identity' in *Journal of Australian Studies* 21 (53), 1997.

_____, 'Kokoda: The Track from History to Politics' in *The Journal of Pacific History* 38 (1), 2003.

Norris, F.K., 'The New Guinea Campaign' in *Medical Journal of Australia* II, 24, December 1945.

Pilger, Alison, 'Courage, Endurance and Initiative: Medical Evacuation from the Kokoda Track, August-October 1942' in *War & Society* 11 (1), May 1993.

Reed, Barry, 'Endurance, Courage and Care: the Kokoda Campaign of Captain Alan Watson and the 2/4 Field Ambulance' in *Journal of Military and Veterans' Health* 19 (2), August 2011.

Sissons, David, 'Sources on Australian Investigations into Japanese War Crimes in the Pacific' in *Journal of the Australian War Memorial*, 30, April 1997.

Thompson, L.C., 'Blitzed Ambulance: the story of an AIF field medical unit by WO/2 L.C. Thompson, NX15734' in *Salt* 7, 29 March 1943.

Tyquin, Michael B., 'Sir William "Mo" Williams, KCMG, CB, KStj, Creator of Australia's Army Medical Services – Maligned or Misunderstood' in *Journal of the Royal Australian Historical Society* 84, 1998.

Wilds, Thomas, 'How Japan Fortified the Mandates' in *US Naval Proceedings* 626, April 1955. Rogerson, E., 'The "Fuzzy Wuzzy Angels": looking beyond the myth', Australian War Memorial, SVSS

Online Publications

Center of Military History United States Army, Papuan Campaign: The Buna-Sanananda Operation (16 November 1942-23 January 1943), U.S. Government Printing Office, Washington D.C, 1945 published online at: https://history.army.mil/books/wwii/papuancamp/papcpn-fm.htm

Cranswick, G.H., 'Some impressions made during nine weeks of Journeys in The Diocese of New Guinea in 1946' published online as: The Diocese of New Guinea in 1946, The First Year after the close of Hostilities with Japan By The Right Reverend G.H. Cranswick, B.A., D.D., Chairman of the Australian Board of Missions, available at:

http://anglicanhistory.org/aus/png/cranswick_diocese1946.html

Grahamslaw, T., 'Recollections of ANGAU' [manuscript] published online at: https://www.pngaa.net/Library/RecollAngau.html

James, Karl, 'The Track', a historical desktop study of the Kokoda Track, Canberra, 2009 published online at: http://www.environment.gov.au/heritage/publications/track-historical-desktop-study-kokoda-track

McAlpine, J.R. and Keig, G., *Climate of Papua New Guinea*, ANU Press, Canberra, 1983, published online at: https://openresearch-repository.anu.edu.au/bitstream/1885/115008/2/b12894229.pdf

Rogerson, E., 'The "Fuzzy Wuzzy Angels": looking beyond the myth', Australian War Memorial, SVSS paper, 2012, published online at: https://www.awm.gov.au/sites/default/files/svss_2012_rogerson_paper.pdf

Papers

Linke, Robert, 'The influence of German surveying on the development of Papua New Guinea' presented at 'Shaping the Change', XXIII FIG Conference, Munich, 8–13 October 2006.

Dean, Peter J., 'Grinding out a victory: Australian and American commanders during the beachhead battles' address presented at 'Kokoda: Beyond the Legend' Conference, Australian War Memorial, Canberra, 7 September 2012.

Horner, David, 'High Command and the Kokoda campaign' presented at 'Remembering 1942', 2002 History Conference, Australian War Memorial, published online at: https://www.awm.gov.au/visit/events/conference/remembering-1942/horner

Websites

Australian Bureau of Statistics, Year Book Australia, No 31, 1938, at: http://www.abs.gov.au/AUSSTATS/abs@.nsf/DetailsPage/1301.01938

Australian Comforts Fund, World War II, 1939-1946, Museums Victoria Collections at: https://collections.museumvictoria.com.au/articles/10608

Australian Dictionary of Biography online edition at: http://adb.anu.edu.au/

Australian Government, Department of Defence, Royal Australian Army Medical Corps, at: www.defence.gov.au/health/about/docs/raamc.pdf

Australian Government Department of Veterans' Affairs, Battle of the Beachheads (November, December, January), The Anzac Portal – The Kokoda Track, at: https://anzacportal.dva.gov.au

Australian Government Department of Veterans' Affairs at: https://www.dva.gov.au/commemorations-memorials-and-war-graves/memorials/war-memorials/papua-new-guinea

Australian Government, Department of Veterans' Affairs, 'Four Peoples at War: The New Guineans', at: http://kokoda.commemoration.gov.au/four-peoples-at-war/new-guineans-at-kokoda.php

Australian Government Department of Veterans' Affairs, 'The Kokoda Track: List of casualties for Kokoda, Milne Bay and Buna-Gona', at: https://anzacportal.dva.gov.au/history/conflicts/kokoda-track/resources/casualties/list-casualtieskokoda-milne-bay-and-buna-gona

Australian Government, RAAF Museum Point Cook, 'Research-RAAF Aircraft', at: http://www.airforce.gov.au/raafmuseum/research/series2.htm

Australian War Memorial, Honours and Awards at: http://www.awm.gov.au/research/people/honours_and_awards/

Australian War Memorial, John Moremon, 'Australian-Japanese Research Project: Remembering the war in New Guinea – Women and war in New Guinea – Australian women,' at: http://ajrp.awm.gov.au/ajrp/remember.nsf/

Australian War Memorial, Military organisation and structure, at: https://secure.awm.gov.au/atwar/structure/army-structure/#1941

Australian War Memorial, 'War History – Sudan (New South Wales Contingent) March-June 1885', at: https://www.awm.gov.au/articles/atwar/sudan

Bell, Jim, AIF reinforcements, 3rd Battalion, Interview 6 'Wounded and back to Myola then on to Moresby,' in Oral Histories collected from Kokoda Veterans, Kokoda Track Memorial Walkway, at: http://www.kokodawalkway.com.au/fsinterviews.html

Commonwealth of Australia, 'World War II Nominal Roll', at: http://www.ww2roll.gov.au/

International Committee of the Red Cross at: https://ihl-databases.icrc.org/customary-ihl/eng/docs/

International Committee of the Red Cross, 'Convention for the Amelioration of the Wounded and Sick of Armies in the Field, Geneva, 27 July 1929', at: https://www.icrc.org/ihl/INTRO/300?OpenDocument

Jervis Bay Maritime Museum Blog 9 April 2014 at: http://jervisbaymaritimemuseum.blogspot.com.au/2014/04/launce-of-maclaren-king-1923.html

Magarey, Major J.R. (Rupert later Sir Rupert Magarey) – 2/6th Field Ambulance, 2/4th A.G.H. SX3668 D.O.B. 21/2/1914 Oral History recording, AWM Accession Number S02366, Interview with Peter Brune 10 June 1987 at: https://www.awm.gov.au/collection/C2078022

Royal Australian Air Force at: http://www.airforce.gov.au

Royal Australian navy: http://www.navy.gov.au/history/feature-histories/australiannaval-and-military-expeditionary-force-first-fight-1914

Trove, digital newspapers, at: https://trove.nla.gov.au/newspaper/

South Australia Medical Heritage Society Inc, 'Sir Rupert Magarey Kt.MB.BS.FRCS. (Eng.), MS FRACS., FRACGP. (Hon.) 1914-1990', at: http://samhs.org.au/Virtual%20Museum/Notable-individuals/Magarey/magarey.htm

US Army Medical Department, Office of Medical History, at: http://history/amedd.army

WW2 US Medical Research Centre at: http://www.med-dept.com

Yoxall, Helen, 'Guide to the Lawrence Hargrave Archive (94/22/1) in the Powerhouse Museum Archives, 1994', at: http://images.powerhousemuseum.com/images/pdfs/322995.pdf

Other

Correspondence with NX15734 Lorence (Lorie) Thompson and NX65150 Alan (Bill) Sweeting, veterans, 2/4th Australian Field Ambulance 7th Division AIF.

In Support, magazine of the Friends of the 2nd Infantry Battalions, Issue 116, October 2008.

Kennedy, Private L.N. NX 21854 2/4th Field Ambulance 7th Division AIF, diary; photograph album, hand-drawn sketch of Soputa MDS after Japanese attack.

Sweeting, A.J. 'The 2/4th Field Ambulance A.I.F. during the Owen Stanleys Campaign 1942: Memories of Sgt A.J. (Bill) Sweeting M.B.E.', unpublished, no date.

Watson, A., 'Kokoda War Diary 1942-1943: The Recollections and Photographs of Dr Alan Watson A.M.' (videocassette), Blackmore-Gocking Production, 1991.

Available now online or at all good bookstores

View sample pages, reviews and more information on this and other titles at www.bigskypublishing.com.au

About the Author

Jan McLeod is a historian, tutor and researcher at the University of Newcastle. Jan's academic interest in the history of Australian military medicine has been inspired by a personal connection to the topic. Her Honours thesis considered popular representations of the Papuan campaign and examined the diary of her great-uncle who served with the 2/4th Australian Field Ambulance during World War Two. Jan's doctoral thesis expanded on this research by critically examining the preparedness, planning, execution and effectiveness of the Australian Army's medical campaign in Papua.

At Templeton's Crossing in October 1942, Private Nick Kennedy paused to write in his diary: 'One wonders why all this strife should be ... these men in the prime of their life cut down like flowers'. As a young nursing orderly serving with the 2/4th Australian Field Ambulance, Kennedy was unenviably well-placed to reflect on the futility of war.

Australian Army was woefully unprepared to fight a medical war in Papua and the soldiers paid the price. Almost 30,000 soldiers suffered from illness and tropical diseases, and an estimated 6000 were killed or wounded during the six-month campaign. These statistics have traditionally been represented as unavoidable consequences of fighting a war in a place such as Papua. This book disputes that narrative. Death and disease were inevitable outcomes, but the scale of the suffering was not. The medical challenges presented in Papua were extreme – they were not insurmountable.

Shadows on the Track considers a wide range of issues that impacted on the health of the Australian soldiers before, during and after the Papuan campaign was fought and won. The strengths, successes, shortcomings and failures of the medical campaign are identified, analysed and evaluated. The focus on the front-line medical personnel – the men of the field ambulance units – brings a new perspective to the battles of the Kokoda Track, Milne Bay and the Beachheads. Shining a light on these Australians who tended the sick, mended the wounded and buried the dead in Papua makes stepping out of the shadows a little easier.

Index

A

2 or 4th Field Ambulance, *105, 172*
   Australian advance, *370, 378, 382, 384, 385, 392, 396, 406, 410, 412, 414, 416, 422, 423, 426, 438*
   Kokoda, *488*
   Myola, *416, 422, 423, 426, 438, 441, 476, 478, 483, 485*

2 or 6th Field Ambulance, *172, 177, 186, 213, 220, 223, 224, 253, 263*
   Australian advance, *370, 382, 385*
   Myola, *423, 426, 438, 444, 452, 478, 488*

7th Division, *78, 213, 253, 392, 438, 456, 487*

abdominal wounds, *240, 277, 423*

accidental wounds, see self-inflicted wounds,

Advanced Dressing Stations (ADS), *7, 48, 360*

aerial evacuation, *164, 186, 354, 363*
   Kokoda, *487, 488*
   Myola, *186, 230, 240, 416, 426, 438, 441, 444, 478*

aircraft, *247*
   aerial evacuations, see aerial evacuation,
   Douglas, *240, 416*
   Ford Trimotor, *240*
   Fox Moths, *240, 416*
   Hudson bombers, *290, 412, 416*
   Junkers, *240, 416*
   Kittyhawks, *290*
   Stinson, *426, 438, 441, 478*

Alexander, Munro, *488*

Alexandria, *65*

Allen, General Arthur 'Tubby', *392, 416, 438, 456*

Alola, *186, 224, 263, 274, 426*

Ambon, *78, 110, 154*

ambulances,

Middle East campaign, *88*
anti-malarial drugs, *27, 30, 33, 131, 308, 324, 340*
  suppressive, *186, 253, 324, 467, 473, 476, 478*
appendicitis, *78*
Army Medical Directorate, *57, 86*
Arnold, Lieutenant Colonel Arthur, *335, 337, 349*
Assistant Director of Medical Services (ADMS), *43*
atebrin, *131, 311, 354, 467*
atrophic tongues, *197*
Australian Army,
  1st Armoured Division, *78*
  5th Division, *370*
  6th Division, *57, 78, 86, 358, 402*
  7th Brigade, *285, 288*
  7th Division, see 7th Division,
  8th Division, *78, 110, 197*
  9th Battalion, *285, 288*
  9th Division, *78*
  11th Division, *370*
  14th Brigade, *161*
  16th Brigade, *396, 402, 406, 426, 487*
  17th Brigade, *358*
  18th Brigade, *285, 290, 335, 358*
  21st Brigade, *186, 213, 456*
  25th Battalion, *288, 290*
  25th Brigade, *385, 392, 396, 406, 416, 426, 438, 487*
  30th Battalion, *164*
  30th Brigade, *164*
  39th Battalion, *153, 164, 177, 186, 195, 197, 259, 385*
  49th Battalion, *121, 131, 164*
  53rd Battalion, *164, 186, 230*
  55th Battalion, *288*
  61st Battalion, *285, 288, 290*
  Drake Force, *335, 337, 349, 351, 354, 365*
  Fall River Force, *288*
  field ambulance units, see field ambulance units,

Hammer Force, *365*
Hanson Force, *360, 363, 365*
interwar structural changes, *48*
Lark Force, *127*
Maroubra Force, *154, 161, 164, 186, 224, 392, 396*
medical care, provision of, *23*
Milne Force, *279, 303, 370*
Mud Bay Force, *337, 340, 347*
Taleba Bay Force, *337, 340*
training, *294, 299*
Australian Army Medical Corps (AAMC), *2, 10, 43*
    funding, *10, 60, 82, 164*
    inspections, *127, 131, 137*
    leadership, *57, 60, 71*
    lessons learned in Middle East, *93, 99*
    Middle East campaign, *78, 82, 86, 88, 93*
    volunteers, *60, 65*

Australian Army Nursing Service (AANS), *143, 315, 318*
Australian Army Service Corps (AASC), *48, 172, 213, 426*
    stretcher-bearers, as, *426*
    equipment shortages, *224*
    Middle East campaign, *82*
    overcrowding, *224, 396*
Australian Imperial Force (AIF),
    divisional support personnel, *48*
Australian Naval and Military Expeditionary Force (AN&MEF), *23*
    New Britain, deployment to, *23, 27, 30, 33*
Australian New Guinea Administrative Unit (ANGAU), *127, 161, 177, 204*
    medical units, working with, *265*

Australian and New Zealand Army Corps (ANZAC), *23*
Australian Special Hospitals,
   3rd ASH, *86*
Awala, *164, 177, 223*

B

Basabua, *153*
Bell, Jim, *478, 483, 485, 487*
Bentley, Staff Sergeant Alan, *265*
Berrima (HMAS), *23*
Berryman, Lieutenant Colonel F., *462*
Bismarck Archipelago, *33*
Bita Paka, *27*
Blackburn, M., *137*
Blamey, General Thomas, *57, 60, 65, 71, 82, 88, 153, 161, 290, 300, 315, 351, 444, 456, 462, 478*
   malaria situation, *467, 472, 473*
   Port Moresby, visit to, *456, 462*
Bootless Inlet, *288*
Borneo, *154*
Bougainville, *33, 154*
Brennan, Lieutenant Colonel E., *121, 127, 164*
Britain,
   Australia's relationship with,
Broadbent, Brigadier John, *444, 449*
Brown, 'Doover', *378, 382*
Brummitt, Major, *253*
Buna, *116, 143, 153, 161, 288, 365, 385, 464*
   malaria situation, *253, 473, 478*
Burston, Brigadier Samuel, *57, 60, 65, 71, 78, 462*
   DGMS, as, *186, 308, 351, 396, 438, 441, 444, 456, 462, 478*
   Downes, and, *57, 65, 71, 78*
   malaria situation, on, *467, 472, 473, 476, 478*
   Middle East campaign, *82, 88, 93*
   Port Moresby, visit to, *456, 462*

C

Camp Hospitals, 46th, *164, 220*
Carlyon, Major, *456*
Caroline Islands, *33, 36*
carriers, Papuan, *177, 265, 349*
  see also stretcher-bearers,
  conditions, *204*
  desertions, *247*
  equipment, *265*
  evacuation of casualties, *204, 230, 234, 240, 247, 249, 253, 426*
  supplies, movement of, *204*
casualties, *177, 349*
  evacuation, see evacuation of casualties,
  Japanese, *392*
  life and death decisions, making, *233, 234, 238, 240, 277*
  Milne Bay, Battle of, *290, 294, 312*
  morphine, administration of, *234, 238, 277*
  treatment, see treatment of casualties,
Casualty Clearing Stations (CCS), *7, 478*
  3rd, *164*
  5th, *402*
  106th, *370*
  110th, *285, 294, 355, 358, 370*
  Disher's recommendations, *99*
  Middle East campaign, *82*
Central Medical Coordination Committee, *57*
Chenhall, Lieutenant Colonel Frederick, *213, 223, 396, 449*
  Myola, at, *414, 416, 423, 426, 438, 441, 444, 449, 452, 485, 488*
China Strait, *288*
Cilento, Captain Raphael, *33*

Citizen Military Force (CMF), *161*
Clowes, Major General Cyril, *279, 290, 294, 299, 300*
communication issues, *10, 131, 385*
  Japanese forces, *385*
  Middle East campaign, *82*
  Milne Bay, *290, 294, 312, 318*
Convalescent Depot, *355*
  113th, *220*
  114th, *452*
Cook, Joseph, *33*
Coral Sea, Battle of, *110, 147, 154*
Crakanthorp, Lieutenant Colonel John, *305, 358*
Crete, *48*
  AAMC activities in, *88, 93*
Curtin, John, *312, 325, 456, 462*
Cyrenaica (Libya), *48, 71, 78, 88*

D

Darwin,
  medical facilities, *121*
Dawkins, Brigadier Alec, *303, 370*
dengue fever, *312*
Deniki, *177, 488*
dental health, *88, 422*
D'Entrecasteaux Islands, *325, 331, 334*
Deputy Assistant Director of Medical Services (DADMS), *488*
Deputy Director of Medical Services (DDMS), *43, 57, 65, 71, 82*
diarrhoea, *131, 197, 265, 272*
Director General of Medical Services (DGMS), *43, 57, 60, 71*
Director of Medical Services (DMS), *10, 23, 65, 71*
discipline issues, *210, 382*
  'waifs and strays', *195, 265*
Disher, Brigadier Clive, *86, 88, 93, 308*
  report on Middle East campaign, *93, 99, 131*
Dobu Island, *23, 325*

Downes, Major General Rupert, *43, 48, 60, 82, 121, 444*
  Burston, and, *57, 65, 71, 78*
  character, *131, 137*
  DGMS, as, *57, 60, 65, 71, 127, 131, 164*
  IGMS, as, *127, 131, 137, 143, 147*
  Middle East campaign, *86*
Drake Force, *335, 337, 349, 351, 354, 365*
dysentery, *43, 88, 131, 147, 195, 272, 312, 315, 324*

E

establishment, *78*
Earlam, Lieutenant Colonel Malcolm, *172, 265*
  report on medical services, *195, 197, 204, 210, 213*
Eather, Brigadier Ken, *392, 396, 426, 487*
Edelman, Captain Howard, *360, 363, 365*
Efogi, *224, 240, 249, 253, 259, 263, 412, 416, 422*
Efogi Ridge, *253, 259*
El Kantara, *78*
Eora Creek, *177, 186, 204, 233, 414, 416, 426*
evacuation of casualties, *224, 230, 233, 234, 238, 240, 277*
evacuation of casualties, *5, 7, 10, 105, 265, 396*
  aerial, see aerial evacuation,
  ambulances, *88, 131, 325, 396*
  Australian advance along Kokoda Track, *396, 406, 416*
  'budding off', *406, 416*
  forward evacuation, *177, 186, 224, 416*
  Goodenough Island, *340, 347, 349*
  issues with, *195, 360, 363*
  Japanese forces, *385*
  Kokoda, *487, 488*
  'leapfrogging', *224, 406, 416*

Milne Bay, *294, 358, 365, 370*
Myola, *426, 438*
native carriers,
see carriers, Papuan,
nutrition issues, *204*
retreat along Kokoda Track, *186, 195, 204, 224, 230, 253, 263*
walking wounded, *186, 204, 259, 265, 272, 396, 406, 478, 483*

F

Fairley, Colonel Neil Hamilton, *186, 464, 467, 473*
famine oedema, *197*
Fergusson Island, *23, 325, 337*
field ambulance units, *2, 5, 223*
   3rd, *164, 220*
   11th, *285, 294, 370*
   14th,
   see 14th Field Ambulance,
   Crete, in, *88*
   Disher's recommendations, *93*
   interwar structural changes, *48*
   Middle East campaign, *82*
   nicknames for personnel, *378*
Field, Brigadier, *288*
filaria, *325*
Flower, Fred 'Tiny', *426*
food supplies, *197, 204, 416*
   evacuation of casualties, *204*
   malnutrition, *197, 272*
foot problems, *272*
Ford, Lieutenant Colonel Edward, *197, 473*
Forde, Francis (Frank), *131, 137, 299, 315*
   Milne Bay, report on, *312, 315, 318, 324, 325*
French, Corporal John, *294*
'Fuzzy Wuzzy Angels', *247*
   see also carriers, Papuan,

G

Galbraith, Lieutenant Colonel, *137*
  report, *137, 143*
Gallipoli campaign, medical disaster, as, *48*
gastric ulcers, *78*
Gatenby, Captain, *488*
Gaza, *65*
Gazelle Peninsula, *27*
Geneva Conventions, *12, 48, 340*
  protection of medical personnel, *195, 197, 340, 347*
Germany,
  New Guinea, in, *16, 17, 23, 27*
  Pacific territories, dispersal of, *33, 36*
Gili Gili, *23, 340, 349, 355*
Gona, *153, 288, 365, 464*
  malaria situation, *473, 478*
Goodenough Island, *23, 279, 288, 290, 325, 331, 335*
  airfield, *351*
  casualty evacuation, *340, 347, 349*
  Japanese control, *294, 334, 335*
  malaria, *325, 351, 354*
  medical services, *340, 347, 349, 351, 354, 355*
Goroni, *294*
Grahamslaw, Major Tom, *240*
Greece, *48*
  AAMC activities in, *88, 93*
Green, Colonel Arthur, *223, 224, 402*
Greenwell, Captain Peter, *485*
Guadalcanal, *154, 279, 392*
Guam, *154*
Gunning, Lieutenant Colonel, *164*

H

Halligan, J.R., *43, 48, 121*
Hammer Force, *365*
Hanson Force, *360, 363, 365*
Hariko, *365*
Harrison, Eric, *36*
Hatton, Brigadier Neville, *164*

Herbertshöhe, *27*
Hobson, Lieutenant Colonel Arthur, *370, 384, 416, 426, 488*
Holmes, Captain Roland, *340, 349, 351*
hookworm, *43, 303, 325*
Hopkins, Brigadier Ronald, *456*
Howse, Lieutenant Colonel Neville, *23*
   AN&MEF expedition to New Guinea, *23, 27*
Hughes, Billy, *33, 36, 41, 43*
Humphrey, Major Ronald, *263*
Huon Gulf, *36*
Hurley, Victor, *444*
hygiene, *23, 43, 82, 186, 253*
   duty personnel, *220*
   poor, *224, 272, 300*
   tropical, *33*

I

Ilolo, *177, 195, 223, 396, 406, 426*
Imita Ridge, *392, 396*
Infectious Diseases Hospital, *172*
influenza, *78*
Inspector General of Medical Services (IGMS), *71, 127*
Ioribaiwa, *253, 263, 392, 396, 412*
Isokaze, *334*
Isurava, *177, 186, 224, 247*
   evacuation of casualties, *224*
Itiki, *223, 396*

J

Japan, *33*
   entry into war, *48, 110*
   League of Nations, withdrawal from, *36*
   Pacific naval bases, construction of, *36*
   Pacific War, *110, 154*
   post-WWI dispersal of German Pacific territories, *33, 36*
Japanese military,
   1st Landing Group, *154*
   8th Fleet, *154*
   17th Army, *154*
   35th Infantry Brigade, *154*

144th Infantry Regiment, *392*
Aoba Detachment, *154*
casualties, *392*
Goodenough Island, see Goodenough Island,
Milne Bay, see Milne Bay,
Papuan campaign, *121, 137, 153, 154, 385, 392*
Ryuto Unit, *154*
Sasebo Special Naval Landing Party, *153, 334*
South Seas Force, *153, 154, 385*
Special Naval Landing Force, *279*
Jason-Lee, *385*
Java, *127, 154*
Jawerere, *406*
Johnston, Colonel William, *57, 71, 449*
    DDMS, as, *93, 186, 223, 253, 300, 396, 402, 414, 416, 438, 441, 444, 476, 478*
    MDS Myola, on, *438, 441, 444, 449, 478*

K

Kabakaul, *27*
Kagi, *177, 195*
Kaiser-Wilhelmsland, *17, 23*
Kanowna, *23*
Katoomba (HMAS), *487*
Kember, Leading Stoker William, *27*
Kennedy, Private Lawrence Nicholis (Nick), *105, 110, 384, 406, 423, 426, 488*
Kennedy, Private William (Bill), *105*
Keogh, Lieutenant Colonel Esmond (Bill), *305, 472, 473*
Kienzle, Captain Herbert, *240*
Kilia Mission, *337*
King's Hollow Hospital, *396*
Koitaki, *143, 147, 220, 223, 396*
Koitaki Plantation, *143*
Kokoda, *17, 153, 161, 186, 274*

aerial evacuations, *487, 488*
Japanese occupation, *164*
malaria situation, *253*
MDS, *487, 488*
Kokoda-Sanananda Track, *175*
Kokoda Track, *17, 175, 279*
  Australian advance, *396, 402, 403, 406, 410, 416, 426*
  Australian re-occupation, *438*
  Australian retreat, *177, 186, 195, 224, 230, 240, 253, 370*
  hostile terrain, *154*
  Japanese advance, *154, 184, 195, 224, 385, 392*
  Japanese withdrawal, *385, 392, 456*
  medical services, provision of, *177*
  mythology,

L

Lae, *36, 154*
Large, Colonel, *86*
Lark Force, *127*
Lavarack, Lieutenant General John, *462*
Lawson, Lieutenant Keith, *456*
League of Nations, *33, 36, 41*
leprosy, *303, 325*
Leslie, Captain Douglas, *416, 422, 423, 438, 485*
Libya, *99*
Lloyd, Brigadier John, *487*
logistics, *10, 48*
Lovell, Colonel Stanley, *370, 378*
Lovett, Corporal Walter, *426*
Luzon, *154*
Lytton Report, *36*

M

malaria, *30, 43, 127, 131, 186, 274, 340, 414, 464, 467, 472, 473, 476, 478*
MacArthur, General Douglas, *116, 153, 288, 290, 315, 351*
  leadership of medical services, and, *456, 462*

Milne Bay, Battle of, *290, 294*
McCallum, Colonel, *467*
McDonald, Major Hew, *382, 412, 416*
McDonnell, Major Stanley, *186, 476*
Mackay, Major General Iven, *57*
Mackerras, Major Ian, *303, 464, 467*
McLaren, Captain William, *177, 186, 230, 238, 240, 253*
   report on August withdrawal, *265*
Maclaren King, *335, 340, 347*
McNicoll, Sir Walter, *36*
Magarey, Major James Rupert, *186, 224, 249, 253, 263, 396*
   Eora Creek, at, *230, 234, 238, 240*
   report on August withdrawal, *263, 265, 272, 274, 277*

Maguire, General Frederick, *23, 27, 30, 71, 127, 137, 444*
Maguli Range, *412*
Main Dressing Stations (MDS), *7, 48, 360, 406*
   Disher's recommendations, *99*
   Kokoda, *487, 488*
   Myola, *416, 422, 423, 426, 438, 441, 478, 483, 485*
Maitland, Lieutenant Colonel George, *93, 99, 305*
malaria, *30, 43, 127, 131, 186, 274, 340, 414, 464, 467, 472, 473, 476, 478*
   AAMC report 1942, *303, 464, 467*
   Anti-Malaria Advisory Committee, *467*
   cerebral, *311*
   deaths, *311, 324*
   epidemics, *253, 467*
   Goodenough Island, *325, 351, 354*
   medical personnel, *305, 358, 467*

Milne Bay, at, *300, 303, 305, 308, 311, 312, 315, 324, 363, 370*
  poor diet and, *197, 274, 464*
  self-inflicted, as, *300, 467*
malingering, *265*
malnutrition, *197, 272*
Manunda (HT), *315, 370, 396*
Mariana Islands, *33, 36, 154*
Maroubra Force, *154, 161, 164, 186, 224, 392, 396*
Marriott, Private, *340, 347, 349*
Marshall Islands, *33, 36*
Medical Equipment Control Committee, *57*
medical history, writing,
medical planning, *213, 240*
medical units, *250, 368*
  adaptation and team work, *265*
  composition of, *195*
  life and death decisions, making, *233, 234, 238, 240*
  malaria, *305, 358, 467*
  protection of, *195, 197*
  staff shortages, *147, 172, 197, 213, 220, 315, 318, 360, 365, 385, 396, 426, 476, 478*
  surgery, *274, 277, 358, 414, 416, 422, 423, 438, 488*
  training, *263, 265, 370, 378, 382, 384, 385*
  walking wounded, aiding, *483*
Menari, *186, 224, 240, 253, 259, 263, 412, 416*
Menzies, Robert, *43, 57, 65, 71*
Middle East war, *48, 57, 65*
  AAMC activities, *78, 82, 86, 88, 93, 382*
  lessons learned, *93, 99*
  map, *82*
Midway, Battle of, *110, 147, 154*
Milford, Major General Edward, *370*
Milne Bay, *23, 33, 147, 282, 294, 299, 318*
  airfields, construction of, *116, 288, 290*
  casualty evacuation, *294, 358, 365, 370*

early exploration, *17, 23*
Forde report on, *312, 315, 318, 324, 325*
Japanese landing and assault, *279, 290*
Japanese withdrawal, *385*
malaria, *253, 300, 303, 305, 308, 311, 312, 315, 324, 363, 370*
medical situation, *294, 299, 300, 355, 358, 360, 363, 365, 368, 370*
military situation, *279, 282, 285, 288, 290, 312, 355, 358*
nurses at, *315, 318*
reinforcements, *365*
strategic significance, *285, 288, 290*
supply issues, *294, 318, 324, 325*
Milne Force, *279, 303, 370*
Minerva, *340*
mobility, *5, 93, 99*
Mochizuki, *334*
Moluccas Islands, *154*
Moodie, Lance Corporal Arthur Mowbray, *382*
morale, *147*
Morris, Major General Basil, *153, 154, 161, 164, 186, 204*
mosquito nets, *27, 30, 127, 143, 147, 300, 324, 464, 467, 476*
Mud Bay Force, *337, 340, 347*
Murray Camp, *131, 137, 147*
Murray, Hubert, *41*
Myola, *186, 224, 230, 240, 247, 249, 253, 412, 416*
evacuations, *426, 438*
MDS, *416, 422, 423, 426, 438, 441, 478, 483, 485*
supplies, *438, 441, 444*

N

Nauro, *177, 186, 195, 253, 259, 263, 396, 412, 416*
Nauru, *33*
Navy,
Australian, *60*
Japanese **83** (map), *154*
Netherlands East Indies, *33, 154*

New Britain, *43, 110, 116, 121*
   AN&MEF deployment, *23, 27, 30, 33*
   evacuations from, *116*
New Guinea, *16, 19, 116*
   civilian and military administration, *121, 127*
   civilians, evacuation of, *121*
   Germany, and, *16, 17, 23, 27, 33, 36*
   Japanese occupation, *154*
   League of Nations Mandated Territory, as, *33, 41*
New Guinea Concert Party, *370*
New Guinea Force (NGF), *127, 186, 402, 444, 456*
Normanby Island, *23, 325, 334*
Norris, Colonel Frank Kingsley, *93, 99, 213, 220, 224, 253, 263, 385, 392, 396, 414, 416, 438, 444, 476*
   malaria situation, on, *473, 476*
nutrition,
   see also food supplies, disease and, *197*

O

outbreaks, *186, 253*
obsolete medical equipment, *82*
Oivi, *177, 274, 487*
Oldham, Captain, *186, 263*
Operation Drake, *294, 335, 337, 347, 349, 351*
Operation Hackney, *351, 354*
Otranto (HMS), *78*
Owen, Lieutenant Colonel William, *153, 177, 234*
Owen Stanley Range, *17, 23, 154, 274, 288, 385, 464, 487*
   front-line medical support, *164, 172, 385*
Owers' Corner, *223, 385, 396*

P

Papua, arrival in, *186*

11th Field Ambulance, *294, 305, 311*
14th Field Ambulance, *164, 172, 197, 213, 370, 406, 416*
  Kokoda Track, on, *177, 186, 195, 220, 224, 230, 385, 396, 426*
  malaria, *274*
17-Mile, *223, 396, 402*
Papua, amalgamation with, *36*
Pacific theatre of war, *114*
Palau, *36, 154*
Palestine, *57, 65, 220*
Papua, *43, 116, 131*
  airfields, *154*
  civilian and military administration, *121, 127*
  civilians, evacuation of, *121*
  defensive fortifications, construction of, *41*
  Japanese invasions (1942), *154*
  New Guinea, amalgamation with, *36*
  pre-war neglect by Australia, *33, 36, 41*
Papuan Infantry Battalion (PIB), *131, 153, 161, 164*
  evacuation of casualties, *234, 265*
  withdrawal along Kokoda Track, *177*
Pearl Harbor, *110, 154*
pellagra (Niacin deficiency), *197*
personnel issues, *93*
Philippines, *116, 154*
plasmoquine, *131, 311, 354, 467*
pneumonia, *78*
Pockley, Captain Brian, *27, 30*
Popondetta, *464*
  malaria situation, *253*
Port Moresby, *41, 43, 127, 131, 288, 392*
  Blamey's visit to, *456, 462*
  defensive fortifications, construction of, *41*
  Japanese advance on, *154*

malaria situation, *253, 274*
medical facilities, *43, 48, 121, 131, 137, 143, 147, 164*
staff shortages, *147, 172, 318, 402*
Porter, Brigadier Selwyn, *164, 177*
Potts, Brigadier Arnold, *186, 224, 240, 253, 456*
Preece, Warrant Officer Robert, *253*
Principal Medical Officer (PMO), *23, 27*
Pygmy movement, *351*

Q

quinine, *27, 30, 33, 147, 265, 324, 467*
  shortages, *473, 476*
  suppressive, *186, 253, 324, 467, 473, 476, 478*

R

Rabaul, *27, 36, 43, 121, 127*
  Japanese occupation, *116, 121, 137, 154, 334*
  medical situation, *43, 137*
  volcanic eruption, *36*
Red Cross, *16, 27, 88, 131, 340*
  comforts, *78, 396*
  flags and identification, *195, 197*
  food supplies, *197*
  Port Moresby, in, *143*
Regimental Aid Posts (RAP), *5, 422*
Regimental Medical Officer (RMO), *177*
Ross, Lieutenant Colonel, *414, 476*
Rouna, *131*
Rowell, Major General Sydney, *153, 186, 392, 462*
  dismissal, *456, 462*
Royal Australian Air Force (RAAF), *290, 416*
  medical services, *444*
  No.32 Squadron, *285*
  No.75 Squadron, *285, 334*
  No.76 Squadron, *285*
rubella, *78*

S

Saipan, *154*

Salamaua, *36, 147, 154*
Salvo Dump, *253*
Samarai, *43*
Sanananda, *175, 365, 464*
Sanaroa Island, *23, 325*
sandfly fever, *303*
Scott, Captain John, *340, 347, 349, 360, 363*
sea sickness, *78*
self-inflicted wounds, *195, 210, 213, 265*
   malaria as, *300*
Senior Medical Officer (SMO), *224*
Seven Mile Drome, *186*
Shera, Captain, *177*
Simpson's Gap, *131*
Singapore, *154*
   fall of, *110*
Slim, Field Marshal Sir William, *290*
Smith, Norman, *426*
Solomon Islands, *116, 154, 279*
Solomon Sea, *288*
Soputa, *17, 382, 464*
South West Pacific Area (SWPA), *48, 110, 116, 143*
   Japanese invasions (1942), *154*
Spender, Percy, *71*
Stantke, Adjutant-General Victor, *71, 131, 444, 449*
   malaria situation, and, *473*
   sterilisation processes, *127, 423*
Stirling Range, *23*
Street, Brigadier Geoffrey, *65*
stretcher-bearers, *93*
   AASC personnel as, *426*
   casualties, *340, 347*
   changing role of, *265*
   Goodenough Island, on, *340*
   native, see carriers, Papuan,
Sturdee, Vernon, *71*
sulphaguanidine, *195, 197*
supplies, *10, 143, 164, 265*
   aerial supply, *164, 412, 414, 416, 444*

AN&MEF deployment to New Britain, *27, 30, 33*
clothing and blankets, *177, 197, 272, 467*
damaged in airdrops, *220, 249, 265, 272, 318, 412, 414, 416*
equipment left behind, *177, 213, 220*
food,
see food supplies,
forward dumps, *197, 272, 274*
issues with, *10, 60, 71, 82, 127, 147, 195, 197, 249*
Kokoda, *488*
Middle East campaign, *78, 82, 88*
Milne Bay, *294, 318, 324, 325*
Myola MDS, *438, 441, 444*
ordnance stores, *197, 213, 325, 416*
sterilisation equipment, *197, 423*
theft of, *363, 365, 396*

surgery, *274, 277, 358, 414, 416, 422, 423, 438, 488*
Syria, *48, 105, 110*

T

Taleba Bay Force, *337, 340*
Taupota, *334*
technology, *10, 99*
　World War I, lessons from, *12, 48*
Templeton, Captain Sam, *177*
Templeton's Crossing, *177, 186, 224, 230, 240, 414, 416, 426*
Thompson, Warrant Officer Lorie, *483*
Tieryo, *340, 349*
Timor, *78, 110, 154*
Tobruk, *99*
Tomitar, Major General Horii, *153*
transport, *2, 10, 23, 48, 93, 154, 240, 290, 385, 396*
　carriers,
　see carriers, Papuan,
　casualty evacuation,
　see evacuation of casualties,

stretcher-bearers,
see stretcher-bearers,
supplies, *186, 213, 249,
318, 324, 325*
Treaty of Versailles, *33, 36*
Tredinnick, Lieutenant Colonel William, *444*
Trobriand Islands, *325*
Truk, *154*
typhus, *312, 340*

U
Uberi, *195, 253, 396, 414, 416, 426*
ulcers, *43*
United States Air Force, *416, 422, 444*
United States Army,
  32nd Division,
  41st Division,
  43rd Engineer Regiment, *285*
  46th Engineer Regiment, *285*
  Milne Bay, at, *279, 285*

V
Vasey, Major General George, *438, 444, 487*

venereal disease, *43, 78, 303*
Verco, Captain, *363*
Vernon, Captain Geoffrey 'Doc', *177, 204, 234*
Vickery, Major Ian Firth, *382, 412, 414, 416*
victory,
Vitamin B deficiency, *197*
'waifs and strays', *195, 210, 265*

W
Waigani, *355, 365*
  malaria situation, *253*
Walker, Private 'Squeaky Joe', *378*
Wall, Lieutenant Colonel Frederick, *285, 288, 308, 355, 370*
Wallman, Captain Douglas, *177, 186, 230, 253, 263*
Ward Hunt Strait, *334*
Warrego (HMAS), *349*
Watson, Captain Alan, *422*
Wedau-Taupota, *360*

Western Samoa, *33*
White, General Sir Cyril Brudenell Bingham, *65*
Whitehead, General Ennis, *444*
Wilkinson, Sergeant J.D., *177*
Williams, Colonel William 'Mo', *2, 10, 48*
Williams, Regimental Sergeant Major Kim, *378*

Y

yaws, *43, 325*
Yayoi, *334*

www.ingramcontent.com/pod-product-compliance
Lightning Source LLC
Chambersburg PA
CBHW010300010526
44108CB00044B/2703